# THE NEW SPAIN

# THE NEW SPAIN

John Radford

MITCHELL BEAZLEY

The New Spain by John Radford

First published in Great Britain in 1998 by Mitchell Beazley,
an imprint of Reed Consumer Books Limited,
Michelin House, 81 Fulham Road, London, SW3 6RB

A CIP catalogue record for this book is available
from the British Library.

ISBN 1 85732 254 1

Typeset in Berkeley, Din Schriften and Helvetica Neue

Commissioning Editor     Sue Jamieson
Executive Art Editor      Fiona Knowles
Editor                    Jamie Ambrose
Design                    Kenny Grant
Cartography               Hardlines
                          Kenny Grant
Production                Rachel Lynch
                          Sally Banner
Picture Research          Claire Gouldstone
Index                     Ann Barrett

Printed and bound by
Toppan Printing Company, China

# Contents

# Foreword

## Miguel Torres

**Above:** The face of Spanish wine. Miguel Torres, head of the world-famous bodega of the same name, has played a crucial role in creating quality wines in Penedès – and in Spain as a whole.

It could be said that the history of Spanish wine is branded with the contributions of those families which, at one time or another, replanted vineyards and introduced new methods of winemaking. These include the historic Sherry houses that created the first Spanish wine; the 19th-century noblemen of Rioja who established the basis of the great *crianzas*; the Catalans who created Cava in 1872; the great families of Córdoba.

Above all, there were the many pioneers – the visionaries of their times – who proudly went out to show the world the products of their vineyards. My father, Miguel Torres Carbó (1909-1991), is an excellent example of those who brought fame and prestige to the wines of Spain. Another was Jean León (born in Santander, later a naturalised US citizen), who planted the first Chardonnay and Cabernet Sauvignon vines in Penedès in 1962. Little did we know then that he was opening another window to the future of Spanish wines – a future that, in today's reality, has seen Spanish wine at last enjoying its full potential.

The ideal natural conditions in our vineyards have allowed us to select the most noble traditional grape varieties – Moscatel, Albariño, Verdejo, Parellada, Macabeo/Viura, Garnacha and Tempranillo – alongside the best international varieties: Riesling, Gewürztraminer, Sauvignon Blanc, Chardonnay, Cabernet Sauvignon, Merlot and Pinot Noir. Investment in the vineyards, the wineries and the cask-cellars completes the contemporary profile. Today's customer knows that such clichés as oxidised whites or maderised reds have given way to aromatic whites and elegant reds in most regions – without losing the style and depth, heritage and colour that denote the great wines of the Mediterranean. This increased knowledge and interest in wine has resulted in increased popularity for Spanish wine as a whole.

The boom in wine culture has been a spectacular phenomenon of the late 20th century. Thanks to the rise in interest and enthusiasm, Spanish wines now enjoy a privileged position on the world's vinous stage. Not only does this renaissance represent a public relations victory, it also respresents the triumph of conscientious work in the vineyards, in the laboratory, in the marketplace and, indeed, in the world's gastronomic culture.

All of which makes the time more than ripe for an up-to-date book on Spanish wine. For the wine-lover, this new and definitive work by John Radford is doubly welcome. Within the pages of *The New Spain*, the reader may explore all the wines of my country, from those of

old Europe – their tradition and history faithfully reflected in their *denominaciones de origen* and their native grape varieties – to those we now call 'New World'. Modern Spanish wines encompass an extraordinary range, thanks to the myriad soil types, grape varieties and styles that go into their creation. They also represent something today's customer prize above everything else: excellent value for money. By reading *The New Spain*, readers can also learn first-hand about the care that is taken in Spanish vineyards, the naturalisation of noble varieties and the environmental conscience of many of the country's growers.

Alongside New-World-style viticulture, characterised by the planting of traditional French varieties from Bordeaux and Burgundy, the reader will discover that, in Spain, wine also has an immensely rich heritage. In Catalonia, for example, once Cabernet Sauvignon and Chardonnay had become established in the 1980s, we began a process of re-establishing the ancient, historic, Catalan grape varieties which had all but disappeared with the arrival of phylloxera in the second half of the 19th century. The results are already encouraging – and exciting.

In the next few years we should see some fascinating new wines coming along to enrich the already wide range of our wine styles, bringing back long-forgotten aromas and tastes we were determined not to allow to disappear. The great variety of soils, sites and microclimates has made and will continue to make it possible to produce wines of rare excellence: the Priorato DO is a good example. Spanish wine has unquestionably achieved its transition from relative obscurity. Today, it is a brilliant success.

This image of Spanish winemaking, the modern reality, is what the reader will find in the pages of *The New Spain*. For many years, John Radford has had a special interest in Spanish wines, as evidenced by his work in all the major English-language wine magazines in Europe, as well as his television and radio career. No one but John, a genuine Hispanophile and an enthusiast for every Spanish region, could have written this comprehensive, contemporary, complex but very enjoyable review of the wines of Spain.

*Miguel A. Torres.*

*Some time in the early 1970s, an independent, single-outlet wine shipper in Nottingham hired a new sales manager. This was done on the basis of an interview conducted (unbeknown to the shipper) after the candidate had spent an intensive weekend reading a book called WINE by Hugh Johnson (still the very best possible introduction to the subject ever written).*

*Within a year or so, the shipper decided that his new member of staff could be trusted abroad with the company reputation and sent him to Jerez – with a selection of reference samples and a modest shipping order – to meet Don Emilio Lustau. The young man (for so he was then) was instantly enraptured with Spain: from the Bougainvillaea climbing the whitewashed walls of the country towns to the shaded, Andalucían courtyards where fountains tinkled in the heavy-lidded afternoons after long, long lunches that had begun with endless tapas and finished with bottomless copas of gran reserva Brandy de Jerez.*

There are many fine books on Spanish wine, but this one is a first in at least three respects. For a start, it is a comprehensive catalogue of all Spain's wine areas as they stand at the beginning of the 21st century.

Second, I have tried to organise Spain into sections that show a family resemblance in styles of wine, in terms of climate, culture and, of course, gastronomy. The idea behind this is to make Spanish wines understandable – to explain why they are like they are from a particular area, and to give the reader an idea of what to expect.

Third, a comprehensive guide to the bodegas within each region has not yet been published. This is not a full list, by any means, nor even a list of all the best bodegas. However, it is a genuine attempt to bring together the names and some basic details of those bodegas in each region that stand out from their peers.

Over the past 30-odd years, I've made a lot of friends in the wine trade and in Spain. It would take another book to list them all, but I would like to say that every single *consejo regulador* I approached offered help, from a working itinerary to bilingual guides, hotel accommodation and structured tastings. Obviously, the bigger and richer DOs have more to give, but even the smallest and newest turned out a *bodeguero* or a *viñero* to explain the wines, match them with local dishes, and talk frankly about their ambitions. However, I feel that I could not have completed my task without the help of the following (in no particular order).

In Spain: José Madrazo, Iñigo Cañedo and Tom Perry in Rioja; Conchi Biurrun in Navarra; Miguel Torres and his impressive team in Penedès; Javier Zaccagnini in Ribera del Duero; Bartolomé Vergara and Luís Bretón in Jerez; 'Paco' Hurtado de Amezaga and his team in Rioja and Rueda; Alvaros Palacio and René Barbier in Priorato; Christopher Garrigós in Valencia (and God-knows-where-else, these days); Carlos Falcó, Marqués de Griñón, in Toledo; Lourdes Fernández López and Ruth Lozano on Tenerife; and Ana Larrañaga of *Gastronomika* magazine, in Bilbao.

In the UK: initially and always the team at Wines From Spain (ICEX-UK) who are absolutely reliable and who, if they don't know something, will always know a man or woman who does. Present and past luminaries include Juan Calabozo, Javier Burgos, Graham Hines, Brian Buckingham, David Balls, Charlotte Hey, Donald Mason, Daniel Brennan and Nicola Speakman.

I've also had enormous support from the specialist UK Spanish wine-trade in terms of samples and tastings, and I ought to mention John Hawes of Laymont & Shaw, David Scatchard, John Comyn of Vinexcell, Manuel Moreno, Félix Benito of C&D Wines and Barry Ralph of The Upper Crust.

And above all: Jeremy Watson, former director of Wines From Spain, now running a successful consultancy in Spain and a man who revealed the magnificent panoply of Spanish wine to a whole generation of wine-writers with inspired visits, tours and tastings; Philip Rowles of DWS-Freixenet, whom I first met at Lustau Sherry on that first visit all those years ago and who, with a single telephone call, can put most of the Cava industry on full alert to provide large lunches and extensive tastings for visiting journalists. And, last and also first: Reg Haward, the former RAF officer who established Vintage Wines Ltd, a small, single-outlet, independent wine-shipping business in Nottingham in 1947– the man who gave me my break in the wine trade and sent me to Spain for the first time.

*John Radford*

# Spanish Wine: a brief history

If Noah really planted the first vineyard around 5,000BC on Mount Ararat, then Spain was a relative latecomer to the practice. Despite the fact that an ancient people known as the Phoenicians dominated trade around the Mediterranean for centuries, they did not establish the city of Gadir (modern Cádiz) until around 1100BC. Even then, wine was a commodity, traded along with olives and wheat.

In those days, wine was transported in clay containers called amphorae, which were heavy, leaky and fragile (fragments are still being fished out of the estuary at Sanlúcar de Barrameda). Sooner or later, it must have seemed more sensible to the Phoenicians to make wine themselves and ship it out of Gadir, rather than to lug it all the way into the city from what is now called the Middle East.

Further inland from Gadir and away from the fierce, westerly coastal winds, the land was low and fertile and the climate hot – an environment that must have seemed similar to the Phoenician traders' own homeland. Such conditions were ideally suited to growing the tough-skinned, sweet grape varieties that were the stock-in-trade of the travelling vintner 3,000 years ago, and this is probably the origin of the 'golden triangle' we now know as Sherry Country.

The next major shift in winemaking style and skills came with the Romans, who ruled Spain (or most of it) from about 100BC until the collapse of the Roman Empire in the fifth century. As was their usual practice in conquered lands, the invading legions planted vines; more importantly, they brought new viticultural methods

**Early Spanish winemakers developed large earthenware vessels called *tinajas* to prevent oxidation. The concrete versions below are proof that some techniques never go out of date.**

with them. As a result, the local tribes – mostly Celts in the west and Iberians in the centre and east – quickly adopted the Roman practices of fermentation in stone troughs and storage in smaller, more manageable amphorae made of finer (and therefore tougher and less porous) clay. This style of winemaking is still in use in the Spanish countryside, where it is known as the *método rural*, or rural method.

## The Moorish invasion

After the fall of the Roman Empire, Spain came under the domination of the Moors of northern Africa, whose occupation lasted from the eighth century until their defeat in 1492. Although the Moors perfected the art of distillation, as a Muslim people they used it mainly in the manufacture of perfumes and cosmetics from plant materials – though undoubtedly stumbling upon various alcoholic distillations in their medicinal research. Wine, meanwhile, was probably made by individual farmers, who may even have traded it with parts of Christian Europe. In terms of advancement, however, Spanish wines remained in a period of stasis until the country was reunified and wine became an export commodity in huge demand in the developing Americas.

Spain's first wines were heavy and heady – a reflection of their eastern Mediterranean heritage – and they were made in either a sweet or *rancio* style (literally 'rancid'; that is, fully oxidised and heavily reduced): the sort of thing that could survive intact if its container were neither airtight nor spotlessly clean. By the 16th and 17th centuries,

Above: By the 15th century, wooden casks or butts allowed some Spanish wines to travel as far as the famed armada itself, slaking thirsts in England as well as in the more exotic Americas.

however, wine was being made all over northern and central parts of the country, and the styles of both red and white wines were much more similar to the wine styles of today.

As always, oxidation posed the main problem for all wines, and a number of methods were devised to prevent it. The first (and most obvious) solution was to develop a taste for *rancio* wines. Although it admittedly takes some getting used to, this style is still made and enjoyed by a small but enthusiastic market in northern Spain.

## Prevention and cure

As to ways of keeping air out: the Greeks had already set a precedent by sealing their amphorae with pine resin, a practice that gave birth to retsina. Similarly, Spanish *viñeros*, or winemakers, developed large clay vats known as *tinajas*, with narrow openings at the top. These they filled to the brim and sealed with a heavy lid to exclude as much air as possible. Even if oxidation did take place, the small surface area meant that its effects were minimal. Old earthenware *tinajas* are still found in parts of southern Spain.

Useful as they were, such vessels were simply too large and cumbersome to move about; they were especially unsuitable as cargo for ships bound for the expanding colonial markets. For this reason, wine was transported in dried animal skins which could be filled and tightly sewn together to prevent oxidation. Given that the curing and cleansing process was a little on the primitive side, however, the wine inside such skins would hardly have remained unaffected, and the several weeks it took to sail from Cádiz to the new colonies inevitably took their toll on the contents.

The late-15th century brought some progress in the form of the butt or cask. Round wooden containers had been used to transport foodstuffs for years; once winemakers began to employ them, laws were passed around the year 1500 which stipulated that barrels made for wine must be of the highest quality, untainted by any other product.

Initially, butts were used for fermentation and storage because the wood swelled when wet, keeping the wine secure. They were little better than skins at keeping air from wine during long sea voyages, but they were hardy enough to keep the strong, fortified wines of Jerez in check – as Sir Francis Drake discovered when he 'singed the king of Spain's beard' in 1587 (by attacking Philip II's armada in Cádiz) and made off with 2,900 of them. This incident coincided with a big demand for what had become known as 'sheris sack' in Shakespearian England, as evidenced by the antics of such fictional characters as Sir John Falstaff.

The real breakthrough in Spanish winemaking took place towards the end of the 18th century. In Bordeaux, cooperage had become much more of a fine art, with the great *châteaux* demanding (and being able to afford) the best workmanship. A *viñero* from Rioja by the name of Manuel Quintano was so impressed with the quality of Bordeaux casks that he purchased some and brought them back to his native vineyards. The French coopers had discovered the art of keeping barrels airtight by means of using a bung on the 'belly' of the cask as well as one in the end. This prevented air from coming in and made it easier for wine to be withdrawn and racked; it also made the casks easier to clean and refill.

Quintano filled the barrels with Rioja wine and sent them to America. He was delighted to find that, not only had the wine arrived in excellent condition, but the time spent in cask rolling around on the deck of the ship had added a pleasantly 'oaky' flavour to it – something modern Rioja-lovers would immediately recognise. His neighbours, however, were less impressed, refusing to have anything to do with him until he stopped using Bordeaux casks. Eventually, Quintano went back to using leaky buckets, but not before the seeds of progress had been sown.

## Riscal and the Rioja transformation

Fifty years later, the foundations of modern Spanish wine were laid by a partnership between Don Camilo Hurtado de Amezaga (later the Marqués de Riscal) and a French winemaker named Jean Pineau. Don Camilo was a journalist, exiled to France because of his political writings. He lived in Bordeaux for some years, learned about Bordelais winemaking methods, and returned from France with Bordeaux casks, French know-how and a belief that his own family land could produce wines at least as good as those he had tasted abroad.

At the same time, Jean Pineau was hired by the local authority in Rioja to show this same Bordeaux technology to local winemakers in hopes of improving their wines, getting a better price for them and developing an export market. In the event, most locals bristled when a foreigner tried to tell them how to make wine, and Pineau received a rather less-than-enthusiastic reception. Spanish *viñeros*, after all, were still using the stone-trough method which had remained virtually unchanged since Roman times. Given this state of affairs, it is not surprising that any proposed changes – particularly from a Frenchman – would have seemed radical indeed.

When Pineau's contract expired, Don Camilo hired him to supervise every aspect of the new *bodega*, or wine estate, he was planning; the rest, as they say, is history. Don Camilo's neighbours watched in amusement as he invested massive amounts of money in his new winery, but the smiles froze on their faces as they saw his wines fetch prices of which they had never dreamed. The new technology had proved its worth, and most of Rioja's winemakers followed suit – although it is still possible to buy Rioja made in the old style.

The Marqués de Riscal is usually cited as the pioneer of new-wave wine in the 19th century; in reality, he was just one of a number of people throughout northern Spain who were experimenting with new ways of making and storing wine. Most importantly of all, perhaps, he was also one of a number developing new methods of quality-control designed to give customers some guarantee of consistency as well as to keep them coming back for more.

A hundred years passed before the next great innovation in Spanish winemaking. The prime mover this time was Miguel Torres, father of the present producer of the same name. Torres had seen stainless-steel winemaking equipment at work in France and Australia in the 1950s, and was impressed with the precise control it gave over fermentation temperatures. He installed the first tanks at his Catalan winery in the 1960s, and such was their success that most of Spain followed his example. Today, in fact, Barcelona is a world centre for the manufacture of stainless-steel winemaking equipment, and it is cheaper to install water-jacketed tanks than it is to rebuild or even repair the older epoxy-lined concrete ones.

## Spanish wine in the modern age

At this point, Spanish winemaking history might well have ended. New-style winemaking existed alongside traditional methods; native and international grape varieties flourished in adjacent vineyards. From the customer's point of view, there was something for everyone. But Spain is not a country to stand still once it finally gains momentum. After centuries of stasis, the *viñeros* have the scent of innovation in their nostrils and they like the aroma. Even in the most obscure regions, at least one maverick is trying out a different type of fermentation, a new yeast strain or a forgotten grape variety. Sometimes their efforts come to nothing; sometimes they yield pure gold. The best news by far is that the *consejos reguladores* (regulating councils) are much more prepared to look at new ideas and innovation. Just 20 years ago, they might have thrown up their corporate hands in despair.

This forward-looking attitude has given rise to a new approach to Spanish wines, which could be dubbed 'post-modern' wines, since they usually involve reinventing some ancient practice. Barrel fermentation is a good example. In the past, it was only in rare autumns, when the temperature fell sharply immediately after picking, that it produced great wines. With today's air-conditioned underground cellars, the coolness of those autumns can be reproduced artificially, with a resulting improvement inside the cask. Similarly, grapes such as the Verdejo, which traditionally oxidised so fast that it was normally used to make *rancio*-type wines, have proved to make outstandingly fresh wines when vinified under a blanket of inert gas.

After 3,000 years (give or take a few), we can enjoy the best of all ages of Spanish wines: nutty, dry olorosos and light, fresh, foot-pressed *cosecheros* (locally crafted wines); oaky reds with all the cinnamon depth and raisiny warmth of a long, golden autumn; crisp, clean whites and ripe, herby reds with enough freshness and ripe fruit for instant enjoyment; and a new generation of sparkling wines – made, of course by the *método tradicional*.

That is the range and panoply of contemporary Spanish wine. And that is what this book is all about.

Below: Vinification, 21st-century style. The ultra-modern Miguel Torres bodega in Catalonia produces some of Spain's – and Europe's – finest wines.

# The New Spain

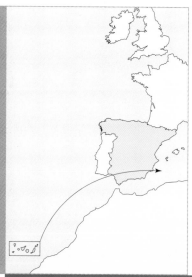

To understand any country's wine, it is first necessary to have a basic knowledge of its structure and geography. In 1978, Spain adopted a new constitution which restored the identity of the ancient kingdoms and regions which originally made up the nation in 1492. The result was a kind of 'United States of Spain', consisting of 17 *autonomías*, or autonomous regions, each with its own parliament and a number with their own languages. To complicate matters, the country is further subdivided into 50 *provincias*, or provinces, and Spain also controls two offshore outposts on the Moroccan coast. Some *autonomías* consist of several provinces; others, such as La Rioja and Navarra, consist of only one.

   Although man-made divisions go some way towards explaining how and why wines develop as they do, other, uncontrollable influences (for instance nature and the human condition) play even more vital roles.

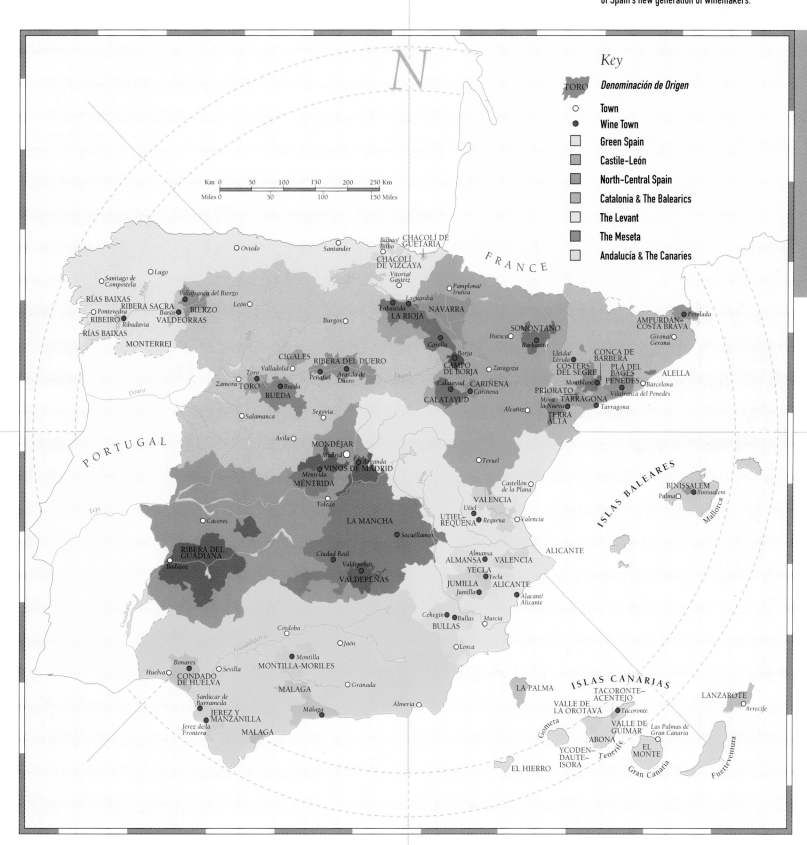

Far Left: The red roofs of the Cava house
Raventos i Blanc, in Catalonia. Investment
and innovation are the key to the success
of Spain's new generation of winemakers.

*Key*

TORO  *Denominación de Origen*

○  Town

●  Wine Town

▢  Green Spain

▢  Castile-León

▢  North-Central Spain

▢  Catalonia & The Balearics

▢  The Levant

▢  The Meseta

▢  Andalucía & The Canaries

Km 0    50    100    150    200    250 Km

Miles 0    50    100    150 Miles

N

FRANCE

PORTUGAL

Oviedo
Santander
Lugo
Santiago de Compostela
CHACOLÍ DE GUETARIA
Bilbao/ Bilbo
CHACOLÍ DE VIZCAYA
Vitoria/ Gasteiz
Pamplona/ Iruñea
RÍAS BAIXAS
Villafranca del Bierzo
Pontevedra
RIBERA SACRA
León
Barco
BIERZO
Laguardia
Labastida
LA RIOJA
NAVARRA
RIBEIRO
Ribadavia
VALDEORRAS
Burgos
Corella
SOMONTANO
Huesca
Barbastro
RÍAS BAIXAS
MONTERREI
CIGALES
RIBERA DEL DUERO
Borja
CAMPO DE BORJA
Zaragoza
Lleida/ Lèrida
CONCA DE BARBERA
AMPURDÁN- COSTA BRAVA
Perelada
Girona/ Gerona
Toro
Valladolid
Peñafiel
Aranda de Duero
Calatayud
CARIÑENA
COSTERS DEL SEGRE
PLÁ DEL BAGES
ALELLA
Zamora
TORO
Rueda
RUEDA
Cariñena
CALATAYUD
PRIORATO
Montblanc
PENEDÉS
Barcelona
Salamanca
Segovia
Alcañiz
Móra la Nueva
TARRAGONA
Vilafranca del Penedès
TERRA ALTA
Tarragona
Avila
MONDÉJAR
Teruel
ISLAS BALEARES
Madrid
Arganda
VINOS DE MADRID
Méntrida
MÉNTRIDA
Castellón de la Plana
BINISSALEM
Palma
Binissalem
Toledo
VALENCIA
Mallorca
Cáceres
LA MANCHA
Utiel
VALENCIA
UTIEL- REQUENA
Requena
Valencia
Socuéllamos
ALICANTE
Almansa
ALMANSA
VALENCIA
Ciudad Real
YECLA
Yecla
RIBERA DEL GUADIANA
Valdepeñas
JUMILLA
ALICANTE
Badajoz
VALDEPEÑAS
Jumilla
Alacant/ Alicante
Cehegín
Bullas
Murcia
BULLAS
Córdoba
Jaén
Lorca
Bonares
Sevilla
Montilla
MONTILLA-MORILES
Huelva
CONDADO DE HUELVA
Granada
Almería
ISLAS CANARIAS
LA PALMA
TACORONTE- ACENTEJO
LANZAROTE
Sanlúcar de Barrameda
MALAGA
Málaga
VALLE DE LA OROTAVA
Tacoronte
Arrecife
JEREZ Y MANZANILLA
Jerez de la Frontera
MALAGA
VALLE DE GUIMAR
Las Palmas de Gran Canaria
ABONA
EL MONTE
Gomera
YCODEN- DAUTE- ISORA
Tenerife
EL HIERRO
Gran Canaria
Fuerteventura

Introduction  **13**

# Regions and Wines

Three main factors influence the way wines develop. First, there is the climate: cool, wet areas foster white-grape vines; warm, dry ones favour reds. A second factor is the food that was most freely available in the days before refrigeration: coastal areas and riverlands yield fish and seafood, while inland and mountainous regions offer game, cattle, sheep and pigs. Finally, there are the cultures and origins of the inhabitants themselves. Celtic seafarers, for example, have very different eating habits to those of the isolated, land-locked shepherds of the Meseta. This evolution of climate, gastronomy and culture has divided Spain into seven major regions, which are reflected in the seven sections of this book.

**Green Spain.** 'Green' Spain stretches from Galicia in the lush, cool, rainy northwest through the *Costa Verde*, or Green Coast, of Asturias and Cantabria in the north, and finally into the Basque Country. These areas share weather influences from the Atlantic and the Bay of Biscay, a tradition of seafood, and a strongly non-Castilian culture – Celtic in the west, Basque in the foothills of the Pyrenees. In Galicia, they speak Gallego, a close relative of Portuguese. In the Basque Country, they speak Euskara, related to no other language in the world.

**Castile-León**, or Old Castile, is the historic heartland of Castilian Spain, where kings and bishops, princes and academics have disported themselves since the Middle Ages. Food comes on the hoof or on the wing, the climate is hot and continental, and the wine style is very 'mainstream' – Spanish wines the way Spaniards drink them. This is traditionally where the best Castilian Spanish is spoken.

**North-Central Spain.** This part of the country lies in the shelter of the Cordillera Cantábrica mountains, which protect it from the excesses of Green Spain's maritime climate. Two provinces of the Basque Country are situated north of the mountain range; one – Álava or Araba – is located south of the mountains and produces Rioja wines.

La Rioja, Navarra and, to a lesser extent, Aragón, have been at the forefront of Spanish winemaking for a thousand years. After the phylloxera, or vine-louse, epidemic that devastated French vineyards between 1860 and 1890, these were also the nearest regions from which the French could buy wine. Then, as now, the Spanish *viñeros* worked hard to keep their customers happy. If these Spanish wines have been designed to please export markets, it must just be a coincidence that this region reflects a strong Castilian heritage, a dry, continental climate and a history of prosperity.

**Catalonia and the Balearics.** There is a strongly independent outlook here, the legacy of the medieval Catalan empire (which included the Balearic Islands). The climate is Mediterranean maritime, the cuisine is based mainly on the sea, and the Catalan people are quick to point out that Spain is not all Castile. This inventive culture has produced some of the country's most exciting and innovative wines. The people of Catalonia speak Catalan, while those of the Balearic Islands use a Catalan dialect called Mallorquín.

**The Levant.** In terms of climate, the Levant (literally 'the getting-up' – where the sun rises) is a hotter version of Catalonia, with similar weather and gastronomy, and an ancient tradition of seafaring and trade. It is divided between Valencia, where the locals speak a Catalan dialect called Valenciano, and Murcia, where Castilian is spoken.

**The Meseta**, according to a Castilian proverb, suffers from 'five months of winter and seven months of hell'. This flat, semi-arid plain is hot and high (700 to 1,000 metres/2,297 to 3,281 feet), and only sheep and the toughest grapes survive here. Thus, local cuisine consists basically of sheep, sheep's-milk cheese and sheep, and until the foundation of Madrid in the 16th century, the local culture was one of isolation. This section covers the wines of Madrid province, Castilla-La Mancha (post-*Reconquista*, or reconquest, Castile) and Extremadura, on the Portuguese border. Castilian is the main language, with regional dialects.

**Andalucía and the Canaries.** Andalucía is Spain's oldest wine-producing area, dominated by Sherry. Its climate is fully Mediterranean, but the style of wine has been determined more by several centuries of export markets than by the local gastronomy. Culturally, Andalucía is highly traditional, and Castilian is its main language, though seasoned with the usual regional dialects.

In contrast, the Canary Islands have a sub-tropical climate, a seafood-eating history and an interesting cultural mix of islanders that is skewed annually by a massive tourist industry. Its wines, however, are astonishing in many ways, ranging from the most modern, cool-fermented styles to those derived from ancient vines that have been cultivated since the Romans left. Here, they speak a soft, gentle dialect of Castilian, and refer to mainland Spaniards as *peninsulares*.

This is how Spain's wine-country breaks down culturally, gastronomically and climatically – but real life is never as well-organised as we might prefer. If ever there were a country in which every rule proves to be an exception and every exception proves to be a rule, then this is it.

## Autonomous communities

As mentioned previously, Spain has 17 *autonomías*, or autonomous communities, each consisting of a number of provinces, of which there are 50 in total. The following is a complete list of all of these divisions in alphabetical order, along with details of the wine areas to be found within each.

Precise details of the *denominación de origen* (DO) zones and *vino de la tierra* (country wine) areas can be found in the relevant chapters; definitions of the various terms may be found in the 'Classification' section on page 22.

Castilian and dialectical differences are indicated where more than one name is listed for a particular word; the Castilian variant is given first.

### Andalucía
*Provinces:* Almería, Cádiz, Córdoba, Granada, Huelva, Jaén, Málaga, Sevilla *DO Wines:* Condado de Huelva, Málaga, Montilla-Moriles, Jerez/Xérès/Sherry y Manzanilla *Vinos de la Tierra:* Cádiz, Contraviesa-Alpujara *Vinos Comarcales:* Laujar, Villaviciosa, Lopera, Aljarafe, Lebrija, Los Palacios

### Aragón
*Provinces:* Huesca, Teruel, Zaragoza *DO Wines:* Calatayud, Campo de Borja, Cariñena, Somontano *Vinos de la Tierra:* Bajo Aragón, Tierra Baja de Aragón, Valdejalón *Vinos Comarcales:* Alto Jiloca, Muniesa, Belchite, Daroca

### Asturias
Asturias is a principality (*see* Notes) *Province:* Oviedo

### Baleares (Balearic Islands)
*Province:* Palma de Mallorca (four islands: Mallorca, Menorca, Eivissa, Formentera) *DO Wine:* Binissalem *Vino de la Tierra:* Plà i Llevant de Mallorca

### Canarias (Canary Islands)
*Provinces:* Las Palmas de Gran Canaria (three islands: Lanzarote, Fuerteventura, Gran Canaria), Santa Cruz de Tenerife (four islands: Tenerife, La Gomera, El Hierro, La Palma) *DO Wines:* Abona, El Hierro, Lanzarote, El Monte, La Palma, Tacoronte-Acentejo, Valle de Güímar, Valle de la Orotava, Ycoden-Daute-Isora *Vino de la Tierra:* La Gomera

### Cantabria
*Province:* Santander

### Castilla-León (Castile-León)
*Provinces:* Burgos, León, Palencia, Salamanca, Segovia, Soria, Valladolid, Zamora *DO Wines:* Bierzo, Cigales, Ribera del Duero, Rueda, Toro *Vinos de la Tierra:* Cebreros, Fermoselle-Arribes del Duero, Tierra del Vino de Zamora, Valdevimbre-Los Oteros *Vinos Comarcales:* Benavente, La Ribera del Arlanza, La Sierra de Salamanca, Valtiendas

### Castilla-La Mancha
*Provinces:* Albacete, Ciudad Real, Cuenca, Guadalajara, Toledo *DO Wines:* Almansa, La Mancha, Méntrida, Mondéjar, Valdepeñas *Vinos de la Tierra:* Gálvez, Manchuela, Pozohondo, Sierra de Alcaraz

### Catalunya/Cataluña (Catalonia)
*Provinces:* Barcelona, Gerona/Girona, Lérida/Lleida, Tarragona *DO Wines:* Alella, Ampurdán-Costa Brava, Cava (*see* Notes), Conca de Barberà, Costers del Segre, Penedès, Pla de Bages, Priorato, Tarragona, Terra Alta *Vinos Comarcales:* Conca de Tremp, Bajo Ebre-Montsiá

### Extremadura
*Provinces:* Badajoz, Cáceres *DO Wine:* Ribera del Guadiana *Vinos Comarcales:* Azuaga, Cilleros

### Galicia
*Provinces:* La Coruña/A Coruña, Lugo, Ourense/Orense, Pontevedra *DO Wines:* Monterrei, Rías Baixas, Ribeira Sacra, Ribeiro, Valdeorras *Vino de la Tierra:* Val do Minho *Vinos Comarcales:* Betanzos, Ribeira do Ulla

### Madrid
*Province:* Madrid *DO Wine:* Vinos de Madrid

### Murcia
(Murcia is a *región* (*see* Notes) *Province:* Murcia *DO Wines:* Bullas, Jumilla, Yecla *Vinos de la Tierra:* Abanilla, Campo de Cartagena

### Navarra
Navarra is a *comunidad foral* (*see* Notes) *Province:* Navarra *DO(Ca) Wines:* Navarra, Rioja (DOCa)

### País Vasco/Euskadi (The Basque Country)
*Provinces:* Álava/Araba, Guipúzcoa/Gipuzkoa, Vizcaya/Bizkaia *DO(Ca) Wines:* Chacolí de Getaria/Getariako Txakolina, Chacolí de Vizcaya/Bizkaiko Txakolina, Rioja (DOCa)

### La Rioja
*Province:* La Rioja *DOCa Wine:* Rioja

### Valencia
*Provinces:* Alicante, Castellón de la Plana, Valencia *DO Wines:* Alicante, Utiel-Requena, Valencia *Vinos Comarcales:* Benniarés, Lliber-Jávea, San Mateo/Sant Mateu

## Notes

**Asturias is a *principado* (principality).** A ninth-century independent kingdom, it absorbed Galicia after the Moors left, then merged with the neighbouring kingdom of León in the tenth century and with Castile in 1230. It has been recognised as a principality since 1388, when the heir-apparent to the Castilian throne took the title *Príncipe de Asturias* – Prince of Asturias. Today, the heir-apparent to the Spanish throne uses the same title, just as the heir-apparent in the UK uses the title 'Prince of Wales'.

**Cava** is made mainly in Catalonia, but also in parts of Aragón, Valencia, Navarra, La Rioja, Castile-León, the País Vasco and Extremadura.

**Murcia is a *región*.** Although part of the Levantine hinterland, Murcia is politically divided from Valencia on linguistic grounds. Whereas Valencia uses Valenciano, a Catalan dialect, Murcia's *lingua franca* is Castilian.

**Navarra is a *comunidad foral*.** Originally an independent kingdom, then linked with France, Navarra joined the newly united Spain in 1512 with the signing of a charter, known as a *fuero* (the adjective is *foral*), in which the king agreed to certain freedoms and privileges for Navarra's citizens in return for their fealty.

# Grape Varieties

Above: Garnacha is probably the most widely planted red-wine grape in the whole of Spain. An important component of Rioja, it is now being used to make new-wave varietal wines.

Experimental plantations of almost every known grape variety can be found in many areas of Spain. So-called 'international' varieties such as Cabernet Sauvignon, Merlot, Malbec, Pinot Noir, Sauvignon Blanc, Riesling and Gewürztraminer are in production or under surveillance from Ampurdán to Cádiz, and some of them have been grown for 300 years or more. The following list details only the most important native Spanish grape varieties. In quality terms, those marked with a full star (★) may be considered the most important. Those marked with an empty star (☆) are showing worthwhile potential.

## Red grape varieties

**Alicante** Another name for Garnacha Tintorera (*qv*).

**Aragón** In certain zones of Castile-León, Garnacha (*qv*) goes by this name. It is also sometimes known as Tinto Aragonés.

**Bobal** A grape with good colouring properties, Bobal yields good, beefy, *rosado* wines and warm reds. In the Levant, it may also be made into a *doble pasta* (literally, ('doubly pasted') wine, in which the grape must is fermented over two lots of lees to provide really hefty body in the finished product. This style of wine is much in demand for blending on the export market by countries that produce red wines which are a little on the 'light' side.

**Cariñena** A variety that produces robust, well-balanced wines, Cariñena is grown most importantly in Rioja, where it is known as Mazuelo. It is the grape which adds colour and body to the Rioja grape 'mix', and it is used in most traditionally made Rioja wines to counterbalance the lightness of Garnacha. Cariñena is also grown in Catalonia. Strangely enough, it plays only a small part in the DO wine of its native region of Cariñena in Aragón. It is known in France as Carignan.

**Cencibel** is used as a synonym for Tempranillo (*qv*) in central and southern Spain – although, rather like twins separated at birth, some Cencibel grown in the south is palpably different from Tempranillo grown in the north. A few growers even have plantations of both types (vines brought in from both north and south) and claim that you can tell the difference.

**Garnacha Tinta** ★ Possibly Spain's most widely planted red grape and a great blender, although the very finest wines made from Garnacha come from Priorato. In (virtual) monoculture, the 100-year-old Garnacha vines of the Clos l'Ermita estate produce the region's finest wine, although the winemaker adds about five to ten per cent of Cabernet Sauvignon to give the wine a perfume. At the Scala Dei cellars (also in Priorato), Garnacha makes a wine as big and bold and as any in Europe at a natural 15 per cent alcohol by volume (abv), and it lasts for ever. Garnacha is an important component of traditional Rioja (usually up to 30 per cent), and at least one Rioja house (Martínez Bujanda) is producing a varietal Rioja made entirely from Garnacha. This grape variety is popular in Navarra and most of the rest of northern Spain. In southern France, it is known as Grenache.

**Garnacha Tintorera** Also called Alicante. One of the few grapes that has coloured juice, it is used in blends to provide colour and weight (particularly with Mencía in Bierzo), but it does not appear in any real wines of quality.

**Graciano** ★ This is a low-yield grape that was almost dying out until Rioja won the DOCa (*see* page 23). A small, tough-skinned variety, it adds tremendous finesse and ageing capability (*ie* tannins) to a blend; even in small quantities, it can produce that final polish which great *gran reservas*, for example, really need. Graciano is used sparingly in Rioja (and to an even lesser extent in Navarra), but it is grown almost nowhere else.

**Juan García** ☆ A variety native to the Fermoselle area of Zamora (Castile-León) where it is widely planted. Recent research has shown Juan García to be a potentially excellent variety in the hands of a skilled winemaker, although it will take serious future investment before it achieves anything spectacular. When well made, however, it gives local *vinos de la tierra* plenty of pleasant, easy-drinking fruit. This could be a grape to watch.

**Listán Negro** ☆ One of the principal varieties of the Canary Islands, especially Tacoronte-Acentejo on Tenerife. In modern wineries it turns out good, rich, ripe red wines of no great distinction but with a pleasant better-than-everyday character. Listán Negro seems to show some potential for the future, should the island's current wine industry achieve 'critical mass'.

**Manto Negro** Native of the Balearic Islands and the leading variety in the wines of Binissalem, Manto Negro yields light, fresh wines (with good fruit and a modest amount of oak) which age well.

**Mazuelo.** *See* **Cariñena.**

**Mencía** ☆ A grape that, according to recent studies, is very similar to Cabernet Franc, with which it may share a common ancestor. It can yield wine of very high quality in the hands of a skilled winemaker, although (quite frankly) it has yet to do so on a consistent basis. Good Mencía wine has lovely, fresh, crisp fruit and elegant tannin, and is built for drinking young. In blends with Garnacha Tintorera, it has shown the capacity for ageing, particularly in Bierzo. It is mainly found there and in neighbouring Valdeorras, where attempts to make a *joven* version have been (mostly) disappointing. This is, however, certainly a grape to watch.

**Monastrell** ☆ A high-yielding, easy-ripening grape which produces some excellent, high-quality wines in new installations, especially in Murcia. After years of disregard, Monastrell has been rehabilitated, due largely to the efforts of a couple of wineries in Jumilla (the late-lamented Vitivino and Señorío del Condestable) and one in Yecla (Castaño). Condestable belongs to the giant Bodegas y Bebidas group, which launched a varietal Monastrell in 1995 and changed a lot of people's ideas about the grape. Its wine has tremendous, vibrant fruit, a delicious ripeness and lip-smacking acidity. Monastrell is also used in Catalonia for the making of pink Cava, and is known in France as Mourvèdre.

**Moristel** This is a rather obscure grape variety found only in the Somontano DO – but it is none the worse for that. It makes good, fruity, early-maturing red *joven* wines and is good for blending with imported grapes which flourish in this area.

**Negramoll** The Negramoll is the grape of the Canary Islands, particularly the Tacoronte-Acentejo DO, where it is most widely grown. Negramoll is used to make light, soft, early-maturing wines, usually in blends with Listán Negro (*qv*). The results are encouraging, but at the moment, production is too small-scale to make a definitive comment.

**Tempranillo** ★ Spain's principal native red grape, it goes by the name of Ull de Llebre in Catalonia, Cencibel in southern Spain, and Tinto Fino, Tinto del País and Tinta de Toro in Castile-León. Recent research indicates a possible common ancestor with Pinot Noir. Vinified on its own, it makes splendid *jovenes*, with strawberry/raspberry aromas on the nose and delicious summer-pudding fruit on the palate. Its finest work, however, has always been in the great Riojas, where it is generally used in a ratio of about 70 per cent with Garnacha, Graciano and Mazuelo; the resulting wine will age to a Christmas-pudding, raisiny, cinnamon richness in great years. Even so, Tempranillo makes lovely, spicy *crianzas* as well as the occasional *reserva* in a good year in Ribera del Duero. In Navarra, Toro and Catalonia, new plantations are producing some spectacular results in Tempranillo/Cabernet Sauvignon blends. The grape is also grown in the Douro region of Portugal, where it is known as Tinta Roriz.

Above: Spain's premier red grape variety. Tempranillo makes light, fruity *joven* wines as well as the classic, spicy oak-aged wines of Rioja.

## White grape varieties

**Airén** This is the most abundant grape in Spain – and (allegedly) in the world. It survives the blistering heat of the great plain of La Mancha, and – when vinified in the modern manner – yields wines that are cool, fresh and creamy. Airén had an appalling reputation until modern winemaking techniques brought out its better character; even so, it will never aspire to wines of more than everyday quality. Most plantations are in Castilla-La Mancha, although a little is grown in Extremadura.

**Albariño** ★ Native of Galicia. However, Miguel Torres is convinced that it is the Riesling brought from Germany as a votive offering by monks on the famous *Camino de Santiago*, or Pilgrims' Road, which runs from northeastern Europe right through to Santiago de Compostela in Castile-León. The *consejo regulador* disagrees with Señor Torres, but whatever its origins, Albariño is the most important grape of the Rías Baixas DO (and other Galician DOs), and has experienced a spectacular boom in recent years – with good reason. At their best, wines made from Albariño have lovely, peachy fruit on the palate, which is rich without being sweet; most are drunk within 18 months of the vintage. Given the opportunity (*ie* with full malolactic fermentation), Albariño can also produce full-bodied, steely, dry wines that age with great grace.

**Albillo** This grape may have originated in the Sherry Country, although it is now grown primarily in the Ribeiro DO, and is the principal (white) variety in the Vinos de Madrid DO. Previously, it was used in small quantities in (red) Vega Sicilia, but these days, it seems to have fallen out of favour almost everywhere.

**Alcañón** The native grape of the Somontano region, Alcañón yields light white wines which possess an individual aroma; it also performs well in blends with other varieties, including French imports. At present, however, it seems to be being neglected in favour of Chenin Blanc.

**Godello** ☆ A high-quality, aromatic grape, which is a native of Galicia. In recent years, measures have been taken to encourage the planting of Godello, especially in the Valdeorras DO. Its best wines show the kind of ripe, rich (though not sweet), crisp, almost peachy fruit exhibited by Albariño, although Godello has a little more acidity. This promises to be one of Spain's great white-wine grapes. Watch this space.

**Listán.** *See* **Palomino.**

**Loureira** ☆ A Galician grape of good quality which yields highly aromatic wines. Loureira is usually found alongside the white grape Treixadura and sometimes in blends with Albariño, but the finished wine always has that typical rich, soft, peachy fruit. If this variety were cultivated more widely, we might have a better appreciation of how it performs as a single variety.

**Macabeo** ★ Also called Viura, Macabeo is cultivated all over northern Spain and in parts further south where areas are licensed to make Cava. In Catalonia, it is blended with Xarel-lo and Parellada to make Spain's best sparkling wines, but Cavas made outside Catalonia tend to be 100 per cent Macabeo. For still wines, Macabeo is the main white grape of Rioja and Navarra. While it is sometimes criticised for being on the neutral side, in the hands of a skilled winemaker it is capable of yielding wines with good aromatics and a herby, spicy nose.

Classic white oak-aged Riojas are likely to be mainly Viura with about five to ten per cent Malvasía Riojana (*qv*). It is known in France as the Macabeu.

**Malvasía** Originally from Greece, this grape variety produces highly aromatic and individualistic wines. It is found especially in Valencia, Zamora and the Canary Islands, where it still produces a sweet, semi-fortified wine which used to be known as Canary sack. There is also a Malvasia Riojana, used sparingly in (mainly oak-aged) white Rioja wines; it provides the spicy edge and is needed for long ageing of white wine. It is known in Catalonia as Subirat-Parent.

**Merseguera** A grape planted in Valencia, Merseguera is the white-wine mainstay of the Levant. Critics accuse it of blandness and neutrality, but the best examples have pleasant fruit and even a little herbiness on the nose. Admittedly, though, its main role is in the production of the everyday white wines that are destined for the supermarkets of Europe.

**Moscatel** ★ This is the grape that is known in France as the Muscat d'Alexandrie: rich and sweet and the basis of Spain's best-value, sweet *vinos de licor*, as well as many of the sweeter wines of Andalucía. A good Moscatel de Valencia must be the best sweet wine, penny for penny, anywhere in Europe.

**Palomino** ★ Palomino is the undisputed grape of Jerez, and is also known as Listán. It flourishes on the chalky soils of the province of Cádiz, and yields a base wine which can grow a coating of *flor* before going on to develop in the *solera* system (*see* page 192). Sherry is a triumph of skill and quality-control over a fairly ordinary base product, as evidenced by the fact that, wherever else Palomino has been planted – usually for its high-cropping characteristics – the results have been decidedly unexceptional.

**Pansà Blanca.** *See* **Xarel-lo.**

**Parellada** ★ One of the mainstays of Cava, this variety is also planted throughout Catalonia for use in the production of everyday white wines. Typically, it is Parellada that provides the soft, creamy base for Cava, while Macabeo adds crispness and acidity, and Xarel-lo

Above: The mainstay of many Galician DOs, Albariño can yield deliciously fresh wines with rich, peachy fruit – which explains its surge in popularity during recent years.

provides the underpinning strength. Single-variety Parellada wines tend to be pleasant, light, easy-drinking everyday whites meant for immediate consumption.

**Pedro Ximénez ★** A Spanish classic, supposedly brought to the country by a German soldier named Pieter Siemens in the 16th century (hence the name – although legend says he told them it was Riesling). This is the great grape of Montilla and elsewhere in Andalucía, where its rich, sweet juice is turned into fabulous dessert wines. The oldest are as thick and black as oil, and are generally enjoyed by the teaspoonful, poured into a hole excavated for the purpose in the top of freshly made vanilla ice-cream.

**Verdejo ★** The principal variety of Rueda, this is the grape that waited 1,000 years for technology to catch up with it. Oxidation problems have been solved by refrigeration and inert-gas blanketing, producing perhaps the greatest white wine of Spain: Rueda Superior.

This must contain 85 per cent Verdejo; the best (look for Riscal, Palacio de Bornos, Martinsancho) has enormous, crisp, mouthwatering fruit, tremendous aromatics and a bone-dry finish. Rueda Superior is truly one of Europe's greatest white wines.

**Viura.** *See* **Macabeo.**

**Xarel-lo ★** The grape that caused all the trouble in Cava circles (known as Pansà Blanca in the Alella DO). Today, it provides the foundation, weight, power and alcohol which underpin everything Cava is about, but in the old days, it suffered from the same oxidation problems as Verdejo did in Rueda. The result was Cavas with a curious 'rooty' flavour that was much vilified by north-European wine-writers with delicate sensibilities. These problems have been solved, however, and one of the latest developments in Cava is a Xarel-lo/Monastrell blend (*ie* white grape/red grape) from Freixenet which offers an entirely new perspective on Catalan sparkling wines.

Left: Baskets of grapes await vinification at a Valdepeñas bodega. While high-tech equipment may be used in the winery, much of the harvesting is still done by hand.

# Climate and Soil

**Chalk**

**Schist**

**Clay**

*Spain's soils vary as much as its regional climates, but three main types are found in the best vineyards. Chalk and schist provide excellent water retention in the driest part of the year, while clay is rich in trace elements such as iron.*

The most popular conception of Spain is of a seaside country that is sandy, southerly and sweltering. While these adjectives can apply (especially on the southeast coast), they no more reflect the reality that is Spain than chalet-strewn Alpine pastures represent the whole of Switzerland. Aside from such misconceptions, Spain has something else in common with Switzerland, as well as with Albania: they are – perhaps surprisingly in Spain's case – the three most mountainous countries in Europe. Spain is the third most mountainous and the second-highest overall, and it is the altitude of many Spanish vineyard areas that explains how quality wines are made at such a southerly latitude.

## Topography

Spain consists of a large central plateau surrounded by mountains, whose peaks reach as high as 3,482 metres (11,420 feet: Mulhacén in the Sierra Nevada), and whose foothills go down to the sea. At 646 metres (2,119 feet), Madrid, situated in the centre of the country, is the highest capital in Europe. The great central *Meseta* (the word means 'table-land') is another study in altitudes: it tilts gently southward, with Burgos in the north at 856 metres (2,808 feet) and Jaén in the south at 574 metres (1,883 feet).

The Meseta is surrounded by mountain ranges. The most important are the Pyrenees, which form the border with France; the Cordillera Cantábrica, a western spur of the Pyrenees which divides Green Spain in the north from the uplands of the centre; the Sierra de Gredos in the west; the Sierra de Morena in the south; and the Sistema Ibérico in the east. In addition, the central plateau is also criss-crossed by smaller mountain ranges which provide the wide range of microclimates found in the country's various wine-producing regions. At its centre is the great plain of La Mancha, which stretches from Madrid in the north to Valdepeñas in the south.

The other major characteristic of Spanish topography takes the form of great rivers. In the north, the two most important are the Ebro and the Duero, both of which rise in the Cordillera Cantábrica. The Ebro flows eastwards and southward, watering the vineyards of Rioja, Navarra and parts of Aragón as well as those of Catalonia, where it meets the Mediterranean south of Tarragona. The Duero flows westward through Castile-León, most notably through the vineyards of Ribera del Duero, Rueda and Toro, crossing into Portugal (at which point it changes its name to 'Douro') and travelling through the vineyards of Port Country until it reaches the Atlantic at Oporto.

West-central Spain's rivers include the Tajo (Tagus), which runs east of Madrid through Toledo into Portugal, where it becomes the Tejo and flows into the Atlantic at Lisbon. Another is the Guadiana, which flows west and south from La Mancha, where it passes for some considerable distance underground and provides much-needed natural irrigation for vineyards in Ciudad Real. The last 100 kilometres (62 miles) of the Guadiana also form the border with Portugal.

East-central Spain has the Turia and the Júcar, which flow into the Mediterranean north and south, respectively, of Valencia. There is also the Segura, which flows through the southern part of the country, running eastwards into the Mediterranean between Murcia and Alicante. The Guadalquivir, meanwhile, flows westward through Córdoba and Sevilla before meeting the Atlantic at the estuary of Sanlúcar de Barrameda. All of these rivers form the arteries of agriculture throughout their respective regions, helping to create microclimates and providing irrigation for the highest and driest areas of the country.

## Geology

The Portuguese and Galician coast is at the leading edge of the European tectonic plate. As a result, most of Portugal's highlands and the western mountain ranges of Spain tend to be composed of primary and crystalline rocks. The most important of these is schist, which provides the bedrock for the best vineyards of both countries. It is significant that schist outcrops come to the surface on the Catalan coast at Alella, in the highlands of Priorato, in Rioja, along the Duero Valley, and in the Port Country of the Douro.

It is even more significant that these are – with the exception of the Catalan coast – highland areas where climatic factors are ameliorated by the altitude. Sedimentary rock formations provide the bedrock for much of the north and east of the country, mainly in the lowland areas outside the rim of mountains which surrounds the central Meseta, and later rock formations make up the remainder. The Canary Islands are mainly volcanic.

In the coastal areas, soils are generally light, sometimes sandy, but not particularly rich in organic matter, which makes them good for vine-growing. The best areas, however, exhibit the characteristics of all great vineyard areas: some calcium carbonate, whether in the form of chalk, limestone or marl, and a wide range of trace elements. For example, the highland areas of Rioja

have clay-based soils which are alternately rich in iron and carbonates, whereas the lowland areas (around Alfaro) are much sandier. The earth in Ribera del Duero consists of nine per cent to 18 per cent active chalk over clay, with a high level of gypsum.

In Jerez, however, much of the soil is *albariza* – that is, so rich in chalk (up to 80 per cent) that some vineyards look as if they have been covered by a recent snowfall. In general terms, though, the very best vineyards in Spain share the schistose bedrock substructures which cross the northern part of the country with limestone and/or chalk soils, with a dash of alluvial matter from a nearby river and a range of trace elements.

## Climate

Spain's climate divides into three main systems. First, there is the system which governs Green Spain – the strip of land situated north of the Cordillera Cantábrica which includes Galicia, Asturias, Cantabria and the northern part of the Basque Country – and the northern (Pyrenean) parts of Navarra, Aragón and Catalonia. Here, rainfall is high: anything up to 2,000 millimetres (80 inches) per year (the UK, by comparison, has an average of around 1,200 millimetres/48 inches). Summers are hot, averaging 24°C (76°F) and winters are relatively cold, with a January average of around 8°C (46°F), although these temperatures vary greatly with altitude.

The second system concerns the Meseta, which has what could be classed as an extreme continental climate, with freezing winters and blazing summers up to and beyond 42°C (104°F). The daily average is around 30°C (85°F) in the summer and well below freezing in the winter, when the daily average temperature is around 4°C (38°F). The Meseta's average rainfall is just 500 millimetres (20 inches) or less.

The third system takes in the strip of Mediterranean coast, which stretches from southern Catalonia right round to the southern Portuguese border. These areas sit between the mountainous rim of the Meseta and the sea, and enjoy a hot climate alleviated by sea breezes. Average temperatures are around 12°C (54°F) in the winter and around 25°C (78°F) in the summer. However, rainfall may be very low, and rivers regularly dry up in the summer.

Statistics notwithstanding, this is a general view of Spain's climate. Most (though not all) of the best vineyards are the result of microclimatic conditions which often go against the normal averages.

# Classification: laws and labels

DO

Vino de Mesa

Vino de Mesa de

Vino de la Tierra

The idea behind wine law is to make it as easy as possible for the customer to know what he or she is getting whenever a bottle comes off the shelf. The basic philosophy sounds simple enough, but it has spawned some of the most complex, bureaucratic and incomprehensible legislation in Europe. Spain came later than most countries to a full classification of its wines, and this has (perhaps) made the subject a little easier to understand.

## Table Wine

This is the European classification for wines of a certain basic quality which do not fit into the classification of Quality Wine. In Spain, there are four types:

**Vino de Mesa (VdM**; literally, 'Table Wine') is simple, basic wine. It is usually blended from various regions of the country to combine the fruit and fresh acidity of the north with the warmth and high strength of the south. *On the label:* 'Vino de Mesa, Produce of Spain' and usually a brand name (Don Darias is probably the best known) but no regional name and no vintage date.

**Vino de Mesa de... (**followed by a region or province name) is living proof that you can buck the system if you have enough influence. This classification is for maverick winemakers who grow unauthorised grapes in unclassified areas using unorthodox methods, such as the Marqués de Griñón in the province of Toledo, who grows Cabernet and Merlot and irrigates, or the Yllera family in Castile-León which makes red wine in a white-wine-only zone. *On the label:* 'Vino de Mesa de Toledo' and 'Vino de Mesa de Castilla-León' provides the legal nicety of a place-name, which thereby allows them to put a vintage date on the label (forbidden for humbler wines). Needless to say, the place-name used on the label may not be the same as, or even similar to, the name of any Quality Wine zone.

**Vino Comarcal (VC or CV**; regional wine) acknowledges that there are *comarcas* (roughly equivalent in size to an English county) which, while of modest quality, do have some definable regional country character. There are 21 areas thus classified – mainly large, sprawling areas of principally local interest and roughly equivalent to the French *vin de pays de région* and *vin de pays de département* classifications. *On the label:* usually branded, sometimes using the words 'Vino Comarcal', or even (confusingly enough) 'Vino de Mesa de' followed by the regional name. What you will

not see is the classification's full legal description, which is *Vino de Otras Comarcas con Derecho a la Utilización de Mención Geográfica en Vinos de Mesa.* This means 'other regions with the right to a geographical annotation in table wines'. This is why we call it 'Vino Comarcal'.

**Vino de la Tierra (VdlT**; 'Wine of the Land') is a classification for country wines, as it were, with attitude: wines that are likely to apply for promotion to Quality Wine status at some time in the future, and roughly equivalent to the French *vin de pays de zone*. There are 25 of them, and they tend to be smaller areas with well-defined local characters. *On the label:* 'Vino de la Tierra de' followed by the district name. Once again, you will not see the full legal name, which is *Vinos de Mesa con Derecho al Uso de Una Indicación Geográfica.* You can see why.

## Quality Wine

Wines bearing the Quality Wine designation must meet Europe-wide standards of supervision and quality-control, and each wine-producing zone has a *consejo regulador*, or regulatory council made up of growers, winemakers, biochemists, viticulturalists and representatives of local government. The *consejo* is there to police all the zone's activities and adjudicate on matters concerning replanting, rootstocks, ageing regulations and everything else. When a new Quality Wine area is created (usually by promotion from VdlT), the *consejo* publishes a *reglamento*, or set of regulations, which becomes the bible of the zone, and which is ratified first by the regional government, then by the Subdirección-General de Vinos de Calidad in Madrid, and finally by Brussels. Only then may it legally carry a Quality Wine designation. There are two levels:

**Denominación de Origen (DO)** is the main Quality Wine classification in Spain. There are 54 DO zones, each with its own *consejo regulador*. The criteria for Quality Wines include all aspects of planting, cultivating, harvesting, vinifying and ageing wines under the inspective eye of the *consejo*, which can withhold its official back labels (*contraetiquetas*) if there is any doubt. *On the label:* the name of the wine zone (eg Ribera del Duero, La Mancha, Tarragona) appears on the main label over the words 'Denominación de Origen' (*Denominació d'Origen* in Catalonia). The two exceptions are Sherry and Cava, upon whose labels the words 'Sherry' and 'Cava' are deemed sufficient. All DO wines, however carry a *contraetiqueta* on the back of the bottle with the logo of the *consejo,* its official seal and the bottle's serial number.

**Denominación de Origen Calificada (DOCa)** is a higher category of Quality Wine introduced in 1988 but not actually awarded until April 19, 1991, to Rioja. Argument still rages in Logroño, Madrid and Brussels over what might or should or could have been done to regulate the new category, and no other region has yet come forward to claim it. However, DOCa allows for lower yields, more rigorous selection of grapes and bottling by the producer, and it aspires to guarantee wines that have performed at the highest quality levels over a large number of years. This is certainly true of the greatest Rioja wines. Whether it should have been applied to all of them indiscriminately is another matter. As the dust finally begins to settle on this, Ribera del Duero, Penedès and Rías Baixas have all been mooted as possible candidates. (They are all denying it hotly, of course.)

## Ageing of wine

As well as the producer's name, or the name of the brand, the DO zone and the official seal of the *consejo regulador,* Spain has its own system of classifying wines by age. Since the 19th century, Spanish winemakers have had a love affair with American oak, whose generously sized pores and rich vanillin content did much to put the Spanish stamp on several generations of wine – particularly Rioja. However, since the late 1970s there has been a growing awareness that French oak, with its smaller, tighter pores, can add a final burnish to a wine, and that bottle-ageing can be every bit as important as cask-ageing – especially for the finest wines. New oak has quite a large impact on the wine, whereas older oak has less and less, and it is the cellarman's job to put the wine through a judicious mixture of old and new that is right for the quality of the vintage. This is summed up in the current Spanish ageing regulations. The following apply to red wines:

**Joven** (young) wines are those harvested in one year and sold the next, with little or no time spent in cask. These are light, fruity wines made for immediate drinking. For example: grapes harvested in the autumn of the year 2000 may be turned into wine and offered for sale immediately, though typically in the spring following the vintage. These wines may or may not spend some small amount of time in oak, though if they do, the time is less than the six months necessary for the next stage.

**Crianza** wines (the term literally means 'raising or rearing' – a reference to the ageing process) must spend a minimum of six months in cask and two full calendar years undergoing *crianza.* Thus, the harvest of 2000 may go into cask in the spring of 2001, be bottled or returned to the vat in the autumn of 2001 (*ie,* six months later) and may be offered for sale on January 1, 2003, having spent two full years in maturation. Some *consejos* (notably those of Rioja and Ribera del Duero) insist on a 12-month minimum period in oak, and many individual bodegas far exceed the minimum. (Wines without oak ageing are also sometimes called *sin crianza,* although the use of this term is actively discouraged by the *consejos.*)

**Reserva** wines must spend a minimum of three calendar years in development, of which at least one must be in oak and one must be in bottle. So, our 2000 vintage may spend 2001 in cask, 2002 back in the tank and 2003 in bottle before being offered for sale on January 1, 2004. Once again, most of the best growers age their wines for far longer than the legal minimum.

**Gran Reserva** wines are made only in the finest vintages or from the best grapes in good vintages (their selection is policed by the *consejo*) and spend at least five years in the cellar, of which at least two must be in cask and at least three in bottle. Thus, our 2000 harvest will spend 2001 and 2002 in cask, 2003 to 2005 in bottle, and be offered for sale on January 1, 2006. In practice, of course, most *gran reserva* wines tend to be much older than this example suggests.

**White and *rosado* (rosé)** wines, in each case above, require only six months in oak and may be released a year earlier than their red counterparts. White and pink *reservas* and *gran reservas* are rare, however.

### Other types of ageing

*Solera* ageing (*see* page 192) takes place in a series of barrels containing increasingly older wines. It is widely used in Andalucía and most spectacularly in Jerez.
*Rancio* wines, most popular in Catalonia and Aragón, are left on ullage (with air between the wine and the stopper) until they turn black and take on a 'rancid' or oxidised character.
*Vinos de licór* are sweet, fortified wines, the most famous of which is probably Tarragona Clásico, which must be aged for a minimum of 12 years before release.

**Joven**

**Crianza**

**Reserva**

**Gran Reserva**

# Green Spain

**G**reen Spain is one of the least 'Spanish' parts of the country. The Galicians and Basques who settled this northwestern corner left behind a decidedly non-Castilian culture that is like no other on earth. This does not mean, of course, that the wines made here are any less desirable – far from it. In fact, any wine-lover who explores Green Spain will soon discover just how much it has to offer in winemaking terms.

The Rías Baixas and Ribeiro DOs produce some of the best white wines in the country; the former's splendid Albariño is already considered to be a modern Spanish classic. The smaller region of Ribeira Sacra creates luscious white wines, too, but it also yields some attractive reds, as do Valdeorras and Monterrei, both of which show good potential. Finally, the Basque Country's wines, made from grape varieties grown nowhere else in the world, are as much a study in individualism as the Basque people themselves.

**Below: The River Sil flows into the River Miño in the province of Lugo. Both rivers are important sources of water in Green Spain.**

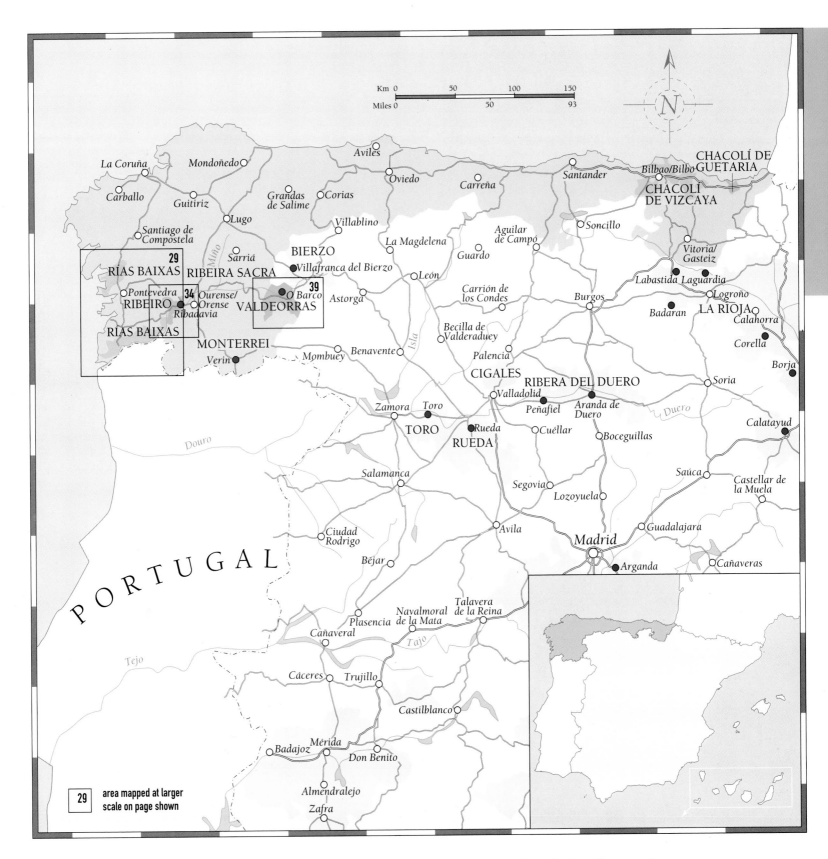

Km 0    50    100    150
Miles 0         50         93

CHACOLÍ DE
GUETARIA

La Coruña    Mondoñedo    Avilés    CHACOLÍ
Carballo    Guitiriz    Grandas    Corias    Oviedo    Carreña    Santander    DE VIZCAYA
de Salime    Bilbao/Bilbo
Villablino    Aguilar    Soncillo    Vitoria/
Santiago de    Lugo    de Campó    Gasteiz
Compostela    Villafranca    La Magdelena    Labastida    Laguardia
Sarriá    BIERZO    Guardo    Logroño
**29**    del Bierzo    León    Burgos    Badarán    LA RIOJA
RÍAS BAIXAS    RIBEIRA SACRA    Carrión de    Calahorra
Pontevedra    **34**    Ourense/    **39**    O Barco    Astorga    los Condes    Corella
RIBEIRO    Orense    VALDEORRAS    Becilla de    Borja
Ribadavia    Valderaduey    Soria
RÍAS BAIXAS    Benavente    Palencia    Calatayud
MONTERREI    Mombuey    CIGALES    RIBERA DEL DUERO
Verín    Valladolid    Duero
Zamora    Toro    Peñafiel    Aranda de
TORO    Duero    Calatayud
Rueda    Cuéllar    Boceguillas    Saúca
RUEDA    Segovia    Castellar de
Salamanca    Lozoyuela    la Muela

P O R T U G A L    Ciudad    Ávila    Guadalajara
Rodrigo    **Madrid**    Cañaveras
Béjar    Arganda
Talavera
Navalmoral    de la Reina
Plasencia    de la Mata
Cañaveral    Tajo
Tejo
Cáceres    Trujillo

Castilblanco

Badajoz    Mérida
Don Benito
Almendralejo
Zafra

Douro

**29** area mapped at larger
scale on page shown

# Galicia: more than just Celtic

**Above:** A young boy plays the *gaita*, or Galician bagpipes, a tradition that has its origins in the region's pre-Christian Celtic roots.

**Far right:** The cathedral of Santiago de Compostela has been the destination of Catholic pilgrims throughout Europe for centuries.

In the streets of Santiago de Compostela, capital of Galicia, you can hear the hurdy-gurdy and the *gaita*, or bagpipes. Truth to tell, you can hardly avoid them while strolling past the souvenir shops filled with postcards of old women in steeple hats and lace pinafores, earthenware *asubios* (a kind of primitive pentatonic flute), effigies of St James, scallop shells, gourds and pilgrim staves.

Alongside Santiago's deeply Catholic tradition, Galicia's pre-Christian Celtic heritage permeates everything in the city, not least in the form of *hórreos*. These stone granaries range in size from that of a dog-kennel to a mobile home, and are supported on legs topped with mushroom-shaped stones designed to keep out the rats. Every home in the vicinity, from the most modest cottage to the grandest *pazo* (country villa) once had its own *hórreo* in which the winter's supply of food was stored. When Christianity arrived in the eighth century following the departure of the Moors, the *hórreos* remained, but the phallic pagan symbols decorating each apex of their pitched roofs were diplomatically replaced with crosses.

All of which shows that Galicia's is a richly diverse civilisation. Archaeological records date from the sixth century BC; the name *Galicia* is a cognate of Gaul (France) and its earliest settlers were the same Celtic peoples who colonised most of the prehistoric European west coast. Incomers, however, have been many and varied. Romans, Swabians, Visigoths and Moors each took over the region until, at length, it was assimilated into the Kingdom of Asturias in the ninth century. Galicia achieved growing international fame throughout the tenth and 11th centuries, due to the pilgrims who journeyed on the long and winding *Camino de Santiago*, or Pilgrims' Road, to pay their respects at the tomb of St James the Greater, the apostle of Spain, which lies underneath Santiago's magnificent cathedral.

## Unification and beyond

Galicia became part of Greater Spain in 1492. In the mid-18th century, the port city of La Coruña (A Coruña, in Gallego) was licensed to trade with the American colonies, a move that resulted in increased fame and fortune. Even so, the enduring icons of Galicia remain the Camino de Santiago, with its extravagant baroque cathedrals and often-palatial *paradors* or state-owned hotels (including Santiago's five-star Hostal de los Reyes Católicos), and the Celtic heritage that is evident in dress, music and custom. Linguistically, however, all Celtic roots have been lost, since the Celts had no written language. Modern Galicians speak Gallego, a dialect that is related to Portuguese.

In addition to its cities, Galicia offers some of Spain's most magnificent scenery. The *rias* (estuaries) of the west coast provide spectacular sunsets, but there are also thickly forested mountain valleys, great slow-moving rivers with terraced vineyards, winding mountain roads, remote villages and, in the wildlife department, golden eagles – if you are lucky enough to spot one, that is.

---

### Galician gastronomy

*Galicia takes its food from the water. The local speciality is percebes, or goose-foot barnacles, which, while delectable in their way, pose particular problems in terms of actually consuming them.*

*A half-hour's stint with special pliers and something like a large hatpin might give you enough sustenance to order another course. This could consist of other local specialities, such as eels and lampreys from the rivers or all manner of seafood: white fish (especially turbot, sea bass, sole and cod), langostinos (prawns), cigalas (crayfish), lobsters, mussels, oysters and every kind of mariscos (shellfish), as well as some organisms without translatable names.*

*The local cheeses consist mainly of hard-to-medium styles made from cow's milk. The most popular of them is something called tetilla, which means... well, look it up for yourself and you'll understand why it is made in that particular shape.*

# Rías Baixas

The *rías baixas* are the 'low estuaries', a name that distinguishes them from the *rias altas*, or 'high estuaries', of the northwest coast. The distinction is merely one of north and south, since the *rías* themselves are all equally breathtaking: some as small and cosy as a Cornish cove, others with all the grandeur of a Norwegian fjord. The province of Pontevedra, in which the Rías Baixas DO lies, occupies the bottom left-hand corner of Galicia, forming Spain's west coast and Portugal's northern border. It is here that most of the best white wines of Galicia are made.

In this cool, lush countryside with its teeming rivers and majestic terraces, the Albariño grape is king (or queen, if you prefer). This is the vine that may once have been Riesling, brought by German monks setting up monasteries on the Camino de Santiago in the Middle Ages, or it may be a variety indigenous to Galicia and northern Portugal (where it is known as Alvarinho). In either case, it produces wines of peerless freshness, with peachy fruit deliciously balanced by crisp acidity. The other two most important grapes are Treixadura and Loureira Blanca, with a further half-dozen varieties found here and there throughout the region. Some light red wine is made mainly from Mencía, but this is a part of the world intended by Nature to produce white wine.

The topsoil in Rías Baixas is mainly dull, grey, alluvial stuff, but the bedrock is made up of pink-tinted granite with tiny shards of quartz; where the latter comes to the surface, the earth sparkles beguilingly with its flakes. Traditional plantations use pergolas for their vines, so that the bunches of grapes hang below a leafy canopy during the hottest months. In contrast, modern vineyards tend to be trained on wires, which aids in spraying and harvesting.

## Climate and yields

The main challenge facing growers in Rías Baixas is the weather. While the cool, wet climate fosters a charming, lush countryside, it also provides the perfect habitat for mildew, other fungal vine diseases and weed-growth which is at least as luxuriant as the vines themselves. Vineyard maintenance is labour-intensive and grapes have to be checked regularly for mould, but the high rainfall does result in high yields. Growers of Albariño are permitted to produce a maximum of 71.5 hectolitres per hectare (hl/ha), while for other varieties the maximum is 87.5hl/ha; in practice, about 50 to 60hl/ha is usual. This is not large by comparison with, say, Germany and Alsace, where 80 to 100hl/ha are the norm, but it is approximately double the production of the average Spanish DO zone.

Three production areas make up the Rías Baixas DO. The largest is the Val do Salnés, located north of the city of Pontevedra and drained by the River Ulla. Its vineyards spread north, south and east of the town of Cambados, and most of the wine produced is Albariño. This area was where new-style Albariño wines were pioneered, and it still makes most of the best of them. Pure Albariño wines bear the name of the grape, and a wine designated as Val do Salnés must be a minimum of 70 per cent Albariño.

The second production area is O Rosal, down in the southwestern part of the region. It runs from the Atlantic coast along the north bank of the River Miño, which at

Below: Traditional vineyards in Rías Baixas use pergolas to support the vines, so that the grapes are shaded by their own leaves in hot weather.

this point forms the border between Spain and Portugal. The climate is warmer here than in the Val do Salnés, since Atlantic influences begin to fade as you head inland. Here, the Loureira grape has equal status with Albariño, and any wine designated as O Rosal must be 70 per cent of either variety or of both blended together. However, the international fame of Albariño is such that most export wines are likely to be made purely from that variety.

Further along the Portuguese border, between the border town of Tui and the neighbouring DO zone of Ribeiro, lies the third production area: the Condado do Tea. The name translates rather picturesquely as 'Torch County', and is derived from the River Tea, which joins the River Miño near Salvaterra do Miño. This area is warmer and drier than O Rosal (although still cool and wet by Spanish standards), and it stretches along the northern upstream

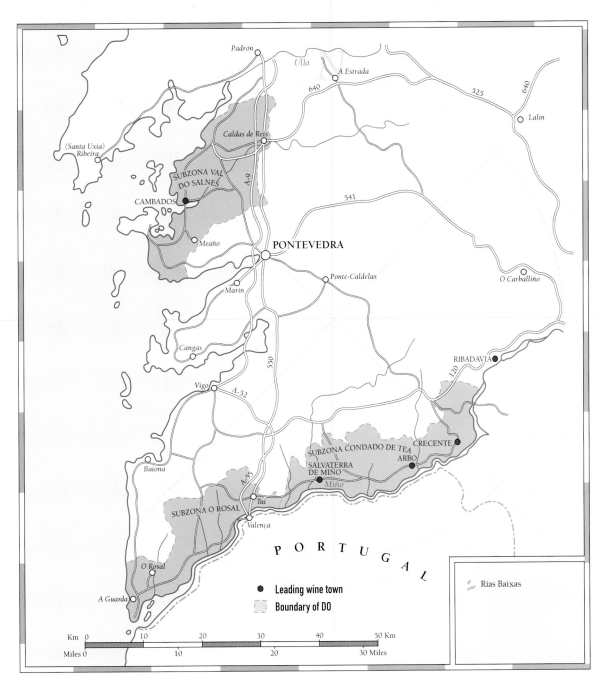

Padrón

Ulla

A Estrada

640

525

640

Lalín

Caldas de Reis

(Santa Uxia) Ribeira

SUBZONA VAL DO SALNÉS

A-9

541

CAMBADOS

Meaño

PONTEVEDRA

Ponte-Caldelas

O Carballiño

Marín

550

Cangas

RIBADAVIA

Vigo

A-52

120

SUBZONA CONDADO DE TEA

CRECENTE

ARBO

SALVATERRA DE MIÑO

Miño

Baiona

A-55

Tui

Valença

SUBZONA O ROSAL

P O R T U G A L

O Rosal

● Leading wine town

Boundary of DO

A Guarda

Rías Baixas

Km 0    10    20    30    40    50 Km

Miles 0        10        20        30 Miles

bend of the Miño. Here, Treixadura shares the limelight with Albariño, and wines bearing the local name may be made from 70 per cent of either or both varieties. Once again, however, in deference to market forces, most of the best wines are likely to be 100 per cent Albariño.

## Winemaking and wine styles

The winemaking process in Rías Baixas is fingertip-light: grapes are crushed in chilled pneumatic presses with as little as 20 grammes of pressure, and the must is fermented under meticulous temperature-control in the most modern stainless-steel installations. There is also some experimentation with barrel fermentation, particularly in native Galician oak.

One interesting aspect of Rías Baixas is the number of producers who give their wines a full secondary (or malolactic) fermentation, in which malic acid in the wine is converted into lactic acid and carbon dioxide. Most Spanish producers of white wine stop the process after the first (alcoholic) fermentation in order to retain acidity. While this practice keeps wine fresh and crisp, it also shortens its shelf-life. Wines that have undergone full fermentation do age gracefully, changing their character into something full-bodied, powerful, steely and dry after a number of years.

Even so, the vast majority of Rías Baixas white wine is enjoyed young, fresh and chilled over a table groaning with local seafood. From a price standpoint, it is never going to be cheap, for there is little economy of scale in the region. Small plantations, labour-intensive harvesting from difficult slopes and careful winemaking may maximise on quality, but it all costs in the long run.

There has been a good deal of debate in recent years over what qualifies as the classic white wine of Spain. Albariño from Rías Baixas is certainly a front-runner, hobbled only by its price levels. Prices aside, it is unquestionably one of the world's finest white wines.

# Notable adegas

*Adega* is the Gallego equivalent of *bodega*. VdS = Val do Salnés; R = O Rosal; CdT = Condado do Tea.

**Agro de Bazán, Vilanueva de Arosa (VdS).** *Founded 1988.* This firm is located in a grand old building surrounded by vineyards; however, grapes are bought in to supplement the harvest. All wines are 100% Albariño. The Granbazán Limousin *crianza* spends a year in oak, and Mainstream Granbazán (*verde*) is excellent. *Best wine:* Granbazán Ambar, made from free-run must.

**Bouza do Rei, Puxafeita-Ribadumia (VdS).** A small joint venture among four shareholders with 30ha of Albariño vines producing a single wine under the adega name. Excellent quality.

**Castro Martín, Puxafeita-Ribadumia (VdS).** *Founded 1981.* Family-owned adega with ten hectares of vines; also buys in grapes (100% Albariño) from other growers. *Best wine:* Casal Caeiro.

**Das Eiras, O Rosal (R).** *Founded 1990.* A smart, modern adega with 60ha of vines, including Albariño, Treixadura, Loureira and Caiño Blanco. Wines include Abadia (100% Albariño) and Terras Gauda bearing the O Rosal designation (70% Albariño, plus the others listed above). Also a barrel-fermented Terras Gauda made in American oak (three months on the lees). All are exemplary.

**Granxa Fillaboa, Fillaboa-Salvaterra do Miño (CdT).** *Founded 1986.* Family-owned adega with 24ha of Albariño vines. Excellent young wines are made in a small, modern winery, but it also keeps back some examples of older vintages. The wines age with consummate grace.

**Lagar de Fornelos, O Rosal (R).** *Founded 1982.* Since 1988, owned by the family which also owns Bodegas La Rioja Alta in La Rioja. Although based in O Rosal, 30% of its Albariño is bought in from the Val do Salnés to supplement the company's own 42ha of vines. Only one wine is made: Lagar de Cervera.

**Marqués de Vizhoja, Arbo (CdT).** *Founded 1980.* The adega produces Folla Verde Condado do Tea (with other varieties) and the non-DO but very pleasant Marqués de Vizhoja, which seems to be the house white in almost every restaurant in Galicia (look for the giant vine leaf). *Best wine:* Torre La Moreira (100% Albariño).

**Morgadío, Albeos-Crecente (CdT).** *Founded 1988.* A modern adega planned around a state-of-the-art winery. The second wine (scarcely less good) is called Torre Fornelos. There is also a Condado wine (Treixadura/ Loureira) called Carballo do Rei. *Best wine:* the flagship Morgadío (100% Albariño), which is as good as or better than anything from the Val do Salnés.

**Pablo Padín, Meaño (VdS).** *Founded 1987.* Small, family firm buying in grapes to boost its own 14ha of vines. It makes good, well-made Albariños, including Segrel Ámbar from free-run must and Segrel from the main pressing.

**Palacio de Fefiñanes, Cambados (VdS).** Founded 1904. The oldest adega in the region and a pioneer of Albariño. It uses its own and bought-in grapes to make just one wine (100% Albariño) in the faded elegance of the *palacio* itself.

**Pazo San Mauro, Salvaterra do Miño (CdT).** *Founded 1990.* Pazo San Mauro was established in a *pazo* dating back to 1582; it has made wine for a century or more under previous ownerships. This small family enterprise has 22ha of vines in production on a 30ha estate and makes two wines: Pazo San Mauro, an Albariño with a fresh, crisp Val do Salnés style; and Pazo San Mauro Condado (with Treixadura, Torrontés and Loureira added to the Albariño).

**Salnesur, Cambados (VdS).** *Founded 1988.* Co-op whose members farm 137ha of vines (all Albariño); self-sufficient in grapes. Three wines are made under the Condes de Albarei brand: Clásico, a classic, fresh-fruit Albariño; Enxebre, made by *maceración carbónico*; and Carballo Gallego (barrel-fermented; three months on its lees).

**Santiago Ruiz, O Rosal (R).** *Founded 1892.* Tiny, beautiful winery with two hectares of vines and 80 contract growers. Makes one wine Santiago Ruiz O Rosal (70% Albariño/20% Treixadura/ 10% Loureira). One of the region's best.

**Valdamor, Meaño (VdS).** Co-op with over 300 growers delivering grapes to a state-of-the-art winery. *Best wine:* Valdamor – a fresh, peachy Albariño presented in a copper-capsuled bottle.

**Vilariño-Cambados, Cambados (VdS).** Another co-op, and the biggest adega in Rías Baixas. Has experimented with whole-bunch pressing (no destalking), split fermentations (alcoholic in tank, malolactic in cask), wood-ageing and *semiseco* styles, all of which show extremely well. *Best wine:* the splendid Martín Códax Albariño, one of the best of the region.

# Ribeira Sacra

The Ribeira Sacra, or 'sacred hillside', is perhaps the most visually stunning of all the DO zones in Galicia, situated as it is in an idyllic riverside setting. The area was popular with monastic orders from the 16th century onwards, and the monks' legacy, evident throughout Ribeira Sacra, also includes the vineyards of the DO itself. Geographically, Ribeira Sacra covers the confluence of the River Sil and the River Miño (along with the River Cabe) in the provinces of Lugo and Ourense, and the main wine centre is the pretty and relatively unspoilt town of Monforte de Lemos, which dates back to Roman times.

But it is the scenery, not the history, that most impresses visitors to the region. Its steep, terraced slopes are planted with vineyards; its lush woodlands teem with wildlife (anything from wild boar to golden eagles); the great, slow-moving River Sil with its placid, deep, olive-green waters meets the mighty Miño in its headlong tumble southwards towards the city of Ourense. Above all, there is a particular tranquillity which settles over the region in late summer, when there is nothing else to do but listen to the grapes ripening while enjoying the fruits of last year's crop.

## Grape varieties and yields

Sixteen grape varieties are grown in the Ribeira Sacra DO. The most important are Mencía for red wines and Godello, Treixadura and Loureira for whites, grown in often impossibly steep, terraced vineyards in the alluvial soils along the banks of the two rivers. The bedrock is slate; the climate is warmer and drier than Rías Baixas – although it is still much cooler and wetter here than in most Spanish DO zones. Maximum production is set at 62 hectolitres per hectare (hl/ha) for Albariño and Godello and 77hl/ha for everything else, although the land is so steep, and planting and harvesting so difficult, that an annual average of 20hl/ha is closer to reality.

There are five subzones, some of which are former *vino de la tierra* areas. They are, from west to east: Chantada, Ribeiras do Miño, Sober, Amandi (the most famous wine of the Ribeira Sacra DO and, according to legend, the favourite of the Roman emperor Tiberius), Ribeira do Sil-Ourense and Quiroga-Bibei. Winemaking styles range from the unashamedly *artesanal* (the word is roughly equivalent to 'craftsmanlike') – perhaps with a tank or two in a converted barn in the farmyard – to the most modern stainless-steel technology. Most producers in this area are small, however, and some of them are very small indeed.

Ribeira Sacra's hopes for the future are pinned on its single-variety wines. In terms of whites, this means wines made from 100 per cent Albariño or 100 per cent Godello; the latter grape is earning itself a reputation second only to Albariño for yielding fresh, crisp, luscious dry white wines. In reds, it means 100 per cent Mencía (at least, that is the recommendation of the *consejo regulador*), and there are high hopes for this grape in the future. When it performs well, it does very well indeed, but these star appearances tend to be on the sporadic side.

Other wines are made from any combination of a dozen other varieties. The best of them are known by the rather dismissive name of *xenérico* (generic), while the rest are of mainly local significance.

## Notable adegas

A = Amandi; RdM = Ribeiras do Miño.

**Moure, Escairón (RdM).**
*Founded 1982.* This family-owned adega occupies a commanding position high on a bend in the River Miño, with stunning views over the valley and a barbecue and a swimming pool for family and friends. Owner José Manuel Moure makes possibly the best Albariño of the region, and an excellent light, fruity Mencía under the brand name Abadía da Cova.

**Priorato de Pantón, Santa Mariña de Eire (RdM).**
Produces a well-made and promising varietal Priorato de Pantón red from 100% Mencía. There is also a cheerful *xenérico* red (Alicante/ Mencía) and a pleasant, if neutral, white made from the Palomino grape. Both are sold under the brand name Ribera de Pantón.

**Rectoral Amandi, Amandi (A).**
*Founded 1889.* Established in the most historic winemaking part of the region, the company buys in grapes and makes only red single-variety wines from Mencía.

*Best wine:* Rectoral de Amandi is one of the region's best reds, though sadly, it is seldom seen outside Galicia.

**Virxe dos Remedios, Diomondi (RdM).** This adega believes in serious hands-on winemaking, with Mencía spending five days on its skins to extract as much colour as possible. TAlso makes *xenérico* red and white (Jerez/Godello) for local consumption under the brand name Viñal de Diomondi. *Best wine:* the varietal Viña Vella (100% Mencía) is possibly the best red wine of the entire region – big and beefy but with plenty of fruit.

**Below:** Vineyards flourish in the valley of the River Sil, east of the city of Ourense. Sixteen grape varieties are grown here.

# Ribeiro

**I**f Rías Baixas has the best coastline and Ribeira Sacra the best riverside scenery, then Ribeiro – or at least its chief town of Ribadavia – undoubtedly has the best architecture of the lot.

Ribadavia's old town centre clings to a steep hill, taking the traveller from a bridge over the River Avia up and eastwards towards the city of Ourense. It is dominated by 18th-century buildings, and boasts an old *plaza mayor* (main square; *praza maior* in Gallego) which has hardly changed since then.

The oldest building is the *Castillo de los Condes de Ribadavia* (Castle of the Earls of Ribadavia) which is mostly ruinous. The church of Santa María de Oliveira dates from the 13th century, and the church of San Juan

has 12th-century elements, including links with the original Knights of St John of Jerusalem. Probably the most spectacular edifice is the church of Santo Domingo: a 14th- to 15th-century Gothic masterpiece. This, then, is the capital of the Ribeiro DO.

## Ribeiro's wine history

Ribeiro really is an old, established wine region, centred around Ribadavia where the rivers Miño, Avía and Arnoia converge in the province of Ourense. Historically, its wine was doing commercial-scale export business when many modern (and better-known) DO zones barely existed. There are records of exports in the 17th century to countries as far away as Italy and England, and it seems that Ribeiro wines

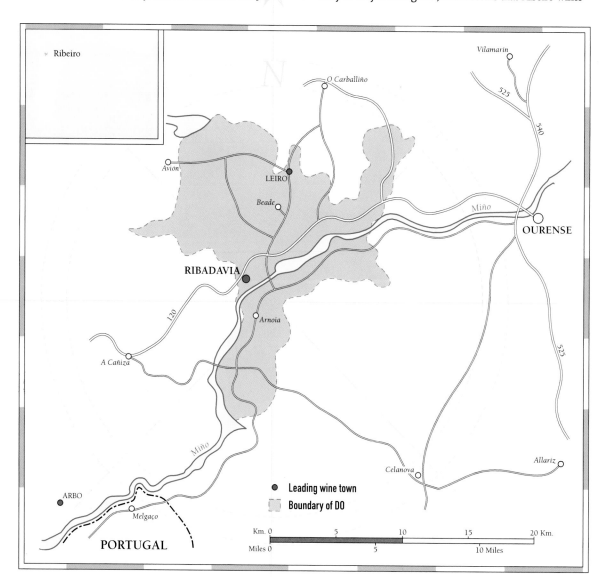

Ribeiro

- ● Leading wine town
- ▒ Boundary of DO

Km. 0      5      10      15      20 Km.

Miles 0      5      10 Miles

Above: Ribeiro may have successfully reinvented itself as a commercial wine-producing zone, but some of its methods remain firmly rooted in the past.

Right: Rootstocks thrive in the valley of the River Miño. Over 12 varieties are grown here, but Treixadura and Caíño are the most important.

were highly prized for their strength and ageing capacity. The zone has been a full DO since 1957, and Ribeiro is the third best-known wine in Spain, after Rioja and Jerez.

## Lure of the status quo

So why isn't it better known outside Spain? The answer must be that Ribeiro saw no reason to change while business was good. When customers started to go elsewhere, it did not have the necessary equipment (or attitude) to win them back. Fortunately, that is all in the past. During the last ten to 15 years, Ribeiro has reinvented itself as one of the most commercially successful DO zones of northern Spain.

One of the guiding lights has been the Cooperativa Vitivinícola del Ribeiro. In most Spanish DOs, one large co-op generally governs the direction the DO will take, since it tends to dominate production. Co-ops, though, are committee-driven creatures; the eternal wranglings of the boardroom can block development in a region for months or even years. In Ribeiro, however, the co-op has led the way, installing stainless-steel equipment, updating quality-control methods, and welcoming new ideas and techniques with open arms. This response has helped smaller producers follow suit, with the result that Ribeiro now produces some of Galicia's best wines – and nearly always at lower prices than its neighbouring DO zones.

A dozen or more grape varieties are grown in Ribeiro, but the most important are Treixadura for white wines and Caíño for reds. Palomino is still quite widespread, a legacy of post-phylloxera replanting and a response to the Franco era's promise to pay a fixed price for any unsold wine –

however undrinkable it might be. Yet Palomino is not recommended for replanting, and its area in the vineyard is gradually diminishing. Some smaller bodegas (the Spanish word in this DO is more common than the Gallego *adega*) are also specialising in Albariño, Godello, Tempranillo and Mencía and other varieties. It is this spirit of experimentation that has marked Ribeiro's return to prominence.

Geologically, Ribeiro's bedrock is granite, covered mainly by alluvial soils. Most vineyards are planted in the river valleys: some occupy terraces while others flourish in larger, higher vineyards up to an altitude of 300 metres (984 feet). The vines used to be trained on pergolas in the Galician style, but this method is giving way to wire-training to make for easier cultivation and harvesting.

Maximum yield is 91 hectolitres per hectare (hl/ha), but again, some of the vineyard sites make a practical harvest fall short of the mark – perhaps 50hl/ha. This is still a higher yield than in most of the rest of Galicia, demonstrating the slightly more hospitable terrain and an increasingly continental climate of hotter summers, colder winters and less rainfall. Pests, however, can be larger than the average insect: in rural areas, some vineyards have fitted automatic security lamps to deter marauding *jabalí* (wild boar), who can easily strip a whole row of vines in about 20 minutes.

## Winemaking and wine styles

Nearly all Ribeiro bodegas are now equipped with modern winemaking equipment, giving *viñeros* free choice over the styles of wines they elect to produce. It is still possible to find fairly heavy, neutral whites made from Palomino, and even a little *enverado* – early-picked, low-alcohol, white wines showing a hint of a prickle on the tongue, rather like Portuguese *vinho verde*.

However, these styles are losing ground to crisp white wines made from Albariño, Treixadura and Torrontés, sometimes with a little Palomino thrown in, or else they are yielding to light reds made from Caíño, Garnacha and other varieties. There is also some competition from the heavier, *semi-dulce* (medium-sweet) styles (red and white) which are popular locally. The white versions of these tend to be the best; in general, the more Albariño and/or Treixadura and/or Godello they contain, the better.

In terms of value for money, it is probably fair to say that the best white wines of Ribeiro offer around 80 per cent of the quality of Rías Baixas at 60 per cent of the price. Unsurprisingly, it is this sector of the market that is winning friends and influencing wine-lovers in the outside world.

# Notable bodegas

## Alanís, Barbantes-Estación.
*Founded 1923.* Now a member of the giant Bodegas y Bebidas drinks group, this bodega has accomplished extensive penetration into export markets. Casal da Barca (Treixadura/Torrontés/Palomino, Albariño) is an excellent everyday white; Gran Alanís (Treixadura/Torrontés/Palomino) is an example of better grape selection. *Best wine:* San Trocado (Treixadura/ Torrontés), which may be counted among the best white wines of the region (it's also the bodega's most expensive).

## Alemparte, Leiro. *Founded 1979.*
This family-owned bodega owns five hectares of Treixadura, Albariño and Palomino vineyards, and buys in more grapes to fulfil its needs. *Best wine:* Airón (Treixadura/Godello/Torrontés).

## Campante, Puga. *Founded 1988.*
Campante owns six hectares of Treixadura, Torrontés and Godello. It buys in enough additional grapes to yield a total production of 10,000hl. *Best wine:* Viña Reboreda.

## Cooperativa Vitivinícola del Ribeiro, Ribadavia. *Founded 1967.*
The co-op which helped start the ball rolling in terms of modernising Ribeiro. With 800 members and 400 contract growers farming 670ha of vineyards, this large organisation produces around 60,000hl of wine each year. The standards are high and the diversity is uncommon for a major co-op. Look for Viña Costeira, a pleasant, everyday white (Torrontés/Palomino) or Alén de Istoria, a spicy, fruity red (Mencía/Caíño/Ferrol); the latter is the official wine of the Fiesta de Istoria, which has been celebrated in Ribadavia since 1868. *Best wine:* the white Amadeus, which comes in a weird bottle but offers excellent spicy, fresh fruit and some considerable complexity, (80% Treixadura/20% Torrontés).

## Emilio Rojo, Ponte Arnoia.
*Founded 1987.* Emilio Rojo was a telephone engineer who decided to switch to winemaking. He established this estate in the late 1980s and has almost single-handedly rehabilitated the Lado grape, an obscure variety found only in the Arnoia area of Ribeiro. Rojo's wine (called, simply, Emilio Rojo) is made from 40% Lado, 30% Treixadura and 10% Torrontés, and it regularly wins prizes at tastings in Spain.

## Lapatena, Santa Cruz de Arrabaldo.
*Founded 1990.* Gigantic, hi-tech vinous palace which was built to state-of-the-art specifications in 1989. It even includes its own distillery for making *orujo* (roughly equivalent to French *marc* or Italian *grappa*), which also forms part of the Galician gastronomic scene. Buys in all its grapes from contract growers. Major varieties are Treixadura and Torrontés, plus the ubiquitous Palomino. Lapatena vinifies the red Rectoral de Amandi (mostly Mencía) from the Ribeira Sacra DO, and makes a sparkling wine by the *método tradicional* (the traditional method of sparkling wine production used in making Champagne, in which wine is refermented in bottle to generate its sparkle). For these and other reasons, the bodega is not currently a member of the *consejo regulador*, so technically, its wines don't have the Ribeiro DO status and must be sold outside the region as *vino de mesa*. However, it is likely that these diplomatic differences will be sorted out in due course. *Best wine:* the white Fin de Siglo.

## Portela, Beade. *Founded 1987.*
Small business situated in a village just outside Ribadavia. The bodega farms nine hectares of vines which provide 75% of its needs; the rest of its grapes are bought in. Wines include a very pleasant, crisp, fruity Beade Primacía from 100% Treixadura as well as a clean, fresh red with good fruit and a surprising amount of tannin. Known as Señorío de Beade, the latter is made from Caíño, Sousón and Ferrol.

## Vilerma, Gomariz Leiro.
*Founded 1988.* Vilerma's vineyards were planted in 1978, and today its vines include Treixadura, Godello, Loureiro and Albariño, which go into its award-winning Vilerma Blanco. Production is limited to 30,000 bottles (22,500hl) per year.

## Viña Mein, San Claudio Leiro.
This small bodega has 11 shareholders and is situated in the middle of nowhere. It is also housed in a splendid 17th-century farmhouse which has a few bedrooms to let for those wanting to get away from it all.

Viña Mein owns 12ha of vines, and produces only white wine from Treixadura, Torrontés, Loureira, Albillo and Albariño. This is one of those outlying vineyards where security lighting has been installed to deter hungry *jabali* from wandering in and demolishing the crop in advance of the harvest. *Best wine:* Viña Mein, a splendid crisp, dry white with the peachy fruit of Albariño and the weight of Torrontés – probably one of the very best wines of Ribeiro.

# Valdeorras

Valdeorras, or 'Golden Valley', may have taken its name from the Roman gold-mines which were reputedly the main industry in these parts a couple of thousand years ago. Or perhaps it refers to the colours along the banks of the River Sil just before harvest time, when the vines are at their autumnal best. In either case, this has been a favoured and prosperous region for as long as anyone can remember, and mineral deposits certainly form the basis of major industries over the eastern border in the *autonomia* of Castile-León.

In today's Valdeorras, however, dominated by the towns of A Rúa, Vilamartin and O Barco, wine is now the main export business. In common with its fellow Galician DO regions, the area has reinvented itself, rediscovered its roots (most particularly those of the Godello and Mencía grapes) and got to work re-establishing itself as a serious wine-producing area.

Valdeorras does not have the spectacular beauty of some of its compatriots, but it does have the River Sil, which flows through the main towns. In many of them, it has been partially dammed to provide a 'beach' area for landlocked towns more than 150 kilometres (93 miles) from the sea. At weekends, the locals barbecue, sunbathe or just lounge around the waterside while the children paddle and splash about to their hearts' content. This is not a jet-setting, southeast coast resort; it is simply life in the comfortable, welcoming, small towns of eastern Galicia.

From a wine point of view, Valdeorras has been through the same high-cropping, over-producing culture that afflicted most of Spain during the Franco era. But just as Rías Baixas rediscovered Albariño and Ribeiro rediscovered Treixadura, so Valdeorras rediscovered Godello: a native grape variety with all the potential (in the right winemaking hands) to make world-class white wines. Add to this the Mencía – a grape which promises much but still stubbornly refuses to give of its best except in exceptional circumstances – and you have, at least, the makings of a quality-wine experience. The battle for the hearts and minds of the winemakers has been won.

However, one still has to win the battle of the vineyards. As the Valdeorras DO approaches the year 2000, the low-grade, high-yield Garnacha Tintorera and Palomino grapes still occupy three-quarters of the entire *denominación de origen*. Much work has yet to be done.

## Climate and geography

Valdeorras is the furthest inland of Galicia's DO zones, and therefore it is the most continental in terms of climate – which means hotter summers, longer autumns and colder winters. The region's soils tend to be alluvial, since most of the vineyard area is situated on the banks of the river, and the bedrock is slate, with limestone outcrops that provide good drainage. The altitude (up to 320 metres/1,050 feet) and the proximity of the river provide some relief from the excesses of the summer heat, and the nature of the Godello grape in particular has shown itself to be a good performer under these circumstances.

Vines tend to be trained on wires on the flatter, lower vineyards and *en vaso* (bush-pruned and self-supporting) on the slopes. The maximum permitted yield is 56 hectolitres per hectare (hl/ha) for hillside vineyards and 70hl/ha for those on the plains. As usual, however, actual production seldom even approaches the legal maximum and may be as little as 25 to 30hl/ha overall.

Regulations governing winemaking in Valdeorras are wide-ranging: reds, whites and *rosados* are permitted with no further stipulation than that they achieve a minimum nine per cent alcohol by volume (abv). However, wines such as these are never going to make the region's reputation. Bodegas serious about the DO's future have specialised in two major grape varieties, Godello and Mencía, while progressive *viñeros* have experimented with more exotic fare, such as Tempranillo, Cabernet Sauvignon and Merlot. Today's Valdeorras *viñero* wants something more than the

**Right:** Mencía is one of the two major grape varieties grown by winemakers who desire a future for Valdeorras as a serious DO zone.

run-of-the-mill wines which characterised the area in the past, and he or she is willing to invest time and money in order to reach important export markets.

## Winemaking and wine styles

The local tradition is for *joven* wines (those with no oak ageing; *see* page 23), and Godello is ideally suited to this fresh, crisp, fruity style. It is encouraged for replanting wherever Palomino grew before. Another grape which does well in blends with Godello is Doña Blanca ('Dona Branca' in the Monterrei DO; 'Valenciana' in some areas). While it lacks the sheer finesse and plump fruit of Godello, it does possess a well-balanced charm and is often used to 'lift' the aroma and attack of wines made principally from Palomino.

There has been little or no experimentation with *crianza* wines, but one or two winemakers have had some success with barrel fermentation followed by three to six months on the lees. Around half a dozen bodegas now produce white Godello wines of exemplary export quality.

Among red wines, Mencía is used for *jovenes* (there have been some trials with *crianzas*). For the most part, however, Mencía as a single variety has some problems with balance – which is why some bodegas are blending it with Garnacha Tinta, Cabernet Sauvignon or the local María Ardoña to see how it develops. Many winemakers, however, believe Mencía has potential on its own, especially given the light, fruity, early-drinking tradition for red wines in this part of Spain.

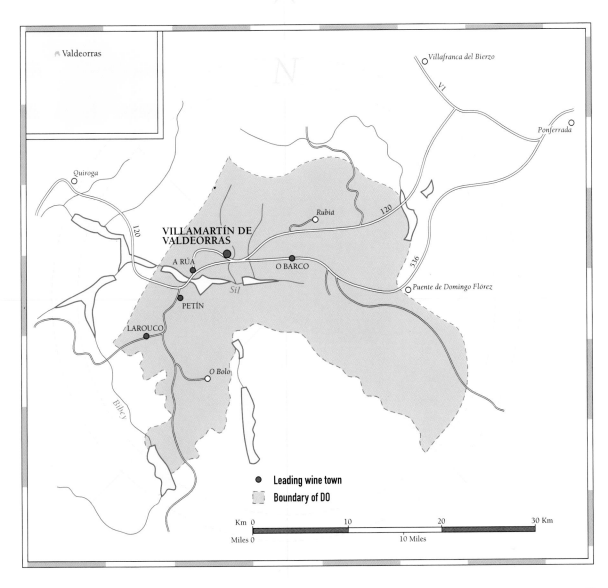

Valdeorras

Villafranca del Bierzo

Ponferrada

Quiroga

Rubiá

VILLAMARTÍN DE VALDEORRAS

A RÚA

O BARCO

Puente de Domingo Flórez

PETÍN

Sil

LAROUCO

O Bolo

Bibey

● Leading wine town

▨ Boundary of DO

Km 0    10    20    30 Km

Miles 0    10 Miles

## Notable bodegas

**Cooperativa Jesús Nazareno, O Barco.** *Founded 1963.* Co-op whose 2,000 members farm 2,000ha of vines (Palomino, Godello, Garnacha Tintorera, Mencía). Production is around 50,000hl and the bodega is changing its epoxy-concrete tanks to stainless steel. Over 100 oak *barricas* (barriques) are used to age its flagship red wine, Menciño (100% Mencía). The white Moza Fresca (Palomino/ Godello/Doña Blanca) is better. *Best wine:* Viña Abad (100% Godello).

**Cooperativa Santa María dos Remedios, Larouco.** *Founded 1962.* Co-op with 317 members tending 218ha of Garnacha Tintorera, Palomino, Mencía, Godello. *Best wines:* white Arume (100% Godello) and red Medulio (100% Mencía). The latter proves Mencía can give plenty of fruit, balance, complexity and length.

**Cooperativa Virgen das Viñas, A Rúa.** *Founded 1963.* Another large co-op (460 members) with epoxy-concrete tanks; however, its investment in over 200 *barricas* of American oak suggests a serious commitment to quality. Its red Pingadelo (85% Mencía/15% María Ardoña) has plenty of aromatic blackberry/strawberry fruit.

**Godeval, O Barco.** *Founded 1986.* Immaculately restored monastery at Xagoaza with massive investment in the very latest winemaking equipment and a commitment to producing the very best Godello wine in Valdeorras from its own 16ha of vines. The result is Viña Godeval, one of the region's best wines.

**Joaquín Rebolledo, A Rúa.** *Founded 1987.* This bodega owns aound 15ha of Godello and Mencía vines as well as experimental plantations of Cabernet Sauvignon,

Merlot *et al*; other grapes are bought in. The estate makes a Cabernet Sauvignon and a Merlot (both *reservas*) which are showing well. *Best wine:* Joaquín Rebolledo Tinto (100% Mencía), the best Mencía of Valdeorras, with deep, dark fruit as well as omnipresent tannins. Joaquín Rebolledo Blanco (100% Godello) is on a par with the region's best.

**Majlu, Vilamartín.** *Founded 1990.* Family firm with eight hectares of Godello on the *bancales* (terraced slopes) below the Finca del Pazo de los Caballeros – an ancient, knightly residence overlooking the main road through Vilamartín. *Best wine:* the brand name is Ruchel; the style is warm, ripe fruit with a good, long finish.

**Medorras, Petín de Valdeorras.** *Founded 1987.* Medorras owns 12ha of vines, including Godello, Mencía and Cabernet Sauvignon, and it is extremely modern. The red (100% Mencía) is called Viña Ladeira. *Best wines:* the white Godellón Oro and Blanco (the former made from free-run must).

**Senen Guitian Velasco, Rubiá de Valdeorras.** *Founded 1989.* Small, ultra-modern winery with sharp quality-control and a desire to make the best Godello wines from nine hectares of vineyards. The basic Viña Guitian has a lovely freshness, a strong, almost savoury palate and excellent fruit. *Best wine:* the excellent Viña Guitian barrel-fermented (six months on the lees in American oak).

**Señorío, Vilamartín.** *Founded 1990.* Señorío owns 27ha of vines and buys in about 1,000 tonnes of grapes – mainly Godello and Mencía, but also Palomino, Alicante (Garnacha Tinta) and Garnacha Tintorera. *Best wines:* the white Valdesil (100% Godello), from old vines; red Valderroa (100% Mencía) crafted in the local fruity, lightweight style.

Below: Vineyards in the Monterrei DO are planted mainly with white-grape varieties, the most popular being Dona Branca.

Yes, there is a mountain (*monte*) located some six kilometres west of the small town of Verín, in the province of Ourense, and yes, it once belonged to the king (*rei*). The town from which this *denominación de origen* takes its name also formed an important part of Spain's defences during the country's war with Portugal in the 16th century. Be that as it may, its history stretches back some 300 years earlier.

Medieval Monterrei was much more than a simple fortified site; it incorporated a small town, a hospital and a monastery. In those days, the latter was actually a seat of learning equal to (or even greater than) a university in terms of significance. The monastery was still in use during the last century, and today it is open to visitors. The local *parador* – a grand building constructed in the *pazo* style – is situated on an adjacent hill and offers excellent views of the surrounding countryside which belongs to the province of Ourense.

Ourense has often been described as a 'tongue' of Galicia, dipping southwards into what would otherwise be north-central Portugal. It is the hottest part of Galicia, mainly because it is the least affected by the Atlantic Ocean. Within the province sits the small market town of Verín, about 15 kilometres (nine miles) from the Portuguese border. A pleasant, old-fashioned place, Verín's atmosphere is marred only by the heavy traffic which bustles by on the N-525, the motorway running from Ourense to Portugal and Castile. The town is well known for its freshwater springs, and one or two of the bottlers even welcome visitors.

## Winemaking and wine styles

There are only four bodegas in the entire Monterrei DO; hence production is slight and exports are virtually non-existent. The majority of the vineyards are situated in the valley of the River Támega, where they are planted mainly with Verdello, Dona Branca (Doña Blanca in Castilian) and Palomino as well as a local variety known as Monstruosa. The most popular whites are made from Dona Branca, but the best tend to be made from the rarer Godello and Treixadura: fresh, lip-smacking, thirst-quenchers with the merest hint of a fizz.

Red wines are lightweights made from Mencía, although there is a little Tinto Fino (otherwise known as Tempranillo). No *crianza* wine is produced here yet, although one or two bodegas are beginning to experiment with the concept.

## Notable bodegas

**Ladairo, Rosal-Oimbra.**
*Founded 1984.* Smart, if small, modern bodega complete with stainless-steel technology. The present building dates from 1995. The main white wines are Ladairo Blanco, a delicious, crisp, fresh mix of Godello and Treixadura (50% each); and Viña Toutelo, a traditionally soft, aromatic style made from Dona Branca. Reds include Ladairo Tinto, a pleasant, light, slightly jammy wine (90% Mencía/ 10% Tempranillo).

**Ribeira del Támega, Albarellos de Monterrei.** *Founded 1995.* A small, modern, industrial-style bodega producing good, everyday wines. Main white wines are Ribera del Támega, (Dona Branca), and Baroncelli Branco which is produced from mixed white varieties. Reds include Baroncelli Tinto, made from mixed red varieties.

# Asturias, Cantabria and the País Vasco

**Above:** This statue of explorer Juan Sebastian Elcano stands in his home town of Guetaria, testimony to the pride of the Basque people.

**Far right:** Fishing boats fill the harbour of Castro Urdialis, near Cantabria's capital city of Santander. The coast in this region is the cleanest in Europe.

Although they were probably among the better known settlers of the times, the Celts were certainly not the only group of people who colonised the western continental edge of prehistoric Europe. Despite the fact that Spain had been part of both the Roman and the Moorish empires, their rulers were never fully able to subjugate the inhabitants who lived along the north coast in what are now the *autonomías* of Asturias, Cantabria and the País Vasco, or Basque Country. This is due partly to the security provided by the mountains of the Cordillera Cantábrica and partly to the independent nature of the people themselves, whose knowledge and defence of their own terrain defeated even the infamous Roman legions.

## Asturias

More than once, Asturias has been compared to Wales, due to its beautiful coastline and rugged, mountainous countryside. The similarities also extend to its people. The region's original settlers belonged to an Iberian tribe known as the Astures, who developed into a hardy race, and – like their Welsh counterparts – eventually took to working in mines.

The old Kingdom of Asturias was established in AD722 by King Fruela. It was occupied briefly by the Moors from 768 to 791, when Fruela's son, Alfonso II, re-established it as a reservoir of Castilian Christianity during the Moorish occupation of the rest of Spain. In 1037, King García expanded the kingdom to include León, and, as the Moors fell back towards Granada, Asturias-León eventually merged with the Kingdom of Castile.

That was in 1230. By 1388, Asturias was recognised as a *principado* in its own right. Since then, the heir-apparent to the Spanish throne has always been styled *Príncipe de Asturias* – Prince of the Asturias. During the 19th century, Asturias and its neighbouring regions thrived on deep-mined coal, shipbuilding and heavy industry. Although a good deal of the industry has now gone, the area is still a prosperous region, with the beautiful old city of Oviedo at its heart.

Gastronomically, Asturias is perhaps best known for its cheeses (the finest of which is *cabrales*) and its apple-orchards. The latter provide some of Spain's best *sidra*, or cider, which is saluted every year in the *Fiesta de la Sidra* (Cider Festival). The action of pouring Asturian cider involves a posture that is rather reminiscent of a flamenco dancer. Even in this region of apples, however, wine is not completely left out. A small area called Cangas de Narcea makes light red wines, mainly from Mencía, but the general opinion is that they are not tipped for stardom.

## Cantabria

Dominated by the capital city of Santander, Cantabria's early wealth came from Spanish exploration of the Americas. Many of the fine houses throughout the region were built by local people returning from the New World with enormous riches. They were known locally as *indianos*, as the Americas were still regarded as the other side of the Indian subcontinent.

Santander itself is situated between a beautifully scenic coastline and the wonderfully dramatic mountains known as the Picos de Europa. The centre of the city is mainly modern in construction, due to two disasters – tornado and a fire – which both occurred in 1941. While much of the old town was destroyed, some parts of the more historic buildings did survive, including the cathedral's early Gothic crypt.

Many visitors, however, come to Cantabria for its scenery – and with good reason: the Cantabrian coast claims the distinction of having the cleanest beaches in Europe. The landscape here is beautiful and wild, and it is extremely popular with well-off tourists who come mainly from Spain itself, although there are usually sizeable contingents from Switzerland and Scandinavia.

The area is fertile and green, so as well as the obvious seafood aspects, cookery focuses on a rich tradition of fruit and vegetables as exemplified by dishes such as *cocido montañés* (a casserole of beans, cabbage and pork) and *cocido lebaniago* (chick-peas and cabbage), which is served as a vegetable with meat and fish. The latter comes from the area around Liébana, which is also home to Cantabria's best cheeses: *ahumado de aliva, pido, picón* and *quesuco*. The only wine made in Cantabria is an unclassified *vino de mesa* also found in Liébana, and it is unlikely to be seen much further afield.

## The País Vasco

This is the Basque Country (*Euskadi* in the Basque language; the word means 'collection of Basques'), and its origins are rather mysterious. The Basques may have been the first people to colonise this part of Europe in Stone Age times, and their isolation in the mountains of the two northern Basque provinces kept them safe from the depredations of Roman, Visigoth and Moor alike. This isolation has also preserved the splendid individuality of the extraordinary Basque language, which is related to no other in the world (the only language found to have any similarity to it at all is Berber, whose roots also go back to the Stone Age). Another unusual fact is that Basques tend to have mainly type-A blood-groups which are usually Rhesus factor (Rh) negative. The rest of the world is mostly Rh positive.

The Basque Country is rich in mineral deposits. Historically, the Basques were metal-workers (the conquering Romans called them *Vascones*, from the Latin *vascularius* – a maker of vessels). Some, however, were also seafarers; there are records of Basque whaling-ships off the coast of Greenland as early as the ninth century. The original Basque Country covered the area of southwest France now known as Gascogne (Gascony), as well as what is now the País Vasco in Spain, but the language on the French and Spanish sides of the border developed in such different ways that the two dialects are now barely mutually intelligible.

## A state of independence

Politically, the Basque Country ruled itself from the town of Guernica (*Gernika* in Basque) during the Spanish Civil War until, in 1937 – and with a little help from Hitler's Luftwaffe – Franco's forces bombed it flat. Today, as a result of the new constitution of 1978, there is a freely elected Basque government in Bilbao which oversees all aspects of life throughout the region.

Geographically, there are three provinces, arranged in an inverted triangle: Guipúzcoa (Gipuzkoa in Basque) and Vizcaya (Bizkaia) are situated along the coast, westwards towards the French border, and Álava (Araba) lies below and between them in the south, beyond the mountains of the Cordillera Cantábrica. In this southernmost province, some of the finest wines of the Rioja DOCa are made (*see* page 74).

Basque cooking is legendary. The fish restaurants of Bilbao and San Sebastián offer probably the best range of seafood in Spain, and every major town in Spain will have one or more Basque restaurants – or at least, a Basque chef or two. There is a Basque tradition of *chiquiteo* (what the Castilians call *tapas*) as well as *chocos*, or food-and-drink societies, which meet to enjoy and celebrate the food and wine of the region.

# The Two Chacolí DOs

## Notable bodegas

G = Guetaria; V = Vizcaya.

### Eizaguirre, Zarautz (G).
*Founded 1930.* This bodega owns four hectares of vines and buys in grapes to make up its total production of about 750hl. There are three different selections, ranging in order from light, fresh and prickly to a more laid-back style: Eizaguirre, Hilbera and Kupela.

### Etxaniz, Guetaria (G).
One of the best-known producers of Guetaria, Txomin Etxaniz' cellars are situated on a delightful old town promontory that sticks out into the sea. His 12ha of vineyards are located 50 metres (164 feet) higher on steep slopes, with the vines trained on pergolas. The wine (Txomin Etxaniz) is classic Chacolí: crisp, fresh, and on a hot summer's day, quite delicious.

### Virgen de l'Orea, Zalla (B).
*Founded 1994.* This estate was begun as a labour of love by a furniture millionaire who painstakingly restored an old house as a bodega and replanted and upgraded its vineyard. The basic wine, Aretxaga, reflects the extra warmth and ripeness of this inland location. *Best wine:* the outstanding Señorío de Otxaran, made from only the ripest grapes.

A word of explanation for wine-lovers. The Basque language is terribly complex, and makes extensive use of the passive voice. For example: 'I drink wine' becomes in Basque, 'By me wine is drunk.' Thus, in the case of its two DOs, Chacolí de Guetaria is Castilian for the Basque *Getariako Txakolina* ('of Getaria, the Txakolina'). The Chacolí de Vizcaya DO in Basque is *Bizkaiko Txakolina*.

Though much warmer than most of northern Europe, the north coast of Spain is still fairly wild and chilly by Spanish standards. The grapes grown here are known nowhere else. The white variety is called Ondarribi Zuri and accounts for more than 80 per cent of vineyards and production. No one knows its exact origins, but it is believed to have developed locally. The red is called Ondarribi Beltza and may share a common ancestor with Cabernet Franc. Folle Blanche is also grown in Vizcaya, and there are small plantations of experimental Chardonnay, Pinot Blanc, Sauvignon and Riesling.

Soils in both areas are similar: loose alluvial or sandy soils over a clay/marl/limestone base, at altitudes ranging from just above sea level (ten metres/33 feet) to about 150 metres (492 feet). Vineyards tend to be very small and are dotted here and there. In Guetaria, around 70 hectares are clustered around the three main towns of Guetaria, Aia and Zarautz. In Vizcaya, 60 to 80 hectares are split into two main groups: the coastal area around Bakio and an inland area around the town of Balmaseda. Some of the plots seem impossibly small, fractions of a hectare tucked away in what looks like little more than a kitchen garden.

A local saying has it that there are 'five days of sunshine, five days of rain' – meaning the coast's maritime climate provides more than ample water. Some coastal vineyards are planted on steeper slopes to shed the rain, and are trained on pergolas to reduce the effects of the sun. Inland areas are hotter and drier, and the vines are trained on wires. Permitted yields range from 63 to 97 hectolitres per hectare (hl/ha), according to the area, but these figures are seldom achieved. Around 40hl/ha is more realistic.

## Wines and wine styles

So what of the wines themselves? The best Chacolis have delicious, fresh acidity and luscious, grapey fruit – perfect for the Basque Country's climate. The wines of Guetaria and the Bakio (coastal) area of Vizcaya have a fresh, crisp, green-fruit style. Those from the inland area around Balmaseda tend to be higher in alcohol and show some similarities to peachy Galician whites. The best are very good but hard to find; because of the minuscule production, they are also expensive. Small amounts of *rosado* and red Chacolí are made, but as this is seafood country, white wines rule.

**Right:** These vineyards growing near Guetaria contain grape varieties that are known nowhere else in the world.

**Far right:** Gorse blooms in the Galician countryside. In addition to its unique culture, the region boasts some of the most magnificent scenery in Spain.

# Country Wines of Green Spain

A reminder: *Vino de la Tierra* (VdlT, or Country Wine) comes from areas which may, one day, aspire to DO status. *Vino Comarcal* (VC) tends to be wine from larger and less well-defined areas but which, nevertheless, possess some local or regional character (*see* pages 22-3).

## Galicia

Provinces appear in brackets.

**VC Betanzos (La Coruña).** Some 114ha of vines are planted around the town of Betanzos, mainly on the slopes of the Mandeo river valley, about 30km (19 miles) southeast of the city of La Coruña. The soil is light over alluvial clay, and more than 40 small bodegas and one co-op turn out around 2,000hl in an average year. Traditionally, the style of the wines has been light reds made from Alicante (Garnacha Tintorera) and Mencía. However, recent developments have seen wines from these parts marketed abroad by the giant Bodegas y Bebidas group, usually light, everyday whites made mainly from Palomino with enough Albariño for aroma and fruit. This area is currently seeking promotion to the rank of VdlT, but many smaller bodegas are still *artesanal* with little investment potential, so it may be a while in coming.

**VC Ribeiro do Ulla (La Coruña).** This area has about 600ha of vines in the Ulla river valley, about 15km (nine miles) southeast of Santiago de Compostela. The chief centre of production is Boqueixón, but most of the land is planted with hybrid vines. In addition, the vast majority of production is either domestic or (at most) on sale at farm gates and tourist centres. However, a little Albarello is grown and used in the production of white wines just as some Caíño is used for making reds, as well as the ubiquitous Alicante and Palomino. If this region has a future, then it lies with white wines made from Albarello.

*The following country wines from Galicia have disappeared since 1996:*

**VdlT Val do Minho (Ourense)** is now part of the Ribeira Sacra DO.

**VC O Bolo (Ourense)** is now part of the Valdeorras DO.

## Asturias, Cantabria and the País Vasco

While the first two regions produce table wines (*see* respecive entries), there are no VdlT or VC wines classified for any of these three *autonomías*.

# Castile-León

In a part of the country where the architecture seems to have leapt straight out of the heroic age, it stands to reason that any wines made here should possess a certain splendour of their own. This they manage to do in Castile-León – and they do it to great effect.

For a start, the Ribera del Duero region is the home of Vega Sicilia, the ground-breaking wine estate that has become one of the most renowned in Spain, if not the world. The red wines produced here and in the rest of the DO zone are famous for their richness and finesse, yet they are by no means all Castile has to offer. After centuries of making traditional, fortified, Sherry-style wines, the Rueda DO has found its true calling in the form of fruity, white Verdejos. With the benefit of technological know-how and greater winemaking skills, they are fast becoming classics in their own right. Meanwhile, the smaller and primarily red-wine regions of Bierzo, Cigales and Toro, with their successful mixture of traditional and high-tech winemaking styles, are proving once and for all that size is not everything.

Below: The turbulent past of Old Castile is reflected in its numerous fortifications. This imposing structure is the Castillo de Peñafiel.

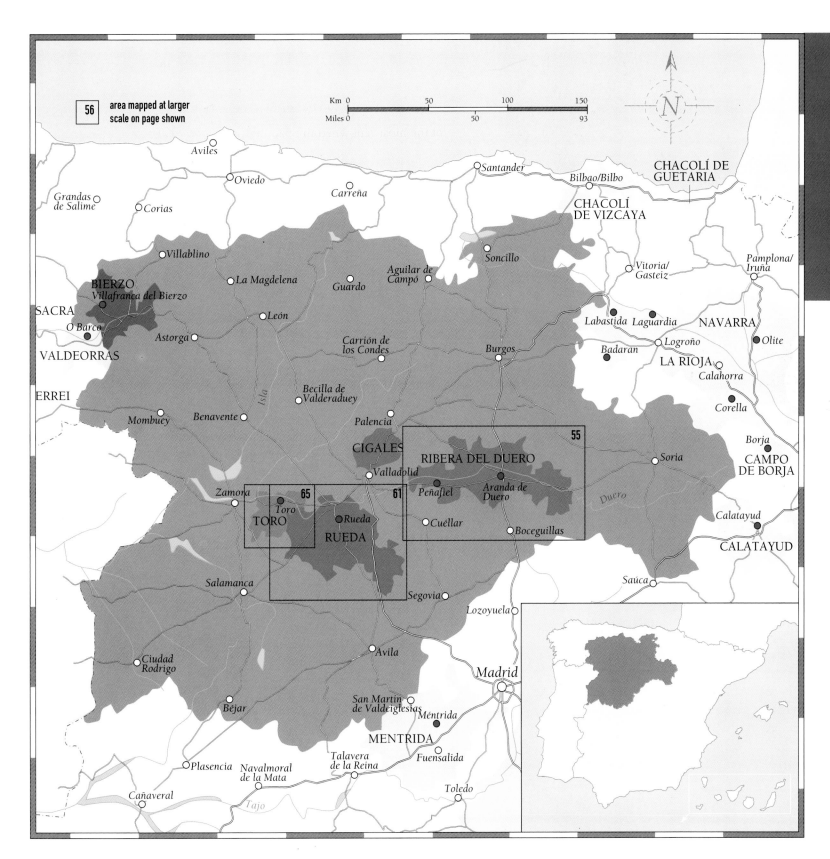

Km 0    50    100    150
Miles 0         50         93

N

Avilés

Oviedo

Santander

Bilbao/Bilbo

CHACOLÍ DE GUETARIA

Grandas de Salime

Corias

Carreña

CHACOLÍ DE VIZCAYA

Villablino

Soncillo

Vitoria/ Gasteiz

Pamplona/ Iruña

BIERZO

La Magdelena

Guardo

Aguilar de Campó

Villafranca del Bierzo

SACRA

O Barco

León

Astorga

Labastida  Laguardia

NAVARRA

Olite

VALDEORRAS

Carrión de los Condes

Burgos

Badaran

Logroño

LA RIOJA

Calahorra

ERREI

Becilla de Valderaduey

Corella

Mombuey

Benavente

Isla

Palencia

Borja

CAMPO DE BORJA

CIGALES

RIBERA DEL DUERO

Soria

55

Valladolid

Duero

Zamora

65

Peñafiel

Aranda de Duero

Calatayud

Toro

Rueda

61

TORO

RUEDA

Cuéllar

Boceguillas

CALATAYUD

Salamanca

Segovia

Saúca

Ciudad Rodrigo

Ávila

Lozoyuela

Béjar

San Martín de Valdeiglesias

Madrid

Méntrida

MENTRIDA

Plasencia

Navalmoral de la Mata

Talavera de la Reina

Fuensalida

Cañaveral

Tajo

Toledo

# Old Castile: kingdom of castles

Old Castile is not named 'the land of castles' for nothing. This former frontier between Christians and Moors was fortified up to the hilt, and formed the crucible from which a unified Spain would be cast in 1492. North of the Cordillera Cantábrica, the invading armies of the Moors made little impression, and the regions of Galicia, Asturias, Cantabria and the Basque Country – situated as they were on the other side of the mountains – emerged more or less unscathed. Thus, the little Kingdom of Asturias became a reservoir of Spanish culture. As the Moors were gradually forced southwards, it expanded, uniting first with León, then with Castile to form the heavily fortified heartland that eventually drove the invaders back across the straits of Gibraltar.

By the beginning of the 15th century, Castile was a bustling community in the throes of *El Renacimiento* (the Renaissance). With a university in Salamanca and the royal court enthroned in Burgos, trade and artistic life burgeoned; wealth flowed in as Christian armies sacked Moorish-held cities in the south. In 1469, in the city of Valladolid, Isabella, heiress to the throne of Castile, married Ferdinand, heir to the throne of Aragón. In 1474, Isabella was officially proclaimed queen of Castile in Segovia, and in 1479, Ferdinand succeeded to the Aragonés throne, effectively uniting Castile and Aragón as well as the lands of La Rioja, which had been hotly contested by the neighbouring Kingdom of Navarre.

When the Moors finally left the country in 1492, Spain's capital moved from Burgos to Valladolid. Navarre – or at least that part of the kingdom south of the Pyrenees – elected to join the newly unified Spain in 1512. In 1561, on the order of King Philip II, the capital moved again, this time to Madrid in 'New Castile' – that part of Spain which had been recaptured from the Moors.

## A flourishing wine trade

What all this means in cultural terms is that, during the 500 years between the 11th and 16th centuries, Old Castile became increasingly rich, academic, ecclesiastical and royal, and the region's business flourished accordingly. The wine industry bloomed as rich customers paid top prices for the finest wines. Producers must have fallen over each other in the race to make something better (and more expensive) to please the palate of the local duke, bishop, professor or physician.

Today, the classic Castilian wine style can be seen as distinct from, say, Rioja, where the export market and French tastes had a significant effect on winemaking. Castilian wines are still made to suit Spanish tastes: powerful, high-strength, full of fruit, and with just a hint of oak rather than the 'full-throttle' approach favoured further east. Given its history, it is not surprising that Castile-León has evolved into a predominantly red-wine area. As elsewhere in the Old World, the region's wines match its foodstuffs perfectly.

---

### Castilian gastronomy

*The River Duero is a source of coarse fishy things for the table in Castile-León, yet this is also hunting and herding country, and one of the most fertile areas of Spain for* huertas, *a term that roughly translates as 'market gardens'. A typical Castilian meal begins with tapas of* chorizos *(sausages), sheep's-milk cheese and* jamón *(ham), always served with* hogaza *– finely textured white bread baked in a wheel shape. Next, the* sopa de ajo: *garlic soup with breadcrumbs and a whole poached egg in the middle. The main course might be game – red partridge, venison or* jabalí *(wild boar) – if served at a rich man's table, but staples for ordinary folk are* cordero asado *(milk-fed baby lamb) and* cochinillo *(suckling pig), roasted in a baker's oven until tender enough to be cut with the edge of a side-plate (a popular restaurateur's trick). These are served with local vegetables and, of course, the robust, high-strength, aromatic red wine for which Castile has become famous.*

# Bierzo

**B**ierzo could be considered the maverick in the Castilian corral, in the sense that it is situated in the province of León, a long way north of the mainstream wines of the Duero Valley, and its western border is contiguous with the eastern boundary of Galicia's Valdeorras DO. It is the home of a transitional type of wine that falls roughly midway between the light, fruity style of Galicia and the serious heavyweights of the Duero. It is also the home of some splendid highland scenery, starting with the ravines of the River Sil and heading southwards to the mountains of the Sierra de la Cabrera.

Cacabelos is at the hub of the zone. It is a pretty market town with a statue of grape-pickers at its centre; it is also the home of the *consejo regulador,* and it forms a staging-post along the Camino de Santiago. The River Cúa passes through Cacabelos; much like the towns in Valdeorras, it has been dammed to provide a 'beach' area which becomes very crowded on summer Sundays. It is also home to one of Castile-León's more eccentric bodegas, Prada a Tope (but more of that in a moment).

The other main wine town in the Bierzo DO is Villafranca del Bierzo. Although small, it boasts a fair amount of monumental architecture, including a castle, a magnificent Jesuit *collegium* and an old ducal palace, which has been transformed into today's Palacio de Arganza (*see* 'Notable bodegas'). Bierzo's main population centre is the town of Ponferrada, but here strip-mining and iron ore have been more important than wine production ever since Roman times.

## Geography and climate

The bulk of Bierzo's vines are planted at between 500 and 600 metres (1,640 and 1,969 feet) along the valleys of the River Sil and its tributaries, including the Cúa, Pradel, Valcarce and Burbia. The vineyards are a mixture of slopes and terraces, the soils being alluvial (often with traces of iron) at river levels and slate at higher positions. The climate falls between the mild, temperate style of Galicia and the hot, continental uplands of the Duero, with sufficient rainfall and top summer temperatures of not much more than 32°C (90°F).

This is the heartland of the Mencía grape, and indeed, the Bercianos seem to be able to coax more warmth and weight out of this variety than their neighbours in Galicia – perhaps because of the slightly warmer climate, or perhaps because of different winemaking techniques. In any case, Mencía occupies 62 per cent of the vineyard and is the only recommended red grape. Garnacha Tintorera is permitted, but it is not found in any wines of real quality.

For white wines, Godello and Doña Blanca are recommended, although between them, they cover only about ten per cent of the total vineyard (the high-cropping Palomino makes up most of the rest). In addition, some experimentation is being conducted with Cabernet Sauvignon, Chardonnay and even Gewürztraminer among the more forward-looking bodegas.

On the whole, however, Bierzo is principally red-wine country, and most of the best wines are made from 100 per cent Mencía, up to *crianza* and even *reserva* level (according to national criteria; *see* pages 22-3). There is also some excellent *rosado,* particularly in lighter years.

**Far right:** The Castillo de los Templarios, or Castle of the Templars, at Ponferrada is a reminder of the Bierzo region's noble past.

**Below:** Bierzo contains other pleasures besides castles and wine – most importantly, its splendid mountain scenery.

# Notable bodegas

### Luna Beberide, Cacabelos.
*Founded 1986.* Family company that owns and works around 50ha of vines, including Gewürztraminer, Chardonnay, Cabernet Sauvignon and Mencía; grapes are also bought in to support a total production of around 250,000hl. The red wines are aged in French and American oak, and are generally of exemplary quality, ranging from the 100% Mencía *joven* to the 100% Cabernet Sauvignon Señorío del Sil. *Rosado* and white wines are equally spectacular. *Best wines:* the Señorío del Sil *rosado* and the Luna Beberide Gewürztraminer, which sells for more than double the price of any of the other wines. A very innovative bodega.

### Palacio de Arganza, Villafranca del Bierzo. *Founded 1805.* This 15th-century ducal palace has belonged to the Vuelta family since 1963. There has been some friction between owner Daniel Vuelta and the *consejo regulador* over pre-1989 wines which were not made under the present DO regulations. For a while, the Palacio stood aloof from the *consejo regulador* altogether. Fortunately, however, matters were brought to a satisfactory conclusion in the early 1990s, and all the Palacio's wines since the 1992 vintage have carried the seal of the Bierzo DO. The firm continues to make wines with bought-in grapes up to *gran reserva* level, with excellent stocks of mature old vintages, some aged in cherry and apple wood as well as the omnipresent American oak. Mature reds from this bodega are among the best Bierzo has to offer. *Best wines:* a mix of 70% Mencía/30% Garnacha Tintorera. Vintages up to 25 years old are still showing very well.

### Pérez Caramés, Villafranca del Bierzo. *Founded 1967.* Owns 30ha of Mencía, Tempranillo, Cabernet Sauvignon, Merlot, Pinot Noir and Chardonnay vineyards; ages its wines in French oak. Brand names are Cónsules de Roma and Casar de Santa Inés. There is an interesting Chardonnay/Malvasía mix under the latter label, as well as varietals Cabernet Sauvignon and Tempranillo. *Best wines:* the Cónsules de Roma red and the Casar de Santa Inés *rosado*.

### Prada a Tope, Cacabelos.
*Founded 1984.* Prada a Tope is a tiny winery run in a very 'hands-on' way by owner José-Luis Prada. The style of winemaking is rather *artesanal*, and the winery boasts a balconied bar and snack-bar overlooking the courtyard, as well as a small shop selling everything from the bodega's wines, olive oil and *jamón* to Prada a Tope T-shirts. In the evening, when the trucks and tankers have left the yard, trestle tables are set up and the whole establishment turns into an open-air restaurant serving excellent, simple, local dishes at very reasonable prices. Don José-Luis, who favours the Che Guevara look, greets guests, signs menus and has his photograph taken with female visitors. If you're visiting Cacabelos, then under no circumstances miss dinner here. The wines (all sold under the Prada label) are excellent, too: pleasant, fresh, gulpable whites (Godello/Doña Blanca) and *rosados*, and very good reds. *Best wines:* the *tinto crianza* and the *maceración carbónica* (both 100% Mencía).

### Vinos del Bierzo, Cacabelos.
*Founded 1964.* A co-op with 1,800 members farming 1,000ha of vines, of which 80% are Mencía. The co-op has been replacing its old epoxy/concrete tanks with stainless steel and also investing in oak *barricas* for more than five years, and the results of all this hard work are starting to be appreciated. There is a good white called Viña Oro (Doña Blanca/ Palomino). *Best wines:* two excellent *rosados* – Guerra (*crianza*) and Viña Oro (*joven*) – as well as an excellent red Viña Oro (*joven*). All three are made from 100% Mencía.

# Cigales

In a landscape that favours big, beefy red wines (from neighbouring DOs Ribera del Duero and Toro) and some of Spain's best whites (from the Rueda DO), it is perhaps unsurprising that Cigales has become best known for its *rosados*. And very good they are, too – especially those with a bit of barrel-age which are made from the Tinto del País grape variety (otherwise known as Tinto Fino or Tempranillo).

It is important to understand that, until very recently in northern Spain generally and in Castile in particular, there has been no tradition of white wine. If you asked for *vino blanco seco* in a bar in Valladolid, they would probably bring you a fino Sherry. If you insisted, they might just be able find a dusty old bottle of some mass-produced *vino de mesa* in the kitchen – but it would probably not be chilled.

In recent years, Rueda has changed all that, but the local gastronomic culture still strongly favours red wine with meat and *rosado* with everything else. This explains why areas such as Cigales (and Navarra, and many of the northern Catalan DOs) have focused on producing excellent-quality *rosado* wines, even though they seem to be a permanent drug on the market anywhere north of Bordeaux. Indeed, in Cigales, although white wine-grapes are grown, there is no such thing as a white wine bearing the Cigales DO; the grapes go into the famous *rosado*.

The town of Cigales lies between Burgos and Valladolid, in what is now a quiet backwater bypassed by the N-620 *autovía*. The DO covers Cigales itself and 11 other *municipios* (municipalities), all but one of which are in the province of Valladolid. The area is drained by the River Pisuerga, and the vineyards are located at an altitude of between 700 and 800 metres (2,297 to 2,625 feet), planted for the most part in lightweight soils over limestone. Limestone is the bedrock of southern Castile; here, as in most neighbouring DO zones, it is honeycombed with tunnels, passages, storage vats and even entertainment rooms, all hewn out of the rock itself.

The wine towns are surrounded with what at first seem to be fossilized termite-hills: oddly shaped, rough-hewn monoliths rising out of the ground to a height of around two metres (around six feet). Called *luceras*, they act as vents, providing fresh air and a little daylight to the cellars situated ten metres (around 30 feet) or so below ground where the temperature never varies, winter or summer.

The climate in Cigales is high continental, with hot summers and cold winters. At these altitudes, the daily temperature variation during the growing season can be very beneficial to the vines, allowing them to 'sleep' during the night (*see* 'Ribera del Duero', page 54, for more details). Late frost is an ever-present danger in the spring, though, so good vineyard management is essential.

## Winemaking and wine styles

Winemaking styles in Cigales vary from the traditional to the ultra-modern. Stainless steel arrived here at the beginning of the 1990s. By that time, however, most forward-looking bodegas had been experimenting with the halfway-house solution of fibreglass tanking, so the philosophy of controlled fermentation was already well established.

As well as the excellent *rosados* (made from Tinto del País, Garnacha Tinta and the white varieties Verdejo, Viura, Palomino and Albillo), Cigales is now turning out splendid red wines, with a minimum 85 per cent Tinto del País and the rest made up of Garnacha Tinta or perhaps even the 'experimental' Cabernet Sauvignon. At least one bodega is working on a 100 per cent Cabernet Sauvignon varietal, but this is not yet permitted the DO accreditation. While the *rosados* of Cigales will, no doubt, always find a ready market in northern Spain and beyond, the DO's export performance is more likely to rest on its quality reds, made from Tempranillo and vinified to *crianza* level or even *reserva* in exceptional years.

**Far right: The church in the little town of Cigales is a hub of activity on market day – a tradition that dates back hundreds of years.**

**Below: Underground cellars, such as this one near Cigales, are commonplace in the hot, dry landscape of Castile-León.**

## Notable bodegas

**Félix Salas, Corcos de Valle.**
Félix Salas is a family-owned bodega
with a production of around 5,000hl
from its own vineyards and bought-
in grapes. Among others, the estate
makes a red Hijos de Félix Salas
(90% Tinto Fino/10% Cabernet
Sauvignon) in both *joven* and *crianza*
styles. *Best wine:* the *rosado* called
Viña Picota (70% Tinto Fino//10%
Garnacha/the rest white grapes).

**Frutos Villar, Cigales.** Frutos Villar
is a third-generation family business that
also maintains interests and vineyards
in Toro and Ribera del Duero as well
as Cigales (where its head office is
located). The Cigales operation has
a capacity of some 20,000hl and is
fully modernised. *Best wines:* Viña
Calderona is the best *rosado*,
made from 60% Tinto del País, 30%
Garnacha and the rest white varieties.
The company also produces a very
good red which sells in the UK under
the brand name Conde de Ansurez.

**González Lara, Mucientes.**
*Founded 1991.* This is a small,
private company with its own 30ha
of vines and an annual production
of approximately 6,000hl.
*Best wine:* the *rosado* Fuente del
Conde (70% Tinto del País/20%
Garnacha/the rest white varieties).

**Rodríguez Sanz, Cigales.**
*Founded 1931.* Rodríguez Sanz
is another small, family firm that owns
and works around 15ha of vines and
produces roughly 2,000hl per year.
*Best wines:* the company makes
the excellent Rosan *joven* (60% Tinto
Fino/20% Garnacha/the rest whites)
as well as a Rosan *crianza* (70% Tinto
Fino/30% Garnacha; six months
in American oak).

# Ribera del Duero

The best time to visit Ribera del Duero is during the first week of June. The *vegas*, or water-meadows, and verges are alive with a carpet of wild flowers in every imaginable colour; the vines are in flower; the last vintage is coming nicely together in the vat or in cask. There is a relaxed atmosphere among the region's people, secure in the knowledge that they will be going on holiday before the real work of the next vintage starts in earnest.

Another noticeable characteristic of Ribera del Duero in June is how cool it is, especially at night. At these altitudes, getting grapes to ripen fully is a challenge for even the most skilled *viñero*. There are only about 125 days during the year – roughly from the first week of June to the last week of September – when growers can be sure that there will not be a frost to destroy their livelihoods. This means that vines must be rugged and vigorous, that vineyards must be kept spotlessly clear of weeds and vine diseases, and that grapes must be harvested in perfect health, dry and fully ripe – ideally the day before the first autumn frost.

All of which is, of course, much more easily said than done. However, when a combination of meticulous attention to detail and consummate skill in the vineyard (coupled with good luck in the meteorological department) allows the average grower to get it right, the resulting grapes are likely to be of the very finest quality grown anywhere in Spain.

## The birth of Vega Sicilia

The first grower to discover this viticultural secret was Don Eloy Lecanda Chaves, who owned a small estate near the town of Valbuena. He came back from Bordeaux in 1864, armed with oak casks, French grape varieties and Bordelais winemaking skills and proceeded to try to recreate a Médoc-style vineyard on his own land at the Pago de la Vega Santa Cecilia y Carrascal.

At that time, winemaking in this stretch of the Duero Valley was largely domestic in scale and *artesanal* in style. What Don Eloy succeeded in doing was actually far more significant than producing a decent pastiche of a French wine type. He discovered that, when given the same care and attention as his imported Cabernet Sauvignon and Merlot, the local indigenous grape (known somewhat disparagingly as *Tinto del País* – 'Country Red'), could produce wines of similarly peerless quality. In fact, in dry years Tinto del País did rather better than the foreign imports.

Today we know Don Eloy's estate as Vega Sicilia and the Tinto del País variety – which is also known as Tinto Fino – as Tempranillo.

Don Eloy's success led other growers and winemakers to the area. What they found was a soil structure that could have been purpose-built for vine-growing: the bedrock is the same schistose substratum that outcrops in the vineyards of Priorato in the east and the Port vineyards of the Douro in the west. Above this, the carbonate subsoil is rich in gypsum and trace elements, but the main factor is the high level of active chalk, which is so prevalent in some areas (notably around the town of Pesquera) that distant ploughed fields seem to have a light coating of snow upon them.

Today, the DO zone is centred around the town of Aranda de Duero in the province of Burgos, with parts of it in the Soria province to the east and Valladolid to the west. There are also some vineyards (but no bodegas) in the northern part of the province of Segovia.

## Geography and climate

The other factor contributing to the quality of grapes in Ribera del Duero is the region's altitude. Vineyards may be planted at heights of up to 850 metres (2,789 feet), although most are positioned at levels between 750 and 800 metres (2,461 and 2,625 feet) on either side of the River Duero. In high summer, daytime temperatures may reach 39–40°C (100–104°F), but this is followed by a big temperature drop during the night of as much as 15 or 20 degrees – hence the danger of frosts at the beginning and end of the season.

Strange as it may seem, the vines actually benefit from this temperature change, because it allows them to 'sleep', or remain dormant at night. In hotter regions during the ripening season, vines draw nutrients from the soil to keep them going 24 hours a day. In Ribera del Duero, however, the vine quite literally 'chills out' overnight. When the sun comes up, the nutrients it would have consumed are still in the soil, waiting to be passed on to where they really need to be: inside the grapes themselves.

Given such natural advantages and Don Eloy's hard work, it is surprising to learn that, for the first 118 years of its existence, wine from Vega Sicilia was classified merely as table wine – despite the fact that it commanded the highest prices in Spain. Only consistent work by other bodegas in Ribera del Duero finally won the DO for the region in 1982.

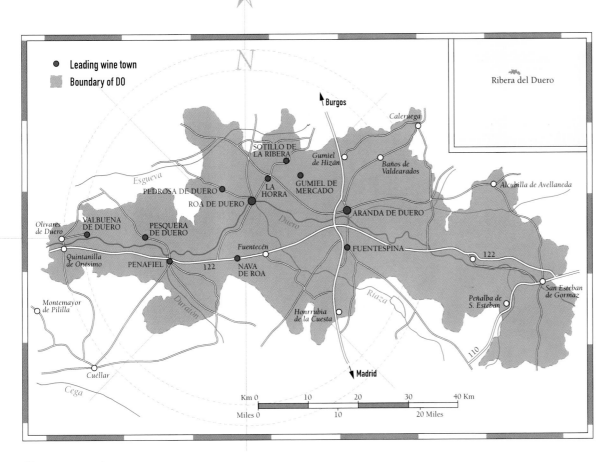

Leading wine town
Boundary of DO

Ribera del Duero

## Slow progression

Even so, during its first few years of existence, the new
DO somehow failed to achieve the expected recognition.
First of all, the traditional winemaking techniques and
long wood-ageing that had served Vega Sicilia so well
simply were not right for vineyards with younger vines on
lighter soils. Secondly, would-be exporters discovered that
a sales-pitch based on the line that, 'This is from the same
region as Vega Sicilia', did not work, since most foreign
importers had no idea where Vega Sicilia was anyway.

Finally, the wines and the region of Ribera del Duero
had no answer to the perceived dominance of Rioja on
world markets. What was sufficiently different about
them? Why should importers buy wines from this
relatively unknown area when Rioja was selling for the
same price – and brought with it the reliability of 150
years of quality-control?

Understandably, some growers became despondent
and tried to cut costs in the short term by using cheaper
grapes. In the process, they unwittingly ensured that
the market would never pick up as they hoped. Others
became so disillusioned that they grubbed up their vines

altogether and replanted the vineyards with other, more
marketable crops. After all, this part of Castile is known
as the market garden of Spain, where vegetables and fruit
grow in glorious, ripe profusion and sell effortlessly.

## The beginnings of success

Over in the town of Pesquera, however, at least one
winemaker stuck to his guns. Alejandro Fernández'
breakthrough with the 1986 vintage rekindled interest.
He proved that wine did not have to come from Vega
Sicilia to make an impact on world markets, and also that
it did not have to be aged for ten years in oak to give it
a world-class taste. As if this were not enough, Fernández
demonstrated that generations of winemaking skills
handed down from father to son were not necessarily
better than hiring a top-class winemaker with a proven
track record – in this instance, Teófilo Reyes.

All of which is even more interesting when you
consider that Fernández is an agricultural engineer who
made his fortune by inventing machinery to increase and
improve the sugar-beet harvest (a major local industry).
When he built his own bodega, he used those skills to

Below: Ventilation shafts spring from the earth, allowing air and a bit of light to reach the cellars of many a bodega in Ribera del Duero.

ensure that it would be as cost-effective as possible by inventing new machinery to clean and move barrels, as well as adapting existing mechanical-handling techniques to be more efficient. Fernández came into wine production in 1972 without any of the preconceptions of family tradition and old-fashioned methods. He simply wanted to make good wine.

## The effects of a catalyst

World interest in the Fernández wines galvanised many other bodegas in the region to rethink their own approaches: if he could do it, then surely so could they. By the late 1980s, many of the existing wineries in Ribera del Duero were replanting or renewing their installations. By the mid-1990s, new investment was running at a staggering rate, with new, internationally funded, state-of-the-art bodegas bringing a new focus to the area.

It seems to have worked. Today, the wines of Ribera del Duero are respected worldwide for their quality and are accepted as among Spain's very finest. They are no longer compared with Vega Sicilia or with Rioja, having earned the right to stand on their own vinous feet in a competitive world.

The important thing to remember about Ribera del Duero, however, is that these are not, and never will be, cheap wines. Vineyard husbandry in this alpine climate demands absolute cleanliness, weed-free plantations and dry, healthy, fully ripe grapes. Winemaking is as natural and as hands-off as possible, conducted in gravity-fed tanks with no pressing of the grapes and with only the ripest free-run juice being allowed into the final selection.

As a result, Ribera del Duero wines have a bold, bright character. In good years, the best of them will be *jovenes*, packed with fruit and mouthwateringly crisp. In very good years, a little *crianza* in mixed American and French oak yields that delicious 'third-dimension' of vanilla and spice. In excellent years, the wines may aspire to *reserva* status with glorious fruit, richness, length and maturity. *Gran reservas* are rare but exceptional.

All of this costs, of course, but Ribera del Duero has learned the lesson of the early 1980s: quality sells, even if it does demand a generous admixture of patience. Most of the wine made here is red, but there is a modest percentage of *rosado*. However, no white wines are allowed under the DO.

## Notable bodegas

**Note:** while the names Tempranillo, Tinto del País and Tinto Fino refer to the same grape, the different names are listed to reflect local usage.

**Alejandro Fernández, Pesquera.** *Founded 1972.* The man who proved that Ribera del Duero had major, world-class export potential even if it was not Vega Sicilia. He continues to do so, year in and year out. Fernández makes 100% Tinto Fino *crianza* and *reserva* wines under the Pesquera label. *Best wine:* in exceptional years, the Pesquera Janus *gran reserva* (also 100% Tinto Fino) is magnificent.

**Alión, Peñafiel.** Recently acquired and revamped by Bodegas Vega Sicilia, Alión shares a 100ha estate with its parent company. The first vintage was released in 1991, and the brief is to produce top-class 100% Tinto Fino wines of *reserva* quality. Early results show extremely well.

**Antonio Barceló, Quintanilla de Onésimo.** *Founded 1876.* Old firm with a brand-new bodega beside the N-122 on the western edge of the DO zone. It farms nine hectares of vines (with additional capacity still coming to maturity) and buys in additional grapes for its annual production of around 7,500hl. *Best wines:* those sold under the Viña Mayor label, which includes *joven, crianza* and *reserva* styles, all made from 100% Tinto del País.

**Balbás, La Horra.** Ancient firm which re-formed and re-equipped itself in 1987 to switch to better-quality wines. The old cellars have been converted into *crianza* naves, and the company produces around 1,500hl each year from its own 30ha of vineyards and bought-in grapes. *Best wine:* Balbás *crianza* (100% Tempranillo).

**La Cepa Alta, Olivares.** *Founded 1988.* La Cepa Alta is one of those estates that had been grubbed-up and

replanted with other crops – until it became apparent that it was situated on prime vineyard land. Around 42ha of vines were replanted in 1988, with a very promising first vintage in 1991. *Best wines:* the estate's Laveguilla label (100% Tinto del País) has gone from strength to strength, and now appears as a 'lightly oaked' *joven* (six months in oak) as well as in *crianza* and barrel-fermented versions.

**Cooperativa Virgen de la Asunción, La Horra.** *Founded 1955.* The 260 members of this co-op make more than 10,000hl per year. They grow Tinto del País and Cabernet Sauvignon, and the vast majority of the wines are *rosados*. *Best wine:* the minority red, Viña Valeria, both *joven* and *crianza* versions, and both 100% Tinto del País.

**Cooperativa Virgen de Fátima, Pedrosa.** *Founded 1957.* This co-op handles 1,000 tonnes of grapes from 200ha of vineyards and still manages to turn out wines of good-to-excellent quality. The brand name is Viña Vilano, which comes in *joven* and *crianza* styles. *Best wine:* the *crianza.*

**Cooperativa Virgen del Rosario, Quintanamanvirgo.** This co-op draws its grapes from its members' 184ha of vineyards and produces *rosados* and reds of very good quality under the Torremorón label. The excellent *rosado* is made from 80% Tinto Fino and 20% Albillo, while the reds are 100% Tinto Fino. *Best wine:* the red *crianza* version in a year classified as *muy buena* or better.

**Cooperativa Virgen de la Vega, Roa.** *Founded 1956.* Co-op whose 275 members farm around 345ha. Makes *rosados* and reds under the Roa and Rauda labels, with the reds (100% Tinto del País) being made up to *crianza* level. *Best wine:* the Roa red *joven.*

**Dehesa de los Canónigos, Pesquera.** *Founded 1988.* Situated in a beguiling *ranchero*-style building

surrounded by 60ha of vines, this estate's house style consists of top-quality *crianza* and *reserva* wines. Typically made from the rather old-fashioned (but none the worse for that) mix of 85% Tempranillo, 12% Cabernet Sauvignon and 3% Albillo, the wines usually spend rather more than the minimum time in *barrica.* In good vintages, they are excellent; in great vintages, they are exemplary.

**Famoro, Pesquera.** *Founded 1989.* Very small, family-run operation located next door to Alejandro Fernández, with 20ha of Tinto Fino vines. Produces red wines from *joven* to *reserva* level, according to the quality of the vintage. Although small, Famoro insists on attention to quality and detail; the wines are very good. *Best wine:* the Emilio Moro label; the *crianza* is often the best.

**Federico Fernández Pérez, Pesquera.** *Founded 1986.* Another small family concern; Federico is the brother of Alejandro Fernández. The estate's 17ha of vines (all Tinto Fino) provide 70% of its needs. The brand name is Federico and the styles are 'oaked-*joven*' (with eight months in *barrica*) and *crianza* (anything up to 18 months in *barrica*). The latter can be excellent in good years.

**Félix Callejo, Sotillo de la Ribera.** *Founded 1990.* Félix Callejo presides over a brand-new, hi-tech, pink palace of a bodega in the midst of his own 30ha of vineyards. The firm is family owned, and the wines are some of the most widely exported of the region. Most of the (red) wines are made from 90% Tinto del País and 10% Cabernet Sauvignon, and there are 'oaked-*joven*' (four months in oak), *crianza* and *reserva* (up to 18 months in oak) styles produced under the Callejo label. *Best wine:* the Callejo Cosecha Especial, which is made from the best selection of grapes in the best years.

**Fuentespina, Fuentespina.** This bodega makes wine with Tinto Fino and Cabernet Sauvignon under two labels: Fuentespina and Vega de Castilla. The Vega de Castilla *crianza* (100% Tinto Fino) shows very well. *Best wines:* the Fuentespina *reserva*, with a 90% Tinto Fino/10% Cabernet Sauvignon grape mix and 24 months in oak. Then there is the Fuentespina *crianza* with a similar grape-mix and the regulation 12 months in oak.

**Grandes Bodegas, Roa.** *Founded 1985.* Grandes Bodegas began by buying in ready-made wines, then buying in grapes, until its own

50ha of vineyards reached maturity. The wines are now showing well; the best of them are 100% Tinto Fino. There is a very good rosado and an excellent red (joven and crianza), all under the Marqués de Velilla label.

### Hacienda Monasterio, Pesquera.

*Founded 1991.* Another example of prime vineyard land neglected during the 'doldrum years'. New vines have been planted, with a magical winery (rather like a pink flying-saucer) built into the hillside overlooking them. Young winemaker Peter Sisseck insists on one-year-old Bordeaux casks for the maturation of his wines, and quality is at the highest level. Sisseck also uses grapes from an experimental plantation called Dominio de Pingus to 'push Tinto Fino to its limits'. Early results are astonishing (as are the prices at which the wine is changing hands). Only *crianza* and *reserva* wines are made (under the Hacienda Monasterio name), typically from 80% Tinto del País, 10% Cabernet Sauvignon and 10% Merlot. These are among the region's finest wines.

### Ismael Arroyo, Sotillo de la Ribera.

Old family firm that built a new stainless steel-equipped winery in 1979. It farms about seven hectares of Tinto del País vines, buying in additional

grapes according to its needs. *Reservas* and *gran reservas* are produced under the Valsotillo label, but only improve on the younger wines in really good years. *Best wines:* Mesoneros de Castilla *rosado* (80% Tinto del País/20% Albillo) is one of the best pink wines of the region, and the red *joven* and *crianza* under the same label are extremely good.

### Montevannos, Baños de Valdearados.

Once an old co-op which, like so many in the 1980s, got into financial difficulty. Now Swedish-owned and partly revamped, it farms 50ha of Tinto Fino as well as buying in grapes to meet its annual production. Although it still has the massive 26,000hl capacity of the original co-op, it currently produces considerably less. Wines include a white called Opinius (which does not have the DO), as well as *rosados* and reds under the Montevannos label. These are 100% Tinto Fino and come as *joven*, *crianza* and *reserva*. *Best wine:* the *crianza*.

### Pago de Carraovejas, Peñafiel.

*Founded 1991.* Very small enterprise sitting in its own vineyards within sight of the famous castle in Peñafiel. It is jointly owned by a restaurateur, a businessman and one of the leading winemakers of the region, who tends its state-of-the-art, gravity-fed tanks in his own time. The wine is made from 70% to 85% Tinto del País, the rest from Cabernet Sauvignon, and it is always given some barrel-age, though often not enough to qualify as *crianza*. Typically, the *joven* spends three or four months in cask, adding a touch of spice to the bouncing, delicious fruit that characterises the basic wine. In better years (and with maturing vines), the bodega also makes *crianza* and *reserva* styles. Another example of excellence in the region's new generation of winemaking.

### Pascual, Fuentelcespied.

*Founded 1986.* Pascual makes around 4,000hl of red and *rosado* wines made with Tinto Fino, Garnacha and Albillo from

its own 15ha. It also supplements its needs with locally bought-in grapes. The main wine is the red Heredad de Peñalosa, which may be *joven* (90% Tinto Fino/10% Cabernet Sauvignon) or *crianza* (100% Tinto Fino). In particularly good years, there is also a Peñalosa *reserva*.

### Peñalba-López, Aranda.

*Founded 1903.* Old, established and one of the prime movers in winning the DO for Ribera del Duero. Owners Pablo Peñalba-López and his wife Pilár are prominent local businesspeople and property owners. The *castillo*-style bodega – which rejoices in the name of Finca Torremilanos – sits magnificently in 170ha of vineyards just outside the town itself, and the winemaking is ultra-modern, with a capacity of some 20,000hl. Wines are uniformly excellent and include a non-DO white called Peñalba-López, a very good *rosado* called Monte Castrillo (70% Tinto del País/20% Garnacha/10% Albillo) and superb reds under two labels: Torremilanos and Torre Albéniz. They tend to be at least 85% Tinto Fino, but the latter is likely to be topped up with Cabernet Sauvignon. Peñalba-López is one of the few bodegas which can make really good *reservas* and *gran reservas* in the best years. It is also one of the few bodegas outside Catalonia to be accredited for the production of sparkling wines under the Cava *denominación*.

### Pérez Pascuas, Pedrosa.

*Founded 1980.* Family firm with some 60ha of vineyards scattered around the village of Pedrosa. Although not a large enterprise, it does have a strong commitment to quality. When it became evident that the winery needed modernising, the owners decided to build an entirely new one 15 minutes closer to the vineyards, rather than refurbish the older building, which now serves for storage. That 15 minutes can be critical at harvest time when the sun is hot. Wines are known as Viña Pedrosa, and are made from 90% to 100% Tinto Fino; the rest is usually Cabernet Sauvignon.

*Best wines:* tend to be *crianzas* in most years and *reservas* in better years. In the best years, these, too, are among the finest wines of Ribera del Duero.

### Protos, Peñafiel.

*Founded in 1927.* Beguiling old co-op situated one kilometre (just over half a mile) from tunnels excavated in the chalky bedrock beneath the castle of Peñafiel. Some of the tunnels pass through what were the castle's dungeons, and there are legends of chained skeletons and even wandering shadows among the casks. The wine, however, has a good reputation. The co-op's 230 members farm 100ha of Tinto Fino vines, and wines range in style from *crianza* to *gran reserva*. All are very good. *Best wine:* the *crianza* is the most consistent.

### Riberalta, Gumiel de Izán.

*Founded 1988.* Newly built, stainless steel-equipped bodega situated right on the N-I *autovía* from Madrid to Burgos, about 12km (seven miles) north of Aranda. There are 12ha of vineyard, and the bodega buys in the extra necessary grapes – mostly Tinto del País and some Garnacha. The wines (*rosado* and red) are all called Vega Izán. The red is made in *joven* and *crianza* styles which are generally of equal quality – indeed, very good.

### Rodero, Pedrosa. *Founded 1991.*

Rodero's is a classic 'new-generation' story. Carmelo Rodero and his wife María Oña took over 37ha of vines – mainly Tinto del País but with a little Cabernet Sauvignon – from their respective families. The grapes had previously been sold to the big names in Ribera del Duero (most notably Vega Sicilia), and they found themselves asking why, if their grapes were so good, they should not make them into wine themselves. The answer was money, of course, and the Roderos embarked on an ambitious plan of mortgaging everything they possessed in order to build a modest winery in the middle of the vineyard. They shared out the various tasks in vineyard, cellar, office and home and lived on bread and cheese (metaphorically speaking) until the first vintage was ready for turning into wine. At this point, they could have opted to make a large amount of wine to sell at middle-of-the-road prices to start recouping their investment. Yet no doubt feeling that another couple of years on bread and cheese was no big deal, they decided to aim for the lowest-yield, highest-quality wine, and duly held out for the best price. They won an award with their second vintage and are now established as one of the very best of the new-wave bodegas of Ribera del Duero. Under the label Ribeño, they make wines ranging from *joven* to *reserva* in style, from 90% to 100% Tinto del País, the rest being Cabernet Sauvignon. All are exemplary.

### Señorío de Nava, Nava de Roa.

*Founded 1986.* Another private takeover of what was once an ailing co-op, now sporting a smart, *château*-style frontage on the main N-122. The bodega owns 140ha of vineyards planted mainly in Tinto Fino, and its wines are made exclusively from its own grapes under the Don Alvaro, Vega Cubillas and Señorío de Nava labels. *Best wines:* the best *rosado* is Don Alvaro (80% Tinto Fino/15% Albillo/5% Garnacha). The best reds are the Señorío de Nava range, *joven* to *reserva* and usually made from 100% Tinto Fino. The *crianza* is consistently excellent, eclipsed only by the *reserva* in very good years.

### Valbuena de Duero, Valbuena.

*Founded 1988.* Modern bodega which farms 21ha of Tinto Fino and produces just one wine: Matarromera. It is a *joven* with barrel-ageing determined by the winemaker according to the quality of the year (typically three to four months). In good years, it is absolutely stunning.

### Valduero, Gumiel del Mercado.

*Founded 1983.* Established in some beguiling old Castilian cellars which (once again) were formerly part of a cooperative, this bodega boasts one of the region's most famous female winemakers: Yolanda García. Valduero has 72ha of vines and also buys in grapes when necessary. The company's non-DO white wine is called Viadero (100% Albillo) and is highly regarded. *Best wine:* the bodega's finest work is its Valduero *crianza*.

### Vega Sicilia, Valbuena.

*Founded 1864.* The bodega that started the whole thing off in these parts, 118 years before the granting of the Ribera del Duero DO. Today, the bodega and the famous family house are immaculately restored in manicured gardens, and the bodega buildings – including the little church of Santa Cecilia – have been spruced up and returned to their original glory. Vega Sicilia has 250ha of vineyard planted in Tinto Fino, Cabernet Sauvignon, Merlot, Malbec and Albillo, and there is a new storage cellar inserted almost invisibly into the hillside opposite the main site. It is still the only bodega in Ribera del Duero with its own cooperage. Since 1982, it has belonged to the Alvárez Díaz family, which has carried on the traditions laid down by the founder while nodding in the direction of modern tastes. Originally, the Unica Vega Sicila was aged for a minimum of ten years in oak before being bottled, and a three-year-old and five-year-old wine under the 'Valbuena' label were released when the winemaker thought it appropriate. These days, the three-year-old has been dropped, and winemaker Mariano García only ages the Unica wines for five to six years before bottling or returning them to the vat. In dry years, the wine is likely to be mainly Tinto Fino; in wetter years, there will be more Cabernet Sauvignon, but in any year García decides to make a Vega Sicilia Unica, you may be sure that it will be one of the finest wines in the world. The current (1999) 'drinking vintages' are the 1990 Valbuena and 1970 Unica, although true *aficionados* will settle for nothing less than the undated Reserva Especial. Only Mariano García knows how old it is – and he's not saying.

# Rueda

## Success with Verdejo

*If ever there were a grape waiting for technology to catch up with it, it has to be Verdejo. Today, top-class winemaking in Rueda starts at harvest time, beginning in the small hours of the morning, well before sunrise. The pickers wear miners' lamps on their heads and load the grapes into plastic-lined trucks or small plastic boxes. There, a blast of heavier-than-air inert gas is blown across them to prevent the grapes from coming into contact with air once they are off the vine. The harvest is transported to the winery as quickly as possible, where the grapes themselves are gently chilled to fermentation temperature (15-18°C/ 58-66°F) in a sealed tank, which is once again filled with an inert gas (usually nitrogen) to prevent contact with air. From here on in, grapes, juice and fermenting must are all blanketed with gas; even the fully fermented wine will be protected until it goes for bottling. This is the way in which the delicate, crisp, gooseberry fruit of Verdejo is captured – after 1,000 years of obscurity.*

Having established that Castile-León is meat-eating country, it may seem odd that it should feature one of Spain's best white wine producing areas. Yet there are reasons both historical and modern for this state of affairs, and for the evolution of the Verdejo-based wine from oxidised obscurity into what is arguably the current classic white wine of Spain.

First, the history. As the Moors retreated southwards during the tenth century, they ravaged and burned everything in their path; the area south of the River Duero and southeast of Valladolid was devastated. This scorched-earth policy effectively reduced the region to a wasteland; what few people who still lived there moved away, and what is now Rueda remained fairly uninhabited for the better part of a hundred years.

Of course, this fallow period did wonders for the soil, allowing it to rest and become fertile again, and providing a habitat for both animal and vegetable wildlife. One of 'vegetables' was an obscure wild grapevine called *Verdejo*, a word that might mean 'greenish' or that might be derived from *verdugo*, meaning 'green shoot' – rather appropriate under the circumstances.

By the middle of the 11th century, King Alfonso VI was installed on the throne of Castile-León, ruling from Burgos. To revitalise the area, he issued an edict to the effect that anyone working land in what is now Rueda would be awarded ownership of it if certain criteria were fulfilled. The policy worked, and monastic orders and farmers began to flood back to the region. Vines were an obvious crop, since there was an unquenchable thirst for the good stuff from the royal courts and seats of learning and religion all over Castile. And here in Rueda was a vine growing wild, just begging to be cultivated.

In those days, Sherry was considered the finest wine in the world, but Jerez was still part of the Moorish empire; thus, the new region of Rueda was appointed to make white wine in the Sherry style. In other words, the market wanted fully oxidised, oloroso-style wines made using the *solera* system (*see* page 192). And behold! Wine made from Verdejo oxidised all by itself, with minimal help from man. It was almost as if the grape had been destined to fulfil this role.

The region prospered. By the 17th century, Rueda wine was considered so good that half its production was earmarked for the court (which by then had moved to Madrid), and the main centre of production was Medina del Campo. By this time, the Sherry Country was back in business, but from Rueda's point of view, it no longer

seemed to matter. Sherry was in the early stages of a boom which – give or take the odd world war – was to continue almost unabated until 1979.

At the end of the 19th century, however, the Rueda bubble burst with the coming of the phylloxera epidemic. During the dead period of grubbing up old vines, replanting with grafted rootstocks and waiting for the new vines to mature, Sherry recaptured Madrid's tastes with a vengeance, and Rueda found itself without a market. The Spanish Civil War, coupled with Franco's policy of paying per litre for any surplus wine regardless of quality, encouraged massive replanting with Palomino. The region remained in a state of stagnation until the 1970s.

At this point, Rueda was producing *pálido* (light and dry) and *dorado* (older and richer) styles of lightly fortified wine which, in their way, were very good. Yet the export markets – particularly in northern Europe – were just waking up to wine; the last thing they wanted to buy was Rueda. Those who wanted *solera* wines bought Sherry (economy of scale made it very cheap – too cheap, in fact, for its own good, as was discovered a few years later), but most people did not want *solera* wines of any sort. They wanted light, fresh, fruity, upfront wines such as those being made in Germany (and subsequently in the New World). Rueda had no place in this scheme of things.

## The Marqués de Riscal

Then along came Francisco Hurtado de Amézaga y Dolagaray ('Paco' to his friends), director of Marqués de Riscal in Rioja and scion of the founding *marqués*, Don Camilo Hurtado. Riscal had never made a white wine, eschewing the traditional oaky style of white Rioja and the perceived blandness of the Viura grape.

As one of Rioja's leading exporters, however, Paco understood the market well and wanted to create a wine full of fruit, freshness and crisp acidity but with good strength and stability into the bargain. He had studied under Professor Emile Peynaud at the University of Bordeaux and invited his old tutor to share his research. They looked at Penedès and what was to become Rías Baixas, as well as areas south of Madrid, before settling on Rueda.

One of the guiding factors for their decision was Verdejo. Peynaud had determined that, with modern technology (stainless-steel vats, cool fermentation and blanketing the grapes, juice and fermenting wine with inert gas; *see* 'Success with Verdejo', left), Verdejo could be prevented from oxidising and would instead produce the crisp, fresh, fruity wine Paco had been seeking. After experiments conducted in 1971, the Riscal estate built a new bodega in 1972 and began to demonstrate Verdejo's capabilities.

## The coming of Sauvignon Blanc

Another innovation pioneered by the Riscal estate was the acceptance of Sauvignon Blanc as an authorised variety. In the early days, this was a financial hedge. Rueda's climate (fully continental with hot summers and cold winters) and soils (alluvial over limestone in the north, sandy/clay over sandstone in the south) are perfect. Sauvignon Blanc's name will sell wine all over the world, but it has done seriously well in this particular region, and many bodegas now submit it to barrel fermentation or *crianza* with considerable success.

Only white wines are permitted to bear the Rueda DO. To achieve it, the wine must contain a minimum of 25 per cent Verdejo; to be Rueda Superior, it must contain a minimum of 85 per cent. The exception is Rueda Sauvignon, which may be 100 per cent of the named variety. There is a new (1992) classification called Rueda Espumoso (*ie* sparkling) which must be made by the *método tradicional* from a minimum of 85 per cent Verdejo, and it must have nine months on its lees before disgorgement. The old *solera* styles, *pálido* and *dorado*, are still made for a niche-market that loves them.

Candidates for the classic white wine of Spain have come forward from Rueda, as well as Penedès (mostly in the form of Chardonnay) and Rías Baixas (Albariño). Until relatively recently, the result of such arguments has been something of a moot point. Given the latest developments in the vineyards and the wineries in this particular region, however, the strongest candidate for standard-bearer of Spanish whites worldwide must be the elegantly crisp, lusciously fresh and deliciously fruity Verdejo wines of Rueda.

**Above:** Despite the innovations pioneered by the Riscal estate, much Rueda wine is still made and aged in the traditional manner.

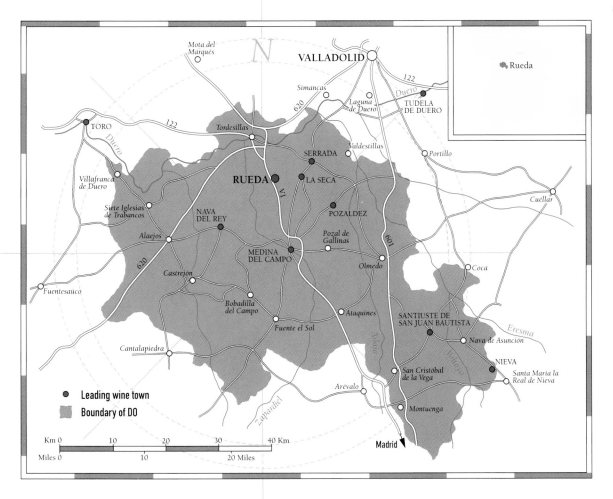

Leading wine town
Boundary of DO

# Notable bodegas

### Alberto Gutiérrez, Serrada.
*Founded 1949.* This family firm pioneered the *dorado* style of traditional Rueda. Its wines generally owe little to fashion and much to careful and consistent winemaking. Many of the best wines are excluded from the DO; these include *generosos* which have been fortified beyond the permitted limits and, of course, red and *rosado* wines. *Best wines:* the best Rueda DO wine is the barrel-fermented Viña Cascarela (100% Verdejo), but *aficionados* of the *solera* style will enjoy (non-DO) San Martín Vino Generoso and San Martín Dry Gold. Non-DO red and *rosado* wines include the very good Viña Valdemoya (50/50 different clones of Tempranillo and Tinto de Toro).

### Alvárez y Díaz, Nava del Rey.
Once the biggest and best of the old *solera*-style producers with 75ha, this bodega changed direction in 1993 to produce fresh, crisp, new-wave white wines but didn't abandon its original commitment to *vino ecológico*: wine made as naturally as possible, with minimal use of sprays and insecticides. The Lurton brothers kicked off the new style with wines bottled under their own label (Hermanos Lurton), including an outstanding basic Rueda (50% Verdejo/50% Viura) and a Sauvignon Blanc. The bodega's own Mantel Nuevo (100% Verdejo) is an excellent, full-fruit example. *Best wine:* the Mantel Blanco *crianza* (100% Verdejo, six months in oak).

### Antaño, Rueda. *Founded 1988.*
Established in restored 15th-century cellars, Antaño belongs to a restaurateur in Madrid, and places as much emphasis on its non-DO reds as it does on its Rueda whites. The best red is Viña Cobranza (60% Tempranillo/40% Cabernet Sauvignon; nine months in American oak). *Best wines:* the white Viña Mocen (60% Viura/40% Verdejo) and Viña Mocen Rueda Superior (85% Verdejo/15% Sauvignon Blanc).

### Angel Lorenzo Cachazo, Pozáldez.
This family firm makes non-DO *rosado* and red wines as well as whites. *Best white wines:* Lorenzo Cachazo Rueda (50% Verdejo/40% Viura/10% Palomino) and Martivilli Rueda Superior (100% Verdejo). *Best red:* a wine called Carmín, a *joven* made from 50% Tinto de Toro/50% Juan García.

### Angel Rodríguez Vidal, La Seca.
*Founded 1780.* An example of living history. Angel Rodríguez, a gentleman of mature years, makes his wine entirely by hand in the *artesanal* way handed down through generations of his family. He has 70ha of his own vines; apart from harvesting, he does all the work himself. The ancient cellars have some fibreglass tanks, but there are also huge oak vats which Angel Rodríguez dismantles, cleans and rebuilds every five years. He avoids oxidation by topping up his casks at least every two weeks, and the bungs are stoppered with a freshly cut goose quill. In spite of the lack of modern equipment, his wines (under the Martinsancho label) have a gorgeous freshness and fruit, a scent of hazelnuts and the apparent ability to live for ever. In 1994, the 1981 vintage was drinking astoundingly well, still maintaining crisp acidity with a touch of oak, rich, golden, ripe fruit and a delicious length without a hint of oxidation – all at 13 years old. This is probably the finest wine of Rueda although, sadly, Don Angel is one of a dying breed of winemakers, uniquely in touch with his land and his vines, and virtually untouched by modern techniques. How can he make wine of this quality, which flies in the face of all the scientific evidence? The secret, he says, is the 'holy trinity' of winemaking: old vines, low yields and slow, patient fermentation. (He also says that there isn't any money in it and he wouldn't do it again.)

### Castilla la Vieja, Rueda.
*Founded 1973.* One of the branches of the Sanz family (here, Ricardo Sanz and his brother) whose members have done an enormous amount to advance the case for Rueda wine. They pioneered night-time harvesting and also a number of improvements in the vineyard, including an ingenious environmentally friendly method of getting rid of the yellow spider, a notorious vineyard pest. Normal insecticides kill everything in sight, even those insects that are good for the vines (ie, those that eat other insects which are bad for the vines). The Sanz family developed a kind of vacuum-cleaner which sucks up soil from around the vine, pulverises it into a powder and sprays it back on to the vine. This has no effect on vine, leaves or grapes but it does cause the insect population to move out pretty rapidly. As the other insects depart with all speed, the poor old yellow spider – which has a very spiky, hairy back – becomes increasingly weighed down with the weight of powdered soil and eventually grinds to a halt, to be killed instantly by the minimum dose of acaricide applied at soil level, which is then immediately neutralised. This avoids insecticides on the vine and, in due course, the good insects come creeping back to re-establish their residency. This kind of thinking characterises this bodega. The classic wine is called Palacio de Bornos and comes in three styles, starting with Rueda Superior (90% Verdejo/10% Viura), which boasts fabulous, crisp acidity and rich, ripe fruit – one of Rueda's very best *joven* wines. There is also a barrel-fermented version (100% Verdejo; six months on its lees), with delicious, warm, oaky notes and a spicy finish; and a sparkling version (under the Rueda *espumoso* [sparkling] regulations of 1992), which has an excellent biscuity flavour and pleasant fruit and freshness. There is a splendid Bornos Sauvignon Blanc, although it does not quite have the zest of the Verdejo. Among non-DO wines, the Sanzes make a ripe-scented, buttery, barrel-fermented Chardonnay with six months on its lees in American oak; a Huerta del Rey *rosado* (100% Gamacha); and an excellent red from 100% Tinto del País called Almirantazgo de Castilla.

There is also a traditional *dorado* called, simply, '62'. *Best wines:* all of this bodega's wines are exemplary, and whether the best of them is the Palacio de Bornos Superior, the barrel-fermented version or the Bornos Sauvignon is purely a matter of taste.

### Cerrosol, Santiuste de San Juan Bautista.
Medium-sized bodega producing about 5,000hl of wine per year. The most important brands are Cerrosol (50% Verdejo/50% Viura), and Doña Beatriz Rueda Superior (100% Verdejo). There is also a Doña Beatriz Sauvignon Blanc. All are first-class.

### Con Class, La Seca. *Founded 1988.*
Situated in 17th-century cellars, this is another offshoot of the Sanz family (Marco Antonio Sanz in this case; see Castilla la Vieja, above, and Sanz, below) making (non-DO) Verdejo, Sauvignon Blanc and Chardonnay wines both tank- and barrel-fermented under the Con Class label. *Best wine:* the (100%) Sauvignon Blanc.

### Cooperativa Agricola Castellana, La Seca. *Founded 1935.*
Co-op with 350 members and an annual production of 30,000hl, but that is not to say its wines are ordinary. Indeed, the Rueda of the Marqués de Griñón is made here (see Viñedos y Bodegas de Malpica, below). In its own right, the co-op makes an excellent Rueda called Veliterra (50% Verdejo/50% Viura) and a Rueda Superior called Azumbre (85% Verdejo/15% Sauvignon Blanc). *Best wine:* the 100% Verdejo Cuatro Rayas, which is the equal of anything else made in the region.

### Cooperativa Viñedos de Nieva, Nieva. *Founded 1989.*
With 50ha of vines, this small co-op turns out excellent wines, including Blanco Nieva (100% Verdejo) and a non-DO *rosado* called Viña Pontel (100% Tinto Fino).

### Los Curros SAT, Rueda.
*Founded 1972.* Not to be confused with Los Curros SA, which is another branch of the family in the town of Fuente del

Sol. In Rueda, members of the Yllera family were nicknamed *Los Curros*, which roughly translates as 'those who get on with the job', because of their dedication to work. This smart, modern bodega draws from 15ha of vineyards and makes the excellent Cantosan (100% Verdejo) as well as a sparkling version (with 10% Viura) with up to five years on its lees. There is also an Yllera *reserva* (12-14 months in American oak). *Best wine:* the non-DO red Yllera (100% Tempranillo).

### Félix Lorenzo Cachazo, Pozáldez.

*Founded 1945.* Family business in a smart, purpose-built bodega situated just outside the town. The basic Rueda is called Larrua (50% Palomino/50% Viura) and is pleasant enough. There is also a non-DO red called Carriles that is aged in oak (though the terms *crianza*, etc, are not permitted on table wines) and made from Tinto Fino/Tinto de Toro. *Best wine:* Carrasviñas (100% Verdejo).

### Garciarévalo, Matapozuelos.

*Founded 1991.* With 17ha of vines, this firm turns out around 1,500hl of wine each year. The basic wine is called Casamaro (Verdejo/Viura). *Best wine:* Viña Adaja (100% Verdejo).

### Garcigrande, Rueda. *Founded 1989.*

With 50ha of vineyards, Garcigrande also buys in grapes, must and wine from other bodegas to supplement its output. The wines are all sold under the Señorío de Garcigrande label. There is also a non-DO red which is made from 75% to 100% Tinto Fino, with the rest Cabernet Sauvignon. *Best wine:* the Rueda Superior (85% Verdejo/15% Viura).

### Grandes Vinos. A bodega located

in Ribera del Duero which has a superb Rueda Superior called Mirador made for it under contract by Bodegas Sanz.

### Marqués de Irún, La Seca.

*Founded 1990.* With 24ha of vines, this estate makes the excellent Marqués de Irún Rueda Superior (85% Verdejo/10% Viura and Sauvignon Blanc).

### Sanz, Rueda. *Founded 1870.* The fount

of the renowned Sanz family, now run by Juan Carlos Ayala Sanz, whose kinsmen run Castilla la Vieja and Con Class. These particular Sanzes farm 100ha of vines planted next door to Castilla la Vieja in Rueda, and were among the first to harvest their grapes in small plastic boxes to minimise damage in transit. They also buy in other grapes from contract growers, paying a premium to get the best. Only wine from the first pressing goes into a bottle under the Sanz label. These, too, are top-of-the-range wines. The basic Rueda (50% Verdejo/50% Viura) is an excellent example of its kind, while the Sanz Rueda Superior (90% to 100% Verdejo/the rest Viura) is exemplary: gorgeous fruit and ripeness and a clean, crisp finish. Sanz Sauvignon Blanc (100%) is one of the best of the region, and the 1993 vintage won all the white-wine trophies in Spain in 1994. Sanz also makes the non-DO Campo Sanz in *rosado* (100% Tempranillo) and red (100% Tempranillo and eight months in oak).

### Vega de la Reina, Rueda.

*Founded 1961.* Bodega with 30ha of vines, turning out two very good whites and a non-DO red. Valle de la Reina (53% Verdejo/47% Viura) is the standard article and, indeed, within a whisker of the quality of the Superior Vega de la Reina (100% Verdejo). The non-DO red is typically 80% Tinto Fino/20% Cabernet Sauvignon with anything up to 42 months in oak.

### Viñedos y Bodegas de Malpica.

This is the Marqués de Griñón, whose main bodega is in the province of Toledo (*see* page 180). The Marqués has his Rueda made (by his own winemaker) on the premises of the Cooperativa Agrícola Castellana. The wine is called Roda and is barrel-fermented from Verdejo and Viura. He also makes the non-DO Durius here, which is also Verdejo and Viura but made from grapes grown both in Rueda and Ribera del Duero, thereby losing its legal right to either name. The quality lives up to

the standard of everything that ever goes into a bottle under the name of the Marqués de Griñón: never less than superb.

### Vinos Blancos de Castilla, Rueda.

*Founded 1974.* The forerunner of the new-wave Marqués de Riscal (*see above*) wines. Since the new grape-chiller was installed in 1994 and night-time picking was introduced, the quality of the wines is better than ever. There are 80ha of Verdejo, 70ha of Sauvignon Blanc; also an experimental vineyard still testing out Riesling, Gewürztraminer, Chardonnay, Albariño

and Treixadura, but Paco is more or less satisfied that Verdejo 'does the business' while Sauvignon Blanc opens doors in markets that are wedded to the varietal concept. The grapes are chilled and then macerated for six hours before spending a painstakingly slow 50 days in fermentation with Champagne yeast at a very low 15°C (58°F). *Best wines:* Riscal Rueda Superior is one of the region's finest (85% Verdejo/15% Viura). The Reserva Limousin (100% Verdejo) spends around 17 months in Limousin oak, according to the quality of each vintage. The Sauvignon Blanc is, like all Riscal's wines, exemplary.

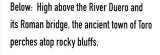 # Toro

One of the most pleasant ways to spend a summer evening before the harvest in Toro is on the terrace of the Hotel Juan II, after a post-siesta swim in the tiny pool and with the prospect of a good dinner to come (the hotel's restaurant is very good). It is a modest, three-star affair, but it is the best that this small country town (population 10,000) has to offer, and the pleasure is enhanced by virtue of the view.

Toro stands on a clifftop, and the hotel's terrace is situated at its edge, offering a panoramic prospect towards the south across the flood-plain of the Duero and Guareña rivers. The view lends some element of scale to the term *Tierra del Pan*, or 'Bread Country', as it is known: in the summer, the rolling acres of wheat curl and unfurl almost to the horizon. Upstream and to the left lies Rueda, with Ribera del Duero beyond. Downstream and to the right is the city of Zamora and, some 40 kilometres/18 miles distant, the border with Portugal.

However, there is no trace of Portuguese influence here, (as there is, for example, in Galicia). Toro is Castilian to the roots of its vinous hair. Its wines reflect a more direct link in style with the tradition of strength, power and fruit that was so highly prized by the medieval movers and shakers of Castile.

The Toro *denominción de origen* is located directly to the west of the Rueda DO. The town of Toro itself – a pleasant, modestly prosperous and cheerfully comfortable place – is situated north of Medina on the Zamora-Valladolid road.

Below: High above the River Duero and its Roman bridge, the ancient town of Toro perches atop rocky bluffs.

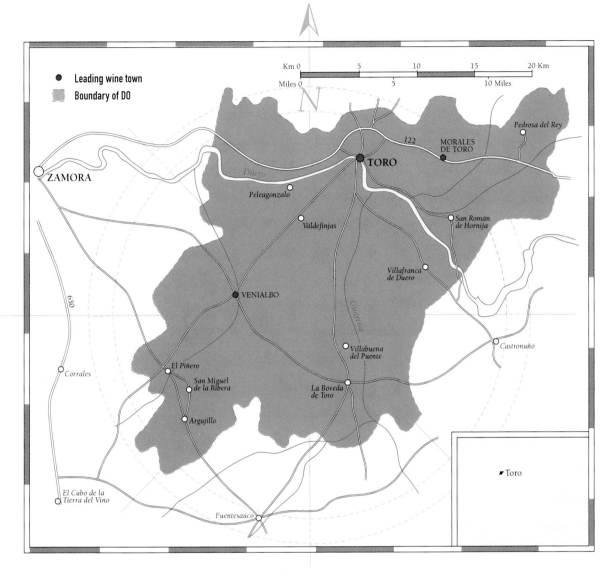

This part of the country could rightly be called the 'breadbasket' of Castile: north of the river are the rolling wheat fields of the Tierra del Pan (*see* above), and south of the river lie the vineyards of the *Tierra del Vino*, the 'Wine Country'. Most of the latter falls within the Toro DO, but some of it, confusingly enough, is part of the Vino de la Tierra de la Tierra del Vino de Zamora (*see* page 68).

## Toro in history

The region of Old Castile was generally populated in the Middle Ages with clerics, courtiers, kings, bishops and princes, all of whom were interested in good wine and (more importantly) had the money to pay for it. As a result of Old Castile's prosperity, the wines of Toro found yet another market when Spain's first university was established in the town. This was founded in Palencia by Alfonso VIII around 1200, but was transferred in 1215 to Salamanca, where it remains to this day. The main evidence of Toro's days as a centre of learning may be found in the beautiful old Romanesque Colegiata, or collegiate church, which lies at the heart of the town. Its west front, known as the Pórtico de la Gloria, is considered to be one of the finest examples of Spanish Romanesque sculpture.

If the clerics and courtiers of Castile had been ideal customers, then the professors and postgraduates of the university were no less enthusiastic in their appreciation of Toro's vinous bounty. In the dark days between the departure of the Moors and the arrival of the Holy Inquisition, who knows what scurrilous and subversive theses may have been written under the influences of the heavy, heady wines of Toro? Characterised by their

Verdejo. On the whole, however, this is essentially red-wine country. When vineyards are replanted, the *consejo regulador* recommends Tinto de Toro.

The northeastern part of the Toro DO falls within the province of Valladolid and is known as Morales; the rest lies within the province of Zamora. The main soil-type is alluvial, since vineyards tend to be planted on the plain of the River Guareña, which flows into the Duero. Some limestone appears in the Morales sub-zone, but clay forms the basis of most vineyards, a factor that assures the vine roots of a good water supply even in the hottest part of the summer.

The region's altitude gives the vineyards full daytime sunshine with cooler nights, which results in nutrients being retained for the grapes, rather than being consumed overnight by the vines. Maximum yield is around 42 hectolitres per hectare, although, as elsewhere in Spain, the actual production is barely half the legal maximum.

## Winemaking and wine styles

Which brings us to the character of the red wine of Toro. Usually made from 100 per cent Tinto de Toro (75 per cent is the legal minimum), it can achieve up to 15 per cent alcohol by volume (abv) by natural fermentation and, uniquely in Spain, it must achieve a minimum abv of 12.5 per cent. This strength and the powerful flavour engendered by it are what made the wine famous all those centuries ago. It was transportable, would keep its flavour and was slow to oxidise, making it highly prized in the days of the mule-train and the leaky wineskin.

Modern Toro wine is no less powerful, although 13.5 to 14 per cent abv is usually the strength nowadays. Its blockbusting, bold, bright Tempranillo fruit drinks well in the year after the vintage, but it can also age disgracefully into a mindblowing *reserva* or even *gran reserva* with more power, fruit and length than is normally accorded to a wine of such venerability.

There are also some non-DO Cabernet Sauvignon/ Tinto de Toro blends which neatly match the fruit and alcoholic characteristics of both grapes, and one or two bodegas produce a deliciously ripe, full-throttle varietal Garnacha – which just goes to show what this grape can do at 13 to 14 per cent abv. These grand, uncompromising, magnificent, Wagnerian wines are not, perhaps, for the faint-hearted, but they are as rich, complex and powerful as they have always been, and remain among the boldest wines in Spain.

**Above: Storks nest on the beautiful Romanesque tower of the Colegiata de Santa Maria, the collegiate church that stands in the heart of Toro.**

**Far right: The vineyards of Toro are rigorously cleared of weeds, and vines are spaced far apart in order to maximise water resources.**

powerful alcoholic strength and bright, upfront fruit, these are perhaps the most authentic examples of the wines of Old Castile that are still being made today.

## Grape varieties

The most widely planted grape variety planted throughout the entire Toro DO zone is the Tinto de Toro (once again, the name is a synonym of Tempranillo), which was initially replanted after the departure of the Moors. Separate development and propagation over the intervening centuries has resulted in a grape which ripens two weeks earlier than its cousins in Rioja. This fact, coupled with the height of the region's vineyards at between 600 and 750 metres (1,969 to 2,461 feet), results in riper, thicker-skinned fruit, which in turn yields wines that have considerably more extract in terms of flavour, colour and strength.

Garnacha and Cabernet Sauvignon are also grown in the region, although the latter is not permitted as an ingredient in any of the DO wines. A small amount of white Toro wine is also made from Malvasía and

# Notable bodegas

**Fariña, Toro.** *Founded 1940.*
This company was originally set up
by Salvador Fariña. His son (and the
present director) Manuel Fariña has
done much to bring worldwide fame
to the Toro region, as well as serving as
the first president of the *consejo
regulador*. The estate's old bodega
is still situated at Casaseca in the Tierra
del Vino, and was originally called
Bodegas del Porto. Here, the company
continues to make *vinos
de la tierra* which reflect the very best
characteristics of Spanish country
wines (*see page 22*). However, Fariña
now has a smart, new stainless steel-
equipped bodega (built in 1990) in Toro
itself, located next door to the Vino de
Toro Cooperativa (*see below*). His wines
are beautifully made, packed with fruit
and are probably

the best Toro has to offer. They are sold
under the labels Colegiata (*joven*) and
Gran Colegiata (*crianza* and *reserva*),
all made from 100% Tinto de Toro.
The *reserva* spends 14 months in oak.
Fariña also makes what are probably
Toro's best white wines: Colegiata
Blanca (100% Malvasía) and the
unusual non-DO Fariña *semidulce*
(medium-sweet) from 50% Moscatel
and 50% Albillo. *Best wines:* the non-
DO red Fariña, made from 50% Tinto
de Toro and 50% Cabernet Sauvignon,
but Gran Colegiata from a good year
is almost unbeatable.

## Frutos Villar, Toro.
This Frutos Villar is an offshoot of the
Cigales bodega of the same name
(*see page 53*), making excellent red
wines under the Muruve (*joven, crianza*)
and Gran Muruve (*reserva*) label from
100% Tinto de Toro.

**Nuestra Señora de las Viñas,
Morales.** *Founded 1964.*
A traditional cooperative that just goes
to show that you really can teach an
old dog new tricks. It has 128 members
farming some 800ha of vines, and
still ferments in epoxy/concrete tanks,
but the results are astonishing.
*Best wines:* a 100% Tinto de
Toro (mainly *joven* but with a little
*crianza* in better years) and a 100%
Garnacha *joven*. These are splendid
wines at everyday prices, sold under
the Moralinos label in export markets
and as Viña Bajoz at home.

**Vega Saúco, Morales.**
*Founded 1991.*
Vega Saúco is a modern bodega
that produces red wines from 100%
Tinto de Toro. Saúco is the *joven* label,
while Vega Saúco is used for *crianza*
and *reserva* wines, the last spending

anything up to 18 months in oak.
*Best wines:* in good years, the older
wines can be quite spectacular.

**Vino de Toro, Toro.** *Founded 1974.*
Another co-op, this time with 250
members farming around 1,000ha
of vines. As recently as 1989, it was
producing nothing much above
everyday quality wines. However,
the success of Toro wines in export
markets encouraged Vino de Toro
to experiment and advance; today,
its top wine (under the Cermeño label)
is excellent. The red is made from
100% Tinto de Toro, while the *rosado*
(second only to Colegiata in quality)
contains 75% Tinto de Toro, 15%
Garnacha and 10% Malvasía.

# Country Wines of Castile-León

## VdlT Cebreros (Avila)

The town of Cebreros is about 70km (43 miles) west of Madrid and 40km (25 miles) south of Ávila. The wine land which takes its name is a westward extension of the Vinos de Madrid DO, although Garnacha rather than Tempranillo is the chief grape. You are likely to encounter these wines in the bars and cafés of Avila, often in screw-top bottles with no pretensions beyond being pleasant, everyday house wines.

Cebreros was awarded a provisional *Denominación Específica* (DE) in January, 1986. This was the old 'halfway house' method of encouraging country wine areas to strive for promotion, but it seems to have had little effect. The local market for wine is as buoyant as ever, and there has been little inducement for bodegas to make the major investments needed to break into the wider world.

This is a pity, as the wines (particularly reds made from Garnacha) are of a good basic quality and could achieve more if they reduced their alcoholic strength (currently up to 15% abv) and retained more acidity. However, until the *bodegueros* of the region decide to make the effort, Cebreros seems likely to remain an area with great potential, but no more than that.

About 9,000ha of vineyards are planted with Garnacha, Albillo and Viura, and the two white grapes are used in the production of *rosado* wines. No white wine is allowed under the Cebreros *vino de la tierra* regulations, although white wines are made as *vino de mesa*.

The climate is hot continental, but rainfall is quite high for these parts and the vineyards tend to be fertile and productive – which probably explains why there has been so little incentive to upgrade. Red wines must achieve a minimum 13% abv, but old-fashioned fermentation techniques mean that most are nudging the 15% mark, a strength that usually burns out any balance or complexity.

There is, however, a small amount of movement. Bodegas of note include the large, family-owned Benito Blazquez

(founded 1939), which turns out some 25,000hl each year of red (*joven* and *crianza*) and *rosado* in bulk, tetrapaks and bottles, as well as an unusual *dulce* made from Moscatel. Brand names are Don Claudio and Perla de Or.

There is also a cooperative (founded 1956) with 820 members farming a staggering 8,000ha of vines. Eighty per cent of production is sold in bulk, with the remainder going out under the El Galayo and Monteperlado brand names.

## VdlT Fermoselle-Arribes del Duero (Salamanca/Zamora)

This area has already indicated that it would like to be considered for promotion at some time in the future. It currently covers about 5,000ha of vines on the Salamanca/Zamora border around the town of Fermoselle, which is some 60km (37 miles) from both Salamanca and Zamora, beside the part of the River Duero that forms the border between Spain and Portugal.

Production is relatively high (up to 80,000hl per year). The main hope for this area is the Juan García grape, which can perform well under the right circumstances and could be developed into something worthwhile, given the right kind of investment. A whole range of other grapes is grown, including Garnacha and Tinto de Toro, but a good deal more work seems to be needed before promotion is a serious consideration.

There is one major bodega, the Virgen de la Banda co-op, whose best wines are the red Viña Borbón and Viña Caracosta (both 100% Juan García).

## VdlT de la Tierra del Vino de Zamora (Zamora)

This is an ancient wine land, the original *Tierra del Vino*, or 'Wine Country'. One of the region's leading winemakers, Manuel Fariña, has maintained his family bodega at Casaseca de las Chanas in a belief that the area deserves better than humble *vino de la tierra* status; he is working hard to re-

establish it as an important wine area. The principal grape is Tinto del País (alias Tinto de Toro), and there are some 1,500ha planted between the towns of Toro and Zamora, producing around 20,000hl annually – mainly red and *rosado* wines. Garnacha and Cabernet Sauvignon are also grown, as well as the white grapes Malvasía, Moscatel and Palomino. A small amount of white wine (and even the occasional dessert wine) is made from Moscatel.

The only bodega of note is that of Manuel Fariña, as mentioned above. His red Country Wine of Zamora sells widely abroad and is excellent value for money.

## VdlT Valdevimbre-Los Oteros (León/Valladolid)

Another promising area situated in the southern part of the province of León, with a well-developed industry already established and ambitions to go further.

There are neighbouring unclassified wine areas (plus the VC Benavente; *see* below) which might usefully be grouped together and reorganised into a potential future DO zone. Names are already being suggested, and the most popular seems to be Vinos del Páramo de León, but so far there has been no official reclassification.

Currently, the zone has around 3,900ha of vines, planted mainly with the local Prieto Picudo ('Dark Pointed') along the River Esla about 25km (16 miles) south of the city of León. There are also Garnacha, Tinto del País and Mencía vines for red wines, and Malvasía, Viura and Palomino for whites.

Traditionally, this area has made *aguja* (slightly fizzy, like Portuguese *vinho verde*) wines from Prieto Picudo, and this is still a major style in the region. Most quality production is red, and the main private winery, Bodegas de León-Vile, turns out an excellent Don Suero from 80% Prieto Picudo and 20% Tinto del País, with 15 months in oak. Other brands from this winery include

Palacio de los Guzmanes (good reds from 100% Garnacha; a decent white from 100% Viura) and very pleasant everyday wine under the name Catedral de León and Palacio de León. There is also a co-op which produces mainly *artesanal* wines.

## VC Benavente (Zamora)

This area is situated next door to Valdevimbre-Los Oteros (above), and if promotion does come along, it seems likely that parts of it will be included in any new classification. The VC covers around 5,000ha of vines, but most of it is planted in very small plots scattered throughout 63 municipalities, often in mixed cultivation with other crops; opportunities for consolidation are few.

As usual, however, there are one or two bodegas trying to achieve something of quality here. The main grapes are the same as for Valdevimbre (*see* above), but there is some serious work being done with Tempranillo (known locally as Cencibel or Tinto Fino). If enough producers can be persuaded to upgrade, we may see a new, combined *vino de la tierra* zone brushing itself up for promotion in years to come.

The only bodega of note is Bodegas Otero, which makes agreeable reds, whites and *rosados* under the brand names Viña Alegre and El Cubeto. The latter is a mix of Prieto Picudo, Mencía and Tinto Fino, with some time in oak, and shows considerable promise.

## VC Ribera del Arlanza (Burgos)

This VC is located about 40km (25 miles) south of Burgos in the valley of the River Arlanza. There are 1,500ha of vines planted in 22 villages between the town of Lerma and the border with Palencia – once again, the vines are located in small and scattered plots.

This is the 'rump' of what was once a 10,000ha plantation that supplied base-wines to Rioja and Ribera del Duero – now illegal, of course. However, it has ambitions to be promoted to *vino de la tierra* level and, since much of the area under vine is growing Tinto del País, there seems to be an opportunity for improvement.

### VC Sierra de Salamanca (Salamanca)

This highland region (over 800 metres/ 2,625 feet) is located in the Sierra de Peña de Francia mountains, about halfway between Avila and the Portuguese border.

Around 2,000ha of vineyards are spread throughout 13 villages, but most of them are terraced into the mountainside, which makes picking difficult. Although the granite bedrock and cool climate seem to offer the prospect of good wines, the local grape, Rufete, is not a high performer.

Rufete occupies about three-quarters of the vineyard, but it is subject to rapid oxidation; unless some inspired winemaking skills can coax something more out of it (as happened, for example, with Verdejo in Rueda), it seems unlikely to progress further. Garnacha, Macabeo (Viura) and Tempranillo are also grown here. Since the altitude and soils would seem to favour good winemaking, perhaps there is a future for this area.

### VC Valtiendas (Segovia)

Valtiendas could almost be considered a southerly extension of the vineyards of Ribera del Duero, situated as it is in the northern part of the province of Segovia. Unlike Ribera del Duero, however, the Tinto del País variety is outnumbered by Garnacha Tintorera in this region – a fact that does not suggest anything too exciting about the prospective quality of the wines produced here.

Some 22 villages are entitled to use the VC name, including Cuéllar and Valtiendas itself, and production is limited mainly to reds and *rosados*.

**Below: Bodegas come in all shapes and sizes. This one in León still uses ox-drawn carts to transport its grapes.**

# North-Central Spain

Two mountain ranges, the Cordillera Cantábrica and the Pyrenees, protect the wine zones of North-Central Spain, providing favourable conditions for red wine grapes. The best known of these DO zones is undoubtedly Rioja. Its vineyards are found in the southern part of the País Vasco, in La Rioja itself, and in southwestern Navarra, an important DO in its own right whose fame has spread rapidly in recent years in the international marketplace. The Rioja Alta and Rioja Alavesa areas, as well as Estella in the highlands of Navarra, consistently yield the best grapes.

To the east along the River Ebro lies the *autonomía* of Aragón. Its southwestern half consists of the Campo de Borja, Calatayud, and Cariñena DOs; the last is the only one of the three to have made a name for itself in export markets. In contrast with these hotter, drier zones, the Somontano DO, some 130 kilometres (81 miles) to the northeast, is a cooler, wetter region of great natural beauty. Over the past ten years it has become one of Spain's most exciting and innovative wine areas.

**Below:** Vineyards in the Rioja Alavesa region, which has more alkaline soils, yield wines full of fruit that are ideal for drinking young.

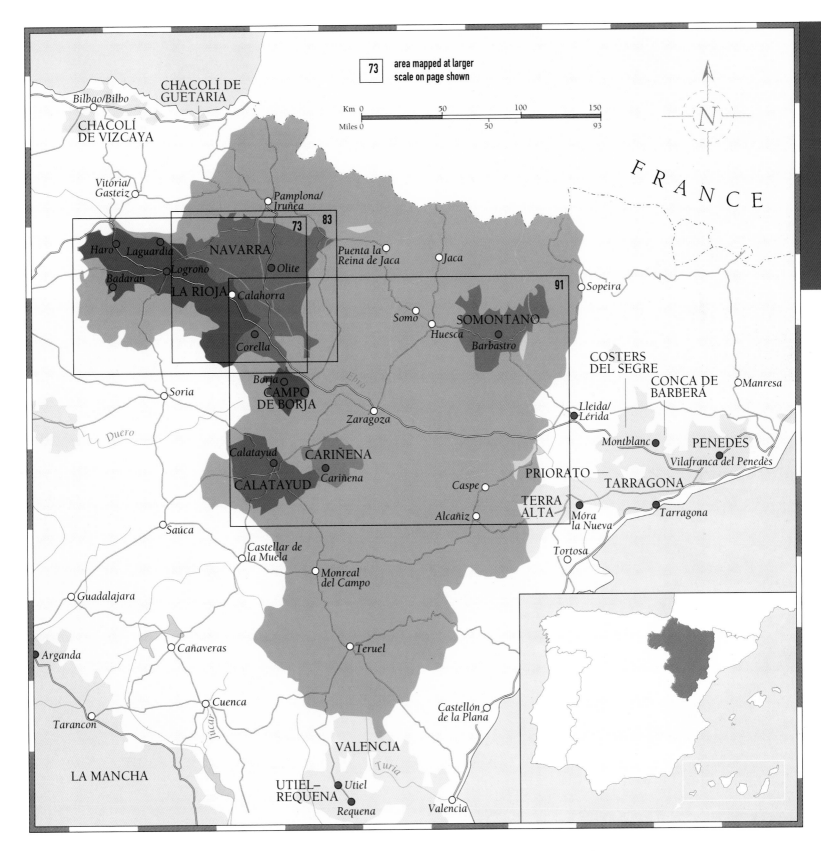

CHACOLÍ DE
GUETARIA

Bilbao/Bilbo

CHACOLÍ
DE VIZCAYA

Vitória/
Gasteiz

Pamplona/
Iruñea

73    83

Haro   Laguardia

NAVARRA

Puenta la
Reina de Jaca

Jaca

Logroño   Olite

Badaran

LA RIOJA   Calahorra

Sopeira

91

Somo

SOMONTANO

Corella

Huesca

Barbastro

Borja

COSTERS
DEL SEGRE

Soria

CAMPO
DE BORJA

Zaragoza

CONCA DE
BARBERÁ

Manresa

Lleida/
Lérida

Duero

PENEDÈS

Montblanc

Calatayud   CARIÑENA

Vilafranca del Penedès

Saúca

CALATAYUD   Cariñena

PRIORATO   TARRAGONA

Caspe

TERRA
ALTA

Alcañiz   Móra
la Nueva

Tarragona

Castellar de
la Muela

Tortosa

Guadalajara

Monreal
del Campo

Arganda

Cañaveras

Teruel

Cuenca

Castellón
de la Plana

Tarancón

VALENCIA

LA MANCHA

UTIEL–
REQUENA   Utiel

Turia

Requena

Valencia

FRANCE

N

# La Rioja: ancient land of wine

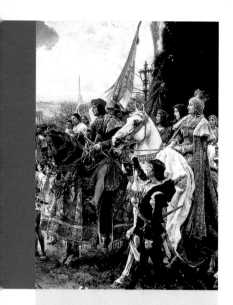

## Los Reyes Católicos

*Even if they did not manage to patch up an ancient quarrel with England, Ferdinand of Aragón and Isabella of Castile certainly set their stamp on Spanish history. Enshrined as* Los Reyes Católicos, *'The Catholic Monarchs', they presided over a golden age of achievement which included the discovery of the New World and the expulsion of the Moors. They also re-established the Roman Catholic faith in post-Moorish Spain, made Castilian the standard of the Spanish language and oversaw the expansion of Spanish colonialism in the Americas. And what of their influence upon wine? The tide of wealth that came flooding in from the Americas meant that more people could afford better-quality wine. Rioja, having established itself as the best light wine of Spain, became the stuff of celebratory banqueting in every noble house as well as in the cottages of those who worked the land. It also became one of the chief items of export to the New World.*

The name of Spain's most famous red wine comes, naturally enough, from the region of La Rioja. The first part of the regional name comes from *río,* Spanish for river. The River Oja – from which the name's second half derives – rises in the Sierra de la Demanda south of Haro and flows north through Santo Domingo de la Calzada before joining the River Tirón just west of the town. This confluence then passes round the back of Bodegas La Rioja Alta to join the River Ebro immediately northeast of Haro.

Even this close to the Ebro, the 'river' is still little more than a stream, so it has always been a puzzle as to why La Rioja should take its name from the Oja rather than the Tirón or the mighty Ebro itself, since the latter dominates microclimates right down to the Mediterranean sea, south of Tarragona. Be that as it may, *La Tierra del Río Oja* ('The Land of the River Oja') was the name given to the surrounding countryside. And really: would the wine taste the same if it came from an area called *Tironia* or *Ebralta*?

## An ancient tradition

Staying on the subject of vinous linguistics: the first words committed to paper in the Spanish language were written by a 13th-century monk named Gonzalo de Berceo. Convinced that the clerical brotherhood needed to get closer to the people it was supposed to represent, Gonzalo wrote a short poem in the vernacular (instead of the usual Latin) which included a reference to the virtues of the local wine.

Such an accolade was not a surprising – by this time Rioja wine was already 1,000 years old. The invading Romans in the first century found the local tribespeople (whom they dubbed *Celtiberi* – the Celts of Iberia) treading grapes in stone troughs and running the fermenting juice off into cisterns and amphorae. The need to supply wine for the occupying forces meant that it was in Rome's interest to develop this industry along its expanding network of roads. The legions duly showed the local inhabitants how to maximise the potential of their grapes and make better wine. This was policy throughout the Roman Empire – which is why much of Italy, France and Germany owes its early winemaking technology to Rome.

By the time Moorish invaders reached as far north as Rioja, wine was an important part of the local economy. Even strict Moslem rules on alcohol could not stamp it out entirely; as the forces of Christian Spain fought back from Asturias, the vineyards of the Upper Ebro flourished almost without interruption.

After all, this was a favourable part of Spain for wine: to the west lay the newly united kingdom of Asturias and León; to the east, the kingdoms of Navarre, Aragón and Catalonia. While disagreements among the kingdoms occurred now and again, the eventual formation of the County of Castile resulted in the creation of a unified force against the Moors which eventually expelled them from Spain.

## Wine as an economic force

Rioja was part of the County of Castile, and counted among its residents and neighbours not only the counts of Castile but also the kings of Navarra and Catalonia, Aragón and León, complete with their courts, clerics, academics and military leaders – in short, a host of rich, powerful people willing and able to pay for good wine.

This early boost towards quality winemaking propelled Rioja into the export business by the 16th century. Rioja wine was going into France, Italy and as far north as Flanders at the same time as Shakespearian England was demonstrating an unquenchable thirst for 'sheris sack'. Spanish wine was big business indeed, and Rioja was in the forefront of its development.

Surprisingly, though, winemaking techniques had hardly changed since Roman times. Grapes were still trodden in stone troughs; transport was largely via animal skins. Not until the 19th century did the region experience a new wave of technology. Wines made today by *cosecheros* ('vintagers': individual small farmers) are produced in much the same way as their original predecessors, and sold – unlabelled and uncapsuled – in the region's wine merchants' shops.

The story of the Marqués de Riscal has already been discussed (*see* page 60). His example did not simply transform the way Rioja made its wines; it proved to be a lesson for the rest of Spain. Well-made casks, fermentation in vats, ageing in oak... all stemmed from those early experiments, and Riscal was not alone in his espousal of Bordeaux techniques. Plantations of Cabernet Sauvignon and other Bordeaux grape varieties dating back to this era survive at Vega Sicilia in the Duero as well as in northern Italy, eastern Europe and Russia. Young men returning from the 'Grand Tour' often came back with bold ideas about having their own wine estates. Not all survived, but those that did have done so with commendable success.

Thus, the revolution in Spanish winemaking can be dated from 1858, when Don Camilo Hurtado de Amézaga planted his first vines in Elciego. Spanish wine in general – and Rioja in paricular – would never be the same again.

La Rioja: ancient land of wine **73**

# Rioja

If Rioja wine advanced two steps forward in the late 19th century, during the early 20th it took one step back many times. Phylloxera hit the region's vineyards around the turn of the century. The sheer time involved in replanting vineyards and waiting for them to mature lost Rioja some of its export market just at the time France was fighting back with newly revitalised vineyards.

Once Spanish vineyards did get back into their stride, the First World War began, effectively closing down the European market; not until the 1920s did things return to relative normality. During this time, Rioja experienced strong growth again and, in 1926, the region established the first *consejo regulador*, therby effectively becoming the first Spanish wine to obtain *denominación de origen* status.

Rioja had wine regulations before the DO; rules and regulations concerning the treatment of grapes, musts and wine were in place by 1560. In 1635, the mayor of Logroño banned traffic from using streets next to bodegas in order to prevent vibrations from damaging the wines. By 1787, most leading growers had formed a body called the *Real Sociedad Económica de Cosecheros de la Rioja Castellana* (the Royal Economic Society of Castilian Rioja Producers), and in 1902, a national law guaranteeing the name of Rioja wine, its origin and labelling was established.

Despite these legal precedents, however, the *consejo regulador* was something new. More than a mere trade-protection society, it had powers to decide what land could be planted, what wines could bear the name 'Rioja' and what actions should be taken against bodegas which broke the rules. These are still the fundamental functions of the modern *consejo regulador*, and Rioja's experiences laid the foundations for all other *consejos* in Spain.

## Wine and war

After the *consejo*'s foundation in 1926, Rioja progressed strongly, making some of its finest-ever wines. It rebuilt export contacts and made headway into European and American markets, although it was still strongest in its Spanish homeland and in Latin America.

In 1936, however, the Spanish Civil War put a stop to most of this expansion, and once again, the wine business as a whole went into decline. The outbreak of the Second World War in 1939 compounded the problem. Even though Spain was not directly involved in the conflict, it was impoverished and demoralised by its own recent hostilities. The few wineries that had the will, money and know-how to market wine abroad found the rest of the world engaged in the business of organised manslaughter. Once it was all over, the serious business of rebuilding Europe and the gargantuan task of feeding its people took priority over other considerations until the 1950s.

The Rioja wine industry used the years of 1945 to 1950 to good effect. In a law passed in 1945, Spain's few existing *consejos reguladores* received full legal status, with Rioja claiming its full accreditation on April 28, 1947. This gave the region full authority over planting, grafting, pruning, harvesting, winemaking and maturation, and it created a budget for promoting wines abroad as well as the authority to police its members and their operations. Once again, Rioja was in a position to go back into the export market with renewed faith.

**Below: Vineyards surround the village of Navaridas in Rioja Alavesa. Soils in this area have striations of chalk and iron, which are of great benefit to the vines.**

It was still a slow progression. During the 1950s, outside the Old World of Europe, wine was still considered an upper-crust pastime. Even here, the market was limited; claret, burgundy, hock, Mosel, Port and Sherry were the choices of the day. Experimentation was not high on the agenda.

As the 1950s gave way to the 1960s, however, a new generation suddenly discovered wine. The bulk market in Spain responded with a wine-lake of spuriously named 'Spanish Burgundy' and 'Spanish Chablis' – a move which did little to promote the country to new consumers who had never heard of Rioja. It must have been a temptation for many Rioja producers to re-label their wines as 'Spanish Claret', but fortunately most stuck to their guns.

The determination paid off. By the end of the 1960s, people were talking about an obscure wine from northern Spain. Restaurateurs found it to be an excellent house red: strong, full of fruit, easy to drink and (most important of all) mature. While French wines still demanded cellaring and careful handling, Rioja was ready to drink as soon as it left the bodega – and it was available at prices the younger generation could afford. As the EEC expanded in the early '70s, labels such as 'Spanish Burgundy' became illegal and

Rioja became Spain's best-known wine. It had taken more than half a century to regain its position, but the sheer integrity of the wine was starting to be appreciated.

And greater things were afoot. If the Marqués de Riscal was the main innovator of the 19th century, then his equivalent in the 20th must be Enríque Forner. The Forner family owns Châteaux Camensac and La Rose Trintaudon in Bordeaux. Like his counterpart a century earlier, Forner had experienced new Bordeaux technology and thought it might benefit winemaking in La Rioja. This time, the innovations took the form of stainless-steel vats, temperature-controlled fermentation and minimal oak ageing.

Stainless steel had been pioneered in the 1950s, especially in Australia and the South of France; the Torres family first used it in Spain in the 1960s, in the Penedès DO. Enríque Forner thought it could be used to make a style of Rioja for the burgeoning export market, where the preference was for lighter, fresher wines with more fruit and less oak. He called in Professor Emile Peynaud of the University of Bordeaux and, in 1970, planned and established a brand-new bodega called Union Vitivinícola in the small town of Cenicero.

Km 0    10    20    30    40 Km
Miles 0         10         20 Miles

- Leading wine town
- Boundary of DO

## The French influence

One of the major factors that contributed to the success of Rioja wine was the export market to France. During the second half of the 19th century, French vines were assaulted first by a plague of mildew, then by the phylloxera disaster, which virtually wiped out the country's vineyards. While French vignerons grafted onto American rootstocks and replanted their vineyards, there was an unabated demand for wine throughout France while its new vines matured.

By pure chance, Rioja's winemaking had been transformed a few years before by pioneers of the Bordeaux winemaking method; thus, the region was turning out wines very similar to their French predecessors – and at good prices. A healthy and vigorous export market developed, and the classic 'burnished-oak' style of old Rioja wine evolved as a consequence of what France wanted to buy. Indeed, mature Rioja still brings tears to the eyes of old men in southern France who remember the way claret used to taste before scientists got their hands on it.

The export market continued strongly until around the turn of the century, when French vineyards were back in production. By then, however, Rioja was fast becoming a well-known name in markets further afield. This international success promoted interest in the neighbouring wine areas of Navarra and Aragón. Rioja has therefore become a world leader in its own right, while Navarra and Aragón have become two of the the most innovative and exciting wine regions in Europe.

**Above:** The village of Samaniego, Rioja Alavesa. Here and in Rioja Alta, Tempranillo is the main grape variety.

Forner's mission was simple: to make fresh, white wines without oak and red wines with the legal minimum oak-age and maximum bottle-age to showcase the fruit and freshness of Tempranillo. He built a splendid winery in Cencicero, and bought grapes exclusively from local independent growers to make a true 'village wine'. Named after a family friend – the Marqués de Cáceres – it is now one of the best-known wines not just of Rioja, but of Spain as a whole.

In the 1990s, Rioja has gone steadily from strength to strength. Traditional bodegas still ferment in oak vats, rack wines by hand, age them for years in oak *barricas*, fine them with egg-whites and release them at full maturity. Modern bodegas turn out crisp, fresh whites and light, fruity *joven* reds for delicious, instant drinking. There is even a new wave of wines, rather fancifully dubbed 'post-modern' Rioja, in which ancient skills such as barrel-fermentation, a touch of oak for red *jovenes* and more bottle-age for older wines offer new styles for the next generation of Rioja *aficionados*.

## The DOCa

Italy created the DOCG (*Denominazione de Origine Controllata e Garantita*): a higher classification for wines with more rigorous standards of grape-selection, a consistent reputation for the highest quality and a stricter approach to quality-control. France already had a higher classification – the AOC (*Appellation d'Origine Contrôlée*). When Spain was offered the opportunity to put forward a candidate for elevation, the new grade was called *Denominación de Origen Calificada*, or DOCa. The term means 'Qualified Denomination of Origin' – 'qualified', in this instance, meaning 'having proved itself in terms of performance'.

The new category was recognised by the Spanish government in 1988, but not awarded to the wines of Rioja until April 9, 1991. The new regime called for more stringent quality and laboratory controls, discarding a higher percentage of grapes before pressing, buying in grapes at higher price levels, and original bottling of wines.

Much of what constitutes the DOCa is still under debate, and the powers that be are still waiting for a second candidate which will, with any luck, give it final definition. Since gaining the DOCa, Rioja has unquestionably shifted upwards in quality terms. There is very little bad wine under the Rioja label these days, and the best has never been better – especially since the stunning vintages of 1994 and 1995.

Rioja wine is not made solely in the *autonomia* of La Rioja; it is also produced on the north side of the River Ebro. In the northwest, this means the province of Álava (Áraba) in the Basque Country, and in the east it means Navarra, but the wine is controlled by the *consejo regulador* in Logroño, the commericial capital, regardless of its origins. A Rioja house can buy grapes or wine from anywhere in the region, so a bodega based in Rioja Alta may not necessarily make its wines entirely with Rioja Alta grapes. Companies outside the region may also own a brand of Rioja wine made under contract under their own label at an existing Rioja bodega.

In winemaking terms, the Rioja region is divided into three parts: Rioja Alavesa (northwest; north of the river, province of Álava as far east as Oyón); Rioja Alta (northwest; south of the river, province of La Rioja as far east as Logroño); and Rioja Baja (southeast; east of Logroño, in La Rioja south of the river, in Navarra north of the river). Each has its own style. In Álava, for example, Tempranillo ripens with a thinner skin, yielding early-drinking wines of great fruit. However, pure Tempranillo wines tend not to be long-lived, so a little help is required the further south one goes.

In Rioja Alta, the temperature is marginally hotter, resulting in thicker-skinned Tempranillo as well as Mazuelo and Graciano. The last two are small, tough-skinned grapes used in minor percentages to add particular characteristics to wine. Graciano has made a bit of a comeback since the award of the DOCa; it adds freshness and aroma, ageing with consummate grace, and is especially useful in blends aimed for *reserva* and *gran reserva* ageing. Mazuelo originates in Aragón, where it is known as Cariñena and is used to add tannins and colour to the wine.

Finally, Rioja Baja focuses on Garnacha. This grape does well after long, hot ripening periods, and flourishes in central and eastern Spain. Grapes from young vines produce fruity, aromatic, early-maturing wines, while those from older vines yield wines that age magnificently.

A few bodegas, particularly in the Basque Country, make 100 per cent Tempranillo wines, give them little or no oak, and sell them soon after the vintage. The great houses on either side of the river often split their efforts between light, fresh, fruity *jovenes* made mainly with Tempranillo, and judicious blends of riper grapes with a view to longer maturation. A typical blend for a *crianza* wine consists of 70 per cent Tempranillo, 20 per cent Garnacha and five per cent each of Graciano and Mazuelo (although this varies according to the quality of the vintage). Some Cabernet Sauvignon, classed as an 'experimental' variety, is also used.

For white Rioja, Viura, Malvasía Riojana and Garnacha Blanca form the main varieties. Viura is most widely used; given the right yeast it can perform spectacularly well, and is much in demand for barrel-fermentation due to its good acidity and herby/fruity characteristics. For longer-lived wines – *crianza* and the increasingly rare *reserva* and *gran reserva* styles – some Malvasía (five to ten per cent) is often used to add a hint of richness and perfume. Garnacha Blanca is useful in years when acidity levels are high and Viura comes in slightly under-ripe; it helps redress the balance with its softer, riper, low-acid juice. In the old days, some white grapes were added to red wines to give them 'fire and brilliance', although this is now a rare practice.

Soils in the north of the Rioja region are clay-based and often alluvial, although Rioja Alta and Rioja Alavesa have outcrops of iron- and chalk-rich subsoil stretching away from either side of the river. The chalky regions – known as calcareous clay – produce the finest grapes, but the iron-rich soils (ferruginous clay) yield grapes with the kind of metallic trace elements that make the difference between good and great wine. A mix of all three varieties of grapes from both areas, and a dash of Garnacha from the hot, sandy vineyards of Rioja Baja is the signature of every bodega's 'house style'.

## Viticultural methods

Vines are trained in two ways: traditional estates use the *en vaso* (gobelet) free-standing style; more modern plantations use wires. Machine harvesting is not widely practised, but it does seem to be increasing, and wire-trained vines are necessary for it. The real benefit of wire-training, however, lies in containing vine diseases and keeping grapes away from encroaching leaves, branches or soil.

Winemaking varies from the traditional to the ultra-modern. Out in the villages, the *cosecheros* still make *artesanal* wines by the old stone-trough method. Traditional bodegas may still use giant wooden vats which, the *viñeros* insist, allow for fermentation in a natural environment. Most, however, have switched to epoxy-lined vats with temperature-controlling *placas* (a device rather like a domestic radiator, lowered into the vat and circulated with ice-cold water) or water-cooled fibreglass tanks.

Modern bodegas use anything from stainless-steel tanks with enclosed water-jackets to the very latest 'alien' technology. In the latter, red grapes are separated into small, flying-saucer-like tanks called *autoevacuaciones,* which have an opening in both top and bottom. The juice ferments

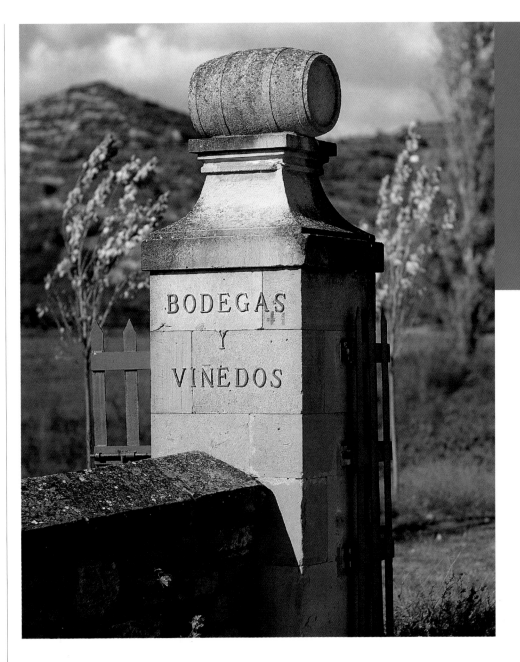

without pressing and is run off; then the 'saucer' is hoisted by mobile crane and the pulp is emptied into the press. In this way, free-run juice is never pumped or roughly handled.

Rioja wines range from new-wave, barrel-fermented whites with spicy, oaky hints to venerable red *gran reservas* with dark, raisiny fruit, depth and amazing complexity. In general, Basques (Rioja Alavesa) like their red wines light, fruity and mainly Tempranillo; Riojanos prefer the firm maturity of the traditional grape-mix; and Navarros opt for warm, ripe, rich Garnacha. All, however, are classic Rioja.

**Above:** The entrance to the Remelluri estate in Rioja Alta. In good years, wines made here are among the best in the entire subzone.

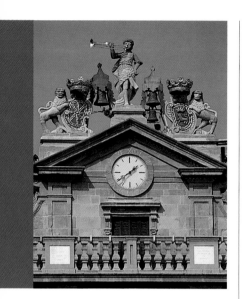

**Above:** The Hotel de Ville in Pamplona, Navarra. Wines made in the southern part of the region can bear the Rioja DOCa.

**Far Right:** Grape-picking boxes are left outside to drain at the López de Heredia estate. Tradition rules here, and the wines are not for the faint-hearted.

# Notable bodegas

There are 250 bodegas in the Rioja region. Those listed below produce higher-quality wines than the good, basic standard to which every Rioja house aspires. Alt = Rioja Alta; Alv = Rioja Alavesa; BjR = Rioja Baja (La Rioja); BjN = Rioja Baja (Navarra); Log = Logroño (La Rioja); Con = contract.

**AGE, Fuenmayor (Alt).**
*Founded 1967.* A merger of three firms, AGE produces around 15,000hl from its own and bought-in grapes. The most famous wine is Siglo Saco (*crianza/gran reserva*) in typical sacking wrap. *Best wine:* the excellent Marqués del Romeral *gran reserva.*

**Alavesas, Laguardia (Alv).**
*Founded 1972.* Alavesas makes very good, typically Basque wines under the Solar de Samaniego label. *Best wines:* the younger wines tend to be better.

**Alejos, Agoncillo (Alt).**
*Founded 1988.* Makes 10,000hl from 20ha of vines and bought-in grapes under the Alabanza label. *Best wine:* the crianza.

**Almenar, Madrid (Con).** Part of the giant Bodegas y Bebidas Group (*see* Campo Viejo, Marqués del Puerto *et al*) making *jovenes* and *crianza* wines; the latter tend to be better.

**Amézola de la Mora, Torremontalvo (Alt).** *Founded 1986.* This is an excellent smaller (2,000hl) bodega with 100ha of vines. Quality is paramount. Only red wines are made under the labels Viña Amézola (*crianza*) and Señorio Amézola (*reserva*); both are outstanding.

**Araco, Laguardia (Alv).**
*Founded 1986.* With 200ha of vineyards, Araco makes good wines in all three colours, mainly *joven,* under the Señorio de Araco label.

**Barón de Ley, Mendavia (BjN).**
One of a handful of Rioja estates to use only its own grapes (90ha Tempranillo; some Cabernet Sauvignon) for its wines. Regarded as the leading bodega of Rioja Baja. After a couple of patchy vintages in the mid-'80s, it bounced back in 1989 and has since been on top form. Most wines are 100% Tempranillo.

**Berberana, Cenicero (Alt).**
*Founded 1877.* One of the most consistent quality bodegas in Rioja Alta, with 130ha of vineyards. Also part of the consortium that makes the Riojas of the Marqués de Griñón. All three colours are made, with reds up to *gran reserva* level. *Best wines:* the *crianzas* and *reservas.*

**Berceo, Haro (Alt).** *Founded 1872.* Berceo has a magnificent electric carousel that drives press-baskets on little railway trucks. Excellent, traditional wines include the Gonzalo de Berceo *gran reserva.*

**Beronia, Ollauri (Alt).** *Founded 1973.* Part of the González Byass group, a modern bodega with traditional aspirations. Good red *crianzas* and *reservas* and an excellent white *joven,* all under the Beronia label.

**Bilbainas, Haro (Alt).** *Founded 1901.* Excellent traditional reds to *gran reserva* level; also rare sweeter wines Viña Pacete and Brillante *dulce.* Makes Rioja brandy and Cava. *Best wines:* the classic Viña Pomal and Viña Zaco *gran reservas.*

**Bretón, Logroño (Log).** Large, quality-oriented bodega with more than 100ha of vines, including 40 in a single estate called Loriñón and 22 in another called Dominio de Conte. *Best wines:* include the Loriñón *crianza* and barrel-fermented whites (both 100% Viura). Reds to *gran reserva* level are excellent to exceptional.

**Campillo, Laguardia (Alv).**
*Founded 1990.* Campillo has 35ha of vineyards planted entirely in Tempranillo.

Also buys in grapes, including Cabernet Sauvignon. *Best wines:* all are excellent, especially red *crianzas* and *reservas;* most are 100% Tempranillo. Very good 100% Viura barrel-fermented white, and an exceptional *reserva especial* (60% Tempranillo/40% Cabernet Sauvignon).

**Campo Burgo, Alfaro (BjR).**
*Founded 1898.* Medium-sized (4,000hl) firm with 35ha of vines; also buys in grapes. *Best wines:* good red *crianza* and a *rosado* (100% Garnacha).

**Campo Viejo, Logroño (Log).**
*Founded 1963.* Riojano flagship of the Bodegas y Bebidas empire, Campo Viejo owns over 500ha of vines. One of the most reliable names for good, very good and sometimes excellent wines. Brand names include Albor (white and red *joven*), Campo Viejo (white joven; red up to *gran reserva*) and the Selección José Bezares. *Best wines:* the excellent Viña Alcorta (barrel-fermented white; 100% Tempranillo red *crianza*) and the Marqués de Villamagna *gran reserva.*

**Carlos Serres, Haro (Alt).**
*Founded 1896.* This bodega makes a good range of wines in the traditional style. Older ones (including *gran reserva*) tend to be better. *Best wine:* the Onomástica *reserva.*

**Casado Morales, Labarca (Alv).**
*Founded 1983.* This small bodega works 25ha of vines and makes good reds and *rosados* from the traditional grape mix.

**Contino, Laguardia (Alv).**
*Founded 1974.* Makes wine solely from the 45ha of vineyards which surround a 17th-century manor in which the winery is situated. Ownership is shared with CVNE (*see* below); the bodega is run by José Madrazo. Makes 2,000hl per year of *reservas* – truly excellent wines, typically 85% Tempranillo.

**Corral, Navarrete (Alt).**
*Founded 1898.* Family-owned firm with 40ha of vines; buys in grapes to produce 7,000hl. Good, classic Rioja under the Don Jacobo label: a fresh white *joven* (100% Viura) and very good *crianza/reserva* wines (80-85% Tempranillo).

**Cosecheros Alaveses, Laguardia (Alv).** *Founded 1985.* Co-op re-formed as a private concern in 1992. Production is around 4,000hl. Main brand name is Viña Artadi: white (100% Viura) is very good; *rosado* (100% Garnacha) and red *jovenes* (85% Tempranillo) are excellent. *Crianza/reserva* styles (branded Artadi-Pagos Viejos and Viñas de Gain) can be very good. *Best wine:* the red *joven*.

**El Coto, Oyon (Alv).** *Founded 1970.* Modern bodega making mainly Tempranillo wines; around half the grapes come from its own 150ha. The basic wine is very good and sells under the El Coto label. *Reservas* and older wines are called Coto de Imaz.

**CVNE, Haro (Alt).** *Founded 1879.* CVNE stands for *Compañía Vinícola del Norte de España.* Pronounced 'COOnee', it is entirely owned by the founding Real de Asúa family, and represents much of what is best in modern Rioja. In 1989, the firm invested heavily in a new winery, which includes a carousel carrying *autoevacuaciones.* Grapes or wines are transferred by gravity; the winemaker makes his selection from anything up to 80 batch samples. There are two wine ranges: Viña Real and Imperial. All types of Rioja are made, in both Rioja Alavesa and Rioja Alta styles; all are excellent – among the finest wines of Spain.

**David Moreno, Badaran (Alt).**
*Founded 1981.* Modern bodega making about 7,000hl almost exclusively from bought-in grapes. Good, value-for-money *jovenes* (all colours) and red *crianzas,* with the occasional spectacular vintage.

**Domecq, Villamediana (Alt).**
*Founded 1973.* Modern bodega controlled by the eponymous Sherry company. Owns 350ha of vineyards, and produces around 50,000hl. *Best wine:* excellent Marqués de Arienzo (95-100% Tempranillo; rest usually Graciano and Mazuelo), from *crianza* to *gran reserva* level.

**Escudero, Gravalos (BjR).**
*Founded 1852.* Good to very good reds, including Becquer Primicia (100% Garnacha) and Solar de Becquer *crianza* Tempranillo/Garnacha/Mazuelo).

**Estraunza, Labarca (Alv).** *Founded 1988.* Buys in ready-made wines, ageing in house. *Best wines:* good Solar de Estraunza *crianza* and *reserva.*

**Faustino Martínez, Oyon (Alv).**
*Founded 1860.* Maker of the famous Faustino range with its frosted bottles and fine-art labels. Main range is Faustino V: very good white and *rosado* wines and an excellent red *reserva* (85% Tempranillo/ rest Graciano and Mazuelo). Also excellent Faustino Martínez *blanco crianza* (100% Viura; six months in oak). *Best wine:* Faustino I *gran reserva.*

**Federico Paternina, Haro (Alt).**
*Founded 1898.* One of the biggest bodegas in Rioja: annual output is around 75,000hl. Success is based on a formula of quality-control over the basic Banda Dorada, Banda Azul and Banda Oro (white, *rosado* and red *joven/ crianza*), and the older Viña Vial *reserva* and Federico Paternina *reserva* and *gran reserva. Best wine:* the red Conde de los Andes *gran reserva* (95-100% Tempranillo plus Mazuelo).

**Florentino de Lecanda, Haro (Alt).**
*Founded 1965.* Known for fine *reservas,* made from 90-100% Tempranillo.

**Franco-Españolas, Logroño (Log).**
*Founded 1890.* Franco-Españolas has 100ha of vines, buying in to make around 30,000hl. Good whites include Viña

Soledad *joven/crianza* (100% Viura) plus a great-years-only Viña Soldedad Tête de Cuvée *gran reserva* (60% Viura/ 30% Malvasía/10% Garnacha). Main reds: Rioja Bordón *crianza/gran reserva. Best wine:* great-years-only Excelso.

**Grandes Vinos, Madrid (Con).**
This firm has a contract white wine made for it in the Rueda DO. Meridiano is a top-class, 100% Tempranillo *crianza.*

**Granja Nuestra Señora de Remelluri, Labastida (Alv).** *Founded 1967.* Single-estate bodega tucked into the base of the mountainous rock face of the Sierra de Toloño. Uses both giant oak vats and modern stainless steel. Annual production is around 2,500hl of *reserva* wines, typically with two years in oak, under the Remelluri label. In ordinary years, these wines are excellent. In good ones, they are among the very best of Rioja Alavesa.

**Herencia Lasanta, Laguardia (Alv).**
*Founded 1935.* Very good reds (*joven* to *reserva*) from the standard grape mix.

**Jesús y Félix Puelles, Abalos (BjR).**
Small family bodega (1,000+ hl) with 20ha of mainly Tempranillo vines. Torrescudo is the brand name. *Best wines: crianzas* and *reservas.*

**Lagunilla, Fuenmayor (Alt).** *Founded 1885.* Owned by the Croft Sherry company. Under the Lagunilla label it makes good *crianza/gran reserva* wines, mainly from Tempranillo, as well as Viña Herminia *reserva* from the classic mix.

**LAN, Fuenmayor (Alt).** *Founded 1973.* Named for the initial letters of the three provinces in which Rioja is made (Logroño/La Rioja, Álava and Navarra). LAN makes around 15,000hl of red and white wines. *Best wines:* red *crianza* and *reserva* under the LAN label.

**López de Heredia, Haro (Alt).** *Founded 1877.* Grape selection and winemaking are done by hand; wines are fined with

egg-whites and aged with a disregard for popular fashion. Wines – white, *rosado* and red – spend far longer in oak than is fashionable and have been known to prosper for over half a century. López de Heredia *rosado crianza* is arguably the classic pink wine of Rioja. The white Viña Gravonia is fresh yet sublimely mature. *Best wines:* reds are the firm's flagship: Viña Bosconia is a classic Rioja (*crianza/ gran reserva*); Viña Cubillo is a lighter style. Viña Tondonia is oldest of all: great *gran reservas* from the 1960s still drink well.

**Luís Angel Casado Manzanos, Labarca (Alv).** *Founded 1990.* Small family firm with 15ha of vines, making about 500hl in all three colours; reds up to *reserva* level. The brand name is Jilaba. *Best wines:* the younger reds.

**Luís Cañas, Villabuena (Alt).**
*Founded 1928.* Became a full-time business in 1970, with 24ha of vines. Good white, *rosado* and red wines up to *gran reserva* level under the Luís Cañas label. *Best wines:* the younger reds.

**Luís Casado Fuertes, Labarca (Alv).**
*Founded 1969.* Makes about 3,000hl under the Jaún de Alzate label. Good-quality wines are aged from *crianza* to *gran reserva* level. *Best wines:* the oldest from great years.

**Above: The newest of the new. CVNE's carousel system uses** *autoevacuaciones* **as part of its ultra-modern vinification equipment.**

**Luís Gurpegui Muga, San Adrián (BjN).** *Founded 1872.* Owns Berceo in Haro and is also active in the Navarra DO. Rioja made in San Adrián includes good wines of all three colours under the Viñadrián label. *Best wines:* the white (100% Viura); also very good *rosado* (60% Garnacha) and good red (60% Tempranillo/40% Garnacha), all *joven*.

**Marqués de Cáceres, Cenicero (Alt).** *Founded 1970.* As Unión Vitivinícola, this bodega changed the face of modern Rioja. All grapes come from local growers; winemaking is state-of-the-art. Makes crisp, fresh, fruity and minimally oaked wines in all three colours from traditional grape mixes. In recent years, the firm has made new, even 'post-modern' wines such as the delicious Antea white *crianza* (90% Viura/10% Malvasía) and a splendid *gran reserva*.

**Marqués de Griñón, Ollauri (Alt).** Carlos Falcó, the Marqués de Griñón, has a simple approach: if the family name goes on the bottle, then what is inside must be worthy of that name. In a joint-venture with Lagunilla and Berberana, the best Tempranillo grapes are now vinified separately under the Griñón label. Only reds are made (*joven* to *reserva especial*) in a modern, full-fruit style. Of their type, they are exemplary.

**Marqués de Murrieta, Logroño (Alt).** *Founded 1872.* Second bodega of the modern Rioja era (along with Riscal) and the other great pioneer of Bordeaux-style winemaking. Since 1983, run by the Cebrian family, Condes (Counts) of Creixell, who increased the vineyards to make the bodega self-sufficient. Today, the winery has everything from old oak vats to modern stainless steel. Wines are among the most traditional of Rioja. The white Dorado de Murrieta *reserva* (91% Viura/6% Malvasía/3% Garnacha Blanca) spends 40 months in oak; the red *reserva* (75% Tempranillo) may have even more. *Best wines:* Castillo de Ygay, red and white; vintages from the mid-1980s are now available.

**Marqués del Puerto, Fuenmayor (Alt).** *Founded 1988.* Smart, modern bodega on the N-232 between Haro and Logroño, it makes a very good barrel-fermented white (100% Viura) and reds to *gran reserva* level (85% Tempranillo).

**Marqués de Riscal, Elciego (Alv).** *Founded 1860.* The pioneer of modern Rioja. Latest equipment includes a hand-sorting station, where individual bunches of grapes are inspected along a moving belt before going to the presses. Elsewhere, winemaking is refreshingly old-fashioned. Traditional reds are heavy (90%+) on Tempranillo, although the bodega's original plantation of Cabernet Sauvignon allows it to beef up *reservas* and *gran reservas* in wetter years. *Best wine:* the stunning Barón de Chirel (35% Graciano/25% Tempranillo/40% 'other varieties'; 28 months in oak).

**Martínez Bujanda, Oyon (Alv).** *Founded 1889.* A new (built 1988–96), state-of-the-art bodega with 300ha of vineyards, this is one of the most successful firms in Rioja Alavesa. The main range is Conde de Valdemar and includes an excellent barrel-fermented white (100% Viura; seven months on its lees) as well as red wines up to *gran reserva*. Most traditional are the Conde de Valdemar Centenario (if you can find it) and the Martínez Bujanda Vendimia Especial. *Best wines:* the *crianzas* and *the* 100% Garnacha *reserva*.

**Martínez Lacuesta, Haro (Alt).** *Founded 1895.* Family firm making about 8,000hl in all three colours. Campeador is the main brand. *Best wines:* the Martínez Lacuesta label (*crianza* to *gran reserva*).

**Montecillo, Fuenmayor (Alt).** *Founded 1988.* Owned by the Osborne Sherry group, producing over 20,000hl per year in all three colours under brand names Montecillo, Viña Monty and Viña Cumbrero. All wines are good to very good. *Best wines:* Viña Monty and Viña Cumbrero (*crianza* to *gran reserva*).

**Muerza, San Adrián (BjN).** *Founded 1882.* Owned by Príncipe de Viana (Navarra DO). *Best wines:* the younger reds (usually 85%+ Tempranillo), sold under the Rioja Vega label.

**Muga, Haro (Alt).** *Founded 1932.* An old dog performing elegant new tricks, with its stunning barrel-fermented white (90% Viura/10% Malvasía). Produces around 4,000hl. Despite its whites, it is known for traditional oak-aged styles (*crianza/ gran reserva*) generally strong on Tempranillo. *Best wine:* Prado Enea.

**Olarra, Logroño (Log).** *Founded 1973.* Big, modern bodega producing 50,000 litres in all three colours. Main brand name is Añares (white, *rosado* and red up to *reserva*). *Best wines:* red *reservas/gran reservas* under the Cerro Añón label.

**Palacio, Laguardia (Alv).** *Founded 1894.* Established by Cosme Palacio, former winemaker at Vega Sicilia (*see page 54*). Palacio belongs to the Seagram Group; it farms a small vineyard but buys in most of its grapes. Today the red and white (*crianza*, according to the year) are among its finest efforts. *Best wines:* Gloriosa *reservas* and *gran reservas* (mostly 100% Tempranillo), but all wines here are excellent.

**La Plana, Andosilla (BjN).** *Founded 1980.* Owns 70ha of vineyards and buys in grapes from Rioja Alta. *Best wines:* tend to be reds (crianza-plus) under the Dominio de la Plana label.

**Primicia, Laguardia (Alv).** *Founded 1985.* Small bodega with 25ha of vines. Best known for good to very good reds strong on Tempranillo (90-100%). *Best wine:* the Viña Diezmo *reserva*.

**Ramón Bilbao, Haro (Alt).** *Founded 1924.* Family firm which makes good red *crianzas* and *reservas* (85%+ Tempranillo) under the Ramón Bilbao label. *Best wine:* the very good 100% Tempranillo *gran reserva* called Viña Turzaballa.

**Real Divisa, Abalos (Alt).**
*Founded 1969.* Small (1,800hl) bodega with 40ha of vineyards. Brand name is Marqués de Legarda (*crianza/gran reserva*). Makes consistently good wines.

**La Rioja Alta, Haro (Alt).**
*Founded 1890.* Family-owned firm maintaining the best Rioja winemaking traditions while keeping abreast of modern advances. Owns 300ha of vineyards. The best wines are still racked by hand and fined with egg-whites, commanding the highest prices for their classic character. Viña Alberdi is the basic *crianza*: good/very good wines from 75%+ Tempranillo. Viña Arana is a *reserva* with excellent fruit and longevity. Viña Ardanza is a *reserva* from a different vineyard selection with a spicy, velvety richness that can age for years. *Best wines:* the Reserva 890 and Reserva 904.

**Riojanas, Cenicero (Alt).**
*Founded 1890.* Still owned by its founding families and still fermenting some of its grapes in ancient oak vats. Some 200ha of vines support around half its production of 18,000hl. Very good-to-excellent wines, especially the Monte Real *gran reservas*.

**San Roque Cooperativa, Alcanadre (BjR).** *Founded 1957.* The best co-op in Rioja, with access to 600ha of vines. Makes around 2,000hl each year. The brand name is Aradón; the white and red *jovenes* are uniformly good, and occasionally rising to excellent.

**Sierra Cantabria, San Vicente de la Sonsierra (Alt).** *Founded 1957.* Makes 7,500hl of wine sold mainly under the Sierra Cantabria label. The white *joven* (90% Viura/10% Malvasía) and *rosado* (80% Tempranillo/ 20% Viura) are good examples of well-made, modern Rioja. Reds go to *gran reserva* level. *Best wines:* the Sierra Cantabria red *crianza*, and the Murmurón red *joven*.

**SMS, Villanueva (Alv).** *Founded 1880.* SMS still ferments partly in oak vats. Grapes come from 60ha of vines plus local growers to yield an annual 2,000hl. Brand name is Valserrano. *Best wines:* the white *joven* (Viura) and red *gran reserva* (mainly Tempranillo).

**Torre de Oña, Laguardia (Alv).**
*Founded 1988.* Small bodega making about 1,500hl of one wine: the excellent red Barón de Oña *reserva* (90% + Tempranillo/the rest Mazuelo).

**Torres Librada, Alfaro (BjR).**
*Founded 1987.* Family firm with 20ha of vines. Only reds are made, mostly from Tempranillo. The label is Torrescudo and the wines are mainly *crianza* and *reserva* of good-to-excellent quality.

**Ugarte, Páganos-Laguardia (Alv).**
Large, modern, family-owned bodega with 100ha of vines, turning out good-to-excellent red wines under the brand names Dominio de Ugarte (*crianza-reserva*) and Cédula Real (*gran reserva*).

**Viña Ijalba, Logroño (Log).** *Founded 1975.* Modern firm with 100ha of vines and a distinctive bottle and label. Wines are among the best new-generation Riojas: a delicate white called Genolí; a very good *rosado* called Aloque. *Best wines:* Ijalba-label reds, especially the *reserva* and varietal Graciano.

**Viña Salceda, Elciego (Alv).** *Founded 1973.* Makes only red wines (*crianza* to *gran reserva*). Viña Salceda is the *crianza/ reserva* label for good-to-very good wines. *Best wine:* the Conde de Salceda *gran reserva*. All tend to be 95% Tempranillo.

**Viña Valoria, Logroño (Log).** *Founded 1989.* Produces around 3,000hl of very good white *crianza* (100% Viura); reds (up to *gran reserva* level) tend to be 70% Tempranillo plus Mazuelo and Graciano.

**Viña Villabuena, Villabuena (Alv).**
*Founded 1987.* This firm makes excellent red wines under the Viña Izadi label, typically from 90% + Tempranillo. The annnual production is around 6,000hl. *Best wines:* the *crianzas* and *reservas*.

**Viñedos Solabal, Abalos (Alt).**
*Founded 1989.* Makes about 3,500hl of wine from 75ha of vines under the Solabal and Muñarrate labels. Wines are mainly Tempranillo and of good, sound quality.

**Above: The shrine at which fans of the most traditional Rioja come to worship: the López de Heredia estate in Haro.**

# Navarra: Spanish by charter

Navarra is unique in the Spanish constitution, being a *comunidad foral*, or chartered community. The charter (or *fuero*) in question was signed by King Ferdinand in 1512, when he guaranteed certain rights and freedoms for the people of Navarra in return for their fealty.

Prior to that time, Navarra – or Navarre as it was once known – had been a medieval kingdom in its own right. In the days of King Sancho the Elder (1005-1035), it expanded to cover a territory stretching from León in the west to Barcelona in the east. Despite its strength, however, this early attempt to unify Spain collapsed with Sancho's death, when a power-struggle ensued between his heirs. The lands of the former kingdom were claimed by both Aragón and Castile until 1234, when they were inherited by the family of Thibaut I, Comte de Champagne, and thence passed to various French dynasties which ruled with widely differing effectiveness.

## A divided empire

The Albret family were the last French family to rule in Pamplona, and they retreated before the Gran Duque de Alba, who claimed all the land south of the Pyrenees for King Ferdinand of Aragón. What had been part of Navarre north of the Pyrenees became part of France (Basse-Navarre in French; capital St-Jean-Pied-de-Port). Accordingly, the kings of France styled themselves *Roi de France et Navarre* up to the reign of Louis XVI, who renounced the title in 1791 and called himself *Roi des*

Below: The beautiful Señorio de Sarria estate in Puenta la Reina, Navarra. Of a total of 1,500ha, around 120 are devoted to vines.

*Français*. South of the Pyrenees, meanwhile, Navarre had become a less turbulent place, now part of a newly united country pushing the Moors back towards Granada.

The original inhabitants of Navarra were the Vascones, who also settled what is now the Basque Country. Navarro culture shows strong Basque influences. The region is now almost more Castilian than Castile in many respects, but the Basque spirit of independence, Basque place-names (alongside their Castilian equivalents) and Basque cookery still show the region's ancient origins.

Today's Navarra is a prosperous, beautiful and bustling region, probably best known abroad for the famous bullfighting festival of San Fermín, immortalised by Ernest Hemingway, which takes place from July 6 to 14 every year. Each morning, the bulls that are to fight in the evening run through the streets of Pamplona, and various would-be *toreros* run in front them – ostensibly to show their courage and skill, but more usually to impress their girlfriends. Other towns in the region have their own versions of these festivities.

## Navarro gastronomy

*Navarra generally (and Pamplona in particular) is as cosmopolitan as the rest of northern Spain. To understand what Navarro cuisine is all about, however, it is necessary to look to the countryside. The wide variety of microclimates provides luxuriant vegetables, and the highland pastures breed a tasty lamb. The Basque influence can be seen in the local bacalao (dried, salt cod). As well as lamb, other Navarro specialities include beans, asparagus, sheep's-milk cheeses (Idiazabal and Roncal), chorizos and artichokes and an obscure local vegetable called* borraja *which grows nowhere else. One of the most popular dishes is cordero al chilindrón: lamb-chops in a spicy tomato sauce with stuffed pepper. It would normally be consumed with one of the region's splendid rosados, for which it is justly famous. Even so, the wines of modern Navarra have progressed well beyond the 'Pamplona pink' which made its name.*

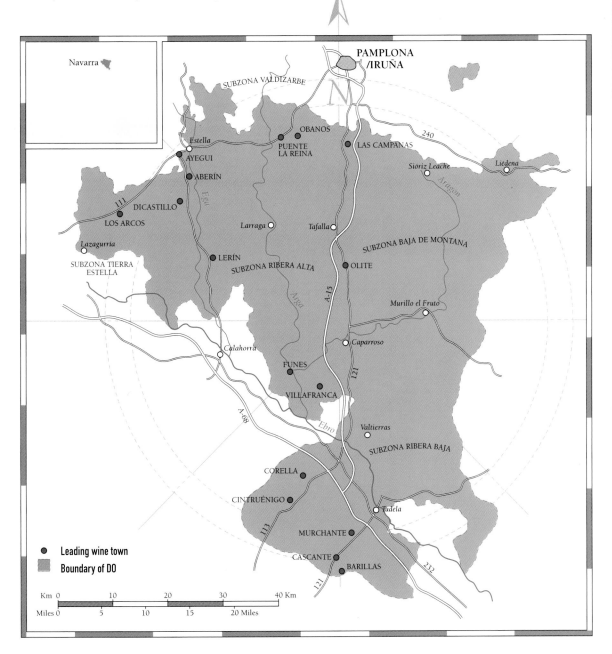

Navarra map showing:
PAMPLONA /IRUÑA
SUBZONA VALDIZARBE
OBANOS
Estella
PUENTE LA REINA
LAS CAMPANAS
AYEGUI
Sioriz Leache
Liédena
ABERÍN
DICASTILLO
LOS ARCOS
Larraga
Tafalla
SUBZONA BAJA DE MONTAÑA
Lazagurria
LERÍN
OLITE
SUBZONA TIERRA ESTELLA
SUBZONA RIBERA ALTA
Murillo el Fruto
Calahorra
Caparroso
FUNES
VILLAFRANCA
Valtierras
SUBZONA RIBERA BAJA
CORELLA
CINTRUÉNIGO
Tudela
MURCHANTE
CASCANTE
BARILLAS

● Leading wine town
▨ Boundary of DO

Km 0   10   20   30   40 Km
Miles 0   5   10   15   20 Miles

**Above: The modern laboratory at EVENA in Olite. The oenological research station has been crucial in the development of the Navarra DO.**

Although Navarra's wine history is as long as that of any other area of Spain, its modern wines represent some of the most exciting and innovative work being conducted anywhere the country. This is due largely to the pioneering work of the *Estación de Viticultura y Enología de Navarra*, the Viticultural and Oenological Research Station of Navarra, better known as EVENA. This foundation, funded by the regional government, is based in an old distillery building on the Pamplona road running north out of Olite.

EVENA's research extends throughout the winemaking process, starting with bedrock and subsoils, and working its way right through to bottling and quality-control. Although every DO region in Spain has a research station to advise on and recommend best practices in vineyard and bodega, EVENA is unique in the scope of its experimentation.

For a start, it has plantations of all major vines scattered throughout Navarra, on most popular rootstocks in every type of soil. Every year, it makes wine from these plantations and uses all the latest techniques to evaluate the results, which are then passed on to the winemakers. This explains how Navarra can still produce the

magnificent Tempranillo-rich *gran reservas* and delicious, fruity *rosados* which made its name, while at the same time turning out elegant, stylish Chardonnay, barrel-fermented Viura and classic, blackcurranty Cabernet Sauvignon.

EVENA's work forms the latest chapter in a long history of winemaking in Navarra – indeed, in the whole of Spain. The oldest surviving commercial-scale winemaking artefact in the country is a Roman wine cistern dating from the second century AD. It is situated in the small town of Funes, where the Arga and Aragón rivers meet (a few kilometres east of San Adrián), and it bears a strong resemblance to the stone *lagares* that are still in use in some rural parts of Spain. It seems likely that this well-watered and fertile region became a major winemaking centre under the Romans and remained so under succeeding civilisations, including the Swabians, Visigoths, Vandals and Moors.

## An early 'tourist trade'

During the 11th century, one of the pilgrimage routes of the Camino de Santiago passed through Roncesvalles and Pamplona, then via the towns of Puente la Reina, Estella and Los Arcos before entering La Rioja to the west. Monks, other clerics and lay-pilgrims journeyed this way, and they all needed food, wine and shelter. The wine of Navarra gained a reputation (along with Rioja) for being among the best available on the Camino. A healthy 'tourist trade' had developed by the 12th century, as travellers returning from Santiago purchased wine to take home with them. By the 15th century, an export trade to France as far north as Normandy had already been established. What few written records survive mention that the area was known for its excellent *rosado* wines.

The wine trade in Navarra boomed even more after the discovery of America. At that time, any wine region of Spain with export experience was called upon to provision ships bound for the New World. Laden with food and drink for the colonists, they returned with gold, silver, tobacco and other exotic commodities. By this time, of course, Navarra was part of a united Spain, but until the foundation of Madrid in 1561, the courts, cathedrals and colleges of Royal Spain continued to focus on the Castile/Navarra/Aragón/Catalonia axis – a ready market for good-quality wines.

When the twin plagues of oïdium (a type of mildew) and phylloxera hit France in the 19th century, Navarra's old French connections played a big part in its easy acceptance as a supplier of wine across the Pyrenees. Along with Rioja and, to a lesser extent, Aragón, Navarra kept France provided with wine until such time as its vineyards could be replanted. Perhaps, given that Rioja had always been famous for its red wines, Navarra's *rosados* showed that this particular region could provide something different.

## The legacy of phylloxera

Phylloxera eventually struck Navarra as it did almost every other wine-growing region in Europe. From a total 49,000 hectares of vineyards in 1891, the area under vine shrank to a little over 700 by 1896 – a reduction of nearly 99 per cent. Replanting took place as quickly as possible, but that vast area was never regained; even today, the Navarra vineyard totals some 30,000 hectares, only around 15,000 of which are actually in full production.

Geographically, Navarra is divided into five subzones. In the north, Tierra Estella (northwest) and Valdizarbe (far north) have altitudes of around 560 metres (1,837 feet). Baja Montaña and Ribera Alta (north of the Ebro) in the centre, and Ribera Baja in the south (south of the Ebro) have altitudes of around 250 metres (820 feet). Throughout most of the region, however, soils are remarkably similar, consisting of loam over gravel with a limestone/chalk bedrock that is excellent for vines. There is more alluvial soil in Ribera Alta, while Ribera Baja has lighter, sandier soils.

The climate becomes increasingly dry towards the south. Parts of the highlands of Valdizarbe and Tierra Estella have microclimates that benefit from the cooler, wetter weather on the north side of the mountains. As in Rioja, however, most major houses source their grapes from various points around the region to achieve their 'signature' house styles. This may involve Tempranillo from the cooler vineyards of Valdizarbe, Mazuelo from the hotter central zone and some rich, ripe Garnacha from Ribera Baja to fill out the blend. This combination of good soils and highland-to-lowland microclimates gives growers the opportunity to plant a wide variety of grapes, and allows winemakers to choose from an equally wide variety of sources.

Garnacha is the most widely planted grape in Navarra, with 54 per cent of the current area under vine, as might be expected in a region particularly proud of its *rosados*. At 23 per cent, however, Tempranillo is rising, and there is a gentle pressure on growers to replant with it when old vineyards are grubbed up – especially as Navarra's red-wine production currently represents about 60 per cent of its total output. Other recommended red grapes are Graciano, Mazuelo, Merlot and Cabernet Sauvignon. The main white grape is Viura (eight per cent of the vineyard), with Garnacha Blanca, Malvasia, Moscatel de Gran Menudo and Chardonnay also recommended.

Red wine is now Navarra's mainstream production, although its classic *rosados* are still strong (about a third of total production) and remain best-sellers in Navarra, Spain and France. However, new-wave winemaking is thrusting Navarra further onto the world stage, due partly to the efforts of EVENA and an enlightened *consejo regulador*, and partly to Navarra's abundant natural advantages.

Hence the growth of top-quality Navarra wine: Chardonnays, Cabernets, Tempranillo/Cabernet blends; the delicately sweet Moscatels and the delicious, fruity *rosados* of yore. Somehow, Navarra also manages to turn out exemplary wines at the lower end of the price-scale: straightforward, cool-fermented whites made from Viura and reds from Garnacha and a little Tempranillo represent excellent value for money. It is perhaps Navarra's unique combination of high-quality highland vineyards in the north and high-yielding, hot, sandy soils in the south that allows its bodegas to excel at both ends of the scale.

Below: The church of Santa María de Eunate, near Puente la Reina, was once a stopping point for pilgrims on the Camino de Santiago.

# Notable bodegas

Bodegas may buy in grapes from any of Navarra's subzones to make their final house blend; a bodega based in one subzone may not necessarily produce wine from grapes grown entirely within that subzone – hence the many excellent bodegas located in the relatively modest subzone of Ribera Baja. Vald = Valdizarbe; TEst = Tierra Estella; BMon = Baja Montaña; RibA = Ribera Alta; RibB = Ribera Baja.

### Beamonte, Cascante (RibB).
*Founded 1938.* Fully refurbished in 1986, and now a subsidiary of Bodegas Julián Chivite with the attention to quality thus implied. Makes a very good *rosado* (Garnacha) and reds from *joven* to *reserva* level under the Beamonte label.

### Camilo Castilla, Corella (RibB).
*Founded 1856.* This firm makes red and *rosado jovenes* of good quality. Brand names include Montecristo and Conde de Castilla. Annual production is 8,000hl. *Best wines:* Camilo Castilla is best known for its unusual sweet (non-DO) whites made from Moscatel de Gran Menudo.

### Castillo de Monjardín, Villamayor de Monjardín (TEst). *Founded 1993.*
Family firm in a smart, modern bodega equipped with the very latest equipment. Owns 120ha of vines to support an annual production of around 4,000hl. The wines are uniformly very good and often excellent. Reds include a Cabernet Sauvignon/Tempranillo/ Merlot *crianza* and a Pinot Noir/ Tempranillo *joven*. *Best wine:* the Chardonnay (which comes both *crianza* and barrel-fermented).

### Fernández de Arcaya, Los Arcos (TEst). *Founded 1990.* This small
(1,000hl) family bodega farms 36ha of vines and makes only reds and a *rosado*. Wines are generally good. *Best wines:* the red *reservas* Fernández de Arcaya and Viña Perguita (65% Tempranillo/35% Cabernet Sauvignon).

### Guelbenzu, Cascante (RibB).
*Founded 1851.* Situated in a lovely old house opposite the bullring. Though well-established, Guelbenzu's present fame goes back to the early 1980s, when the eight children of the family (doctors, lawyers, an archaeologist and an artist) replanted the vineyards (currently 36ha) with Cabernet Sauvignon, Tempranillo and Merlot. For ten years, the grapes were sold to the local co-op in Cascante while the vines fully matured. Then, in 1989, winemaker Joseba Altuna turned out the first new vintage under the Guelbenzu label. The wines are exemplary, an example of what a boutique winery can do, given financial backing. Current production is 1,600hl of red wine under two labels: Guelbenzu for *crianza*, and Guelbenzu Evo for *reserva/gran reserva*. The *crianza* is typically 70% Tempranillo/ 15% Cabernet Sauvignon/ 15% Merlot; the *reserva* is 70% Cabernet Sauvignon/15% Tempranillo/ 15% Merlot. The *gran reserva* is 50% Cabernet Sauvignon/40% Tempranillo/ 10% Merlot.

### Inversiones Arnótegui, Dicastillo (TEst). *Founded 1991.* Another
modern installation with 300ha of vineyards and an eye for French grapes. Production averages 16,000hl under the Palacio de la Vega label. Wines are uniformly excellent and include a white *joven* (100% Chardonnay), *rosado joven* (50% Cabernet Sauvignon/50% Garnacha, a red *crianza* (70% Cabernet Sauvignon/30% Tempranillo) a 100% Merlot *crianza*, and two red varietal *reservas*, one Tempranillo, one Cabernet Sauvignon. The oak-aged wines have a minimum of one year in wood except for the Cabernet Sauvignon varietal, which has perhaps 14 months.

### Irache, Ayegui (TEst). *Founded 1891.*
Traditional bodega with its own little wine museum and wine-fountain for

passing pilgrims on the Camino de Santiago. The Camino runs along a footpath beside the winery, and in 1990 the ebullient chief executive, Jesús Santésteban, inserted an iron gate into the wall with a drinking-fountain dispensing both wine and water. Pilgrims (and other passers-by) are welcome to help themselves to either without charge – although if they wish to fill their gourds against future thirst, they are asked to pay a modest fee. Irache went through considerable expansion and modernisation in 1991 and now farms 50ha of vines as well as buying in grapes and ready-made wines from neighbouring producers. Wines are traditional, although more attention is being paid to younger styles. New equipment has helped create slightly more modern Navarra wines. Makes a very good *rosado* (90% Garnacha/10% Tempranillo) under the Castillo Irache label.
*Best wines:* (all reds) are the Gran Irache *crianza* (70% Tempranillo/30% Garnacha) and the excellent Real Irache *gran reserva* (70% Tempranillo/10% each Graciano, Mazuelo, Garnacha). *Reservas* and *gran reservas* keep very well and age gracefully.

### Julián Chivite, Cintruénigo (RibB).
*Founded 1647.* The company as it is today dates from 1860, although the winery itself was completely refurbished in 1990. Don Julián the elder died in 1996, after having taken Chivite to extensive export markets and large-scale international success (in the early 1980s, 70% of all Navarra wine exported was Chivite). Today, the firm is run by his four children: sons Julián, Carlos and Fernando and daughter Mercedes. The wines represent some of the best Navarra has to offer. Chivite owns 250ha of vines, including the single-estate Señorío de Arinzano at Aberín. Its basic range is called Gran Feudo: white and *rosado jovenes* (the Garnacha *rosado* is excellent) and red *crianza* (70% Tempranillo/30% Garnacha). The firm celebrated its

125th anniversary in 1985 and launched a Tempranillo *gran reserva* called '125 Aniversario'. This style has been continued, and now forms a suite of wines including a white barrel-fermented Chivite Colección 125 (Chardonnay) and Chivite 125 Aniversario *gran reservas* of succeeding vintages (Tempranillo). There's also Chivite *reserva* (85% Tempranillo/15% Garnacha) and Viña Marcos (60% Tempranillo/40% Garnacha) from the Arinzano estate. House style is to give the wines the legal minimum of oak and then age in bottle for supreme elegance; these are excellent. Chivite is generally considered one of the two leading Navarra bodegas (the other is Ochoa).

### Luís Gurpegui Muga, Villafranca (BMon).
*Founded 1921.* Family firm which also owns Bodegas Berceo in Rioja and has a Rioja bodega in San Adrián under the Gurpegui name (in the 'Rioja' bit of Navarra, or the 'Navarra' bit of Rioja, if you prefer). In Navarra, the family farms 25ha of vines and buys in large quantities of grapes to produce around 30,000hl. Main brand name is Monte Ory.
*Best wines:* red *crianzas* and *reservas*, typically 70%+ Tempranillo, the rest Garnacha and sometimes 10% to 15% Cabernet Sauvignon.

### Magaña, Barillas (RibB).
*Founded 1968.* New-wave bodega and one of the first to plant French varieties in Navarra, now amounting to 110ha of mainly Cabernet Sauvignon and Merlot, with some Tempranillo, Malbec, Mazuelo, Cabernet Franc and Syrah. Wines are among the best of their type, from *crianza* to *gran reserva.* *Best wines:* Eventum *crianza* (Merlot/Tempranillo/Cabernet Sauvignon/Syrah/Malbec/Mazuelo), Viña Magaña *reserva* (Cabernet Sauvignon/ Merlot), Viña Magaña Merlot *reserva* and Viña Magaña *gran reserva* (Cabernet Sauvignon and Merlot). All are excellent.

The bodega ranks with Guelbenzu as one of the most successful modern wineries in Navarra.

### Marco Real, Olite (RibA).
*Founded 1989.* Marco Real has a hotel-chain as its major shareholder and is famous for one wine: Homenaje, white, *rosado* and red up to *reserva* level. The *rosado* (Garnacha) is very good, but best are probably the reds, especially the oak-aged styles. These are mainly Tempranillo, but may include a little Cabernet Sauvignon. The *reserva* is likely to be Tempranillo, Garnacha and Graciano.

**Above: From water into wine. The fountain at Bodegas Irache offers both *gratis* to pilgrims on their way to Santiago de Compostella.**

**Far left: Navarra's scenery is often as stunning as its wines. The Lumbier gorge near Liédena is just one of many examples.**

Below: The Castillo de Monjardín wine estate lies in the middle of Villamayor de Monjardín, where it makes modern-style Navarra wines.

### Nuestra Señora del Romero Cooperativa, Cascante (RibB).

*Founded 1951.* Major refurbishment in the mid-1970s. Another enlightened co-op which turns out good, workmanlike quality wines with occasional departures into excellence. The members farm 1,600ha of vines, the bodega produces 60,000hl of wine under the labels Señor de Cascante, Plandenas, Torrecilla, Señorío de Yániz and Malón de Echaide.
*Best wines:* the Malón de Echaide white (Viura), Torrecilla red *crianza* (60% Tempranillo/40% Garnacha) and Señor de Cascante *gran reserva* (80% Tempranillo/20% Garnacha).

### Ochoa, Olite (RibA). *Founded 1845.*

Current head of the family Javier Ochoa is well-known in Navarra for his commitment to quality and the time he gives to EVENA and the *consejo regulador*. The firm has 20ha of vineyards and buys in grapes to produce around 6,000hl. The style is 'modern Navarra', with deference to the classic varieties of the region; there is also a willingness to experiment with French varieties. Ochoa shares with Chivite a reputation for exemplary quality-control. All its wines are excellent and occasionally exceptional, especially the award-winning Vino Dulce de

Moscatel, which comes in a half-litre bottle. All are called Ochoa. The basic range provides very good white (Viura), *rosado* (Garnacha) and red *jovenes* (50% Tempranillo/50% Garnacha). Next come the *crianza* varietals: Cabernet Sauvignon, Merlot and Tempranillo, all with 12 months in oak. The third range covers the classics: red *crianza*, *reserva* and *gran reserva*, all made from (typically) 75% Tempranillo and 25% Cabernet Sauvignon. The wines are beautifully made and, in the best years, of peerless quality.

### Orvalaiz, Obanos (Vald).

*Founded 1993.* Very modern operation with 250ha of vineyards producing 15,000hl of wine with a strong bias towards French varieties and Tempranillo. Under the Orvalaiz label there are three *joven* wines: a *rosado* (Cabernet Sauvignon) and two reds – one Cabernet Sauvignon, the other Tempranillo. These are truly excellent; although classified as *jovenes*, the reds spend about three months in oak. The more traditional Viña Orvalaiz offers three more *jovenes*: white (75% Viura/25% Malvasía), *rosado* (50% Tempranillo/40% Garnacha/10% Viura) and red (75% Tempranillo/25% Cabernet Sauvignon). *Best wine:* the Orvalaiz Cabernet Sauvignon.

### Piedemonte Cooperativa, Olite (RibA). *Founded 1992.* In addition to

its 400ha of vines, this very modern co-op has all the latest equipment and access to good grapes (both native and French). Production is 21,000hl, entirely of *joven* wines. Confusingly, it produces four wine ranges, although nearly all are outstanding. The basic (*joven*) range is called Agnes de Cleves, and includes a white (Viura) and *rosado* (Garnacha/Cabernet Sauvignon). Next is Viña Egozque, also *joven*, with a *rosado* (Garnacha) and a red (Tempranillo/Garnacha). Under the Bodegas Piedemonte label are three further *jovenes*: a white (Viura), *rosado*

(Garnacha) and red (Tempranillo). *Best wines:* those called Olígitum (the Roman name for Olite). There's a 50% Cabernet Sauvignon/50% Tempranillo with about three months in oak, as well as a pure Cabernet Sauvignon.

### Príncipe de Viana, Murchante (RibB). *Founded 1983.* Formerly

known as Bodegas Cenalsa, this big, modern, industrial bodega owns 700ha of vines and produces an annual 40,000hl. Quality-control is strict, however, and the firm's large export market reflects the care with which its wines are made. The basic range is called Agramont and includes *jovenes* in all three colours: the white is Viura, the *rosado* is Garnacha and the red is Tempranillo. All are very good wines, beautifully made. The upper range is sold under the Príncipe de Viana label, with a white *joven* (but barrel-fermented) Chardonnay, a *rosado joven* (Cabernet Sauvignon) and a red *crianza* (Cabernet Sauvignon), all excellent.

### Señorío de Sarría, Puente la Reina (Vald). *Founded 1952.* The most

beautiful bodega in Navarra, set in a private estate (*señorío*) of 1,500ha, of which 120 are devoted to vines to support a production of 4,900hl. The rest offers magnificent landscapes and beautifully restored buildings. Restoration was begun in 1952, when Félix Huarte, a local building contractor, bought the estate and used the income from the vineyards to fund the work. In 1981, he sold it to the Caja de Ahorros de Navarra (the Navarra Savings Bank), which made further improvements to the winery, buying more new oak casks; the bodega now has over 8,000. All wines are sold under the Señorío de Sarría label, and the range offers five wines: a white *joven* (Viura), *rosado joven* (Garnacha), a classic red *crianza* (60% Tempranillo/15% Garnacha/15% Mazuelo/10% Graciano) and a varietal Cabernet Sauvignon *crianza*. *Best wines:* the red *reserva* (70% Tempranillo/10% each Mazuelo/

Garnacha/Graciano) and *gran reserva* (80% Tempranillo/7% each Mazuelo, Graciano/6% Garnacha). Quality is very good, with the *gran reserva* and the varietal Cabernet Sauvignon taking most of the honours. Also makes a white *semidulce* and a *rosado* called Vendimia Seleccionada, both *jovenes*.

**Vinícola Navarra, Campanas (Vald).** *Founded 1864.* Former co-op now part of the Bodegas y Bebidas empire. Twelve hectares of vines provide a small proportion of its needs to service an annual production of 56,000hl. However, in spite of the size of the operation, quality is generally very high, with some exceptional wines under no fewer than seven labels. Castillo de Javier is a *rosado joven* Garnacha, reckoned to be one of the region's best. Bandeo, Viña del Recuerdo and Viña Alaiz are the three basic ranges of white, *rosado* and red *jovenes* (Viura for the white, Garnacha for the others). Las Campanas is the premium range, with a white *joven* (Viura/Chardonnay 50/50), *rosado joven* (Garnacha), red *crianza* (70% Tempranillo/20% Cabernet Sauvignon/10% Garnacha), red *crianza* varietal Cabernet Sauvignon and red 'classic' *reserva* (70% Tempranillo/20% Garnacha/10% Mazuelo). There is also an older red *reserva*, Castillo de Tiebas, from the same mixture of classic varieties. *Best wines:* those under the Las Campanas label, particularly the varietal Cabernet Sauvignon.

**Virgen Blanca Cooperativa, Lerín (RibA).** *Founded 1956.* Virgen Blanca is currently farming 415ha of vines (in Ribera Alta and Tierra Estella). The concern is owned by about 300 members, producing a total of 12,000hl. This is probably the best old-style co-op in Navarra, with good-to-very good wines, including the white Viña Ezkibel (Viura), *rosados* Campo Lagaza and Viña Sardasol (both Garnacha) and red *reserva* Viña Sardasol (80% Tempranillo).

# Aragón: Spain in microcosm

The story of Aragón is the story of Spain in microcosm. In the ninth century, as the Moors were being pushed southward, an independent country between the kingdom of Navarre and the County of Catalonia emerged under Louis the Pious. In 1035, Ramiro I Sánchez proclaimed Aragón a kingdom in its own right with its capital at Jaca, in what is now the province of Huesca. Forty years later, Aragón merged with neighbouring Navarre.

Aragón then experienced an empire-building period after the *Infanta* (princess) Petronilla married Ramón Berenguer IV, Count of Barcelona, in 1137. The real turning-point in Spanish history, however, came in 1469, when Ferdinand, prince of Aragón, married Isabella, the young queen of Castile. He acceded to the Aragonés throne in 1479, uniting the old County of Castile, the Kingdom of Aragón and the County of Catalonia under one royal house. This move provided the impetus necessary to transform the country into a united Spain.

In 1492, the twin achievements of the expulsion of the Moors and the discovery of America heralded a golden age for the newly united country. In 1501, Ferdinand and Isabella offered the hand of their daughter Caterina (Catherine of Aragón) in marriage to Arthur, Prince of Wales, heir-apparent to the English throne. Arthur died before his accession, and Catherine married his younger brother, who became Henry VIII.

So what did all this do for the wine business? Quite a lot, really. The early years of the *Reconquista* provided a concentration of royal, political, religious and academic power in northern Spain, establishing a ready market for good wine among those with the money to pay for it. In addition, Aragón's French connections gave it an export market in the days when even Rioja and Navarra were still selling solely on the domestic market.

From an objective standpoint, this state of affairs may well have locked Aragón into a rather old-fashioned style of winemaking. As its neighbours responded to the French need for Bordeaux-style wines in the late 19th century, Aragón was still producing pre-phylloxera styles, including *rancios*, *generosos* and *dulces*. These had served it well for generations, but they were certainly on the way out as far as exports were concerned.

Today, Aragón is much more dynamic, offering a wide range of wines from an astonishing range of vineyards, but in some ways it missed the boat a hundred years ago and is still trying to make up the difference.

**Right:** The Pyrenean mountains tower over the village of Riglos, near Huesca. Besides such spectacular scenery, Huesca province also boasts the Somontano DO.

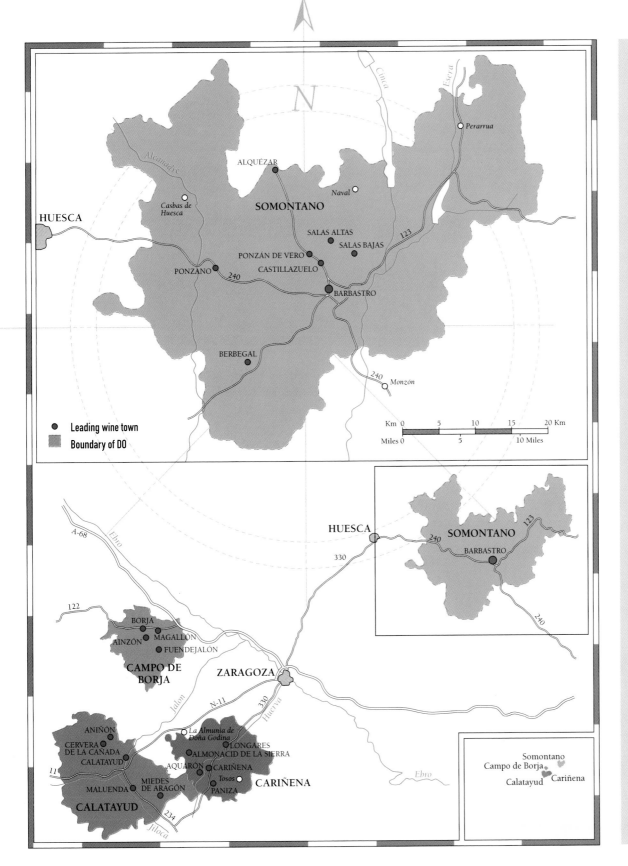

**Leading wine town**

**Boundary of DO**

Km 0    5    10    15    20 Km

Miles 0    5    10 Miles

### The structure of Aragón

*The autonomía of Aragón consists of three provinces: (from north to south) Huesca, Zaragoza and Teruel. The main vineyard areas lie in Zaragoza (which contains the Calatayud, Campo de Borja and Cariñena DO zones) and Huesca (which boasts the Somontano DO zone). The region also incorporates seven country-wine areas, located mainly in the south of Zaragoza and the east of Teruel. Placed as it is on the way to Catalonia and on the main road network between the Basque Country, La Rioja and Navarra, Aragón admittedly has several hard acts to follow. Still, it manages to hold its own, since it is a region full of lush river valleys, mountainsides and semi-desert areas. Its variety of landscapes is unparalleled in Spain, and so it justly takes a quiet pride in its pivotal history and prosperous present.*

# Calatayud

## Notable bodegas

**Langa, Calatayud.**
*Founded 1982.* Modern winery run by a brother-and-sister team with 21ha. The main range of *joven* wines (white, *rosado*, red) is called Portalet. Also makes a red *reserva*.

**Niño Jesus Cooperativa, Aniñón.**
*Founded 1978.* Co-op with more than 300 members. The brand name is Estecillo, and offers white (Viura), *rosado* and red *jovenes* (both 90% Garnacha). The wines have a robust, rustic character.

**San Alejándro Cooperativa, Miedes.** *Founded 1962.* Largest co-op in the region, with 700 members farming about 1,500ha. The standard range includes *jovenes*: white (Viura), *rosado (Garnacha)*, and red (mainly Garnacha).

**San Gregorio Cooperativa, Cervera de la Cañada.** *Founded 1965.* Nearly 500 members farm over 1,000ha, making about 14,000hl. The brand name is Monte Armantes; standard three *jovenes* (white, *rosado*, red) are made from Viura and Garnacha. *Best wine:* delicious, fruity newcomer (since 1996) Viña Armantes Tempranillo *joven* (14.5% abv).

**San Isidro Cooperativa, Maluenda.**
*Founded 1945.* The best of the co-ops, which exports its Marqués de Aragón and Don Aragón brands (white, *rosado,* red). The red Marqués de Aragón is a full *crianza* (70% Tempranillo/30% Garnacha) with a classic toasted style. In Spain, the wines are sold under the labels Viña Alarba (*jovenes*) and Castillo de Maluenda (white/red *jovenes*, red *crianza*).

**Right: The village of Belmonte de Gracian, in the Calatayud DO, another wine region whose viticultural history dates back to Roman times.**

The rather unusual name of the Calatayud DO comes from a Moorish governor called Ayub who built a castle (*qalat*) at the confluence of the Jalón and Jiloca rivers. Names aside, however, there was a thriving population in this area as far back as Roman times, when the old city of Bilbilis (which has been extensively excavated nearby) was used as an important staging-post for the Roman legions on their way north to Gaul.

Roman citizens other than members of the legions lived in the area, of course: the poet Martial, for example, was born in Calatayud about AD40, returning here to die some 67 years later. The presence of poets and other artists indicates an learned upper class – and upper-class tastes. It is quite likely that winemaking would have played an important part in local business, for the Romans – military or civilian – seldom went anywhere without ensuring easy access to a flagon or two.

Modern Calatayud is still an important winemaking centre; indeed, it is the largest DO zone in Aragón. Along with the neighbouring DO zone of Cariñena, Calatayud

forms part of what is Aragón's southernmost winemaking region, situated approximately 87 kilometres (54 miles) southwest of Zaragoza. Yet despite its long winemaking history, its wines have yet to realise anything like large-scale export potential.

The River Jalón flows north through the town of Calatayud to join the Ebro, but even this large water source is not enough to keep the area from being the hottest and driest part of the Upper Ebro Valley. The vineyards themselves manage to avoid the worst of the heat, planted as they are at high altitudes of between 500 to 900 metres (1,640 to 2,953 feet). In addition, the local soils are rich in limestone, marl and slate, so there is plenty of opportunity to make good wines on a regular basis. The climate is continental, verging on the semi-arid in places. Rainfall in the best areas averages about 550 millimetres, falling to 300 in the driest (22 to 12 inches).

## Grape varieties

As might be expected, the Garnacha grape variety is the mainstay of the Calatayud vineyards, making up roughly 65 per cent of the total vineyard. Tempranillo trails a long way behind at just ten per cent, but its percentage is increasing as the *consejo regulador* encourages replanting with it. There is also some Monastrell and Mazuelo. The main white wine-grape is Malvasía, with a small amount of Garnacha Blanca, and about two per cent of the vineyards are planted in Moscatel Romano.

## Winemaking and wine styles

The bulk of wine made in Calatayud is produced by the major cooperatives which, by virtue of their committee-driven nature, are often slow to change their winemaking methods. Fortunately, as in most wine regions of Spain, this static state of affairs is counteracted by the inevitable mavericks: someone is always experimenting with new ideas, and one or two growers are already working with plantations of Cabernet Sauvignon.

Most of the wine produced is *joven* in style; the local *rosado* (which typically accounts for 50 per cent of production) is very popular due to its combination of fruit and freshness, weight and strength. Calatayud has potential for making some good red wines, and there is no reason (except for slow market penetration) why these should not be made up to *gran reserva* levels at some time in the future.

# Campo de Borja

Yes, the Borjas of Aragón are the same as the Borgias of Italy. The spelling changed to the Italian when Alfonso de Borja, formerly adviser to King Alfonso V of Aragón, was elected pope, took the title Callistus III and moved to the Vatican in 1455. The Borgias became notorious in their new country, but the old Aragón Borja estates retained their staid, medieval existence. Much of that lifestyle is evident today.

The main civilising influence in the region seems to have been the monastery at Veruela. Like most monasteries, it grew vines to make wine for celebrating mass or for selling or trading the surplus to the local community. Although Veruela is now outside the official Campo de Borja DO zone, the monastery itself has been restored to its former glory. It is now an exhibition centre for Aragón generally and the local area in particular, celebrating the countryside, its people and its products – including wine.

Geographically, Campo de Borja is an extension of southern Navarra, situated south of the River Ebro. Its vineyards climb up the slopes of the Sierra del Moncayo at altitudes of between 350 and 700 metres (1,148 to 2,297 feet). The soils consist of light loam over limestone, some

active chalk and iron-rich clay on the mountainsides, and offers excellent drainage. Rainfall is average (350 to 450 millimetres/14 to 18 inches) and the combination of altitude, climate and soils provides all the necessary raw materials to make wines of excellent quality. All that is needed now is sufficient investment.

Garnacha is king here, with 75 per cent of the vineyard. Tempranillo and Macabeo (*aka* Viura in Rioja/Navarra and Maccabeo in Catalonia) have 12 per cent each and Mazuelo, Cabernet Sauvignon and Moscatel less than one per cent each. The wines are mainly *rosado* and red; white wine accounts for just eight per cent of production. *Rancios* and *vinos de licor* are also made, both with and without the DO.

White and *rosado* wines are generally *jovenes* made from Macabeo and Garnacha respectively: light and fresh, for instant drinking and with no pretensions to greatness. Red *jovenes* tend to be made mainly or entirely from Garnacha, sometimes with a little Tempranillo or Cabernet Sauvignon for added perfume and character. Wines for ageing (*crianza* to *gran reserva* level) are mainly Tempranillo or Cabernet Sauvignon or a combination of both.

## Notable bodegas

**Aragonesas, Fuendejalón.** *Founded 1984.* This firm bottles and markets the wines of two local co-ops: San Juan Bautista in Fuendejalón and Santo Cristo de Magallón. There are four ranges. The first three are Don Ramón (*jovenes* in all three colours); Viña Tito red *joven*, white and *rosado aguja* (slightly sparkling); and the very good Mosen Cleto red *crianza*. The fourth range is relatively new, offering traditional (although cool-fermented) *jovenes* in all three colours, a barrel-fermented white and red, and a new red *crianza*, all under the Coto de Hayas label. *Best wine:* the Duque de Sevilla *reserva*.

**Borsao, Borja.** *Founded 1958.* Co-op whose 800 members farm 1,000ha. Winemaking equipment is modern and standards are high, with very good-to-excellent results in most years. Borsao is the basic *joven* range, with good white (Viura) and *rosado* (Garnacha) wines and an excellent red (Garnacha/Tempranillo/Cabernet Sauvignon). *Best wines:* Gran Campellas *crianza* and Señor Atares *reserva* (both Garnacha/Tempranillo).

**Santo Cristo Cooperativa, Ainzón.** *Founded 1955.* Along with the Borsao co-op in Borja, this is the region's leading bodega. Its basic range is called Viña Collado and offers *jovenes* in all three colours. *Best wines:* Viña Ainzón is the *crianza* and *reserva* range – very good to excellent (typically 80% Tempranillo/20% Garnacha).

Left: Vineyards near Fuendejalón. The most popular grape variety in the Campo de Borja DO is Garnacha, which makes up some 75 per cent of the vineyard.

**Cariñena**

# Cariñena

**Far right:** The mountains of the Sierra de Algairen range form the backdrop for these vineyards near the village of Aguaron.

**Below:** Despite the fact that it is hugely important in northern Spain, the Cariñena grape is little used in its homeland.

Cariñena has been the most high-profile of all of Aragón's DO zones, perhaps because it has been around the longest. The zone was first demarcated in 1932 and received its official *denominación de origen* documentation in 1960. It has therefore had more time than most to establish itself – so long, in fact, that it begs the following question: why does it not have an even higher profile?

Modesty would seem to be one reason – especially considering the fact that this is the birthplace of one of northern Spain's most important grape varieties: Cariñena (known as Mazuelo in Rioja/Navarra). Here in its home region, Cariñena represents less than ten per cent of the vineyard. Can you imagine what would have happened if the good citizens of the village of Chardonnay had treated their own native grape with such disregard? Where is the fabled Cariñena de Cariñena, a marketing-man's dream? At the moment, there simply isn't one.

What there is, however, is some very good wine. The Romans, as ever in this part of Spain, were the first to organise winemaking on a commercial level, but Cariñena had its own regulations in place as early as 1696. As we have seen, it was also one of the first wine-producing regions in Spain to have its borders delimited.

## Geography and climate

The vineyards, like those of the neighbouring Calatayud region, spread upwards from the flood-plain of the River Ebro into the mountains of the Sistema Ibérica at altitudes between 400 and 800 metres (1,312 to 2,625 feet). The soils are good for vines: limestone and a little chalk with some slate and alluvial deposits at the lower levels. The climate is fully continental, with long, hot summers and even longer autumns. Rainfall is relatively low at 300 to 350 millimetres (12 to 14 inches), so yields are not likely to be high.

Garnacha is the main grape variety, accounting for more than half the vineyard, followed by Tempranillo (15 per cent) and Cariñena (six per cent). There is also a small percentage of Cabernet Sauvignon, Juan-Ibañéz and Monastrell. For white wines, the main variety is Macabeo, which accounts for 20 per cent of the vineyard, supplemented by some small amounts of Garnacha Blanca, Parellada and Moscatel.

The wines of Cariñena tend to be mainly *joven* in style, produced in all three colours. However, a few bodegas are marketing excellent *crianzas* made from Tempranillo and Garnacha – sometimes with a bit of Cabernet Sauvignon thrown in – and this would seem to be a beneficial way ahead. Some old-fashioned *rancio* wine is also made.

Cariñena's are some of the best-known wines of Aragón, and are thus given pride of place in many of the region's restaurants. They are served alongside *migas*, a dish of fried breadcrumbs and leftovers – typically bits of ham and cheese but also fish, vegetables and even sweetmeats. Roast lamb, kid and suckling-pig (the standard cuisine of northern Spain) are prominent menu items, and beef is often served raw alongside a plate of baked rock-salt to allow diners to cook it the way they want.

# Notable bodegas

**Covinca Cooperativa, Longares.**
*Founded 1988.* This co-op's members farm 3,000ha of vines and produce a staggering 100,000hl of wine. However, quality is very good and quality-control consistent. The main brand name is Torrelongares, which covers *joven* wines, white (Macabeo), *rosado* (Garnacha) and red (Garnacha). There is also a Torrelongares *vino de licor* which can be very good, and a red *crianza* called Marqués de Ballomar which has yet to make an impression. *Best wine:* unusually for these parts, the white *joven*.

**San José Cooperativa, Aguarón.**
*Founded 1955.* Co-op whose 500 members produce 45,000hl of wine. Another large bodega that turns out some very good wines, thanks to recent investment in stainless-steel technology. There are two ranges. Monasterio de las Viñas offers white (Macabeo) and *rosado* (Garnacha) *jovenes*, with reds from *joven* to *gran reserva* level (typically Garnacha/Tempranillo/Cariñena), as well as a varietal Tempranillo *joven* and a Cabernet Sauvignon *crianza*; these can be very good. The other range is called Valdemadera and offers a *rosado joven* (Garnacha) and a very good red *crianza*

(Garnacha/Cariñena/Tempranillo).
*Best wine:* the excellent Valdemadera white *joven* (Macabeo).

**San Valero Cooperativa, Cariñena.**
*Founded 1945.* San Valero put Cariñena on the map in export markets, having been responsible for around half the DO's exports. 1,000 members farm 5,500ha, but the co-op has its own programme of experimentation and its quality-control is excellent. It was among the first to try Cabernet Sauvignon and encourages its members to replant with Tempranillo. Its most famous wine is Don Mendo, which used to be unlabelled and wrapped in parchment.

*Best wines:* the Marqués de Tosos *reserva* and the Monte Ducay range: white *joven* (Macabeo/Moscatel), *rosado joven* (Garnacha/Cabernet Sauvignon) and reds from *joven* to *reserva* level (typically Garnacha/Tempranillo/Cabernet Sauvignon). Excellent in good years.

# Somontano

**Above:** Vines grow below the Monasterio del Pueyo, near Barbastro. Monasteries such as this were responsible for promoting the export of Somontano wine in the Middle Ages.

Somontano, the most recent of Aragón's DO zones, owes little in style, climate, or marketing to its compatriots in the rest of the *autonomía*. Centred around the town of Barbastro, in the province of Huesca, it is for the most part a lush, green place with ancient villages, prehistoric caves, river gorges, rich red soil, white-blossomed almond trees and vines.

Indeed, Somontano is such a beautiful place that when the Roman Empire collapsed in the late-fifth century and the legions could return home, quite a few elected to stay. To many, Italy was only a distant memory; others had never even been there, born to Romans already living in the land known as *Hispania*. These expatriates may no longer have had an empire, but one thing they did have was technical knowledge about winemaking on a commercial basis, and they were happy to share that knowledge with their new countrymen.

By the Middle Ages, Somontano was the centre of a burgeoning religious establishment, whose monasteries extended the vineyards and set up a growing export business with France – which was, after all, just up the mountain and over the other side. This French connection stood the winemakers of Somontano in good stead when the phylloxera disaster struck in the 1860s: they were able to expand both their export business and their vineyards, and replant with grafted vines when their own time came.

Because the region is relatively small and very close to the French border, Somontano managed to maintain its links with France, and a good deal of its production routinely went over the mountains. In 1974, however, local growers decided that the time had come to establish themselves, and applied formally for elevation to DO status. In the event, this took quite a while (nearly 11 years), but, once approved, a great deal happened in a very short time.

## Geography and climate

Somontano covers a wide variety of terrain: river valleys, terraced mountainsides, the rolling foothills of the Pyrenees. Soil conditions are good: rich, fertile sandstone and clay with some chalk and excellent drainage – which is important, since rainfall is greater than elsewhere in Aragón (550 millimetres/22 inches). Vineyards grow at altitudes ranging from 350 to 650 metres (1,148 to 2,133 feet); microclimates provide excellent exposure to the ripening sun as well as the cool nights needed to rest the vines. Prospects here were perfect for making top-class wines as soon as the DO was granted.

At the time, however, most production lay in the hands of a couple of sleepy old co-ops and a few enthusiast wineries; fortunately, this situation did not last long. Surveys of the land showed that it was ideal for cultivation, and the *consejo regulador* was more than amenable to companies wanting to come in and invest. Even the co-ops started to get excited. With its good conditions and low land prices, Somontano, it seemed, had promise.

One of the first companies to come to Somontano after it gained DO status was CoViSa – *Compañia Vitivinícola Aragonesa* – at Salas Bajas. This firm belongs to an organisation called DAYSA, which stands for *Desarollo Agrícola y Social de Aragón* (Agricultural and Social Development Company of Aragón). DAYSA is a group made up of banks and other local companies whose brief is to invest, develop and expand local businesses in the agricultural field, and to do it in a socially worthwhile manner.

CoViSa originally built an experimental winery in the village of Salas Bajas and worked with soils, rootstocks and grape varieties, as well as different methods of winemaking. Once the the best combination of variables had been discovered, a brand-new, state-of-the-art winery was constructed on a greenfield site, and planting began in earnest. Today, CoViSa's wines are among the best of the area, and the firm's example has been taken up by most of its neighbours.

## Grape varieties and wine styles

The grapes grown in Somontano were originally restricted to Garnacha (Tinta and Blanca) and Macabeo, along with some obscure local varieties: two reds – one called Moristel (no relation to Monastrell), the other Parraleta – and a white called Alcañón. Today, these are still important varieties, but they have been joined by a few newcomers. Tempranillo, Cabernet Sauvignon, Merlot and Pinot Noir have joined the red pack, while whites now include Chardonnay, Chenin Blanc and Gewürztraminer. Others are under consideration.

Wines in Somontano fall into two groups: old-style *jovenes* in all three colours made from Macabeo, Garnacha and Moristel (although these are becoming less and less common). Much more prevalent are new-wave blends using traditional and French grapes, experimenting with oak and generally pushing viniculture to its limit. This new approach has revitalised what was a relatively sleepy area, brought back to life over two decades by the hard work of a few *bodegueros* trying to bring their wine to public notice.

Below: The village of Alquézar, Somontano,
is one of the most picturesque in all Aragón.
Its skyline is dominated by a 12th-century castle.

## Notable bodegas

### Alto Aragón, Salas Bajas.

*Founded 1991.* Under the brand name
Enate, this bodega set out to produce
low-yield, high-quality wines from its
own vineyards. The range is impressive:
Enate Blanco (70% Chardonnay/30%
Macabeo) is excellent quality, bettered
only by the Enate Chardonnay (barrel-
fermented), which is exceptional.
There is also Enate Riesling, Sauvignon
Blanc and Gewürztraminer; the
Sauvignon tends to show the best, but
all are top-quality examples. There is an
excellent Cabernet Sauvignon *rosado*,
and red wines include a splendid *joven*
(Tempranillo/Monastrel/Cabernet
Sauvignon) and an even better *crianza*
(70% Tempranillo/30% Cabernet
Sauvignon; nine months in barrel).

### Borruel, Ponzano. *Founded 1983.*

Family-run bodega with 14ha which
also buys in grapes to produce 3,500-
4,000hl. Makes a number of ranges,
including Villa de L'Ainsa and Villa Osca
(*jovenes* in all three colours), Villa de
Benasque (white and *rosado jovenes*).
Red *crianzas* carry the labels Villa de
Benasque (50% Tempranillo/50%
Moristel; 12 months oak) and Castillo
de l'Ainsa (70% Moristel/30%
Tempranillo; 12 months in oak).
Also a Gran Eroles *reserva*
(50% Tempranillo/25% Moristel/25%
Cabernet Sauvignon; 14 months
in oak). *Best wines:* the *crianzas*
show particularly well.

### CoViSa, Barbastro. *Founded 1986.*

Currently farms 600ha and is one
of the most modern wineries in Spain.
The range is large. Viñas del Vero
offers white (Chenin Blanc/Macabeo/
Chardonnay), *rosado* (Tempranillo/
Moristel/Garnacha) and red
(Tempranillo/ Moristel) *jovenes*.
There are also white *joven* varietals
of Chardonnay, barrel-fermented
Chardonnay, Chenin Blanc,
Gewürztraminer and Riesling,
as well as red *joven* varietals of Merlot

and Tempranillo. Next come the
*crianzas*: Duque de Azara (Tempranillo/
Moristel; eight months oak) and a
varietal Pinot Noir called Val de Uga
(also eight months oak). *Reservas*
are called Gran Vos (Merlot/Cabernet
Sauvignon/ Pinot Noir) and Val de Vos,
a varietal Cabernet Sauvignon. All are
beautifully made, with meticulous
attention to detail. *Best wines:*
the varietal Tempranillo (*joven*) and
the Gran Vos.

### Monclús, Radiquero. *Founded 1980.*

Family-owned bodega run by Mercedes
Monclús who farms 12ha and turns out

around 200hl. Doña Mercedes worked
particularly hard to achieve DO status
for Somontano, and her efforts deserve
to be recognised. She makes very
pleasant *jovenes* in all three colours
under the Monclús label, as well as
a *crianza* (Tempranillo) called Inés
de Monclús.

### Pirineos, Barbastro. *Founded 1993.*

Once the Somontano de Sobrarbe
co-op, and the engine of the region.
It remains a co-op whose members
farm 1,000ha. Recently Pirineos has
reinvested and renewed its equipment,
encouraged replanting in the fields and

revamped its range. Produces a
bewildering array of labels and ranges.
*Best wines:* the very good Montesierra
*rosado joven* (Tempranillo/Macabeo/
Moristel/Garnacha), the Villa de
Alquézar red *joven* (Tempranillo/
Moristel), the Monasterio del Pueyo
red *crianza* (Tempranillo/Cabernet
Sauvignon) and the Señorio de Lazán
red *reserva* (Tempranillo/Moristel/
Cabernet Sauvignon).

# Country Wines of North-Central Spain

### VdlT Bajo Aragón (Teruel)

This a large area (some 10,000ha of vines) located in the east of the province of Teruel. It is south of the river and contiguous with the western border of Catalonia, and is centred around the town of Valderrobres.

Bajo Aragón divides into three subzones: east, central and west. The eastern section has the most vines and makes the most wine; the central area is the largest, although with less concentrated areas of cultivation; the western section is least important.

The main grape varieties are Garnacha Tinta, which makes up around 60% of the vineyard, and Garnacha Blanca with most of the rest (30%), although there is a little Macabeo and Mazuelo. There is even some experimentation with Cabernet Sauvignon (every region seems to have its mavericks).

Winemaking is varied, to say the least, with some bodegas still vinifying mixed grapes to produce light reds, or turning out high-alcohol red wines from Garnacha in the time-honoured style. However, there is an influence for improvement. The regional *Estación de Viticultura y Enología* (Viticultural and Oenological Station) has a local branch at Valderrobres, and is doing its best to encourage higher quality among the *viñeros*.

It does this by encouraging them to install new equipment, ferment at lower temperatures and make wines to sell younger and fresher. Some progress is being made, although the region's production (approximately 200,000hl) is still heavily geared to the bulk-wine market.

### Notable bodegas

**Santa María La Mayor Cooperativa, Valderrobres.** *Founded 1957.*
Typical *cooperativa comarcal* (district co-op) making wine from more or less anything thrown at it. It does have a range of bottled wines under the Valderrobres and Peña Lagaya labels,

which consist of *jovenes* of up to 13% abv in all three colours. In general, they are all made from different mixtures of Garnacha, Macabeo and Mazuelo. Quality is modest.

### VdlT Valdejalón (Zaragoza)

Another large area, this time situated in the west of the province of Zaragoza, filling the triangle of land between Campo de Borja in the north and Calatayud and Cariñena in the south. Its main centre is La Almunia de Doña Godina.

This is bulk-wine country. The annual production averages some 200,000hl from 15,000ha of vines, and although it produces as much wine as Bajo Aragón, the yield per vine is less. Sadly, this does not mean that quality is higher – simply that methods are not as efficient. The main grape variety is Garnacha Tinta (90%), and the wines made from it tend to be heady, hefty reds, often produced by the *doble pasta* method and high in alcohol.

Once again, a few small producers are turning out better examples. The ubiquitous Cabernet Sauvignon has been seen here and there, and the better wines of the region owe something to the style of Campo de Borja in the north, rather than to Calatayud in the south.

The most interesting part of Valdejalón is in the northwest around Moncayo. Higher vineyards, a cooler microclimate and more rain are helping forward-looking winemakers to produce wines which are lighter, fresher and lower in alcohol. If Valdejalón has a future as a serious wine-producing area, then Moncayo is its crucible.

### VdlT Tierra Baja de Aragón (Zaragoza)

Not to be confused with the similarly named VdlT Bajo Aragón (above), this small area is situated east of the town of Caspe on the River Ebro, about halfway between Zaragoza and Lleida

(Lérida). Six villages between Caspe and the border with Catalonia make wine in all three colours, mainly from Garnacha, although once again some Cabernet Sauvignon and Tempranillo vines are in evidence. Anything of note has yet to emerge.

### VC Alto Jiloca (Teruel)/ VC Daroca (Zaragoza)

These two areas are linked together since all that divides them is the Zaragoza/Teruel border. They are, in all other respects, the same area.

The VC Daroca covers two dozen villages in the south of the province of Zaragoza, located between Calatayud and Cariñena and the border; the area is centred around Daroca itself. The vines are planted mainly in the valley of the River Jiloca.

The vineyards of the VC Alto Jiloca continue southwards without a break, into the north of the province of Teruel. Around 21 villages are centred around Calamocha – again in the valley of the River Jiloca, but spreading westwards to the border with the province of Cuenca (*autonomía* of Castilla-La Mancha). Between them, the two regions have about 10,000ha of vines.

The style of wine made here would be familiar to anyone who has visited other country-wine areas of Aragón: mixed cultivation, unexciting varieties and – quite simply – what seems to be a lack of interest in producing anything other than the hefty, heady table wines (up to 14% abv) which have been made here for centuries. The main grape varieties are Garnacha and Macabeo; there is also some Monastrell, so there is really no reason why good wines should not be produced here. All that is needed is the will – and the investment – to do so.

### VC Belchite (Zaragoza)

Belchite and 16 other villages in the south of the province of Zaragoza (situated between the city itself, southwards to the border with Teruel) may use this name for simple country wines produced from Garnacha and Macabeo.

The style is typically heavyweight (the legal minimum strength is 12% abv for whites, 13% abv for reds) and the wines show similarities to those made in Muniesa, which lies to the south.

### VC Muniesa (Teruel)

This is more or less a continuation westwards of the VdIT Bajo Aragón (above) in the north of the province of Teruel, although winemaking is not nearly as developed or focused.

Some 2,200ha of vines are planted around the town of Muniesa, mainly Garnacha (70%) plus Macabeo. These turn out heavyweight wines of up to 15% abv. The rest of the vineyard is made up of the rather obscure Provechón, Miguel de Arco and Royal varieties. There has not been much in the way of noticeable development.

# Catalonia and the Balearics

The 'Catalan corner' between France and Spain has been a turning point in Mediterranean history ever since seaborne trade began here some 3,000 years ago. What we now know as Catalonia, an *autonomía* of Spain, is just part of a region that once dominated business and cultural life much further afield. In Spain, Catalonia, or *Catalunya* as it calls itself (*Cataluña* in Castilian Spanish), comprises four provinces: Girona (Gerona) and Lleida (Lérida) in the north, bordering France; Barcelona and Tarragona in the centre and south, down the coast. The winemaking style is eclectic, demonstrating the independence of spirit that characterises almost everything Catalan. If the local climate, soils and gastronomy favour light, fresh, whites and *rosados* (which they do), then expect the Catalans to decide to make fine reds, powerful *crianzas* and *reservas*, and the world's second-favourite sparkling wine (which they do). The Balearic Islands have a similarly shared history, language and cuisine, and remind us that here was once one of the most significant civilising forces of the medieval era.

**Below: The futuristic bodega of Raïmat, in Costers del Segre. The interior has been described as imperial Rome meets the starship Enterprise.**

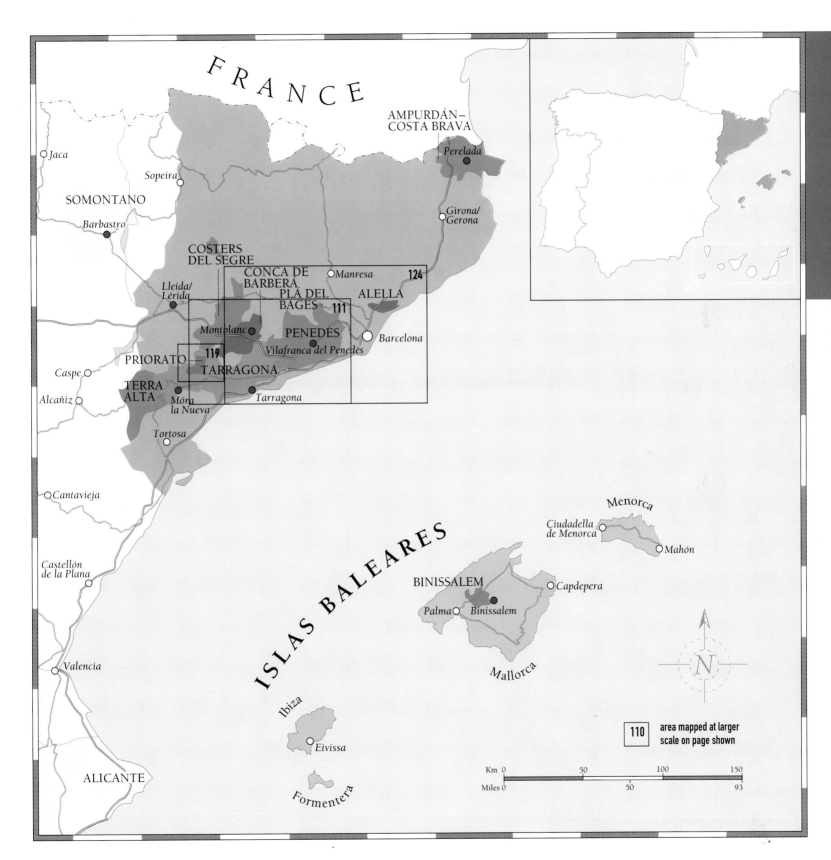

FRANCE

AMPURDÁN–
COSTA BRAVA

Jaca

Sopeira

SOMONTANO

Barbastro

Perelada

Girona/
Gerona

COSTERS
DEL SEGRE

CONCA DE
BARBERÁ

PLÁ DEL
BAGES

Manresa

ALELLA

124

Lleida/
Lérida

111

Montblanc

PENEDÉS

Vilafranca del Penedès

Barcelona

Caspe

PRIORATO

119

TARRAGONA

Alcañiz

TERRA
ALTA

Móra
la Nueva

Tarragona

Tortosa

Cantavieja

Menorca

Ciudadella
de Menorca

Mahón

ISLAS BALEARES

Castellón
de la Plana

BINISSALEM

Capdepera

Palma

Binissalem

Mallorca

N

Valencia

Ibiza

110    area mapped at larger
scale on page shown

Eivissa

ALICANTE

Km 0        50        100        150
Miles 0            50            93

Formentera

# Catalonia: a centre of trade

## Catalan cuisine

*Catalonia is fish country, with a long Mediterranean coastline and an ancient tradition of seafood. It is no surprise to discover the many restaurants which deal exclusively in* mariscos *and* pescado. *However, just as it has a microclimate for every type of vine, so Catalonia has a microclimate for every other form of garden produce in the central Meseta, which ranges in altitude from sea level to 800 metres plus. From peas and beans to asparagus, peppers, artichokes and olives to wild mushrooms, Catalonia is rich in vegetables. There are also ham and other pork products (particularly a local 'white' version of black pudding called* butifarra*), and a Provençal-style garlic sauce called* alioli. *In addition, Catalonia is the source of Spain's favourite dessert:* crema Catalana. *This is a version of the classic* crème brûlée, *often served with the sugar-caramel still melting on the top, and enjoyed in every town in Spain. The most famous Catalan cheese is probably Garrotxa, a goat's-milk cheese made all over the region, but look out for* Valle de Aran *and* Montsec *from Lleida,* Serrat *and* Tupi *from the foothills of the Pyrenees and* La Selva *from Girona.*

Catalonia's position in the northeastern corner of the Mediterranean, straddling the border of modern France and Spain, gave it excellent ports (including Barcelona) and political and military significance. The result meant early trade and prosperity, but its long coastline and legendary riches made it ripe for attack from all comers: the Greeks in the sixth century BC, then the Carthaginians and the Romans, and finally the Moors in the ninth century AD. Desperate for independence, the citizens of Catalonia joined forces with Charlemagne, king of the Franks, who helped liberate their lands from the Moors. Charlemagne, however, liked the area himself, and duly incorporated Catalonia into the Frankish empire.

In 865, the Counts of Barcelona took control of Catalonia; by the end of the ninth century, the magnificently named Count Wilfred the Shaggy had made the region virtually independent from the Franks. Considerable prosperity followed as the trading nation explored further east and along the coast of Africa. In 1137, Count Berenguer IV of Barcelona married Petronilla, daughter of the king of Aragón, and the two nations merged when she came to the throne. The name of this joint kingdom became Aragón, even though Catalonia was by far the dominant partner.

## The golden age of Catalonia

The alliance heralded a golden age. At its height, what might be called 'Greater Catalonia' stretched from what is now the Languedoc in the north to Valencia in the south, with possessions right across the Mediterranean, including the Balearic Islands, Corsica, Sardinia, Sicily, Naples and parts of Greece and Turkey. This position of strength lasted until 1387 and the death of King Pedro IV. Squabbles among his heirs fragmented the empire, allowing outside forces to claim much of the territory. Meanwhile, the axis of power shifted westwards as Ferdinand, heir to the throne of Aragón, married Isabella of Castile in 1469, forging one of the last links in a chain of influence which included Castile, León, Asturias, Cantabria, Aragón and Catalonia.

Naturally, the citizens of Catalonia were not happy with their loss of power. As late as the War of Spanish Succession (1702-14), the region sided against Castile with the French, who promised independence if France won. The struggle for self-rule continued, and Catalonia finally gained regional autonomous status in 1932, under the second republic. Yet even this was doomed to failure, since the Spanish Civil War (1936-39) took its toll of

Republican and separatist regions. The nationalist government of General Francisco Franco banned the Catalan language and Catalan symbolism altogether.

Autonomy returned only after Franco's death, confirmed by the new constitution of 1978 which enshrined Catalonia's rights, individuality, language and self-government. Today, Barcelona is more flamboyant than ever. As Spain's biggest port, it is still an artistic and cultural centre of international repute, revelling in the legacies of Gaudí, Miró, Picasso, Dalí and Tàpies.

## The region and its wines

In wine terms, Catalonia has virtually reinvented itself in a generation. Its original wines included heady, oxidised *rancios* and sweet *vinos de licor* made with one or other of the Moscatels (Muscats) which flourished in these warm, fertile parts. As recently as the 1950s, these wine styles, together with Garnacha-based *rosado*, were the mainstay of Catalan wine production. There was also Cava, of course, born in the valley of the River Anoia. In some ways, the growing of Cava grapes and the care, cleanliness and acidity they require provided a clue to the future of still wines from the region.

The major change began in the 1940s. With Europe embroiled in the Second World War, the only export market for Catalan wines was the Americas. A young Miguel Torres, head of the family firm of the same name, set off across the Atlantic with his wife Margarita to try to promote Torres wines abroad. When Torres returned to Catalonia two years later, the company name was established throughout North and South America. This proved tremendously beneficial once the hostilities were over: Europe was not ready to ship wine in what few cargo ships remained, but the vast cities of the Americas were only too pleased to have something to celebrate. Sales boomed.

The work done by Miguel Torres became self-perpetuating, and as the Pacific rim and Australia emerged from the 1940s, there, too, Torres wine became well-known. At this time, the firm was still shipping wine in cask. As other wine companies re-entered the export market, Miguel Torres realised that if he wanted 'branding' in the most effective sense, his wines would have to be sold in bottle. This was a remarkably bold step at a time (the 1950s) when only a few of the world's most famous wine estates insisted on bottling their wines themselves, but it further reinforced the prestige of the brand. Torres became a byword for quality-control and innovation.

In the early 1960s, Miguel's son, Miguel Agustin Torres, graduated from university with degrees in chemistry and œnology. Straightaway, he set about bringing even more new thinking into the business. Stainless-steel fermentation technology was in its infancy, but Miguel Agustin realised it pointed the way to the future, and Torres was the first to install new equipment in Catalonia. Miguel Agustin was also quick to explore planting Cabernet Sauvignon, Merlot, *et al* in selected plots with the right microclimates.

By this time, Torres was not the only company involved in dragging the Catalan wine industry into the modern age. Another pioneer was Jean León, a Catalan who went to live in California in the 1950s and founded a chain of successful restaurants. He returned in 1962 to buy a parcel of land in the Penedès DO zone, with the idea of making a Bordeaux-style wine from classic French grape varieties and bottling it on the estate. Cabernets, Merlot, Chardonnay – even Pinot Noir and Syrah – are now found throughout the region.

Modern Catalan wine is an astonishing mixture of ancient and modern. Here, some of Spain's most modern wineries make impeccable wines to world-class standards, while boutique wineries produce individual wines from single plots. Alongside them, *artesanal viñeros* create the old *rancios* and *licorosos* the way their grandfathers did, sleepy country co-ops still sell only in bulk to their local communities, and factory-farmers turn out vast quantities of good, honest everyday wine for seaside towns and city cafés and bars at modest, value-for-money prices.

**Below:** The face of Catalonia remains traditional, but beneath its old-fashioned exterior lies a flourishing modern wine region.

# Alella

## Notable bodegas

**Alella Vinícola Cooperativa, Alella.**
*Founded 1906.* The co-op's 106 members farm 140ha. The brand name is Marfil, which covers good whites and *rosados*. *Best wine:* one of the region's few remaining old-style *semiseco* whites (60% Pansà Blanca/30% Garnacha Blanca/10% Chardonnay).

**Parxet, Tiana.** *Founded 1920.*
Home of Alella's most famous wine under the Marqués de Alella label. Wines are all white. The basic Marqués de Alella Clásico is 100% Pansà Blanca – full of fruit, fresh with crisp acidity and a hint of grapey sweetness. Marqués de Alella Seco is a dry version of the same wine and is equally good, as is the varietal Chardonnay. *Best wine:* the 100% Chardonnay Marqués de Alella Alliers (six or seven months in Alliers oak), with a spicy/oaky character.

**Roura, Alella.** *Founded 1981.*
Smart, modern bodega with an excellent reputation for quality, making wines from its own 35ha as well as bought-in wines. Roura Voramar is the basic white: dependable, with excellent quality. There is also a varietal Chardonnay. Roura's fame rests on its delicious 100% Merlot *rosado* and its red wines – probably the region's best. Roura Memory is the basic red (80% Tempranillo/20% Cabernet Sauvignon). Better is the varietal Roura Merlot. *Best wine:* the Roura *crianza* (Cabernet Sauvignon/Merlot/Tempranillo; up to 20 months in oak).

**Right: Xarel-lo grapes, known in Alella as Pansà Blanca, yield the DO's light, fresh wines that are designed for immediate drinking.**

Sixty years ago, the area known as Alella was important enough to be counted among the first group of Spanish wine-producing regions to have its vineyards officially delimited; 30 years ago it was three times the size it is today. Even just a few years ago, Alella was a pleasant, rural area situated about six kilometres (three miles) north of the River El Besós, which marks the northeastern city limit of Barcelona.

Today, however, Alella has unfortunately metamorphosed into commuter-land, and much of what was its lower vineyard area has been taken over for building development. Four highland areas (known as *valles*, or valleys) were released for additional planting in 1989, but this is a small concession. The fact remains that the Alella region is little more than a shadow of its former self.

### Geology and viticulture

On the credit side, the *valles* areas have the advantage of containing some of the finest base material for vine-growing in the world. The eastern outcrop of schistose/limestone bedrock from the stratum that runs across the whole of Catalonia disappears underneath the central Meseta and resurfaces towards Ribera del Duero. The older, lower-lying vineyards grow over granite bedrock. The combination of the two types of soil and a hilly location on the eastern side of the Sierra de Montseny provide this small area with a relatively wide choice of vineyard types and microclimates.

Small though it is, there are three main climatic regions in the Alella DO zone. The coastal area, up to 90 metres (295 feet) in altitude, is planted mainly in Garnacha Blanca. The intermediate zone, which has altitudes of between 90 and 150 metres (295 and 491 feet), covers much of the *denominación de origen's* 'old' vineyard area with its granite bedrock and is planted in Pansà Blanca (Xarel-lo), Pansà Rosado, Garnacha Tinta and Ull de Llebre (Tempranillo).

Finally, there is the Valles region which, at altitudes of between 160 and 260 metres (525 and 853 feet) is the coolest of the three microclimates. It is planted mainly in Pansà Blanca; even so, this is also where the experimental and developing plantations of the so-called 'international varieties' – Chardonnay, Chenin Blanc, Cabernet Sauvignon, Pinot Noir *et al* – are currently found.

### Winemaking and wine styles

Traditionally, Alella made semi-sweet white wines, a style that was prominent right through to the 1970s; now it has almost (but not quite) faded away. Today, a small amount of *rosado* and (surprisingly good) red wine is produced here and there, but Alella's international fame rests firmly upon its white wines: typically light, fresh and made mainly from the Pansà Blanca for immediate drinking. Given the plantations of international varieties currently growing in the Valles region, excellent Chardonnay mixes and even varietals are being made here, too.

At last count, only three bodegas were active in the entire DO zone: Parxet, Roura and the local co–op, which has been at the forefront of modernisation. All are doing reasonably well. Parxet, for example, is now based in a smart modern winery in Tiana, while Roura is well-known for its experimental work with French varieties – not just the big-name internationals but also traditional varieties from the south of France. Both Parxet and Roura also make wine under the Cava DO. We may only hope that they and the co-op continue to resist any further development that might arise from the ever-encroaching city.

# Ampurdán-Costa Brava

The DO zone where Spain meets France. Known as *Empordà* in Catalan, its northern limit is the Franco-Spanish border, and some vineyards meander from Spain to France and back again with a fine disregard for national boundaries. The main town is Figueres (home of the legendary Dalí museum). As the name implies, the DO's eastern boundary is the wild coast of northeastern Spain.

Traditionally, French influence extended only slightly to winemaking styles. Ampurdán's *vino de licor* and Banyuls' *vin doux naturel* bear a strong family resemblance, but apart from that, Roussillon is famous for its red wines, while Ampurdán concentrates on *rosados* made principally from Cariñena. Recently, this has all changed. New plantings of experimental varieties are now found alongside Garnacha and the three main Catalan white varieties (Cava is also made here).

Altitudes in Ampurdán rises to about 200 metres (656 feet). Many of the vineyards are situated in *concas* (Castilian *cuenca*: a crater-shaped valley), and some lowland vineyards come down almost to the sea. Soils tend to be light, fairly fertile and well-drained, with limestone bedrock, especially in the Pyrenees foothills. The climate is fully Mediterranean, although the eastern Pyrenees and the *Tramontana* (a cold north wind) moderate the temperature.

All of which could explain the success of new experimental varieties, including Tempranillo, Cabernet Sauvignon and Chardonnay. One or two growers are also working with Syrah, Chenin Blanc, Riesling, Muscat and even Gewürztraminer. From a production point of view, this is very much co-op country, and some of the larger ones turn out very good wines from old-style epoxy/concrete vats. The signature wine is still largely *rosado* made from Garnacha and Cariñena. These can be very good, but the most exciting developments have come from new-wave whites and reds.

The former may be made from Parellada, Xarel-lo and Macabeo, perhaps with some Garnacha Blanca and often a little Chardonnay. The latter are likely to be Tempranillo/Cabernet mixes or varietals in their own right. The local speciality is a classic *vino de licor* called Garnatxa: 100 per cent Garnacha, 15.5 per cent alcohol by volume.

## Notable bodegas

### Cavas del Ampurdán, Perelada.
*Founded 1947.* Modern firm whose still wines under the Castillo de Perelada label are among the region's classics. There's a basic white, a 100% Cabernet Sauvignon *rosado*, and red *crianzas* and *reservas* as well as a varietal Cabernet Sauvignon. *Best wines:* the *blanc de blancs* (typically Parellada/Macabeo/Xarello/Chardonnay) and the varietal Chardonnay.

### Comercial Vinícola del Noreste (CoViNoSA), Mollet de Perelada.
*Founded 1977.* Joint venture between Cavas del Ampurdán (above) and the Cooperativa de Mollet de Perelada; CoViNoSA takes the wine from the co-op and markets it. As regards still wines, this bodega pioneered Vi Novell: a fresh, fruity, early-drinking red. Also makes non-vintage, everyday wines in all three colours under the Vinya Farriol label, and older reds called Garrigal. *Best wine:* the excellent Cabernet Sauvignon varietal (with 15% Garnacha).

### Ricardell Cooperativa, Pont de Molins. *Founded 1934.* Co-op whose 87 members farm 300ha to produce around 15,000hl. Makes one of the region's better 'new' wines, Empordà Novel (50% Garnacha/50% Cariñena) as well as a white Garnatxa de Ricardell *vino de licor.* Main range is Vinya Orlina: good quality and value.

### Trobat, Garriguella. *Founded 1965.* Tends to buy in musts. *Best wines:* the Noble Blanc de Blancs (Macabeo) *joven*; the Vinya Noble Cabernet Sauvignon (15% Tempranillo), and the classic sweet 15.5% abv Garnatxa Trobat (six months in oak).

Left: The sun sets over the village of Campany, whose vineyards produce grapes for the Ampurdán-Costa Brava DO.

# Conca de Barberà

## Notable bodegas

**Cava Sanstrave, Solivella.**
*Founded 1984.* A small bodega dealing mainly in the region and throughout Catalonia. It makes a very good varietal Chardonnay called Gasset Blanc Sastrave, and a good red *reserva* (Gasset Negre Sastrave) with 80% Cabernet Sauvignon and 20% Tempranillo. *Best wine:* the red *joven* of the same name: Gasset Negre Sastrave (60% Tempranillo/ 20% Cabernet Sauvignon/ 20% Merlot).

**Concavins, Barberà de la Conca.**
*Founded 1988.* This is the bodega that pioneered 'double vintaging' in the region, under the tutelage of flying winemaker Hugh Ryman. A former co-op, it went private in 1988, but still buys in the grapes of its former members and produces two ranges of wine. The 'early' wines are sold variously under the labels Santara or Castillo de Montblanc and offer a Catalan white (50% Macabeo/50% Parellada), a varietal Chardonnay and a red *joven* (70% Tempranillo/15% Cabernet Sauvignon/15% Merlot); all are very good wines at value-for-money prices. *Best wines:* the main vintage produces excellent varietal Chardonnay, Cabernet Sauvignon and Merlot wines under the Xipella or Concavins brand names.

*Right:* **Cabernet Sauvignon grows in the hills near Monestir de Poblet, just one of many 'international' plantations in the Conca de Barberà DO.**

West of Penedès, north of Tarragona and east of the largest chunk of Costers del Segre, Conca de Barberà's main claim to fame used to be that it grew some of the best grapes for the Cava producers of the Anoia Valley. This is a result of the zone's soil and altitude (averaging 400 metres/1,312 feet); both give its vineyards just the right microclimatic exposure to yield dry, healthy, fully ripe grapes boasting the perfect acidity for sparkling wine.

Yet the still-wine producers in the region felt that they, too, deserved recognition. After all, Miguel Torres grows the grapes for his most expensive Chardonnay in the vineyards of the ruined fortress of Milmanda. If the grapes in these parts are this good, why not give them a name?

The region is named after the village of Barberà de la Conca, but the main town is Montblanc, a modest settlement of some 5,000 people which, like the rest of the DO zone, is situated in the province of Tarragona. Years of hard work were needed to gain the DO, but they resulted in major investment in brand-new wineries. Producers also acknowledged that, if Conca de Barberà were to have an international profile, then it was likely to be for top-quality wines instead of everyday ones. In practice, the region achieves both, as we shall see below.

### Geography and grape varieties

A *conca* (Castilian *cuenca*) is a crater-shaped valley that provides shelter from winds and frost, and exposes at least 135 degrees of arc to the best ripening phases of the sun. In Conca de Barberà, that shelter is enhanced by the surrounding mountain ranges, and the valley is drained by the rivers Francolí and Ganguera – excellent conditions for the healthy, productive vines that grow in the chalky, alluvial soils over a limestone bedrock.

Two-thirds of the vineyard is planted with white grapes, including Macabeo and Parellada, as well as some Chardonnay. For red wines, recommended grapes are Trepat (thought to be a variant of Garnacha), Garnacha Tinta and Ull de Llebre (Tempranillo). There are also extensive plantations of Cabernet Sauvignon and Merlot.

Winemaking is generally ultra-modern. One of the great successes in this region has been a management system that creates two wines in each vintage – a technique that has become an art-form in Conca de Barberà. It works as follows. In well-exposed vineyards, fully ripe grapes are gathered anything up to a month before the main harvest is ready. These are made into wine in less than three weeks, with minimal skin-contact, maximum fruit-extraction and

no malolactic fermentation. Costs are low and the wine can be sold during, or even before, the spring after the vintage. The real benefit is that these wines are run-off into storage tanks before the end of September, when the harvest proper begins. At this time, the main grape crop is gathered and made into wine using the same fermentation vessels as the early crop – effectively halving infrastructure costs for the bodega, as well as allowing it to make both price-sensitive 'supermarket' wines and longer-term, finer wines.

The result is red and white *joven* wines with instant appeal at modest price levels, plus excellent varietal whites (usually Chardonnay) and reds of *crianza* level and above (from Cabernet Sauvignon, Merlot and Ull de Llebre). The style is similar to that of Penedès.

DENOMINACIÓ D'ORIGEN
Pla de BAGES

Formerly known as Artès, the region of Pla de Bages was only recently promoted to the status of a *denominación de origen*. It is centred around the town of Manresa in the west of the province of Barcelona, approximately 70 kilometres (43 miles) northwest of the city of the same name. *Bages* is the name applied to the whole *comarca*, but wines bearing the DO symbol are produced in only 18 towns and villages, including Artès and Manresa itself.

Interestingly enough, the name *Bages* derives from the ancient Roman city of Bacassis, thought to have gained its own name from Bacchus, the god of wine. Whether this means that the region was an important winemaking centre during the Roman occupation or not remains unknown. What we see today is some smart, modern winemaking in the middle highlands of the province of Barcelona, about halfway between the coast and the border with the province of Lérida (Lleida).

The foundation of quality winemaking in these parts is largely intertwined with the history of the Cava business – which is precisely the reason that much of the vineyard land in Pla de Bages is given over to the production of grapes and base-wines for Cava. This heritage notwithstanding, it has also led a number of growers to embark upon their own quest for excellence in non-sparkling wines. The award of the DO is a recognition that the quality standards which apply to Cava grapes are also being realised for grapes being grown for still wines.

## Geography and grape varieties

There has been extensive replanting with French varieties in the Pla de Bages region, mainly in order to take advantage of the area's favourable microclimatic conditions. Altogether, there are some 350 hectares of vines in the DO, located mainly in the valleys of the River Llobregat and its tributaries. They are planted at altitudes ranging between 200 and 500 metres (656 to 1,640 feet) on alluvial and carbonate-based soils.

The climate is inland-Mediterranean, with warm summer nights and hot autumn days, and an average of around 500 millimetres (20 inches) of rainfall. The north – which is roughly 20 kilometres (nine miles) from the Pyrenees – is wetter and slightly cooler than the south, but the overall style is typical of central Catalonia.

At present, the main grape varieties are the Catalan Picapoll and the Macabeo, but plantings of other mainstream varieties such as Tempranillo, Cabernet Sauvignon, Chardonnay and Merlot are increasing all the time. Most of the everyday wines are white, crafted in the traditional light, fresh, *joven* style, but more forward-looking bodegas are turning out some very respectable reds using state-of-the-art equipment.

One such bodega is Ramón Roqueta in Manresa, a smart, modern winery which concentrates primarily on varietal styles. The quality of the wines produced here ranges from good to excellent, and it is this style of winemaking that probably points the way forward for Pla de Bages as a region, once full quality-control is firmly established.

## Notable bodegas

**Cellers Cooperativa d'Artès, Artès.** *Founded 1908.* The biggest and oldest established winery in the region, with 250 members farming some 3,000ha of vines. Not all of the co-op's wares, of course, will carry the DO. The bulk wine is everyday stuff, largely white, and sold throughout the region; only a small minority is bottled and sold nationally and abroad. The brand name is Artium and there is a white *joven* varietal Picapoll and two red *crianzas*: one is made of 80% Cabernet Sauvignon/20% Merlot, while the other is 75% Tempranillo with the rest 'other varieties'; both spend six months in oak. At their best, these rise above the generally perceived quality of co-op wines.

**Masies d'Avinyò, Avinyò.** *Founded 1983.* A smaller, modern bodega with some export business. It makes a white *joven* that is 80% Chardonnay/20% Picapoll, a red *joven* varietal Merlot and a red *crianza* made from 50% Cabernet Sauvignon, 35% Tempranillo and 15% Malbec, with 14 months in cask. A good deal of experimentation takes place here. *Best wine:* the *joven rosado* made from 80% Cabernet Sauvignon and 20% Garnacha.

**Ramón Roqueta, Manresa.** Wines made here are beautifully presented, with labels designed by the modern Catalan artist, Tere Vila Matas. There are whites made from Macabeo (for which they use the French spelling 'Macabeu') and Chardonnay, a *rosado* from Garnacha ('Garnatxa'), and reds from Tempranillo ('Ull de Llebre') and Cabernet Sauvignon.

# Costers del Segre

The Raïmat name is derived from a stone tablet showing a human hand – *mat* in Old Catalan – and a bunch of grapes, or *raïm*. This symbol appears over the entrance to the castle (above).

The Costers del Segre DO is an arid land that has been transformed. The River Segre flows down the Pyrenees near Andorra to join the River Ebro south of the city of Lérida (Lleida in Catalan), and it and its tributaries drain a wide expanse of agricultural land east and west of the city.

The DO zone is divided into four subzones, three of which lie in the east; they are (from north to south) Artesa, Vall de Riucorb and Les Garrigues. These form the vast bulk of the land under vine, but to understand Costers del Segre fully, we must first focus on the westernmost and smallest of the subzones: Raïmat. Well-separated from the others and with almost nothing in common with them in terms of soil, climate or tradition, this subzone is nonetheless responsible for the birth of the DO.

## Manuel Raventós and Raïmat

Its origins lie in one man's vision, conceived nearly 90 years ago. In 1914, Manuel Raventós, boss of Cava company Codorníu, discovered what would become the Raïmat estate. At that time, it was little more than a derelict landscape with poor, salty soils and a ruined castle, but its history of vine-growing stretched back centuries. However, the grapes were not of great quality, and no one bothered to replant vines at all after the phylloxera disaster of the late 19th century.

Raventós realised Raïmat's soil structure would need radical change, but he also knew a canal project linking Catalonia and Aragón was to pass through the estate, providing opportunities for irrigation. He bought the estate and set up an agricultural plan that would, in quality-wine terms, only be fully realised more than 60 years later.

Between the purchase of the estate (1914) and its first commercial vintage (1978), Raventós changed the nature of the soil by gradual and environmentally friendly means. Initially, he planted agricultural plants and pine trees to reduce the saltiness of the soil, starting major work 20 years later once the trees had been harvested. By that time, the new canal was in place and Raïmat could construct its own irrigation systems. The landscape was levelled to allow large-scale planting of fruit orchards and cereals – the next stage in the process of rehabilitating the land. These crops still form part of the estate's output.

In the meantime, a new winery was constructed by Rúbio Bellver, one of the Gaudí school of architects, and experimental vineyard plantations were put into constant trials. (The new winery made history by being the first building in Spain to be made of concrete.)

It quickly became apparent that the classic Catalan grape varieties simply did not flourish at Raïmat – and not just because of its salty soil. Much further inland than most Catalan vineyards, the estate is drier, with an average rainfall of 300 millimetres (12 inches). There are also wide temperature swings during the ripening season. The answer to Raïmat's problems lay in finding grapes which did well under similar conditions. In Spain, that meant Tempranillo, but French varieties that had evolved in a cooler climate might also be suitable.

The Raventós family had close contacts with Fresno and Davis universities in California, both of which are leaders in the field of viticultural and oenological practice. After a thorough study of the soil and climatic conditions at Raïmat, it was suggested that the right combination of French vines on new-wave American rootstocks (notably Agro-2000) would do the trick. Early vintages were successful, and a new winery was commissioned in the early 1980s (see page 100). Designed by architect Domingo Triay, it sits half-buried in the ground (to maintain constant temperatures) with a working vineyard on the 'roof'. There is nowhere like it in Spain.

## The DO as a whole

And the rest of the region? The *consejo regulador* has six members, including Codorníu at Raïmat; the other five range from established boutique wineries to co-ops. Some cynics claim the DO was originally cobbled together simply because it was embarrassing to have a giant operation such as Raïmat in a region with no other contenders. Whatever the case, Costers del Segre has certainly encouraged smaller, more obscure producers to give of their best. Today, it offers a range of very good to exceptional wines, from classically Catalan to... what shall we say: Catalifornian?

For red wines, the DO authorises Cabernet Sauvignon, Merlot, Ull de Llebre (Tempranillo; often called *Gotim Bru* or 'brown bunch'), Monastrell, Garnacha, Pinot Noir, Trepat and Mazuelo (Cariñena). For whites, Chardonnay, Macabeo, Xarel-lo, Parellada and Garnacha Blanca are grown. There are also experimental plantations of Syrah, Sauvignon Blanc and Albariño grapes which are not currently permitted in wines with DO status. Quality is generally high, as the smaller wineries have struggled to capitalise on their individuality, the local climate and soil conditions. In the three eastern subzones, the style is geared more towards Tempranillo and Garnacha for reds and the 'big three' Catalan white grapes (Parellada, Macabeo, Xarel-lo) for white wines.

# Notable bodegas

Rai = Raïmat; Art = Artesa;
VdR = Vall de Riucorb.

## Castell del Remei, La Fuliola (VdR). *Founded 1871.* Unusual site

including a beautiful *ermita* (chapel), a working restaurant and a stately home as well as extensive vineyards (40ha) and ancient cellars. Relatively small-scale (about 1,500hl), and its wines are sold under the Castell del Remei brand name. The basic white is called Blanc Planell, and there is a very good white *joven* (50% Chardonnay/50% Sauvignon Blanc). The *rosado* (100% Merlot) is excellent, but the red *crianza* wines are the most famous. There is an excellent varietal (100%) Merlot with nine months' oak. *Best wine:* the varietal Cabernet Sauvignon (15% Tempranillo; eight months in oak).

## L'Olivera Cooperativa, Valbona de las Monges (VdR). *Founded 1989.* Very small operation based on

a previous co-op, farming 10ha and buying in to make up the difference. The wines (all white) are exemplary. The basic one is called Blanc de Scré (60% Macabeo/30% Parellada/10% Chardonnay); better still is L'Olivera *crianza* (same grape mix but with six months in oak). Next up in quality are three barrel-fermented varietals with six months on the lees: L'Olivera Missenyora (selected Macabeo), L'Olivera Chardonnay and L'Olivera Macabeo; all are excellent.
*Best wine:* L'Olivera Parellada/ Chardonnay (66% and 34% mix) barrel-fermentedl with six months on the lees.

## Parnás, Raïmat (Rai). Wholly owned

subsidiary of Raïmat (*see* below), producing a range of wines under the Parnás label. The white Parnás Garbi is good; the *rosado* is better, with an eclectic and expensive grape mix (50% Cabernet Sauvignon/40% Pinot Noir/ 10% Chardonnay). *Best wine:* the red Parnás Mistral *crianza* .

## Raïmat, Raïmat (Rai). *Founded 1914.* Some 1,200ha of 3,000ha of

land are devoted to vines, winemaking is state-of-the-art and the style is very much California-on-toast. All wines are sold under the Raïmat label. Classic varietals include Chardonnay *joven* and Chardonnay Selección Especial. There is also a Clos Casal white *joven* and two *rosados*, both *joven*. Raïmat red varietals include Cabernet Sauvignon, Merlot, Pinot Noir and Tempranillo, made to *crianza* or *reserva* level. *Best wines:* Raïmat Abadía is a Cabernet Sauvignon/Tempranillo/Merlot blend in *crianza* and *reserva* styles (both with 18 months oak). Raïmat Clamor is a single-vineyard *crianza* (typically 45% Cabernet Sauvignon/20% Tempranillo/ 10% Cariñena and Pinot Noir/5% Garnacha; 12 months oak).

## Vall de Baldomar, Baldomar (Art). *Founded 1989.* Small firm with around

25ha; originally made *rosados* from Cabernet Sauvignon and Monastrell. Now also makes Baldoma white *joven* (90% Macabeo/10% Müller-Thurgau), Cristiari white *joven* (100% Müller-Thurgau) and a red Baldoma *joven* (40% Cabernet Sauvignon/40% Merlot/10% Monastrell).

**Far right:** The old bodega of the Raïmat estate at Lérida, designed by one of the students of the Gaudí school of architecture.

**PENEDÈS**
DENOMINACIÓ D´ORIGEN

# Penedès

The shift in Penedès' fortunes as a wine region can be traced back to 1960, when Barcelona began to prosper. At that time, the city's mayor, irritated by inferior local examples, promised financial help to any winemaker who turned his or her production over to red wines.

The nearest large-scale wine region was Penedès, but frankly, it was not promising red-wine country. Its climate, soils and seafood tradition all suggested white and *rosado* wines. Still, many of the best Cava vineyards were located there, which meant that high-quality vineyard practice was already being used; replanting with Cabernet Sauvignon and Tempranillo was but the work of a few years. By the early 1970s, it looked as if Penedès could produce more or less anything it wanted. Its secret? Microclimates.

There are three levels of land between the Penedès coast and the great central Meseta of Spain, starting with the low Penedès (*baix-Penedès* in Catalan), which ranges from sea level to 250 metres (820 feet) in altitude. Here, vines yield Garnacha, Monastrell and Cariñena for red wines and the 'big three' Catalan varieties (Macabeo, Xarel-lo and Parellada) for everyday whites. Next is the middle Penedès (*mitja-Penedès*), at between 250 and 500 metres (820 and 1,640 feet). Most of the 'big three' Cava grapes are grown at this generally cooler level, but it is also where the best Cabernet Sauvignon, Merlot and Tempranillo are found.

Highest of all is the high Penedès (*alt-Penedès*), which reaches from 500 to 850 metres (1,640 to 2,789 feet). Here, the most delicate grapes are grown: Chardonnay, Pinot Noir, Cabernet Franc, Gewürztraminer, Riesling *et al*. The climate is similar to that of northern France, but with one important difference: nights may be cold and the danger of frost omnipresent, but summer and autumn routinely offer the long, golden days necessary to deliver fully ripe grapes.

Altitudes aside, Penedès is really a mixture of bluffs and coves, hillsides and *concas*, terraces and hidden valleys, all dominated by the magnificent Montserrat mountain range (symbol of the Catalan nation) and offering almost every imaginable microclimate. Vine-growers in general (and Miguel Torres in particular) have not been slow to capitalise on them. Many of Penedès' best wines are sourced from grapes grown in small quantities from individual vineyards at the higher levels.

## Viticulture

The 'big three' Catalan white grapes and Chardonnay represent about 80 per cent of the vineyard, but Subirat-Parent (Malvasía Riojana), Moscatel de Alejandria (Muscat d'Alexandrie), Moscatel de Frontignac (Muscat de Frontignan), Chenin Blanc and Sauvignon Blanc are also grown for white wines. Additional red varieties include the local Samsó grape, but more than 120 varieties are native to Catalonia: any of them could suddenly find a new lease of life if it reveals hidden talents in on-going tests. Not surprisingly, Miguel Torres has the largest plantation of Catalan grapes in the entire region.

Penedès had overseen the development of Cava, the introduction of French and other north-European grape varieties, and the establishment of modern stainless-steel winemaking technology. Yet the region is also the leading source of another development in the winemaking world – and this, too, has been implemented by Miguel Torres.

Below: Regular samples of wine are taken from stainless-steel fermentation tanks at the Torres estate, one of the region's main innovators.

In the past, people planted as many vines as could be squeezed into the available land; since all were fighting for the same water and nutrients, many of them withered and died. For this reason, every *consejo regulador* sets a maximum number of vines which may be planted in any one hectare – typically from 2,500 to around 4,000.

At 4,000 to 5,000 vines per hectare, the limit in Penedès is higher than most, due to its favoured soils and exposure, but Torres is trying out a new theory. He is planting at 6,000 to 7,000 vines per hectare, which means that while the vines have to fight in order to produce grapes, they do not have to die trying. Instead, an inspection prior to the vintage will reveal which are producing the best grapes. Those on the 'losers' can then be removed and ploughed back as fertiliser, thereby channeling all the goodness to the best vines. This technique is also being tested in the Priorato and

Ribera del Duero DOs in Spain, and the Bordeaux AC in France. It lowers production quantities but increases quality, and represents a probable way for mature vineyards to achieve the highest levels – yet vineyard owners must be sure of a commensurately higher price for the better wine to make it work.

The result of this experimentation is that Penedès now offers three ranges of wine. There are good, everyday *jovenes* in all three colours selling at modest prices; individual, high-quality vineyard wines made from 'noble' grapes (Cabernet Sauvignon, Chardonnay *et al*); and finally, the old *rancios*, *vinos de licor* and Moscatels a returning Roman ghost would recognise. Penedès has almost become a wine-producing country in its own right, producing a style to suit every taste – which partly explains its brilliant commercial success.

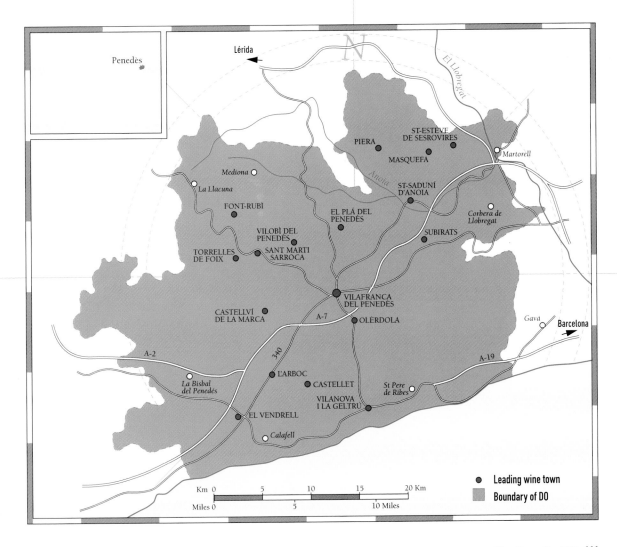

# Notable bodegas

**Note:** most bodegas listed below also produce Cava, but *Cavas* in a company name does not necessarily imply that sparkling wine is made there. In Catalonia, the term is used for 'cellars' in the same way as *bodegas* is used elsewhere in Spain. Similarly, *can* is the equivalent of the French *chez*, and *mas* or *masía* implies a small agricultural settlement which may or may not belong to one family.

### Albet i Noya, San Pau d'Ordal Subirats. *Founded 1980.*
Family-run estate with 26ha, and vines and wines are classified as 'ecological': a halfway stage between mainstream and organic. The wines are excellent, with varietals to the fore, including a white Xarel-lo *joven* (they use the term *anyada* but it means the same thing) and a barrel-fermented Chardonnay with six months on its lees, which makes it *crianza*. There are also splendid varietal red *crianzas* from Cabernet Sauvignon and Tempranillo with 12 months in oak. *Best wine:* a stunning Tempranillo *joven* – one of the best of its kind from anywhere in Catalonia.

### Alsina i Sardá, Plà del Penedès. *Founded 1986.*
Primarily a Cava house making some Penedès DO wines. *Best wines:* the reds Alsina i Sardá *crianza* and Castillo de Fontellada *reserva* (both Cabernet Sauvignon).

### L'Arboç 'Caycra' Cooperativa, L'Arboç del Penedès. *Founded 1919.*
The co-op's 400 members farm 800ha, and have the very latest winemaking kit and a passion for quality. The main business is Cava, but the members turn out some very good Penedès DO wines, with *jovenes* in all three colours under the D'Arcyac label. *Best wines:* those

called Pupitre, which include three varietals: Chardonnay, Xarel-lo and Cabernet Sauvignon.

### Can Feixes, Cabrera d'Anoia. *Founded 1945.*
Family firm with 75ha producing around 1,000hl, mainly Cava. Still wines with the Penedès DO offer a white and a red under the bodega's own name. The white *joven* is typically 50% Parellada, 25% Macabeo and 25% Chardonnay. The red is a *crianza* made from 70% Cabernet Sauvignon/30% Tempranillo, with eight months in oak. Both wines are very good, but the white occasionally achieves excellence.

### Can Rafols Dels Caus, Avinyonet del Penedès. *Founded 1980.*
This firm occupies a splendid old *masía* and was a pioneer in the planting of French grape varieties. Today, it owns 35ha and makes wine solely from its own grapes, both Cava and still wines with the Penedès DO. Wines are exemplary and include Petit Caus white *joven*; Gran Caus barrel-fermented Chardonnay; Gran Caus *rosado* (100% Merlot); Caus Lubis red *crianza* (100% Merlot; eight months in oak) and Gran Caus *crianza* (typically 55% Cabernet Franc/30% Cabernet Sauvignon/15% Merlot; nine months in oak).

### Can Suriol del Castell, Fontrubí. *Founded 1980.*
Small, private firm farming 20ha, mainly for Cava. Also makes a couple of worthwhile Penedès wines: Suriol (a 'big-three' mix) and Suriol Chenin Blanc, both *jovenes*.

### Capita Vidal, Plà de Penedès. *Founded 1990.*
Mainly a Cava company, though it makes some good still wines from its own 50ha. Capita Vidal *rosado* is a *joven* made from 60% Garnacha/20% Tempranillo/20% Cariñena. *Best wine: a* white made from 40% Xarel-lo/35% Macabeo/25% Parellada, also *joven*.

### Cavas Gramona, Sant Sadurní d'Anoia. *Founded 1921.*
Cava house, now run by the fourth generation of the same family, farming 15ha as well as buying in grapes. Still-wine production under the Penedès DO totals about 500hl. *Best wines:* the Gramona Chardonnay Gran Cru *joven* and the *aguja* (slightly sparkling) Moustillant Brut (70% Parellada/30% Macabeo).

### Cavas Hill, Moja Olderdola. *Founded 1887.*
One of the best-known and most stylish (in packaging terms) Penedès bodegas with 60ha plus bought-in grapes to make a total of around 3,500hl. Quality is uniformly excellent; the range is wide, including: (whites) Blanc Bruc Hill (60% Xarel-lo/30% Macabeo/10% Parellada), Blanc Cru Hill (60% Macabeo/40% Xarel-lo), Chardonnay Hill (100% barrel- fermented Chardonnay; four months on the lees) and Timón Hill *aguja* (60% Macabeo/40% Xarel-lo). Also an interesting *semiseco* called Oro Penedès (50% Xarel-lo/50% Parellada). There are two *rosados*: Castell Roc Hill and an *aguja* Timón Hill; all are *jovenes*. *Best wines:* reds Masía Hill *joven* (100% Tempranillo), Gran Civet Hill *crianza* (60% Garnacha/40% Cariñena; ten months oak), Cabernet Sauvignon Hill *crianza* (12 months oak) and Gran Toc Hill *reserva* (60% Tempranillo/40% Garnacha; 18 months oak).All are excellent.

### Cavas Josep Masachs, Vilafranca del Penedès. *Founded 1920.*
Primarily a Cava house but with some excellent Penedès wines. *Best wines:* (white) Josep Masachs Chardonnay *joven* and Painous *joven* (35% Xarel-lo/35% Parellada/30% Macabeo), and an interesting Painous *semidulce* (40% Parellada/30% Xarel-lo/30% Macabeo).

### Cavas Lavernoya, Sant Sadurní d'Anoia. *Founded 1890.*
Owns 100ha and produces around 1,200hl per year, including Cava. *Best wines:* the Lavernoya white *joven* (30% Chardonnay/30% Xarel-lo/25% Macabeo/15% Parellada) and the Lavernoya Cabernet Sauvignon *reserva* (eight months in oak).

### Conde de Caralt, Sant Sadurní d'Anoia. *Founded 1969.*
Part of the Freixenet empire and largely devoted to Cava, but turns out some very good Penedès wines, including a *blanc de blancs joven* (40% Xarel-lo/ 30% Macabeo/30% Parellada) and a varietal Chardonnay with two months in oak. *Best wine:* an excellent red *reserva* (typically 85% Tempranillo/ 15% Cabernet Sauvignon; 18 months oak).

### CoViDes, Vilafranca del Penedès. *Founded 1962.*
Very large co-op (the name is an acronym of *Cooperativa Vinícola del Penedès*) with three major bodegas throughout the region, and 800 members producing 300,000hl. Mainly in the Cava business, although there are some excellent Penedès wines. Main label is Duc de Foix and the range includes a white *joven* (35% Parellada/35% Xarel-lo/30% Macabeo), two varietal *jovenes* (Xarel-lo and Parellada), a Chardonnay *crianza* and two red *reservas*, one 70% Cabernet Sauvignon/30% Tempranillo and the other a varietal Cabernet. The more 'traditional' label Moli de Foc offers *jovenes* 'big three' (white), 50% Tempranillo/50% Cariñena (*rosado*), and 70% Tempranillo/30% Cariñena (red). These are very good wines, occasionally excellent.

### Grimau de Pujades, Castellví de la Marca.
Small firm dealing mainly in Cava and producing about 1,000hl. Penedès wines include a good white *joven* called Grimau Blanc de Blancs

(45% Macabeo/35% Xarel-lo/20% Parellada) and a *rosado joven* called Grimau (60% Cabernet Sauvignon/ 40% Tempranillo).

### Grimau Goll-Duart de Siò, Vilafranca del Penedès.

*Founded 1987.* Makes around 4,000hl of wine, mainly Cava. Under the Penedès DO, the main brand name is Duart de Siò (DdS) and the white-wine range includes a *joven aguja* varietal Macabeo called DdS Brisasol, a varietal *crianza* Parellada called DdS Caliu and a 'big three' mix called DdS Primavera. For reds, DdS

Gitana is a varietal Cabernet Sauvignon *joven*, and DdS Grana offers a red varietal Tempranillo *joven* and a Cabernet Sauvignon *crianza*. Very good.

### Heretat Mont-Rubí, Esplugas de Llobregat.

Single-estate winery with 110 acres under vine, producing mainly Cava. However, there are two excellent Penedès *joven* wines (one white, one *rosado*) under the Heretat-Mont Rubí label: Blanc d'Anyada (45% Parellada 35%/Macabeo/20% Xarel-lo) and Rosat Nature (80% Cariñena/ 20% Tempranillo).

### Jané Ventura, El Vendrell.

*Founded 1914.* Buys in most grapes but also has 15ha; makes about 1,500hl of Penedès wines and some Cava. Wines are uniformly good and include a white *joven* (50% Xarel-lo/ 50% Parellada), a *rosado joven* (50% Tempranillo/50% Cariñena) and a varietal Cabernet Sauvignon in both *crianza* and *reserva* styles.

### Jaume Serra, Vilanova i la Geltrú.

*Founded 1943.* Since 1986, this firm has been based in a fine old *masía* in the seaside town of Vilanova, with 30ha of vines. Buys in grapes to

**Below:** Sheep graze on vines left over from the harvest at the wine estate of restaurateur Jean León, in Torrelavit.

make up its total needs and makes Cava as well as Penedès wines. Wines carry the Jaume Serra label and are of reliably good quality, most notably the white *joven* Opera Prima (40% Macabeo/30% Parellada/30% Chardonnay); two good *rosados*, both *joven* – Albatros *aguja* (50% Tempranillo/50% Garnacha) and a varietal Cabernet Sauvignon; and two varietal reds.

### Jean León, Torrelavit.

*Founded 1963.* The other great pioneer of French grape varieties. Jean León made his fortune in the restaurant business in America and returned to Catalonia to set up a winery. The first commercial vintage was in 1969 and the wines achieved international recognition by the mid-1970s. In 1995, León returned to California to concentrate on his restaurants; his wines are now marketed on his behalf by Miguel Torres. Today, the estate has 60ha and yields an average annual 1,500hl. Quite simply, León's best wines are among the best Penedès has to offer. There's a white varietal Chardonnay *crianza* and *crianza* and *reserva* reds made from (typically) 85% Cabernet Sauvignon and 15% Cabernet Franc. *Best wine:* the red *reserva* from a great vintage year – it must be one of the best Cabernet-based red wines of the world.

### Joan Raventós Rosell, Masquefa.

*Founded 1985.* Has 60ha and buys in grapes to yield an annual 1,400hl. The brand name is Heretat Vall-Ventos; the quality is never less than excellent. There are four white *jovenes:* Blanc Primer (60% Macabeo/ 30% Chardonnay/10% Pinot Noir), a varietal Chardonnay, a varietal Pinot Blanc and a varietal Sauvignon Blanc which can attain 13.5% abv. There are also two *rosado* varietal *jovenes* – a Pinot Noir and a Merlot.

### Juvé y Camps, Sant Sadurní d'Anoia. *Founded 1921.* Big outfit (*see* Cava) with a reputation for high quality in all it does. Owns 380ha in various parts of the region and turns out 20,000hl, of which 90% is Cava. Penedès wines are the white *joven* Ermita d'Espiells (40% Macabeo/ 40% Parellada/20% Xarel-lo) and the varietal *crianza* La Miranda d'Espiells Chardonnay with six months in oak.

### Manuel Sancho y Hijas, Castellví de la Marca. *Founded 1975.*
This bodega produced its first commercial vintage in 1981. The vineyard amounts to 48ha which, with bought-in grapes, yield a current production of 6,000hl. Most is of Cava, but Penedès wines are made under the Mont Marçal label. *Best wines:* the white *joven* Vi Novell (40% Xarel-lo/ 30% Macabeo/20% Parellada) and the red *reserva* (80% Tempranillo/20% Cabernet Sauvignon; 12 months oak).

### Marqués de Monistrol, Sant Sadurní d'Anoia. *Founded 1882.*
Primarily a Cava house but also produces some excellent Penedès wines under the company name. These include two white *jovenes:* Vin Nature Blanc de Blancs ('big three' grapes) and Vin Nature Blanc en Noirs (Xarel-lo/Parellada). *Blanc en Noirs* in this context means 'white wine made in the manner of red wine' – *ie* with skin-contact, and should not be confused with *Blanc de Noirs:* white wine made from black grapes. There is also a varietal Chardonnay. *Best wines:* a red *reserva* (Cabernet Sauvignon/Tempranillo; 22 months in oak), and varietal Merlot *crianza* (nine months in oak).

**Below:** Vineyards such as this one in the Penedès DO turn out grapes destined for some of Spain's most popular red wines.

**Masía Bach, San Esteve de Sesrovires.** *Founded 1921.* This company was taken over by Codorníu in 1975. The elegant *masía*, the grounds, extensive vineyards and bodega have been immaculately preserved. There are 300ha planted with both Catalan and French varieties, and the company also buys in grapes to produce an annual 36,000hl of wines of uniformly excellent quality. Main brand name is Bach, and the range includes two white *jovenes*: Extrísimo Seco (35% Chardonnay/30% Xarel-lo/15% Macabeo/10% Chenin Blanc) and Magnificat (75% Chardonnay/25% Sauvignon Blanc; two months in oak). There is an interesting 55% Cabernet Sauvignon/45% Tempranillo *rosado joven*; red wines include a splendid Cabernet Sauvignon (15% Tempranillo) *crianza* with 12 months in oak. *Best wines:* the medium-sweet Extrísimo Bach and the Viña Extrísima red *reserva*; in great years, the latter is one of the finest wines of the region.

**Masía Vallformosa, Viloví del Penedès.** *Founded 1978.* Family-owned firm in a beautiful neo-Catalan building with a smart, modern winery and 307ha of vines. Best known abroad as a Cava house, but around 55% of its 20,000+ hl production is of Penedès wines, made from both Catalan and French varieties. White wines are all *joven*, and come in *aguja* and *semidulce* (70% Macabeo/30% Muscat) styles, including a varietal Chardonnay. Reds are generally very good, and include a classic *gran reserva* (75% Tempranillo /25% Cabernet Sauvignon; 30 months in oak) as well as a varietal Cabernet Sauvignon *reserva* (15% Merlot; 24 months in oak).

**Miguel Torres, Vilafranca del Penedès.** *Founded 1870.* The pioneering company profiled on pages 102-3. Torres maintains a unique plantation of more than 100 obscure native Catalan grape varieties at his *finca* (farm) Rabell de Fontenac and is constantly experimenting with new ways of using them. The firm's international fame has been built on innovation, impeccable winemaking, inspired marketing and quality-control. Until relatively recently, the Torres name was worth more on international markets than the Penedès DO, but all the firm's wines are now labelled under the auspices of the *consejo regulador*. Torres' vineyards now extend to nearly 1,000ha throughout Penedès; its winery is one of the most modern in the world. The range of wines is exemplary: whites include the *jovenes* Viña Sol (Parellada), Gran Viña Sol (85% Chardonnay/15% Parellada; three months in oak), Viña Esmeralda (85% Muscat/15% Gewürztraminer), and Waltraud (Riesling) named after Miguel Torres' German-born wife. There are two white *crianzas*: Milmanda (single-vineyard barrel-fermented Chardonnay; eight months on its lees) and Fransola (single-vineyard 85% Sauvignon Blanc/15% Parellada; six months in oak). The *semidulce* San Valentín is made from Parellada. De Casta is a *rosado joven* (65% Garnacha/35% Cariñena). Red wines start with the *jovenes* Viña Magdala (85% Pinot Noir/15% Tempranillo), Mas Borras (single-vineyard 100% Pinot Noir; two months in oak) and Viña Las Torres (100% Merlot; two months in oak). In the *crianza* zone there are Coronas (85% Tempranillo/15% Cabernet Sauvignon; 15 months in oak) and Sangre de Toro (65% Garnacha/35% Cariñena). *Reserva* wines include Gran Coronas (85% Cabernet Sauvignon/15% Tempranillo; 18 months in oak), Gran Sangre de Toro (70% Garnacha/30% Cariñena) and Mas la Plana (single-vineyard Cabernet Sauvignon; 18 months in oak), which used to be known as Gran Coronas Black Label. *Best wines:* the single-vineyard wines are among the best Penedès has to offer, but nothing is less than first-rate.

**Molí Coloma, Subirats.** *Founded 1984.* Family firm with 60ha which also buys in grapes to produce 3,000hl, split between Cava and white-only *joven* Penedès wines. Brand names are Claverol Blanc de Blancs (50% Parellada/30% Macabeo/20% Xarel-lo) and Sumarroca for varietals Chardonnay and Gewürztraminer. All wines are very good to excellent.

**Olivella Sadurní, Subirats.** *Founded 1987.* Begun in a 15th-century *masía* surrounded by 85ha of vineyards, this family-owned company makes very good wines from both Catalan and French grapes. All wines are *joven*, and include the white Prima Lux (75% Xarel-lo/15% Chardonnay/10% Parellada), *rosado* Prima Juventa (85% Cabernet Sauvignon/15% Merlot), and red Prima Vesper (85% Cabernet Sauvignon/15% Merlot).

**Parató Vinícola, Plà del Penedès.** *Founded 1975.* Bodega with 75ha, producing over 1,000hl of wine per year, including a substantial proportion of Cava. Penedès DO wines (all *joven*) include a 'big three' white called Parató Blanc Coupage (50% Macabeo/30% Parellada/20% Xarel-lo), a varietal Xarel-lo and a *rosado* varietal Pinot Noir.

**Puig Roca, El Vendrell.** *Founded 1991.* Small bodega with ten hectares producing about 700hl per year. The brand name uses Roman capital letters – AVGVSTVS – and the range is entirely varietal (with additions): the barrel-fermented Chardonnay with five months on its lees is still technically *joven*; the Merlot *joven* has two months in oak; Cabernet Sauvignon *crianza* has a little Merlot and Cabernet Franc and six months in oak. These wines are uniformly excellent.

**Raventós i Blanc, Sant Sadurní d'Anoia.** *Founded 1986.* Begun by an offshoot of the Raventós family which owns Codorníu. Mainly a Cava house with 130ha of vines and an annual production of some 5,000hl. *Best wines:* the excellent whites El Preludi ('big three') and Chardonnay (both *jovenes*).

**René Barbier, Sant Sadurní d'Anoia.** *Founded 1880.* Now part of the Freixenet group (*see* Cava DO) and not to be confused with René Barbier *fill* (*see* Priorato DO), this bodega makes only Penedès wines from its own vineyards as well as bought-in grapes and ready-made wines. There's a very good *rosado joven* (Tempranillo/ Garnacha/ Monastrell). Most interesting, however, is the classic Viña Augusta *semidulce*, and best value must be the red and white *jovenes* sold simply as 'Mediterranean White' and 'Mediterranean Red' at very modest prices (the white has the edge). *Best wines:* a white *joven* called Kraliner, made from 'big three' grapes; also a red *reserva* (Tempranillo/ Garnacha/Cabernet Sauvignon), though there is a good varietal Cabernet Sauvignon *crianza* (12 months in oak).

**Sadeve, Torrelavit.** *Founded 1984.* This estate has 100ha of vines and 90% of its production is Cava, but also turns out about 750hl of Penedès wines. *Best wines:* the Manuela de Naveran barrel-fermented Chardonnay (three months on its lees), and the red *gran reserva* varietal Cabernet Sauvignon.

# Terra Alta

As its name implies, *Terra Alta* is a highland region located in the extreme south of Catalonia. It borders the *autonomía* of Aragón in the east and comes within a few kilometres of the *Comunidad de Valencia* in the south. The main town is Gandesa, which boasts a local co-op in a magnificent art deco building as well as a couple of more modern, new-wave wineries.

Out in the countryside, however, this is still a land of sleepy local co-ops, many of which do not even bottle their wine. In Gandesa there is some movement; the major co-op has made great strides, and there is evidence of boutique wineries taking an interest in the region's potential (Bàrbara Forés is a good example). Sadly, these are still in the minority.

On the face of it, there is no real reason why Terra Alta should not produce wines at least as good as those of Tarragona and even approaching Priorato standards. The vineyards are positioned at heights of about 400 metres (1,312 feet), providing excellent microclimatic opportunities. The soils are good, with plenty of limestone and good drainage. They are also relatively easy to work. Perhaps what is lacking here is investment; after all, it has taken several centuries for the new-wave bodegas of Priorato to overtake those making traditional wines. Tarragona is starting to flex its muscles. Perhaps Terra Alta will be next.

## The Cava dilemma

Cava grapes are a factor here, too – but in a comparatively negative way. Whereas elsewhere, the example set by growers of grapes for the Cava industry has been followed by other growers wanting to turn out still wines of similar quality, in Terra Alta it seems to have had the opposite effect. The Cava business brings in good money from outside; they can sell all their own wine locally – without even bottling it in many cases. Why should they worry? In addition, there is still a buoyant local market for *rancios*, *dulces* and *mistelas* (unfermented grape-juice plus spirit) made in the old style. What are the incentives to reinvest?

Fortunately, however, that point of view is not universal. The Gandesa co-op has grasped the nettle and is re-equipping itself with new winemaking technology, and several smaller independent bodegas have sprung up in the past five to ten years. The *consejo regulador* has been quick to respond to the new needs of the marketplace; originally the major grape hereabouts was Garnacha Blanca (75 per cent of the vineyard) with Macabeo, Cariñena and Garnacha making up most of the rest.

Garnacha Blanca is a pleasant and reliable grape, but not the stuff of which great wines are made. Therefore, in 1995 the *consejo regulador* approved an addition to the recommended varieties, adding Parellada and Moscatel to the white-grape list and Tempranillo, Cabernet Sauvignon and Merlot to the reds. It is perhaps a bit early to assess the development these grapes have enjoyed, but at least it means that someone, somewhere, is pushing for quality.

The ingredients are certainly all in place for quality wine production, giving the region enormous potential. In the next century, we may well see great wines originating from Terra Alta.

**Below: The main wine town of Gandesa lies on the plateau, or 'high land', of the Terra Alta DO. Conditions here produce high-quality grapes.**

## Notable bodegas

**Bàrbara Forés, Gandesa.**
*Founded 1994.* This bodega began in a lovely old building dating from 1889, which is in the process of being restored. Bàrbara Forés (1825-1905) was a winemaking pioneer of the 19th century, and her son, Rafael Ferrer, built the bodega and equipped it for bottling wine – something of an innovation in the last century. Their descendant, Carme Ferrer, and her husband, Manuel Sanmartín, did the restoration work and put the bodega back to work

in 1994. Today, they farm 15.5ha in four individual plots around the town of Gandesa. Wines are only white and *rosado*, both *jovenes* (although they have grander ambitions for the future); both are sold under the Bàrbara Forés label. The white is mainly Garnacha Blanca with a little Macabeo, and the *rosado* is mainly Garnacha Tinta with a hint of Alliers oak. However, the vineyards also have plantations of Cariñena, Cabernet Sauvignon and Syrah, so who knows what we may see in a few years' time? At the moment, the wines are good to very good.

**De Muller.** This Tarragona-based house has some holdings in Terra Alta and turns out an excellent traditional *dulce* under the name Vino de Misa.

**Gandesa Cooperativa, Gandesa.**
*Founded 1919.* Situated in one of those magnificent art nouveau buildings designed by Cèsar Martinell, a pupil of Antoní Gaudí. Its 400 members farm some 1,200ha, producing around 28,000hl of wine. Much of this is of everyday quality and sold under the Antic Castell label, but the co-op is also making

some very good wines under the Garidells label. *Best wine:* the red *joven* Garnacha.

**Pedro Rovira, Gandesa.**
Tarragona-based house making communion wine, Moscatel and *dulces* in the traditional style. *Best wine:* an excellent white *joven* called Blanc de Belart (75% Macabeo/25% Garnacha Blanca).

# Priorato

Priorato is Spain's most traditional and yet most modern, exciting region. In the tiny village of Scala Dei, wine styles have hardly changed in 500 years. In the town of Gratallops, there are wines of such quality (and price) as to gladden the heart of an international auctioneer. All this from one of the most remote highland locations in Catalonia.

Priorato lies in the Tarragona province. It is almost entirely surrounded by the Tarragona DO zone, but its microclimates and soil structure are unique. The vineyards are situated between 100 to 700 metres (328 to 2,297 feet), planted on terraces up craggy escarpments or buried deep in lonely mountain valleys. The range of microclimates includes Alpine meadows, windy natural amphitheatres and valleys surrounded by astonishingly steep cliffs.

The name *Priorato* means 'priory', and the zone takes its name from the Priorato de Scala Dei. The story goes that some 800 years ago, a shepherd boy out tending his flocks awoke one night to see angels descending from a celestial ladder. He told the local priest about his vision, and in 1163, an order of Carthusian monks came to the area and established the *Priorato de Scala Dei* – the 'Priory of the Stairway of God'. The *comarca* took the name of the monastery, and a small village grew up nearby. The monks are gone, but the village remains, with some 28 inhabitants and one of the region's most famous bodegas – Cellers Scala Dei – making wine in the old priory cellars.

There are 11 villages within the DO, and the wines they make are unique in Spain. Part of this is due to the region's topography. The River Siurana (a tributary of the Ebro) runs through Priorato, fed by sources high up the mountainsides. The bedrock is also vital, part of the schist stratum that also provides the bedrock for the finest Port vineyards of the Douro in Portugal.

## Geology and viticulture

Schist is almost perfect for vines. Its crystalline structure provides apertures for vine-root tendrils as well as space for storing rainwater for use during the ripening period – especially important in highland areas such as Gratallops, where the topsoil can be eroded and dry.

Down in the river valleys, the bedrock is slate with alluvial topsoils. Here, too, is abundant water for vines – although the style of wine made from them is very different. The most characteristic soil of the region is called

Right: The new face of Priorato. The natural amphitheatre that is Clos l'Ermita is home to 100-year-old Garnacha vines. Yields are small, but the wines are among the finest in Spain.

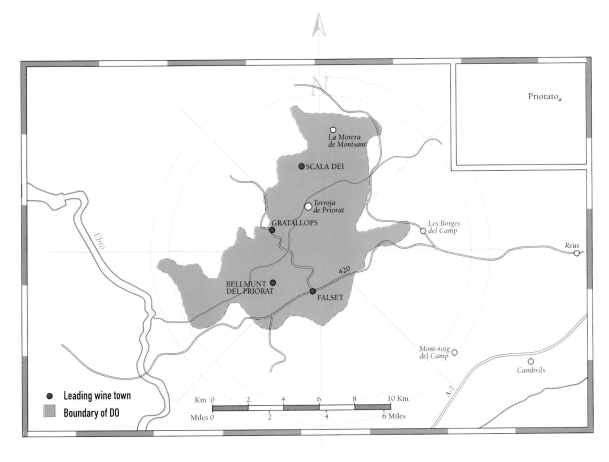

La Morera
de Montsant

SCALA DEI

Torroja
de Priorat

GRATALLOPS

Les Borges
del Camp

Ebro

Reus

420

BELLMUNT
DEL PRIORAT

FALSET

Mont-roig
del Camp

Cambrils

A-7

Priorato

● Leading wine town

Boundary of DO

Km 0    2    4    6    8    10 Km
Miles 0        2        4        6 Miles

Here, in the mid-1980s, a group of winemakers invested jointly in eight plots of vineyard land, high up in the Siurana Valley on schistose soils. The idea was to plant the best grapes, harvest low yields, and make wines in a small cooperative winery. All would be called *Clos-* something to differentiate them from the region's traditional wines. The grapes used by the group and the methods it employed (including drip-feed irrigation) ruled the resulting wines out of the DO, but this did not concern those involved. Once their wines started to win medals at national and international tastings, the *viñeros'* theories were vindicated.

The survivors of this original group include Alvaro Palacios, Costers del Siurana, Mas Martinet and René Barbier *fill* ('son' – not the same as the René Barbier company in Penedès; *see* below). All are now independent and members of the *consejo regulador*, producing wines with the Priorato DO.

## The Gratallops legacy

The 'Gratallops pioneers' proved beyond doubt that Garnacha and Cariñena are perfectly capable of producing highly complex, quality wine – as long as yields are low. The result is that Gratallops wines are among the most stunning in all of Spain: cooler, fresher and less oaky than the traditional north-Spanish red. Their concentration and character are outstanding – as is their price.

Meanwhile, the old ways are still used in more traditional Priorato villages. But here, too, low yields result in deeply concentrated, high-alcohol wines of tremendous individuality. They need five years in bottle before drinking, and will age gracefully up to 25 years. The tiny winery at Scala Dei still ferments in concrete vats (albeit with cooling *placas* suspended in the wine) and makes an almost-black Garnacha wine called Cartoixa Scala Dei with a natural strength of up to 15 per cent alcohol by volume (abv). It is something of a niche-market wine, but those who love it do so with a passion.

There are other wines in Priorato, including some experimental *novel* styles and a good supply of light, fresh, everyday *joven* wine in all three colours made from Macabeo and Garnacha. True, most of the region's wine companies are little more than cottage industries in comparison with the giant co-ops and great houses of Penedès and beyond. On the other hand, the wines they make are limited in quantity, and people seem willing to pay the prices that allow Priorato's winemakers to continue making them – which is what a successful winemaking business is all about.

**Above:** The vine-covered landscape that surrounds the village of Scala Dei, site of the famous priory where wine is still made.

**Far right:** The hermitage that lent its name to the L'Ermita vineyard, an integral part of what has become known as the Gratallops project.

Llicorella; its alternate layers of slate and quartzite present a black-and-gold 'tigerskin' quality in bright sunlight. Vines are planted wherever they will grow, vintaging is difficult and yields are pitifully small, even by Spanish standards – yet the wines make up for this in a number of ways.

The main quality grape has always been Garnacha, though Cariñena occupies more vineyard space. Other traditional varieties include Garnacha Blanca, Macabeo and even a little Pedro Ximénez, yet white varieties make up less than five per cent of the vineyard. New and experimental plantings include Cabernet Sauvignon, Merlot, Syrah, Pinot Noir and Chenin Blanc, but new-wave winemaking is mainly the preserve of the Gratallops enclave.

# Notable bodegas

### Alvaro Palacios, Gratallops.

*Founded 1989.* One of the founders of the Gratallops project, Alvaro Palacios is the scion of the great Rioja house of Palacios Remondo. His original wine was named Clos Dofí, although he plans to rename it 'Finca Dofí' in due course. Today, his pint-sized winery produces three wines, all red. Las Terrasses is a 13.5% abv *crianza* (45% Cariñena/40% Garnacha/15% Cabernet Sauvignon; 12 months in oak). Clos Dofí is a 13% abv *crianza* from the single vineyard of the same name (60% Garnacha/20% Cabernet Sauvignon/10% Merlot/5% Cariñena/5% Syrah; 17 months in cask). *Best wine:* Clos l'Ermita. This is a single vineyard on a 45° slope in a natural amphitheatre in the highest part of Gratallops. The vines are Garnacha and about 100 years old, with some of the lowest yields in Spain. They create a wine of intense concentration, ripeness, fruit and depth. Palacios blends in 10% Cariñena for colour, 10% Cabernet Sauvignon for aroma. The 1993 vintage spent 19 months in oak. The result is arguably the finest individual red wine in Spain and certainly the most expensive, with a price outstripping Vega Sicilia and Dominio de Pingus in Ribera del Duero. To sum up: Las Terrases is excellent, Clos Dofí is outstanding, and Clos l'Ermita is unbelievable.

### Cellers de Scala Dei, Scala Dei.

*Founded 1973.* Begun in the old cellars of the tiny village of the same name. Current winemaker is Manuel Peyra, and his one concession to technical modernity has been the use of cooling *placas* during fermentation. In these parts, fermentation is a slow process, with full malolactic and plenty of skin contact to extract as much colour as possible. This does not mean that the bodega lacks an innovative spirit. There are two very good whites, one *joven* and one barrel-fermented with six months on its lees (both 80% Garnacha Blanca/ 20% Chenin Blanc). There is a *rosado joven* (*rosat* in Catalan) (100% Garnacha) and a Novell red *joven* (100% Garnacha); both are very good. *Best wines:* Negre Scala Dei is a gesture towards a more modern style (80% Garnacha/20% Cabernet Sauvignon; six months in cask). Most classic is the *reserva* Cartoixa Scala Dei (100% Garnacha; 22 months in cask). Ideally, it should have up to five years in bottle – or 25, depending on your willpower. At up to 15% abv, the longer it's kept, the better.

### Costers del Siurana, Gratallops.

The original company which, in the 1980s, brought together the pioneers of the Gratallops project, guided then as now by Carles Pastrana, a visionary even among the visionaries of Priorato. Miserere is a *crianza* (Garnacha/ Cabernet Sauvignon/Tempranillo/ Merlot/ Cariñena; 14 months in cask). Clos l'Obac, the bodega's flagship wine, is also a *crianza* (Garnacha/ Cabernet Sauvignon/Merlot/Syrah/ Cariñena). Both these wines are outstanding. *Best wine:* Dolç de l'Obac (Garnacha/Cabernet Sauvignon/ Syrah; 12 months in oak). At 16% abv it brings together all the ripeness and sweetness of warm summer fruits, following the tradition in Catalonia of old, sweet red wines with a hint of fortification (*see* Tarragona DO for the most famous example). This is an exceptional wine, even for Gratallops.

### Masía Barril, Bellmunt del Priorato. *Founded 1931.*

Small family firm in the old tradition of Priorato, with 20ha and a small but discerning export market. Current director Rafael Barril has his own ideas about what he wants to produce. There are some 'new-wave' wines, notably the red *jovenes* Virgen (80% Garnacha/20% Cariñena) and Tipico (70/30 ditto). *Best wines:* this bodega does classic wines best: old vintages of (unoaked) white wine (80% Macabeo/20% Garnacha Blanca) at 15% abv; Aromatizado, a non-DO *semiseco* (50% Macabeo/30% Garnacha Peluda/20% Garnacha Blanca) at 15% abv and spiced with herbs from the bodega's own kitchen garden; Clásico, a high-strength (16% abv) 70% arnacha/30%Cariñena mix; and the original Rancio, fully oxidised 70% Garnacha/30%Cariñena of the type that was Catalonia's main style only half a century ago.

### Masía Duch, Scala Dei.

*Founded 1987.* Restored monkish vineyard, formerly part of the Scala Dei Priory holdings, which lies in the foothills of the Sierra de Montsant. There are 20ha (with a further ten coming forward) on slate-based soils yielding about 500hl from Garnacha and Cabernet Sauvignon. The style is modern with a nod to tradition, and director Delfí Duch i Martorell insists that his wines will only cope with a year in oak; the rest must be in bottle. A bodega to watch. *Best wines:* an excellent *joven* (Garnacha) and *reserva* (Cabernet Sauvignon).

### Mas Martinet, Falset.

*Founded 1986.* Another of the Gratallops pioneers, run by the Pérez Ovejero family on a small estate on the road to Falset. The vineyards have drip-feed irrigation and the winery is small but immaculately modern. In common with the other Gratallops bodegas, Martinet makes only reds. The two basic wines are Martinet Bru *joven* and Clos Martinet *reserva* (both Cabernet Sauvignon/Garnacha/ Merlot/Syrah). *Best wines:* a series of 'Martinet Especial' wines, including a Cabernet Sauvignon/Cariñena, varietal Cabernet Sauvignon, Merlot, Syrah *jovenes* and a Syrah/Merlot blend.

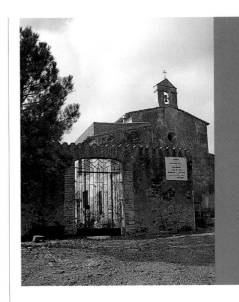

### René Barbier fill, Gratallops.

*Founded 1987.* Yes, it is confusing, so let's explain. René Barbier the elder owned and ran a firm called René Barbier in Sant Sadurní d'Anoia making wines under the Penedès DO. He sold it to the Freixenet group, where it remains. His son, René Barbier the younger, is one of the Gratallops pioneers; as well as building his own bijou winery, he has also built a house into a mountainside nearby. His wine is called Clos Mogador and is a *reserva* (30% Garnacha/30% Cabernet Sauvignon/ 25% Syrah/15% 'others'; 12 months in cask). Exemplary.

# Tarragona

A lesson in how far Catalonia has come in wine terms, even since the 1960s, can be learned in Tarragona. A strong, sweet, red fortified wine called Tarragona Clásico is still produced in these parts, and it has had legal recognition since 1933. Thirty years later, it was still, for many people, the only Catalan wine they had encountered outside of Catalonia itself. In the UK, it was known as 'the poor man's Port'. Fortunately, much has changed since then.

The Tarragona DO occupies most of the province of the same name (with the excision of Priorato). It is the largest DO in Catalonia, divided into two subzones: Tarragona Campo covers 75 per cent of the DO north and east of neighbouring Priorato; Falset covers the southern part of the zone, and further subdivides into the Comarca de Falset (on the southern borders of Priorato) and the Ribera d'Ebre (or Ribera de Ebro) which, as its name implies lies along the banks of the River Ebro. In general terms, Campo is the region that makes the old-fashioned sweet, fortified red wines as well as modern supermarket styles. Falset – certainly the northern part – has greater ambitions, having seen what its neighbours are achieving in Priorato.

## Geology and climate

Geologically, Tarragona Campo ranges from sea level to about 200 metres (656 feet) in altitude before rising sharply at the border with Priorato. The bedrock is limestone and the topsoil tends to be alluvial, generated from the many streams and rivers that flow down into the Ebro. Falset is higher, situated at an altitude of some 363 metres (1,191 feet) in a *conca* surrounded by mountain ranges. The soil here is loam and limestone over granite.

Ribera d'Ebre drops to about 100 metres (328 feet) along the riverside, where soil is (understandably) mainly alluvial. Interestingly enough, the lowest vineyards in Tarragona are in the Campo subzone, at an altitude of just 40 metres (131 feet); the highest are at 450 metres (1,476 feet) in the Falset subzone. As with all the coastal Catalan DO areas, the climate is rather Mediterranean along the east coast and becomes increasingly continental as the terrain rises inland. Once again, this favours Falset as potentially the best production area for grapes.

Of course, grapes for Cava are grown in the province and, once again, the example provided by the careful husbandry of these vines has been followed by makers of wines bearing the Tarragona DO. In the Campo subzone and the Ribera d'Ebre, the recommended grapes are Garnacha, Cariñena and Tempranillo for red wines and Macabeo, Xarel-lo and Parellada plus Garnacha Blanca for whites. In the Falset area, however, only Garnacha and Cariñena are recommended – but this is Catalonia, after all, so also look for Cabernet Sauvignon, Merlot, and other imports from France.

## Winemaking and wine styles

The wines are legion. Tarragona Clásico is still made, typically from 100 per cent Garnacha. When you consider that it must achieve an alcoholic strength of 13.5 per cent alcohol by volume (abv) and spend a minimum of 12 years in oak, it is hardly surprising that it has priced itself out of a dwindling market. Traditional *rancio* wines and *mistelas* are also made from the versatile Garnacha. From Roman times until about 1960, these and *clásico* were among the best-selling wines of the world, exported everywhere and underpinning the prosperity of most of the region. In addition, there has always been a substantial religious market: communion wine for Christian churches throughout Europe very often had its origins in Tarragona.

However, the Cava example – both in the vineyard and in the winery – has led to rethinking and re-equipping. Tarragona's main commodity these days is well-made, modestly priced, everyday *jovenes* in all three colours, made from the 'big three' grapes for white wines, Garnacha for *rosados*, and Garnacha and Cariñena for reds. And there are the inevitable pioneers with their Syrah, Pinot Noir and what-have-you. Tarragona's future in vinous terms would seem to be one that encompasses a two-tier structure.

The Falset wines, while not achieving the sheer hights of their neighbours in Priorato, do have an economy of scale that Priorato lacks. If subsequent development in Falset is towards individualistic, quality wines, and if that development is underpinned by solid, dependable, quality-controlled supermarket business from Campo, then Tarragona could, once again, become the source of the some of the world's most exported wines.

The area was first delimited in 1933, and the first Tarragona DO certification was granted on April 24, 1947, for *clásico* and *rancio* wines only. Beverage wines were added to the DO in 1959.

# Notable bodegas

Co = Campo; FC = Falset/Comarca; FR = Falset/Ribera d'Ebre.

### Capçanes Cooperativa, Capçanes (FC). *Founded 1932.* Re-invented in the 1990s, an independent business with a very independent streak when it comes to winemaking. This former regional co-op is a village winery situated in its own *conca*, still owned by its original members (142 farming 268ha of vines) but the business style has changed radically. Half the grapes harvested here are now sold off to other co-ops, allowing Capçanes to concentrate on the best 50% of its production. Investment in new equipment and some inspired winemaking have made this bodega the envy of many older, more dinosaur-like co-ops throughout Tarragona. The top wines are called Flor de Maig, and the range includes four varietal whites, one *joven* (Macabeo) and one *crianza* (Garnacha Blanca; six months in oak), and two Chardonnays, one fully and one partly barrel-fermented. The *rosado* is another *joven* (70% Garnacha/20% Cariñena/10% Merlot). It is for its reds, however, that Capçanes is best known. The basic Flor de Maig is a very good *joven* (50% Garnacha/30% Cariñena/10% Tempranillo). However, Capçanes also produces traditional *rancios*, *dulces* and *mistelas*, including the very good Marmellans Garnatxa in both red and white (Garnacha Tinta and Garnacha Blanca – very unusual). One of the reds, Flor de Primevera, is a kosher wine carrying the certification of the chief rabbi of Barcelona. *Best wine:* an excellent varietal Cabernet Sauvignon with three months in oak (not enough to be called *crianza*). Probably one of the best wines of the entire region.

### De Muller, Tarragona (Co). *Founded 1851.* One of the firms which helped to make the name of classic Tarragona wines throughout the world, especially in the field of communion wine. Today, the firm is active in Scala Dei (Priorato DO ) as well as in Tarragona, and it is the custodian of many of the region's traditional vinous skills. De Muller's fame rests on sweet, fortified and *rancio* wines, but there is also a brace of good *jovenes* – red and white – called Viña Solimar.

### Falsetença Cooperativa, Falset (FC). *Founded 1919.* Another co-op with a lot of new equipment and new thinking. There are joint plantations of vines (particularly Cabernet Sauvignon and Pinot Noir) with Bodegas Pedro Rovira (*see* below) and a good deal of experimentation. The 150 members farm 300ha, and although they make traditional Garnatxa wines in *rancio* and *dulce* styles, the future here lies in lighter things. There is a very good *rosado joven* (80% Cariñena/10% Garnacha/10% Tempranillo). *Best wine:* the *crianza* Vinya Candida (30% Garnacha/ 30% Cabernet Sauvignon/ 30% Tempranillo/10% Cariñena).

### José Anguera Beyme, Darmós (FR). *Founded 1830.* Run by Josep Anguera Beyme, who farms just 30ha and makes only a few wines. However, this has been enough to establish the firm in international markets (including Germany, Switzerland and England). The bodega is well-equipped with the latest equipment and, perhaps most importantly, the latest thinking on winemaking. *Best wine:* Joan d'Anguera (45% Syrah/35% Garnacha/ 20% Cabernet Sauvignon). In good years, it is excellent; in great years, it's exceptional.

### Mitjavila, La Secuita (Co). *Founded 1987.* A Cava firm that also makes still wines under the Tarragona DO. The range comprises good white and *rosado jovenes* plus a red *crianza* (90% Tempranillo/10% Cabernet Sauvignon; eight months in cask).

### Pedro Rovira, Móra la Nova (FR). *Founded 1864.* This firm went into the wine business in 1917 and also has a joint-development relationship with the Falsetença co-op (*see* above); it is active in the Terra Alta DO as well. Tarragona wines include a popular *rosado joven* called Raquel (60% Garnacha/40% Cariñena). *Best wines:* the reds *reserva* Viña Mater (80% Tempranillo/30% Garnacha; 18 months in oak) and *gran reserva* (100% Tempranillo; 18 months in oak).

**Below: This vineyard growing near Cornudella is part of the Tarragona DO. The grapes it yields could be made into anything from Tarragona Clásico to communion wine.**

# CAVA | Cava

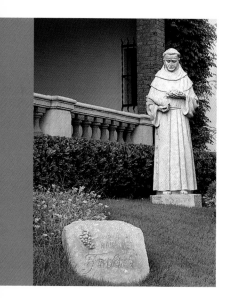

**Above: This statue of Dom Pérignon, considered to be the father of Champagne, stands outside the Freixenet Cava house.**

Only two wines in Spain do not have a legal requirement to carry the words *denominación de origen* on the label. One of them is Sherry, the other is Cava. Legally, in Spain and throughout the EU, the term *Cava* means 'sparkling wine made by the traditional method of fermentation in the bottle and produced in specified areas notified to the relevant authorities'. The *consejo regulador* styles itself *Consejo Regulador de la Denominación Cava*; notice that the words *de Origen* do not appear.

The first Cava was made in 1872 by Josep Raventós in the town of Sant Sadurní d'Anoia, in the valley of the River Anoia, in the *comarca* of Alt-Penedès, in the province of Barcelona, in the *autonomía* of Catalonia. You are allowed to call Cava made in this town by any of these geographical names except the obvious one: Penedès. As it happens, the vineyards of the Penedès DO occupy many of the same fields, valleys and coverts as those of the Cava DO, but it is not permitted under EU law to describe a quality wine as coming from another quality wine's area – even if it does. Is that clear?

The brutal truth is that some 95 per cent of all Cava wine comes from Catalonia, and some 75 per cent of that is made in and around the town of Sant Sadurní. However, because Cava also comes from elsewhere, we are forbidden to use the geographical name. Hence there is no *de origen*; just *Cava*. For convenience, we shall use the term 'Catalan Cava' to distinguish it from 'non-Catalan Cava'.

It was Champagne which gave the world its thirst for bubbles, and the world has never been able to get enough. Catalonia, however, has an independent spirit and prefers to fulfil its own needs rather than import them – even from the rest of Spain. Thus, once the bars and cafés of the major cities (especially Barcelona) began to ring with the sound of popping corks, the winemakers of Barcelona province turned their minds to the matter of sparkling wine.

The technology was no mystery in itself; indeed, most local wine producers had made small quantities of sparkling wine for many years. What was needed was a foolproof way of making it at high-quality levels, with minimal numbers of exploding bottles, and with proper quality-control.

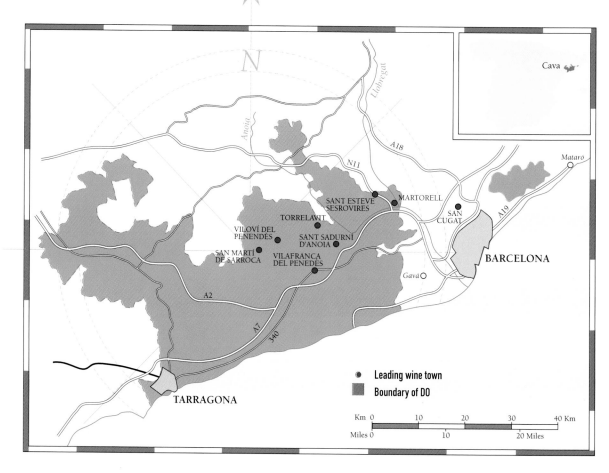

• **Leading wine town**
▪ **Boundary of DO**

A group of Sant Sadurní's leading winemakers (nicknamed the 'Seven Greek Sages') got into the habit of meeting every Sunday to discuss their latest experiments with sparkling wines. Problems were common: flawed bottles; poor-quality corks; high temperatures during bottling; slow, inefficient disgorgement techniques; and (not least) the dry, oxidised quality of many of the grapes delivered to the bodegas.

As the years passed, it became apparent that the only way anyone could make a sparkling wine of passable quality would be as a result of massive investment in vineyards and contract growers, new fermentation vats, the very latest machinery in the winery and the most expensive bottles and corks. Then there was the problem of convincing the Catalan people that a local sparkler could meet the standards of a wine they had been importing from France. The risks were astronomical.

## Searching for suitable grapes

Still, a great deal of work had already been done – particularly in the selection of suitable grape varieties. The first act of many would-be sparkling wine producers was to copy the Champenois by planting Chardonnay, Pinot Noir, *et al*, but this exercise was not a success. Champagne's vineyards were mature, for one thing. In any case, the soils and climate of Catalonia were completely different from those of Champagne. It became apparent that if Catalonia were to achieve a quality sparkling wine, it would have to use grapes already well-adapted to the region. It must also realise that vinification in oak vats or concrete tanks was not an option if the sparkling wine were to have universal appeal.

The first breakthrough took place in the vineyards. The three landscape 'levels' (as exemplified by the *baix-mitja-* and *alt-*Penedès; *see* page 110) had always produced grapes with differing characteristics. The lower vineyards turned out good, ripe grapes for sweet and *rancio* wines. The middle range provided smaller quantities of grapes which took much longer to ripen. The highlands irritatingly provided frost, which damaged what small quantity of grapes actually appeared on the vines.

It did not take long, of course, for the inspired winemakers among the 'Seven Sages' to realise that this was just what they needed. The crisp acidity imparted to Chardonnay by the cold climate of Champagne could be reproduced in the higher vineyards. All that was needed was to determine which grapes performed best at which levels. To leap forward a century or more, we now know

that the 'big three' grapes flourish best in the middle levels, and that the best (although most expensive) Chardonnay comes from the highlands.

The next task was down to the wineries. With no stainless steel, no epoxy-resin and no fibreglass, the only way to ferment wine with absolute cleanliness was in specially constructed vats lined with glazed tiles to ensure that the wine never came into contact with concrete or metal. Even though Catalonia is one of the ceramic capitals of the western world, this was still going to be considerably expensive.

Add to that the cost of allowing the wine its year or so in the *pupitres*, the cost of staff to do the *remuaje* (remuage) and the labour-intensive, highly skilled matter of *dégüelle* (disgorgement). And don't forget the high-quality bottles, corks and cages, or that there was no guarantee anyone would show the slightest interest in buying the product once it was on the market. The financial risks were enormous, and it would take a company of great courage to risk the kind of investment required just to get started. Yet all that was needed now was for one man to make the first move.

In the event, this was Josep Raventós. His company, Codorníu, was founded in 1551 and has one of the longest histories in Spain outside the Sherry region. Raventós could certainly afford the investment; he could not, however, afford to fail. As it turned out, he need not have worried. Not only did Barcelona and the rest of Spain take to Cava with an unquenchable thirst, the wines turned out to be perfectly in tune with Catalan and Mediterranean tastes. Unlike Champagne, the new wines were ready to drink at just over a year old. They proved to be fresh, light and relatively low in acidity. They were also modestly priced and could be sold within Spain without import duties.

## Barriers to success

That, however, is not the end of the story; indeed, in many ways it is only the beginning. By the turn of the century, every wine-producing country in the world was turning out sparkling wine of one sort or another. All wanted to export and all stood in the shadow of Champagne. Cava had experienced a modest boom during the phylloxera disaster in France, but there were still three more hurdles to overcome before it gained its ascendancy in the world of sparkling wine.

The first was nomenclature. At the turn of the century, no one thought that sparkling wine was called anything other than Champagne. In Catalonia, they

Above: The red rooftops of Raventós i Blanc, founded by another branch of the family which created the first Cava in 1872.

cheerfully labelled Cava as *Xampàn* (*Champán* in Castilian) and announced to the world that it was made by the *método champañés*, or Champagne method. This did not go down well in Reims and Épernay. With the establishment of the European Economic Community (EEC) in 1957, only wines from the Champagne district of France could use the name within the six countries of the Common Market: France, Germany, Italy, Holland, Belgium and Luxembourg.

Elsewhere, you could call your wine anything you liked. Cava continued to use the French name well beyond 1957 in export markets outside the EEC. Once it became apparent that an expanding Europe would one day include Spain, however, producers realised a distinctive name was needed to distinguish the Catalan sparkler from all the others.

## The origins of Cava

The origin of the name is probably the result of the differentiation in Spain between the words *bodega* and *cava*. Both mean 'cellar', but a bodega is traditionally a ground-level cellar, while a cava is underground. Because sparkling wine develops underground to benefit from constant temperatures during the time spent on its lees, winemakers might refer to their *bodega* wines (still wines stored above ground, probably in cask) and their *cava* wines (sparkling wines stored underground, in bottle). This is how the wines were labelled within the EEC, and as other countries joined what has now become the European Union (EU), more and more found that what they had known as 'Spanish Champagne' became 'Cava'.

This was fortunate for the winemakers, since by the time Spain joined the EU, Cava had become well known as a term, and was ripe for marketing. This separate identity really came into its own after September 1, 1994, when the term *méthode champenoise* and its translations were banned worldwide. The phrase *método tradicional* replaced it, but for Cava, there was no problem: the name was well known and the wine was second only to the French product in world markets.

The second hurdle was a legal one. In the great Cava explosion of the early 20th century, production spread all over Spain. Some of the wines carrying the Cava name were not doing its reputation any good, and the first attempt at regulation came in 1959 with the creation of the Cava *Denominación Específica* (DE).

This controlled the method of production without controlling the areas in which the grapes were grown. To be accepted as Quality Wine under EU law, however, the

vineyards had to be mapped in detail – a thorny political problem. Catalonia wanted the name Cava to be restricted to wines made within its own boundaries, but some large and powerful companies outside Catalonia were making Cava, and many of them claimed to have been doing so for at least as long as the major Catalan houses.

In 1986 (the year of Spain's accession to the EU), a compromise was reached whereby Europe would recognise Cava as a quality wine on a provisional basis until the vineyards were mapped in detail and registered with Brussels. This was a long and often painful process. Towns and villages that had made Cava for decades lost the right to the name altogether. Growers who were able to fight for the right to keep it had to replant with approved varieties, provide details of their vineyard holdings and specify precisely which ones were given over to Cava production. These requirements were completed to international satisfaction in January 1992, and Cava finally became, legally, a QWPSR – Quality Wine Produced in a Specific Region – throughout Europe.

Grapes used in making Cava must come from listed vineyards. The wine may be made only from Parellada, Xarel-lo, Macabeo (Viura), Subirat (Malvasia Riojana) and/or Chardonnay grapes, and Monastrell and/or Garnacha for the pink version, known in Catalonia as Cava *rosat*, *rosado* or rosé for export markets. There is still heated debate over the admission or proportion of Chardonnay which should or should not be permitted in the wine, although there have been plantations of the grape for at least a century and a half. A good deal of unnecessary unpleasantness on this subject still erupts in Sant Sadurní from time to time, often between companies big enough and old enough to know better.

## A question of style

The final hurdle for Cava was the style of the wine. With a few exceptions (notably Italy and Germany), all the world's sparkling wines were made either in France, or from French grapes, as winemakers worldwide tried to make ersatz Champagne. This strategy was doomed to failure, since wine is a result of a myriad factors, not just the grape varieties used to make it.

While some excellent sparklers are created from Chardonnay and Pinot Noir (particularly in the New World), the best to which they can aspire is to be 'very like Champagne'. Cava was always (in typically Catalan style) stubbornly and unashamedly different. In its early days, it was often criticised for having a rooty, earthy, even gamey character. This was a fair comment: the Xarel-lo grape provides the weight and foundation for the wine, and all too often it was being harvested too late, in an overripe and oxidised state. Similarly, Parellada, which provides the 'creamy' base for good Cava, was allowed to overripen and become at best bland and at worst blowsy; Macabeo, which provides acidity and freshness, was sometimes over-fermented and completely neutral.

## Finding the right balance

Such problems were not solved overnight. The larger houses got there first simply because of the scale in which they worked, and the rest followed. Boutique wineries sprang up, with inspired winemakers harvesting earlier and earlier, pressing and fermenting with greater refinement. The conundrum of Xarel-lo was solved by early harvesting (sometimes in the small hours of the morning) and rapid transit in small plastic boxes to the presses. The careful balance between the soft, voluptuous nature of the Parellada and the crisp, fresh acidity of the Macabeo was finally achieved.

By law, Cava must spend nine months on its lees and may not be sold for a year. This allows it to be called *crianza*, if the bodega wishes. Most quality Cava spends much longer on its lees: after 18 months it may be called *reserva* and after 30, *gran reserva*. The result, in good winemaking hands, is a wine of great freshness, fruit and citrous flavours with a warm, ripe palate and a pleasant, lingering finish. Hard work over many years has been required to achieve this, but by the end of the 1980s, Cava had become a worthy world-class wine, owing nothing to Champagne except its sparkle.

Cava's success had been achieved against a cacophony of protest from trendy wine-writers who were almost united in their distaste for it. Heavyweight articles in respected journals detailed the 'lumpen, bucolic, uninspiring' character of the wine compared with Champagne and the burgeoning Champagne-wannabes from the New World. There was no shortage of wine 'gurus' only too anxious to explain exactly why Cava would never achieve anything, and why people should be buying Australian or Californian or South African or anything else – as long as it came from a place where the hotels were well-appointed and the local language was English.

Fortunately, the world's wine-lovers were more sanguine about spending their money, and perversely insisted on buying something they actually enjoyed and could afford. Cava sales boomed. By the mid-1990s, it had become the world's favourite sparkling wine, after Champagne.

Today, Cava is still made principally in Catalonia, mainly in Sant Sadurní d'Anoia; however, in the following *autonomías*, some towns and villages are also allowed to produce the wine: Aragón (province of Zaragoza); Navarra; La Rioja; País Vasco (province of Álava); Valencia (province of Valencia); Extremadura (province of Badajoz); and Castile-León (province of Burgos). In some cases, special regulations apply for the benefit of just one company; in most cases the wine is made with 100 per cent Macabeo grapes. By law, the base of the Cava cork must carry the symbol of a four-pointed star and the word *Cava*.

The epithets used to describe the sweetness/dryness of the wines are similar to those used worldwide in the production of sparkling wines. They refer to the amount of sugar-syrup added to the *dosaje* (*dosage*, in French), after disgorgement and before the wine is finally sealed. *Extra Brut* has less than six grammes per litre (g/l) of sugar and may be considered bone-dry; *Brut* has six to 15g/l and is dry; *Extra Seco* has 12 to 20g/l and may be off-dry to medium-dry; *Seco* has 17 to 35g/l and may be medium to medium-sweet; *Semiseco* has 33 to 50g/l and is sweet; *Dulce* has more than 50g/l and is very sweet.

**Below: Vineyards flourish around Sant Sadurní d'Anoia. This deep into Cava country, the grapes are Xarel-lo, Parellada, or Macabeo.**

# Notable bodegas

Unless otherwise stated, all wines below are made from the 'big three' Cava grapes. Otherwise, grapes are coded as (X)arel-lo, (P)arellada, (M)acabeo/Viura, (C)hardonnay.

**Agusti Torelló, Sant Sadurní d'Anoia.** *Founded 1955.* Begun by Agusti Torelló Mata, a master of the craft of making Cava. His wines are uniformly excellent. *Best wines:* the fabulously expensive Kripta, presented in a pointy bottomed bottle in the style of a Greek amphora, although the *brut reserva* is better value.

**Albet i Noya, Sant Pau d'Ordal.** *Founded 1980.* Family firm with 40ha, most of which is farmed 'ecologically'. *Rosat* and *semiseco* versions are made. *Best wine:* the straight *brut*.

**Can Feixes, Cabrera d'Anoia.** *Founded 1945.* Another family firm with 75ha; making excellent wines. *Best wine:* the *brut nature gran reserva* (PMC).

**Canals i Nubiola, Sant Sadurní d'Anoia.** Part of the Freixenet group via Castellblanch, with 30ha of vines. *Best wine:* the *brut reserva*.

**Castell de Vilarnau, Sant Sadurní d'Anoia.** *Founded 1982.* This estate turns out around 4,500hl of Cava every year that is uniformly excellent. *Best wines: brut nature* and (in good years) a *brut gran reserva*.

**Castellblanch, Sant Sadurní d'Anoia.** *Founded 1908.* Part of the Freixenet group since 1984, Castellblanch makes wine from its own 250ha as well as bought-in grapes; production approaches 100,000hl. All wines are excellent. *Best wines:* Gran Castell *gran reserva* and Brut Zero.

**Castillo de Perelada, Perelada.** *Founded 1925.* Cava firm in the cellars of the castle in the village of Perelada. Only the excellent top-of-the-range Gran Claustro is aged here; others are made in Sant Sadurní d'Anoia. All wines are good. *Best wines:* the *brut nature* and the varietal Chardonnay.

**Chandón, San Cugat Sesgarrigues.** *Founded 1987.* Owned by Champagne house Moët & Chandon; buys in around 50% of its grapes to make around 3,500hl of Cava. Wines are sold in Spain as Chandón or Masía Chandón; in export markets as Torre del Gall. *Best wine:* the excellent Masía Chandón *brut*.

**Codorníu, Sant Sadurní d'Anoia.** *Founded 1551.* One of the two great houses of Cava (the other being Freixenet). Biggest of all Cava houses, with the most glamorous winery set in landscaped grounds; the buildings were designed by architects of the Gaudi school. The old bodegas are now a museum and the cellars go down five levels. The site is now a national monument. Codorníu's range includes traditional styles and those using Chardonnay. Anything made here is at least very good, often exceptional. *Best wines:* the outstanding Codorníu 1551 ('big three') and Jaume Codorníu (Chardonnay/Pinot Noir/Parellada).

**Conde de Caralt, Sant Sadurní d'Anoia.** Part of the Freixenet empire. Cavas bear the bodega name and come *brut*, *blanc de blancs* and varietal Chardonnay. *Best wine:* the *blanc de blancs*.

**Covides, Sant Sadurní d'Anoia.** *Founded 1962.* Co-op with high standards, turning out Cava under the Duc de Foix label. *Best wine:* the excellent Duc de Foix Xenius.

**Freixenet, Sant Sadurní d'Anoia.** *Founded 1889.* The other great house of Cava and the largest sparkling wine producer in the world. Its magnificent art

deco cellars are situated beside the railway station, and its wines sell all over the globe. Carta Nevada and Cordón Negro are the best-sellers. New wine to watch is the black-grape/white-grape Monastrell/Xarel-lo made for the first time in 1996. Early results show extremely well, and when it has a little more maturity this could be a new direction for Cava. *Best wines:* Brut Barocco, Freixenet Vintage and Cuvée DS. *Best of all:* (and very expensive) is Reserva Real, made from base wines from the finest plots in finest vintages. Arguably the best Cava made today.

**Gramona, Sant Sadurní d'Anoia.** *Founded 1921.* Farms 15ha as well as buying in grapes. *Best wines:* Tres Lustros *nature extra brut* and Reserva Vintage *brut*; both reliably excellent.

**Heretat Mont-Rubí, Esplugas de Llobregat.** Single-estate winery with 45ha under vine. Makes 650hl of Cava. All are sold under the Mont-Rubí name. *Best wine:* the *brut nature.*

**Joan Raventós Rosell, Masquefa.** *Founded 1985.* Has 60ha and buys in grapes to make 1,400hl. Makes two excellent Cavas: *brut* (75% M/25% C) and *brut nature* (65% M/20% P/15% C).

**Josep Masachs, Vilafranca del Penedès.** *Founded 1920.* Respected house with 40ha, buying in grapes to make 15,000hl. *Best wines:* the Josep Masachs *brut de brut* and the Louis de Vernier *brut.*

**Llopart, Sant Sadurní d'Anoia.** *Founded 1881.* Family firm with 25ha making just over 1,000hl of Cava under the Castell de Subirats, Integral, La Mesa del Rey and Leopardi labels. *Best wine:* the Llopart *brut nature.*

**Marqués de Monistrol, Sant Sadurní d'Anoia.** *Founded 1882.* One of the oldest bodegas with the most vineyards in the area, after the two great houses. There are 400ha and a smart, modern

winery turning out a massive 45,000hl of wine, most of which is Cava. All are good, especially the Gran Tradición *brut nature. Best wine:* the Brut Selección.

**Masía Bach, San Esteve de Sesrovires.** *Founded 1921.* Taken over by Codorníu in 1975. Has 300ha and also buys in to produce around 36,000hl of uniformly excellent wines, much under the Penedès DO, but a small amount of Cava is made. *Best wine:* Masía Bach *brut nature.*

**Masía Vallformosa, Viloví del Penedès.** *Founded 1978.* Family-owned firm with a smart, modern winery and 307ha; makes over 20,000hl, nearly half of which is Cava. *Best wine:* the splendid *gran reserva.*

**Nadal, Pla de Penedès.** *Founded 1943.* Family firm with 100ha making 4,500hl of Cava. Also an interesting *rosat* made (80% Tempranillo/20% Monastrell). *Best wines:* Nadal *brut* and Nadal Brut Salvatje.

**Parxet, Tiana.** *Founded 1920.* One of Catalonia's leading boutique wineries, with 40ha. All wines are excellent, including a fascinating Parxet Cuvée Dessert *rosat. Best wines:* the varietal Parxet Chardonnay and the straight Parxet – both *brut nature* but the second from 'big three' grapes.

**Puig Munts, Martorell.** *Founded 1940.* Owns large vineyards (254ha), much of which is not yet in production. Buys in grapes to make 6,000hl. Wines are very good, sometimes excellent. *Best wine:* the *gran reserva extra brut.*

**Raïmat, Raïmat.** *Founded 1914.* *See* Costers del Segre DO for full history. Raïmat Cava has become a legend in its own lunchtime. Basic *brut nature* (CMP) is very good, but eclipsed by the varietal Chardonnay *brut nature. Best wine:* the Gran Brut (60% Chardonnay/40% Pinot Noir).

**Raventós i Blanc, Sant Sadurní d'Anoia.** *Founded 1986.* Mainly a Cava house farming 130ha and making 5,000hl. As well as basic Raventós i Blanc *brut*, excellent wines include Clos de Serral and L'Hereu, both *brut.*

**Recaredo, Sant Sadurní d'Anoia.** *Founded 1924.* Popular among *aficionados* of traditional, classic Cava. Two wines: a *brut nature* and a *brut de brut nature.* Both are excellent.

**Rovellats, Sant Martí Sarroca.** *Founded 1940.* Beautiful 15th-century bodega in a lovely garden making classic Cava from its own vineyards to the tune of 2,500hl. All wines are *gran reserva. Best wines:* Rovellats Masía SXV (CXMP) or the varietal Rovellats Chardonnay, both *brut.*

**Sadeve, Torrelavit.** *Founded 1984.* Has 100ha, and 90% of its production is Cava (the rest is Penedès DO), amounting to 7,500hl. Main brand name is Naverán, with an excellent traditional *brut* and a varietal Chardonnay.

**Segura-Viudas, Torrelavit.** *Founded 1954.* Part of the Freixenet group, and one of its best outposts, situated in a beautiful old 13th-century *masía.* All wines are excellent, without exception. *Best wines:* Aria *brut nature*, Heredad *reserva* and the standard Segura-Viudas *brut vintage.*

**Signat, Alella.** *Founded 1987.* Small bodega (1,200hl) producing three exemplary wines: *brut nature*, *brut* and *brut reserva*, all under the Signat label. *Best wine:* the brut nature.

**Sumarroca, Subirats.** *Founded 1986.* Family firm with 60ha. There are two wines under the Sumarroca label: *brut nature* (PMXC) and a varietal Chardonnay (85% C/ 15% P), both *gran reservas.* Also a *brut* Claverol (PMXC). All are excellent. *Best wine:* the *brut nature.*

Above: The glamourous exterior of the Codorníu winery in Sant Sadurní d'Anoia. one of the Cava DO's two 'great houses'.

# The Balearics: an island kingdom

First of all, a word about nomenclature. In the Balearic Islands, the natives speak a dialect of Catalan called Mallorquí (*Mallorquín* in Castilian), and in it, the four main islands are called Mallorca, Menorca, Eivissa and Formentera. Tourism development in the Franco era (when regional languages were suppressed) meant that an entire generation grew up knowing only the Castilian name for Eivissa: Ibiza. For reasons known only to God, the British chose to spell Mallorca with a 'j' – Majorca – in spite of the fact that the consonant in question is pronounced 'y'. Visitors will make friends much more quickly in the Balearics if they remember to use the local Mallorquí names.

### The legacy of Catalonia

The Catalan language connection goes back, naturally enough, to the days of the Catalan empire, which ruled most of the Mediterranean during the 12th century and beyond. However, Mallorca was once a medieval kingdom, ruled by James I of Aragón. The islands were occupied by the Moors along with the rest of Spain in the last quarter of the first millennium, but as the Moors were beaten back towards Granada in the 13th century, the opportunity arose to expel them from the Balearics altogether, thus re-establishing trade routes to Italy which had been previously cut off.

In the autumn of 1229, James I took his fleet to Mallorca, where he won the final battle against the Moors in the Bay of Palma on December 31st of that year. Nonetheless, it took a further 30 years to create the new Kingdom of Mallorca, which included not only the Balearic Islands, but also the French possessions of Roussillon and Montpellier. James' son, James II, and grandson, Sancho, brought immigrants from Catalonia into the islands. They also fortified the coastal towns against attack, ushering in a period of short-lived prosperity which started to crumble in 1343, when Pedro IV of Aragón attacked the islands and reclaimed them for Aragón. By 1349, Mallorca was once again part of what was to become a united Spain, and Montpellier and Roussillon had drifted into the hegemony of France.

Despite the fact that the kingdom lasted only 87 years, the nature of the Balearic Islands had become irrevocably Catalan-Mediterranean, due to the immigrants who settled there – and the culture continues to thrive in the modern age. Naturally it is a heritage which translates into the gastronomic field.

Seafood is more than a passion; it is almost a religion in the islands, with every imaginable shellfish, white fish and cephalopod represented in a myriad recipes.

### Balearic gastronomy

Each May, a food and wine festival is held in Palma de Mallorca, where local produce, cookery and wines are demonstrated to a highly appreciative public. What much of the modern world calls mayonnaise (the sauce of egg-yolks and oil) was first made in the town of Maò (Mahón in Castilian) on Menorca, where it was known *Maonès* or *Mahonesa*. There is also a Mahón cheese made on the island. Other cheeses include Mallorquín (made from a mixture of cow's and sheep's milk), which is made on the island of Mallorca.

Of course, in a tourist paradise such as this, it is now possible to eat the food of every region of Spain and, indeed, most of western Europe. Even so, there are still places where it is possible to find old-fashioned Mallorquín cooking, and the search is well worth the effort.

### Early wine history

In winemaking terms, the Balearic Islands have just one *denominación de origen* – the Binissalem DO zone – which is based on the island of Mallorca. Small though it is, the wines of Mallorca have an honourable and, indeed, quite propitious history which is not as well known as it deserves to be.

The oldest winery on the island, Hermanos Ribas, was founded in 1711. Even as early as this, writers in Spain were singing the praises of Mallorca's riches in the produce department – and they included its wines in the list. In the late 1700s, a mission of Franciscan monks, led by the Mallorcan Junípero Serra, sailed to the Americas and journeyed to the wild west of California to baptise the populace – and, of course, to plant vines. Some of the first vineyards in Sonoma and the Napa Valley owe their origins to this latter-day Balearic gyrovague.

Today, the Binissalem DO is too small to make great inroads into the international export business, but the locals take a characteristic pride in the older-style wines, which can hold their own capably against many of their colleagues from the mainland. As is usual with any region's wines, it is these that make the best partners for the Balearics' wealth of seafood dishes.

**Above:** Fish nets dry in the sun at Puerto de Soller, Mallorca – a testimony to the island's wealth of seafood.

**Far right:** Vine cuttings await grafting at Bodegas Franja Roja, one of the leading lights of the Binissalem DO.

# Binissalem

## Notable bodegas

**Antonio Nadal Ros, Binissalem.**
*Founded 1960.* Owns 25ha and makes about 800hl of wine, mainly red. The red wines are called Tres Uvas (70% Manto Negro/20% Callet/10% Monastrell). There are *joven, crianza* and *reserva* styles according to the year. *Best wine:* the *reserva* in good years.

**Franja Roja, Binissalem.**
*Founded 1931.* The biggest of the island's bodegas, still run by the Ferrer family. The firm owns 70ha and produces about 4,500hl from a smart, refurbished winery. Brand name is José L Ferrer. There is a very good *joven blanc de blancs* and a barrel-fermented Viña Veritas. The main production consists of reds: the *joven* is 85% Manto Negro/10% Tempranillo/5% Garnacha; the *crianza* and the *reserva* from 85% Manto Negro/15% Callet, both with 18 months in oak.

**Jaume de Puntiro, Santa María del Camí.** *Founded 1980.* Small boutique bodega with 11ha turning out some seriously good examples. Main production is of *jovenes* in all three colours, but there is a red with a little oak ageing made from Manto Negro, Callet and Tempranillo called Carmesi.

**Ribas, Consell.** *Founded 1711.* The oldest winery on the island, very small but excellent. *Best wine:* the red *crianza* (70% Manto Negro/ 25% Cabernet Sauvignon/5% Tempranillo; 18 months in oak).

*Right:  The entrance to the bodega of Franja Roja, founded by José Ferrer. It was the first to export Mallorcan wine in any quantity.*

After Junípero Serra had taken Balearic vines to the New World in the 18th century, they effectively disappeared into what would become the California wine industry. Back home in Mallorca, however, what had once been an established wine business was in a bit of a rut. There was plenty of wine for the inhabitants of the island and its neighbours, but little chance of exporting any of the surplus.

To the west lay mainland Spain; to the north, Provence; to the east, Italy. All were more than self-sufficient in terms of their own wine production. To the south, the countries of the Mahgreb were mainly Islamic and teetotal, so no export market could be hoped for there. It was all a bit of a shame, really, for Mallorcan wines tended to be simple country stuff made good by the natural benefits of excellent soil and a

Mediterranean-maritime climate. The artists, writers and poets who passed that way throughout the 19th and early 20th centuries thought them very fine.

This state of affairs continued until the mid-1960s, when Spain in general and Mallorca in particular opened up to mass tourism. Suddenly, the coastal developments of hotels and apartments could not get enough wine to supply their needs – in fact, they would take anything the island could produce. The result of this sudden demand was that, once again, there was little enough incentive for winemakers to strive for quality.

Thankfully, a few Mallorcan *viñeros* retained a passion for quality wines and harboured a desire to see their bottles on the international stage. One such was José Ferrer, who founded Bodegas Franja Roja in 1931 (*see* listings, left). He and a few stalwarts in the early part of the century worked hard to establish the name of Mallorcan wine at least as far as the mainland, and his descendants used the tourist boom of the second half of the century to win the *denominación de origen* for the region.

## Geography and climate

The DO zone occupies much of the centre of the island of Mallorca, on a gently rolling plain which radiates around the town of Binissalem itself at an altitude of 250 to 300 metres (820 to 984 feet). The soils here consist of fertile loam over limestone and clay. Although there are no rivers on the island, this central depression, surrounded by highlands, retains water quite well throughout the ripening season. Summer temperatures are cooler than on the mainland, providing the long, golden autumns beloved of all vinegrowers. Winters are so mild as to be mainly frost-free.

The main grape varieties are almost all native to Mallorca. The most widely planted is (red) Manto Negro, with 89 per cent of the vineyard; all red wines with DO must be made up of 50 per cent or more of this variety. The other main red grape is Callet (five per cent of the vineyard). The main white variety is Moll (five per cent; also known as Prensal Blanco), and the remaining one per cent is made up of Tempranillo, Monastrell, Cabernet Sauvignon, Parellada, Macabeo, Chardonnay and Moscatel – but these are little more than experimental.

The wine style is divided into two strands: *jovenes* in all three colours which are snapped up by the tourist industry on the island, and reds up to *gran reserva* standard which, given skilled handling, can achieve greatness in the right years.

# Country Wines of Catalonia and the Balearics

## Catalonia

### VC Anoia (Barcelona)
Formerly known for making unclassified wines under the name of its chief town, Igualada, this VC area now officially covers 18 municipalities in the valley of the River Anoia, in the *comarca* of Alt-Penedès. Three of these (Odena, La Pobla de Claramunt and Vallbona d'Anoia) are already classified for grape production for the Cava DO. Understandably, these are mainly planted with the 'big three' Cava grapes (Xarel-lo, Macabeo and Parellada) and are responsible for the bulk of production. Wines from these three villages under the Anoia VC are in the minority, and mainly white.

The rest of the region (which totals about 800ha) is devoted mainly to red-wine production from the Sumoll grape, which does not lend itself to quality wine.

### VC Bajo Ebro-Montsiá (Tarragona)
This area covers six municipalities north of the town of Ulldecona in the *comarca* of Montsiá, west of the Ebro delta. The VC only officially applies to white wines made from Macabeo and/or Garnacha Blanca. The official minimum strength at 9.5% abv does not suggest that great things are afoot.

There are around 2,500ha of vineyards (receding in the face of cereal production) scattered across the *comarca*. Most grow the obscure local variety Esquitxagos, which is not known for making quality wines (to be fair, almost no research has explored its potential). Red grapes are also planted, including some small amounts of Garnacha and Cariñena, but production methods are generally old-fashioned, and quality-control is very patchy.

### VC Conca de Tremp (Lleida)
This is a tiny area situated in the comarca of Pallars Jussà, comprising six municipalities around the town of Tremp. The guiding factor here is the River Noquera, which forms two long lakes north and south of Tremp. This provides excellent opportunities for vine growth, but the vineyard area is less than 50ha, and production is virtually domestic in scale. The VC is classified for white wines made from Macabeo, but there is some (fairly undistinguished) red made from Monastrell and Garnacha.

## The Balearic Islands

### VdIT Plà i Llevant de Mallorca (Baleares)
When the Binissalem DO was created in 1991, this is what was left behind: the remnants of an area known as Felanitx, dominated by the bulk-wine business which has faded away here as it has on the mainland. The zone includes 18 municipalities centred around Felanitx and enjoys a wide selection of grapes classified for the production of white wines of 10% abv and reds and *rosados* of 10% abv, and up. Principal grapes are Chardonnay, Prensal Blanco, Macabeo, Parellada, Callet, Tempranillo, Cabernet Sauvignon and Manto Negro. Subsidiary varieties are the Monastrell and the Fogoncu.

There are about 1,000ha of vineyards, planted a little above sea level on the fertile soils which characterise the island. The wines they make tend to be light and fresh and are intended for immediate drinking under the auspices of the island's ever-burgeoning tourist trade. However, as always, there are those enthusiasts who have greater ambitions (*see* below).

### Notable bodegas

**Miguel Oliver, Petra.** *Founded 1912.* Produces about 2,500hl of wine, sold largely throughout the island. *Best wines:* varietal Gran Chardonnay Miguel Oliver; a splendid dry Muscat (60% Moscatel de Alejandría/40% Moscatel de Frontignan); and a red Celler Son Calo *joven* (70% Callet/30% Fogoneu).

**Trevin, Manacor.** *Founded 1969.* A family firm which bottles enormous amounts of wine. There are white varietals from Parellada and Chardonnay, which make this a forward-looking bodega. However, only wines made from grapes grown in the area are permitted the VdIT. *Best wines:* the *rosat joven* (60% Manto Negro/40% Callet) and the red *crianza* (60% Manto Negro/30% Tempranillo/10% Callet).

**Below:** Ancient olive trees grow alongside vineyards near Móra de Ebro, in the Tarragona *denominación de origen*.

# The Levant

The Levant gets its name because, in Mediterranean Spain, this is where the sun 'gets up' (*levantarse* in Spanish) in the morning. Geographically, the Levant is made up of two *autonomías*: Valencia and Murcia. Valencia consists of three provinces – Alicante, Castellón de la Plana and Valencia itself – and includes Spain's third major city, which also shares its name. The DO zones within it are Alicante, Utiel-Requena and Valencia, although some 'cross-fertilisation' in wine-trading terms occurs among the three.

Murcia consists of a single province, but also comprises three DO zones of its own: Bullas, Jumilla and Yecla. Within Spain itself, this enormously fertile area is better known for oranges than for wine, since so much of what it produces goes to the export market. However, while the wines may be of modest pretensions compared to their neighbours to the north, Levantine winemaking expertise and the value-for-money factor of the finished product are unrivalled in Europe.

Teresa de Cofrentes, in Valencia province. Like many towns in the Levant, it catches the clear, diaphanous light known as *La Clara*, beloved by artists for centuries.

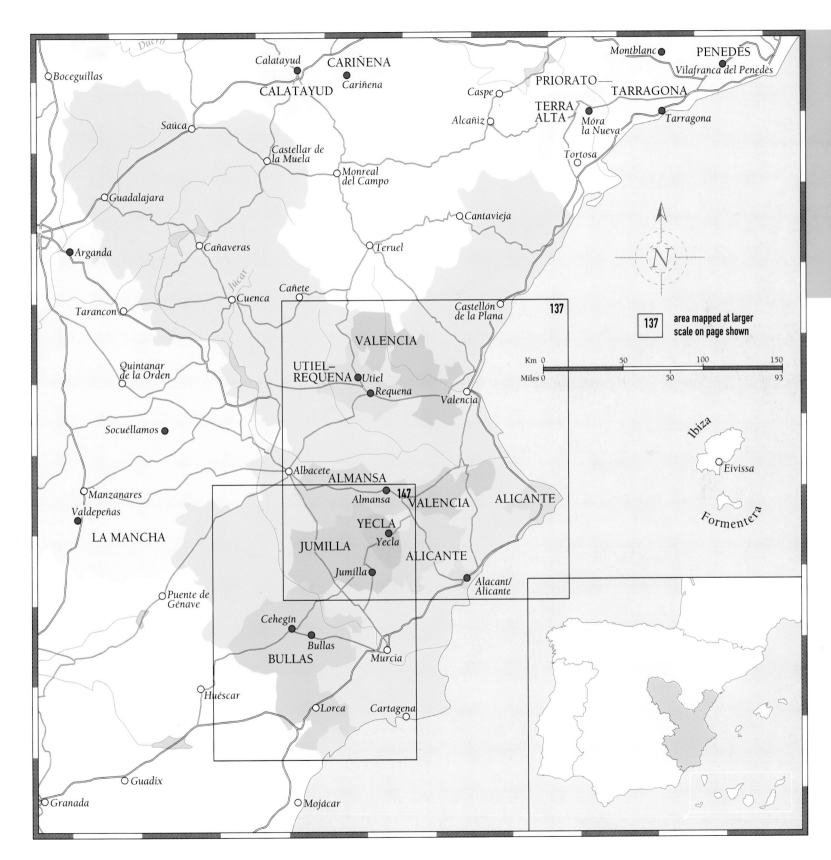

Boceguillas

Calatayud
**CARIÑENA**
**CALATAYUD**
Cariñena

Montblanc
**PENEDÈS**
Vilafranca del Penedès

**PRIORATO**
Caspe
**TARRAGONA**
Alcañiz
**TERRA**
**ALTA**
Móra
la Nueva
Tarragona

Saúca

Castellar de
la Muela

Monreal
del Campo

Tortosa

Guadalajara

Cantavieja

Arganda
Cañaveras

Tarancon
Cuenca
Teruel

Cañete

Castellón
de la Plana

**137**

**137** area mapped at larger
scale on page shown

**VALENCIA**

Km 0        50        100        150
Miles 0              50              93

Quintanar
de la Orden

**UTIEL–**
**REQUENA** Utiel
Requena
Valencia

Ibiza

Eivissa

Socuéllamos

Manzanares

Albacete **ALMANSA**
Almansa **147**
**VALENCIA**
**ALICANTE**

Formentera

Valdepeñas

**YECLA**
Yecla

**LA MANCHA**

**JUMILLA**

**ALICANTE**

Jumilla

Alacant/
Alicante

Puente de
Génave

Cehegín
Bullas
**BULLAS**
Murcia

Huéscar

Guadix

Lorca
Cartagena

Granada
Mojácar

# Valencia and València

The differences in spelling of Valencia may seem small, but they are sufficiently important for the city fathers to have decreed that road-signs carry the name in both versions. The problem, of course, is linguistic. Valenciano is a dialect of Catalan, dating back to the days when greater Catalonia spread down the east coast to Granada, courtesy of the armies of Navarre, who eventually came to free the region from Moorish control. Be that as it may, Valencia had an even longer period of Moorish occupation than most areas – all of which means that Valenciano, Catalan dialect or not, received far more Arabic loan-words than Catalan. Today, it is a language in its own right.

To complicate matters further, *Valencia* (with or without its grave accent) is the name of the capital city, the *autonomía* and one of three provinces in the Levant (the other two are Alicante and Castellón de la Plana) as well as the title of the main DO zone for quality-wine production. The city and the region have a bold and ancient tradition of exporting their most famous item of produce – so much so, in fact, that it is said that, elsewhere in Spain, no one knows that Valencia produces wine at all; they think only of the eponymous oranges.

## A bustling wine port

The city and port of Valencia were exporting goods before many of Spain's major business centres were even founded, and that commerce continues to this day. Although Barcelona is the country's biggest port, Valencia is its largest wine port. Bottled, casked and bulk wines leave here by road, rail and sea-going tankers, as well as by air.

Nothing is allowed to get in the way of trade. At one point in its history, the harbour became so crowded with heavy shipping that local fishermen complained of being elbowed out. The result was not what you might expect of corporate planners. Rather than compromise the shipping trade, the city officials had a brand-new harbour built alongside the old one and reserved it exclusively for the fishermen.

Similarly, the railway which carries so much of the freight northwards to the French border used to pass through a dozen level-crossings as it traversed the old port area of El Grau. To make things more efficient, the city of Valenica paid to have a tunnel excavated and put the whole line underground from south to north. Even with this improvement in place, however, there were so many wine companies in El Grau that it became impossible for them to expand – or even to get their lorries in and out. Valencia duly provided incentives for firms to move to the outskirts of town, where some brand-new, state-of-the-art wineries have since been built from scratch.

Such planning has even extended to natural elements. The River Turia used to flood in the autumn and cause endless hold-ups and expense in the city centre, so it was diverted into a newly excavated course to the west and south of Valencia. It now forms a rather beguiling, long, thin, winding park that has been enhanced by some spectacular Baroque bridges. And, just for good measure, once El Grau was cleared out by companies moving to newer industrial estates, the city officials put in a magnificent boulevard running in a straight line from the city centre to the sea.

That, it seems, is just the way they do things in Valencia.

## Regional gastronomy

In gastronomic terms, Valencia is the rice capital of Spain, with bigger paddy-fields than anywhere else in the world outside southeast Asia. *Paella* was invented here, allegedly at Denia, and other seafood specialities include *arroz abanda*: a dish of rice cooked in the juices of the shellfish and then served alone (the shellfish are eaten separately). Fish is the mainstay, naturally enough, in this fishing area, and local specialities include *calamari* (squid), *chipirones* (whole baby squid) and *pulpo* (octopus). A favourite way of cooking *lenguado* (sole), *dorada* (John Dory) and other white fish is to bake them in a salt crust and then fillet them straight from the oven. One of the local dessert specialities is called *turrón*, a nougat from Alicante which is flavoured with honey, nuts or pine-kernels. It makes a splendid end to a meal when served with the sweet local Moscatel de Valencia.

## Wine style and development

One important factor in the style and development of the wines of Valencia is a special dispensation which allows a proportion of wine made in the Utiel-Requena DO to be blended and bottled in Valencia and sold under the Valencia DO. In an *autonomía* in which 'bespoke' wine is a vital export-earner, this added flexibility allows exporters to match their international clients' requirements perfectly. The bodegas hope eventually to have the regional DO confirmed, perhaps with the names of Utiel and Alicante as subzones.

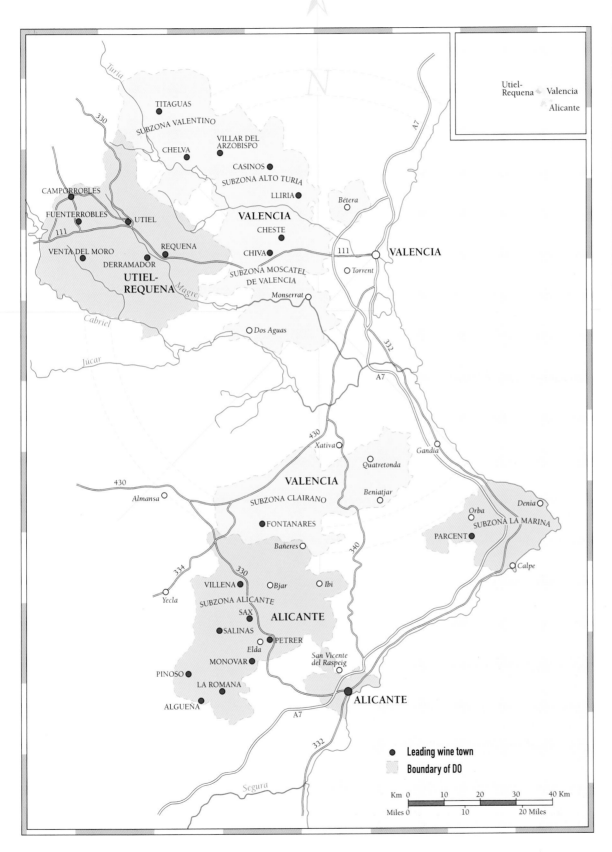

Turia

330

TITAGUAS

SUBZONA VALENTINO

VILLAR DEL
ARZOBISPO

CHELVA

CASINOS

SUBZONA ALTO TURIA

CAMPORROBLES

LLIRIA

Bétera

A7

FUENTERROBLES

UTIEL

VALENCIA

111

CHESTE

REQUENA

VALENCIA

111

VENTA DEL MORO

DERRAMADOR

CHIVA

Torrent

UTIEL-
REQUENA

Magre

SUBZONA MOSCATEL
DE VALENCIA

Cabriel

Monserrat

Júcar

Dos Aguas

332

A7

430

Xativa

Gandia

Quatretonda

VALENCIA

Almansa

SUBZONA CLAIRANO

Beniatjar

Orba

Denia

SUBZONA LA MARINA

FONTANARES

PARCENT

334

Bañeres

340

Calpe

330

VILLENA

Bjar

Ibi

Yecla

SUBZONA ALICANTE

SAX

ALICANTE

SALINAS

PETRER

Elda

San Vicente
del Raspeig

MONOVAR

PINOSO

LA ROMANA

ALICANTE

ALGUEÑA

A7

332

Segura

Utiel-
Requena    Valencia

Alicante

● Leading wine town

Boundary of DO

Km 0     10     20     30     40 Km

Miles 0          10          20 Miles

**Above:** Famed for its oranges, rice and wine, the city of Valencia also hosts the Fiesta del Patron, a springtime festival in which effigies known as *ninots* are ceremonially paraded, then burnt.

# Alicante

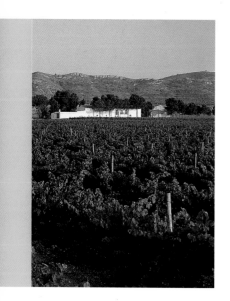

**Above: Vineyards all over the Alicante DO tend to have the same sort of topsoils, made up of clay, sand and limestone – although some (far right) have a higher chalk content than others.**

It has been said that Valencia's wines are suitable partners for the appetizers of a meal, while Utiel-Requena's are perfect for the main course. It follows, then, that the wines of Alicante were born to go with desserts. This is not to say that the DO produces exclusively sweet or *rancio* wines, just that dessert-style wines have been one of its traditional strengths.

The Alicante DO is divided into two subzones. The first, La Marina, covers the east coast from Miraflor in the north to Calpe in the south, and inland as far as Castell de Castells; it produces mainly sweeter wines. This area was added to the original Alicante DO ten years after its foundation, and takes advantage of lower, hotter vineyards to produce mainly dessert wine grapes.

The original DO area, now known as *Subzona Alicante* or *Subzona Clásico*, includes the city and its hinterland to the northwest in the valley of the River Vinalopó. As well as its share of *Fondillón* (*see* below) and *rancios*, it also produces *jovenes* in all three colours. The Alicante subzone is contiguous with the Valencia DO (specifically the Clariano subzone) in the north, the Almansa DO (*autonomía* of Castilla-La Mancha) in the northwest and the Yecla and Jumilla DOs (*autonomía* of Murcia) in the west. Indeed, some Alicante vineyards are situated over the border in the Murciano district of Abanilla. (The new Spanish constitutional politics of 1978 did not always match the pragmatics of the wine-producing areas.)

## Geography and climate

Their locations notwithstanding, the highest vineyards in Alicante (those which are furthest inland) rise to 400 metres (1,312 feet), and there is a good deal of limestone in the bedrock and the subsoil. Topsoils all over the Levant tend to be made up of the same limestone, sand and clay mixtures. Similarly, climates are fairly uniform all over the *autonomía* of Valencia: hot, humid and Mediterranean on the coast, becoming drier and more continental further inland.

This far south, however, the increasing altitude does little to reduce vineyard temperatures as it does in Penedès. While the range between day and night temperatures may be very wide during the ripening season, it is still very high overall: highland vines throughout Valencia have been known to sink their roots as deep as seven metres in search of water. Vines tend to be trained low to reduce the heat on the grapes: the higher and hotter the climate, the lower the training.

The main red-wine grape grown in Alicante is Monastrell (known in France as Mourvèdre). It has enjoyed a magnificent renaissance in recent years. Once it was thought of as nothing more than a workhorse variety turning out hefty, everyday reds, but skilled husbandry and winemaking have shown that Monastrell can yield some superlative wines, full of fruit and delicious for early drinking – even capable of a bit of ageing in the right hands. Garnacha, Tempranillo and Bobal are also grown and used in red wine production. The main white-wine grape is Merseguera (as in the Valencia DO itself) as well as Moscatel Romano, but there are also plantations of Macabeo/Viura, Planta Fina, Airén and even Riesling and Chardonnay.

## Wine styles

Although Alicante shares with its fellow Levantine DOs the desire, capability and willingness to produce low-cost, high-quality wines in large quantities to the customer's specification, its 'natural' or traditional wines fall into two groups. The first comprises *jovenes* in all three colours. These are produced from Merseguera (white), Garnacha (*rosado*) and Monastrell (red); there is also a small amount of older red wine, often made with the help of a little Tempranillo. The Moscatel wines are made purely from the Moscatel Roman as *vinos de licor* – ie fortified during fermentation to 15 per cent alcohol by volume (abv).

The Alicante DO also encompasses a unique dessert wine which may be made in either sweeter or *rancio* styles. This is called *Fondillón*, and it is usually made with Monastrell, fortified to 16 per cent abv and kept in oak for a minimum of eight years, sometimes in a variant of the *solera* system (*see* 'The Sherry Process', page 192). *Fondillón* is an unusual wine, often sold in Sherry-style bottles sporting a flanged cork, and it is much favoured in the locality and among *aficionados* further afield. At its best, it possesses something of the nutty character of a tawny Port combined with the delicate sweetness of fine cakes. *Meriendas* (afternoon teas) were made for this.

From a business point of view, there is a great deal of 'cross-fertilisation' going on between the Alicante and the Valencia *denominaciones de origen*, with the result that many of the same bodegas are represented in both regions. To simplify matters, only those unique to Alicante are listed under 'Notable bodegas' (right).

## Notable bodegas

Subzones: A = Alicante; M = Marinera

**BOCOPA, Petrel (A)**. *Founded
1987-8.* The result of a merger of no
fewer than 11 older, smaller co-ops
in the area, this leviathan has 4,000
members farming 10,000ha of vines.
However, the approach to the market
is still rather old-fashioned; 90% of the
wine is sold in bulk. The range of
*jovenes*, under the Viña Alcanta label,
is workmanlike and reasonably
reliable. Better is a new-style dry
Moscatel called Marina Alta.
*Best wine:* the traditional *Fondillón*
(100% Monastrell). Alone is the brand
name and the 1970 vintage, on sale
after 22 years in cask, is exceptional.

**Enríque Mendoza, Alfaz del Pi (M).**
*Founded 1989.* This forward-looking
young bodega counts Tempranillo,
Cabernet Sauvignon, Cabernet Franc,
Shiraz, Pinot Noir, Merlot, Chardonnay
and Parellada among its 65ha of
vines. Equipped with all the latest kit,
the bodega has set itself firmly and
successfully on the varietal route.
The brand name is Viña Alfas;
examples include 100% Chardonnay
(good) and Pinot Noir (very good).
*Best wines:* the Cabernet Sauvignon
and Merlot. The former runs to *reserva*
level but, strangely, is sometimes
better *joven* (especially from the great
mid-'90s vintages). The Merlot is also
outstanding, carries a little *crianza*
ageing and, if anything, is better
than the Cabernet.

**Gutiérrez de la Vega, Parcent (M).**
*Founded 1978.* Mainly a sweet-wine
bodega specialising in Moscatel and
doing it very well. The brand names
are legion and devoted mainly to
writers and their works. Viña Ulises
(Ulysses) is dedicated to James
Joyce and is an ancient *rancio gran
reserva*. Rojo y Negro ('red and black')
is dedicated to Dashiel Hammett and
is a red *crianza* (60% Garnacha/30%

Cabernet Sauvignon/10% others).
Cavatina Tender is an *aguja* (slightly
sparkling) sweet Moscatel, of which
there is also a dry white version.
Cosecha Dorada ('golden harvest')
is a dry-fermented Moscatel of style
and grace. *Best wine:* the Cosecha
Miel ('honey harvest') made only in
the best years from 100% selected
Moscatel with six months in oak and
an intensely sweet and yet perfectly
fruity, fresh palate.

**Primitivo Quilés, Monóvar (A).**
*Founded 1780.* An ancient family
firm that made its name in *Fondillón*
and Moscatel and continues to do so
triumphantly. The bodega is equipped
with old wooden vats as well as new
American oak *barricas*, and the firm
now produces modern-style wines as
well as its beloved traditional product.
There is a light, fresh, fruity Rosado

Virgen *joven* made from Monastrell,
and a slightly heavyweight, non-
vintage red *crianza* called Cono 4
(a *cono* is a large barrel, typically of
600 litres). *Best wines:* the traditional
fare. Opinion is divided between the
magnificent El Abuelo *rancio generoso*
(Monastrell) and the Primitivo Quilés
Moscatel Extra; both are exemplary.

**Salvador Poveda, Monóvar (A).**
*Founded 1919.* This family firm
has been a pioneer in re-establishing
*Fondillón* as a speciality of the region,
as well as maintaining its own
reputation for quality and reliability.
The family owns and buys in from
a total of 150ha of vines, making wine
both at home and at the local co-op
in nearby Mañan. Light wines include
a splendid Salvador Poveda Riesling
*joven* as well as Cantaluz (a *joven*
made from Merseguera); both are

very good, but perhaps the Riesling
has the edge. Rosella is a *joven
rosado* (80% Monastrell/20%
Cabernet Sauvignon), and there is
a pleasant red called Viña Vermeta
(100% Monastrell) up to *reserva* level.
*Best wine:* as almost everywhere in
Alicante, the magnificent *Fondillón*: the
1970 vintage (described as *semiseco*)
is 100% Monastrell, and much of it
is still in oak even as you read this.

# Utiel–Requena

The Utiel-Requena DO is part of the reason for the 'special dispensation' that allows wines to be transferred between Valenciano DOs without losing their quality-wine designations. Along the coast, Valencia produces good light, white, quaffing wines that are excellent with the food served in its myriad seafood restaurants. When it comes to red wines, though, the Valencia style is a little too light.

Fortunately, weightier examples are not far away. Utiel and Requena are two towns located within Valencia province; the DO zone named after them is the largest and furthest inland of Valencia's three wine zones. Its *métier* is red wines made from Bobal: honest, simple stuff that is excellent for blending with the lighter wines of Valencia to create a wine with the right balance.

Unsurprisingly, then, this area is famous for a style of blending wine called *doble pasta*. During its production, grapes are crushed and their juice fermented over the skins as normal; then the wine is run off and another consignment of crushed grapes is put into the same vessel on top of the previous skins and pulp. The result is a wine of enormous extract and colour, much in demand for blending – not just within Valencia, or even within Spain, but far beyond Spanish boundaries.

## Geography and climate

The vineyards of Utiel-Requena are hot and high, planted between 600 and 900 metres (1,969 to 2,953 feet) above sea level. The climate here is the second most harsh in Spain (after La Mancha), with summer highs up to 40°C (102°F) and winter lows down to -15°C (6°F) – although such actual extremes are rare. The River Magro runs down from the north, bringing alluvial soils with it, and the limestone outcrops of the highlands give way to sandstone bedrock covered with marl and clay topsoil.

As well as Bobal, which takes up around 80 per cent of the vineyard, other red grapes grown in the DO include Tempranillo (recommended for replanting in former Bobal sites) and Garnacha. For white wines, the main grapes are Macabeo, Merseguera and Planta Nova. There are also experimental plantations of Cabernet Sauvignon and Chardonnay.

As well as blending wines, Utiel-Requena makes distinctive wines of its own. There are the inevitable *jovenes* in all three colours; the best are made from Merseguera and Macabeo for whites, Garnacha and Bobal for *rosados*. Reds come from Bobal, with more or less Tempranillo according to the quality level. A small amount of red *crianza* (mainly Tempranillo) is also produced, but the area's intense heat and altitude makes the wines mature much more quickly than in the cool, northern bodegas. A Tempranillo from Utiel-Requena will be fully mature after six months in oak and a year in bottle – less than half the time required in the Rioja DOCa.

There is also a category called Utiel-Requena Superior, designed to encourage winemakers to strive for quality. It applies to white wines made from Macabeo, *rosados* from Bobal (both with a strength of 10.5 to 12 per cent alcohol by volume [abv]), and reds from Tempranillo and Garnacha with 11.5 to 13.5 per cent abv. If the *consejo regulador's* hopes are fulfilled, these will become the middle- to upper-range quality wines of Utiel-Requena in the 21st century.

Below: Bobal vines such as this flourish in the red soil of Utiel-Requena, yielding grapes which make excellent blending wines.

## Notable bodegas

### Augusto Egli, Valencia.
*Founded 1904.* This Swiss-owned company makes wines at all levels, both here and in the Valencia DO, but it is best known for its estate called Casa lo Alto in Utiel-Requena. The wines are all estate bottled and include a white (50% Macabeo/50% Merseguera), *rosado* (100% Bobal) and red *joven* produced under the brand name Rey Don Jaime. There is also a range including a red *crianza* (70% Tempranillo/ 30%Garnacha) called Casa lo Alto.

### Beltrán, Jaraguas.
*Founded 1940.* Beltrán has 150ha of vineyards and also buys in grapes from the region for its production which, in big years, may be as much as 20,000hl. Most of it is sold in bulk, but some 10% of the company's red and *rosado* wine is bottled under the name Viña Turquesa, made from 85% Tempranillo and 15% Garnacha. *Best wines:* the reds.

### Campo del Requena, Utiel.
*Founded 1919.* This family-run firm owns 40ha of vines which, with bought-in grapes, allow it to meet an annual production of approximately 750hl. The wines are consistently good and include a white *joven* called Flor (85% Macabeo/15% Chardonnay); a *joven rosado* called Viña Angeles (100% Bobal), a red *crianza* called Viña Mariola (100% Tempranillo; 30 months in oak); and a red *reserva* called Vera de Estenas (65% Tempranillo/ 35% Cabernet Sauvignon; 42 months in cask).

### Coviñas Cooperativa, Requena.
This is another conglomeration of various small co-ops designed to create a greater entity with a better economy of scale. The speciality is good-to-very good red and *rosado*

wines made under the Viña Enterizo label. *Best wine:* in good years, the red is made for *gran reserva* and can be excellent.

### Ernesto Cárcel, Rebollar.
*Founded 1948.* This company owns 35ha of vineyards and buys in grapes to support an annual production of about 1,400hl. Only 10% goes into bottle under the labels Valle del Tejo and Rebollar. All the reds are 50% Garnacha/50% Tempranillo. *Best wine:* the *rosado joven* (50% Bobal/50% Garnacha).

### Gandia. *See* Valencia DO.

### Murviedro. *See* Schenk, Valencia DO.

### Schenk *See* Valencia DO.

### Torre Oria, Derramador.
*Founded 1987.* The main interest in this company is that it is one of the few outside Catalonia that is allowed to produce sparkling wines under the Cava DO. Here in Utiel it produces pleasant *jovenes* in all three colours. *Best wines:* the *rosado jovenes* (100% Bobal).

### Vinival, Alboraya.
Vinival is a Valenciano company which is part of the giant Bodegas y Bebidas group (*see* page 151). It is mentioned here (as well as under the Valencia DO) because it owns a single estate in the region called

Viña Calderón, dominated by a hunting-lodge and surrounded by private walled gardens. The wines are *rosado joven* (80% Bobal/20% Garnacha) and red *crianza* (Tempranillo; 12 months in oak). *Best wine:* in good years, the red can be excellent.

# Valencia

The city and province of Valencia dominate the winemaking and business life of the entire *autonomia* – understandably so, since most of the wine for export passes through the port and railways of the city. As mentioned earlier, wines carrying the Valencia DO may, as a temporary measure, include 30 per cent of the production of certain vineyards: that is, of wine made from Bobal in the Utiel-Requena DO.

The need for this flexibility in the legal department may be explained as follows. First, under EU wine law, one Quality Wine Produced in a Specific Area (QWPSR) may not be blended with another QWPSR and still retain quality status; instead, it must be downgraded to the category of Table Wine. A good example of this is Durius, the *vino de mesa* from Castile-León made by the Marqués de Griñón (*see* Toro/Ribera del Duero DOs). So why is Valencia permitted to have an exception?

## Community spirit

One reason is because there is a separate campaign afoot in the *Comunidad de Valencia* (the Community of Valencia) to change the entire structure of the DO (*see* page 136). In neighbouring Castilla-La Mancha, for example, the central DO (La Mancha itself) covers a vast area stretching out over four provinces. The winemakers and *bodegueros* within it are allowed to decide their own particular needs in terms of blending wines that will suit their customers: generally the mass-markets and supermarkets of western Europe.

Recent attempts to split up the La Mancha DO into more manageable, smaller DO zones have failed simply because exporters want to take powerful red wine from the hot south and blend it with lighter reds to make a blend that represents the right price/quality ratio for the market. They may often want to include some white wines from the north and west in that blend. This system has worked well. In a dozen years, La Mancha has come from nowhere to a position as a major player in the field of everyday, low-cost wines.

'Right,' say the *viñeros* of Valencia. 'We want to be able to do the same thing.' The basic plan proposed for the region would establish an overall Valencia DO (perhaps called Vinos de Valencia in the manner of Vinos de Madrid) covering all three of the existing zones, each of which would then become a subzone of the main *denominación de origen*. This would have the dual benefit of allowing cross-blending to meet the needs of export markets while at the same time giving small, individual regions with their own microclimates the possibility of producing something unusual, special or different under the DO system.

The Valencia DO **143**

This has certainly happened in La Mancha. Based on its success, a number of small (and not so small) growers in the *Comunidad de Valencia* might like to have a go. In the meantime, Valencia takes in a good deal of Bobal red for cross-blending, and this is permitted – for the time being.

The importance of the export market to Valencia cannot be overstated. Some of the DO's major companies are foreign-owned (the Swiss are well-represented) and wine has been exported from here in vast quantities since the last century. This does not mean that everything produced here is everyday, supermarket wine. Every region has its mavericks and its individualists, and they are not always necessarily the smallest companies.

## The subzones and their structures

Geographically, Valencia's vineyards are divided into three subzones. Valentino and Alto Turia lie east and northeast of the city itself, over towards the east coast, while Clariano is separated entirely from the other two, situated south of the city. Valentino covers a wide range of terrain from the coastal plain up to an altitude of 550 metres (1,805 feet), with the main vineyards positioned at about 180 and 260 metres (591 to 853 feet). At the lower levels, the soil is dry and sandy with some alluvial deposits over limestone. There are similar but lighter soils on higher ground.

Alto Turia is higher still. At an average of 620 metres (2,034 feet), it is as hot and high as the lower slopes of Utiel-Requena, but without such extreme temperature ranges since it is located that much closer to the coast. Clariano is lower – around 350 metres (1,148 feet) – with more clay in its subsoil. In general, the soils of the region are well-adapted to vine-growing. Given the right training, there is no reason why quality vines should not flourish here.

## Main grape varieties

The main grape for white wines is Merseguera (covering about 25 per cent of the vineyard). Here, as elsewhere in the Levant, it yields light, fresh wines which can be pleasantly herby when well made and rather neutral when over- controlled. Malvasía Riojana (called Subirat-Parent in Catalonia) is grown in the Clariano and Valentino subzones; other white-wine grapes include Planta Fina and Pedro Ximénez, and Moscatel Romano for *vinos de licor*. Yet another native white grape is the Verdil (also known as Tortosí; quite promising in places, it seems). Chardonnay has also been planted.

The main grape for red wines is Monastrell, going through a renaissance in the Clariano subzone, as elsewhere in the winemaking world (thanks largely to work done in the neighbouring Jumilla DO). Others include Garnacha Tintorera, the black grape with the pink juice; it is an important blending grape even if it does not have the finesse of its cousin, Garnacha Tinta. A very small quantity of Tempranillo is grown in the region, which the *consejo regulador* recommends for replanting to replace any other red vine, and there is also a local variety called Forcayat (in Clariano). Then, of course, there are the inevitable experimental plantations of Cabernet Sauvignon.

## Winemaking and wine styles

So what of the wines themselves? The Valencianos are proud of the fact that customers can go to one of the new, state-of-the-art wineries on the outskirts of the city and virtually specify any wine they like, defining it by colour, strength, acidity and sugar levels, label, bottle, price and everything else. What this tends to mean is that a large output of pleasant *jovenes* is produced in all three colours, at every level of sweetness, tailor-made for the supermarket business. The white wines will be made mainly from Merseguera with a dash of Macabeo, *rosados* are mainly Garnacha and Bobal, and the reds come from Bobal with some Monastrell. These are likely to surface as supermarket and restaurant own-brand house wines at suitably modest prices.

There are also some speciality wines. The Valentino subzone makes semi-sweet and sweet wines from Moscatel and Pedro Ximénez, as well as the classic Moscatel de Valencia *vino de licor*. *Licorosos* and *rancios* are also made throughout the region and require a minimum of two years in oak.

However, the most promising category for the lover of serious quality wines is likely to be that of the experimental wines made on individual estates, often from Monastrell, Tempranillo and Cabernet Sauvignon (*see* listings below). Valencia's extreme climatic conditions mean that it is rare to find anything above *reserva* level, but *crianza* wines are made with the minimum six months in oak and are beginning to show that there is considerable potential. Such potential has become particularly evident since drip-feed irrigation was permitted on an experimental basis after the near-death drought years of the early 1990s. It remains to be seen what might be achieved in these parts with a few regular drops of water per day during the ripening season.

# Notable bodegas

## Augusto Egli, Valencia.
*See* Utiel-Requena DO.

## Belda, Fontanares.
*Founded 1931.* This family-run firm
is of mainly regional significance,
but it also adopts a modern approach
to its winemaking. Belda produces
a white *joven* (Verdil) and a *rosado
joven* (Cabernet Sauvignon) under the
Ponsalet label, as well as varietal reds
called Eusebio la Casta. There are
also *crianza* varietal wines made from
Tempranillo (ten months in oak) and
Monastrell (12 months in oak).
*Best wine:* the varietal Tempranillo
*crianza* can be excellent.

## Gandía, Chiva. *Founded 1885.*
Gandía is now situated in a smart
new state-of-the-art bodega located
outside the city. It is one of the
most successful producers (some
100,000hl) and biggest exporters
in Spain, with 90% of its massive
production going abroad.
Gandía wines may be found under
supermarket own-brand labels all
over the world, but the company does
make wines under its own brand,
Castillo de Liria. There are good-
quality *jovenes* in white (Merseguera),
*rosado* (Bobal) and red (80% Bobal/
20% Monastrell). There is also a *dulce*
made from Moscatel Romano.

## Murviedro, Valencia.
*See* Schenk (*below*).

## Schenk, Valencia. This firm includes
Cavas Murviedro (*above*) but makes
a distinct range of wines under each
bodega's name, as well as the
inevitable own-brands for the export
market. Cadrillo and Las Lomas are
brand names used in Utiel-Requena
for a basic range of everyday wines.
*Best wines:* Those bearing the
Murviedro brand name. In Utiel,
Murviedo is used for an excellent
varietal Tempranillo *crianza*, while in

Valencia the same name is used for
two varietal white *jovenes* (variously
Merseguera, Moscatel and Macabeo),
a Garnacha/Bobal *rosado* and a very
good red *crianza* (Monastrell/Garnacha;
12 months in oak).

## Torrevelisca, Fontanares.
*Founded 1990.* A large bodega
with 221ha of vines, including
Cabernet Sauvignon, Tempranillo and
Chardonnay. It turns out workmanlike
wines under its own label as well
as some for contract customers.
*Best wines:* the reds, *joven* and
*crianza,* including a varietal Monastrell.

## Vinival, Alboraya.
One of Valencia's biggest firms and
part of the Bodegas y Bebidas group
(*see* page 151). Vinival produces
millions of litres of wine each year,
and yet its name is hardly noticed
in the small print of the own-label
brands it supports. There is a local
brand called Torres de Quart, under
which *jovenes* in all three colours
are produced, plus a Vival d'Or
Moscatel, but the company's
real strength still lies in its enormous
and almost anonymous export
market. *See also* the Vinival entry
in the Utiel-Requena DO.

**Below: Grapes are weighed at Valencia's
Godelleta co-op. The chief white variety is
Merseguera, which yields fresh, herby wines.**

# Murcia: a separate society

Periodically, someone asks why the little region of Murcia, which is patently part of the Levant in terms of its export culture, climate and (to a large extent) gastronomy, should be an *autonomia* in its own right, rather than part of nearby Valencia or other, larger regions. The answer lies partly in the history of its language.

The town of Murcia was founded in the ninth century by the Moorish caliph, Abdu'r Rahman, and known by the Arabic name of *Mursiyah*. Once its Muslim settlers began farming in the vicinity, it prospered immediately due to its fertile plains or *huertas* (the meaning in this instance is of a huge natural 'garden'), which boast well-drained soil and – for these latitudes – plentiful rainfall.

Because of these natural advantages, Murcia the region quickly grew rich in produce of all types: oranges, melons, rice, vegetables in profusion and (naturally enough) grapes, which the Moorish Muslims enjoyed as fresh fruit and raisins since they were not so keen on wine. Not surprisingly, given its background, the region today has become a fruit-canning centre (mainly apricots and peaches), and it also specialises in the production of almonds and olives as well as wine.

## Castilian settlement

The *Reconquista*, or reconquest, of Moorish Spain came from the north, driven by Castilian power and money. When the region finally came back within the ranks of an expanding Spain in 1266, it was due to Castilian armies – who, of course, spoke the Castilian tongue. Many settled in the area, and most of the Murcians of today are their descendants.

Meanwhile, after experiencing a brief period of independence under Rodrigo Díaz de Bivar, Duke of Valencia – otherwise known as El Cid – neighbouring Valencia reverted to Moorish rule. It was then liberated some 28 years earlier than Murcia by James the Conqueror, of the Kingdom of Navarre. Navarre, in spite of its name, was heavily influenced by Catalonia; the Catalan language became dominant there and subsequently in Valencia – which is why the Valenciano language is vastly different from Castilian. Hence, Valencia and Murcia began as separate entities with separate languages, and they have remained so to this day. In any case, the citizens of Murcia are happy with this state of affairs, and view themselves as something of a transitional culture between the seagoing, fish-eating, Mediterraneans of Valencia and the farming, meat-eating New Castilian peoples of the Meseta.

One of Murcia's most famous early inhabitants was the Moorish mystic poet Ibn Al-Arabi, who was born here in 1165. Today, congenial little Murcia town displays its cultural heritage both a cathedral city and a university city. The cathedral, which boasts a splendid baroque façade, is dominated by an unusual high tower and was built by four different architects between 1521 and 1792. For many years, the town provided a safe inland haven for the papal see, which had formerly been dangerously exposed to seaborne attack on the coast at Cartagena.

## Early winemaking history

After the *Reconquista*, when Valencia provided export goods in the form of oranges, wine and rice, Murcia produced different but just as vital commodities in the form of fresh vegetables, cereals, meat and livestock. In winemaking terms, it fulfilled a similar role to that of Utiel-Requena, by providing heavy, heady, mainly red (and *doble-pasta*) wines designed to beef up the lightweight, Mediterranean wines of Alicante and Valencia. Today, however, this role has changed rather radically due to the rise of the Monastrell grape (*see* following DOs).

## Murcian gastronomy

Elsewhere in the gastronomic life of Murcia, its frugal and prudent past still shows through in the way its foodstuffs are used to their best advantage. In spite of its lack of coastline, one of the region's signature dishes is something called *rin-ran*, made from *bacalao* (dried salt cod) with potatoes and peppers. The major local cheese is a simple goat's-milk product, sold fresh or after having been aged in vine-leaves.

The most ingredient-efficient dish of all is a pancake called *alojaharina*, which is made from flour flavoured with garlic and contains anything the cook happens to have left in the fridge: typically *chorizo*, *embutido* (sausage), mushrooms and peppers of various colours, all fried together and usually served with *patatas a la brasa* (new potatoes braised from raw on the grill).

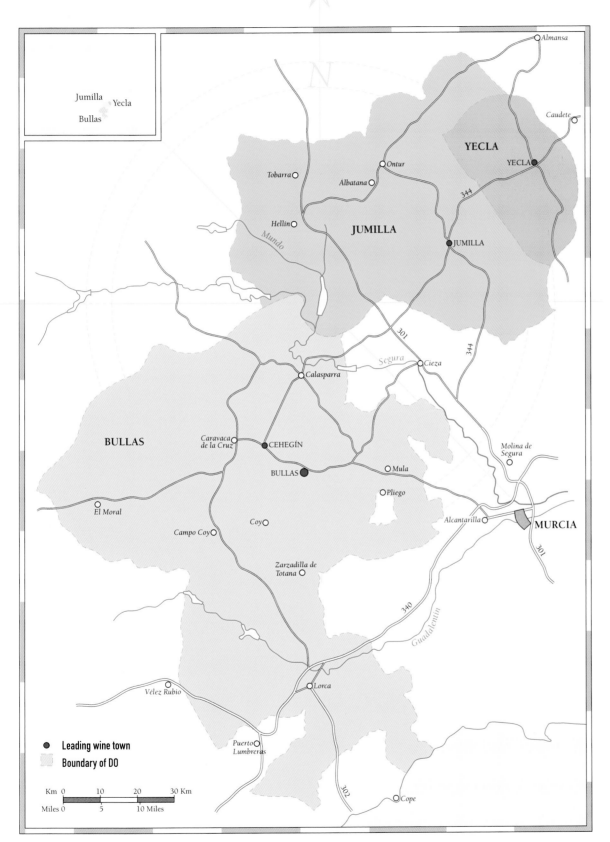

Jumilla   Yecla

Bullas

Almansa

YECLA

Caudete

Tobarra    Ontur    YECLA

Albatana    344

Hellín    JUMILLA

Mundo    JUMILLA

301

Segura    Cieza

344

Calasparra

BULLAS    Molina de Segura

Caravaca    CEHEGÍN
de la Cruz

BULLAS    Mula

Pliego

El Moral    Alcantarilla    MURCIA

Coy    301

Campo Coy

Zarzadilla de
Totana

340    Guadalentín

Lorca

Vélez Rubio

Puerto
Lumbreras

● Leading wine town

░ Boundary of DO

Km 0    10    20    30 Km

Miles 0    5    10 Miles

302    Cope

**Above:** Small but perfectly formed. The little town of Murcia is a congenial place, home to both a cathedral and a university as well as wine.

Below: Vineyards in Murcia province. Those serving the Bullas DO are located in the western half, and are planted mainly with Monastrell.

# Bullas

**B**ullas is the newest of the Murcian *denominaciones de origen*. Even though it covers a large area, it is not one that is heavily planted. The Bullas DO makes up most of the western half of the province, including eight towns and villages radiating around the town which bears the DO name. Bullas itself is a typical inland market-town whose teetering, narrow streets are filled with small, comfortable houses positioned cheek-by-jowl with tiny churches and bell-towers – and the inevitable bars and cafés which offer a warm welcome all over Spain.

The town of Bullas has Roman origins. It was heavily fortified in the eighth century during the reign of the Moorish Caliph Abd-Al Rahman. During the 13th century, it was taken by King Alfonso the Sage, and official records of 1254 state that the *castillo*, or castle, of Bullas was intended to extend its protection to the neighbouring village of Mula. Mula, as it happens, is another of the eight municipalities that have the right to make wines under the Bullas DO.

## Geography and climate

Geographically, Bullas divides into three subzones, which might be designated northeast, central and western. The most important of these is the western subzone, which accounts for just over half the land under vine and boasts the highest altitude – from 500 to 800 metres (1,640 to 2,625 feet). Second most important is the central subzone, which covers most of Bullas itself, at an altitude of 500 to 600 metres (1,640 to 1,969 feet); it provides about 40 per cent of production. Finally, the northeast subzone is an area of low yields, with less than ten per cent of the vineyard situated at altitudes ranging from 400 to 500 metres (1,312 to 1,640 feet).

As we have seen in our progression southwards from Catalonia, these inland, high-altitude areas have tremendous potential. True, they may not have the benefit of the microclimatic conditions of the Alt-Penedès, for example; this far south, the effect of even 800 metres of altitude can be rather less dramatic than might be expected in the north. Yet just as in its neighbouring DO zones, sterling work is being done in the Bullas DO with the Monastrell grape.

Monastrell accounts for around 95 per cent of the Bullas DO vineyard. Until as recently as the mid-1990s, however, it was regarded as little more than a workhorse grape, turning out vast quantities of good, solid, red blending wine which was reliable, generous – and dull. While the French make something much more stylish from the same grape (which they call Mourvèdre) in the Rhône Valley and the south of the country, their vineyards are much further north and their winemaking tradition is different.

Well, for 'northern' read 'high-altitude' and for 'tradition' read 'old-fashioned under-investment', and you have what Bullas and its neighbouring DO zones of Yecla and Jumilla had at the beginning of the 1990s. As always, it takes a few bodegas with forward-thinking ideas and a willingness to risk some money to change the way an entire DO works.

This has taken place, not just in Bullas but in all three Murcian DO zones. The details are split between developments in Jumilla and Yecla (*see* respective DOs) but suffice it to say that, since being awarded the provisional DO in 1982, Bullas has had a number of excellent examples to follow in the now-familiar fields of early harvesting, maceration control, temperature control and ageing, and the auguries are good.

## Main grape varieties

As well as Monastrell, a small amount of Tempranillo is grown here, along with some Macabeo and Airén for white wines, as well as experimental Cabernet Sauvignon, Garnacha, Syrah and Merlot. Yet the present Bullas is principally Monastrell red and *rosado* wine country – roughly one-third and two-thirds of production, respectively.

The wines as we know them today consist of *jovenes* in all three colours (but overwhelmingly *rosado*). Until relatively recently, that was the top and bottom of it. However, since the award of the DO, one or two bodegas have been galvanised into trying something new. This mainly takes the form of lighter, fresher, early-picked reds with more acidity and upfront fruit and a little judicious oak-ageing, perhaps not even to *crianza* level. These, it seems likely, are the wines that will mark Bullas' future, along with its Murciano compatriots.

The local co-op has been one of the prime movers in modernising winemaking in Bullas, which has set an example to other, smaller producers. There are also a number of small, family bodegas waiting to make their mark as the region expands: Bullas is a wine to watch.

## Notable bodegas

**Carrascalejo, Bullas.**
*Founded 1850.* A family-owned bodega with 140ha of vines and a total output of around 2,800hl. The wines are a cut above the local norm. *Best wines:* the varietal *jovenes* made from Monastrell, both *rosado* and red.

**Nuestra Señora del Rosario Cooperativa, Bullas.**
*Founded 1950.* With 1,200 members, this co-op has become the flagship winery of Bullas. It has been re-equipped with the latest automated stainless-steel kit as well as a large contingent of new American oak casks. The Las Reñas label offers *jovenes* in all three colours; the white is made from Macabeo and the *rosado* and red from Monastrell. These are very good wines and among the best of the region. *Best wine:* a premium *rosado* called Tesoro de Bullas, made from selected Monastrell grapes and macerated for 16 to 24 hours to extract the colour. This can be excellent in good years.

# Jumilla

Twenty-five years ago, only the bulk-wine trade had heard of Jumilla. A giant industrial bodega called SAVIN dominated production and conducted most of the business, and local co-ops did most of the rest. And why not? The area is dry and high, conditions which make for a good production of simple wines. It was precisely this simple wine which was in enormous demand from the surrounding areas – especially Valencia, in the days when no one particularly cared what your DO was, and much of Europe, still outside the EC, could call its wines whatever it liked. Given this state of affairs, Jumilla did good business, sold everything it produced, and wondered (when it thought about it at all) what all the fuss was about.

Conditions, however, were changing fast. Most notably, because of its sandy soils and hot climate, Jumilla had never suffered from phylloxera, a situation which allowed its growers to plant European vines on their own roots. The inevitable bug arrived in 1988-89 – roughly a hundred years later than the rest of the world. Production fell to one-third of what it had been previously as the vineyards were hurriedly grubbed-up and replanted with grafted vines in an attempt to regain its former status. But the act of grubbing-up made the *consejo regulador* pause for thought: since vineyard owners were replanting anyway, was there anything they could do to revitalise the rather tired, low-production vines – and even, perhaps, make something rather better?

**Monastrell vines, such as these near Hellín (below), are now harvested earlier to maximise acidity and provide better balance in the finished wine.**

The *Estación Enológica* (Oenological Station) in Jumilla duly started to conduct research into the matter. One or two of the local bodegas showed an interest in the subject as well. There had long been a belief in some quarters that Monastrell could perform better than it had been performing, and this proved to be precisely the case. For a start, new, virus-free clones of Monastrell could replace the old vines. With earlier picking to retain acidity, new investment in winemaking equipment and a new approach to the marketplace, Jumilla could re-invent itself as an island of quality winemaking in an area better known for bulk wines. After all, hadn't the Valdepeñas DO done exactly the same thing many years ago?

Such a momentous step forward required the support of some fairly heavyweight producers in the region, and there is none heavier than the drinks giant, Bodegas y Bebidas. The company is the owner of Señorío del Condestable, the giant installation which had been known as SAVIN all those years ago. In the laboratories here, as in many others throughout Jumilla, grapes were harvested at different times, vinified in different ways and scrutinised – not just by the oenologists, but by the firm's export directors with a view towards foreign markets.

As well as Condestable, a small independent winery called Vitivino (now, sadly, no longer with us), was producing improved wines from its own private estate.

Its strategy included taking advantage of the rich colour of Monastrell, macerating longer, fermenting cooler and even ageing judiciously in bottle as well as (or even instead of) barrel. The results were surprising to many of Jumilla's traditional winemakers: richly ripe wines with consummate fruit, good strength and honest backbone started to appear where there had been little more than bulk wine before. Some bodegas even began experimenting with an admixture of wine made by *maceración carbónico*, and other bodegas decided to join in. All of which means that today's Jumilla is poised to be a strong force in 21st-century southern Spanish winemaking.

## Geography and grape varieties

The town of Jumilla itself is a very pleasant place, beautifully restored in the centre and with a couple of decent restaurants, small town-centre parks and that kind of discreet prosperity which appears when a place is 'on the up'. The DO's wine is produced in the surrounding areas as well as just over the border in the province of Albacete (*autonomía* of Castilla-La Mancha). Its vineyards are located at heights of 400 to 800 metres (1,312 to 2,625 feet), planted in light, sandy soils which lie over limestone bedrock. Almond trees and olive groves grow alongside the vineyards – such is the heat generated even on these upper slopes. But, as we have seen, early harvesting and modern winemaking methods have taken advantage of this situation to drive the new Jumilla wines back to the export market with a vengeance.

Although the main grape is Monastrell, which makes up over 85 per cent of the vineyard, other red varieties are grown: Cencibel/Tempranillo, Garnacha (both Tinta and Tintorera) and Cabernet Sauvignon. For white wines, the main grapes are Airén and Macabeo, and for sweet wines (*vinos de licor*), there is Pedro Ximénez – also Monastrell, when it is harvested over-ripe and full of natural grape-sugar.

Although the DO regulations recognise all the old blending-wine criteria, the new Jumilla rules (which became law in November 1995) very much encourage better-quality wines. Main production today is aimed at red wines made from at least 85 per cent Monastrell with at least 12.5 per cent alcohol by volume (abv) and *rosados* with at least 12 per cent abv. There are also categories for *jovenes* in all three colours, as well as Jumilla *dulce*.

Right: The bodegas and vineyards of Casa Castillo, which produces pure Monastrell wines that grow old with grace.

## Notable bodegas

**Agapito Rico, Jumilla.**
*Founded 1989.* Very much a
'new-wave' bodega whose 70ha
include Cabernet Sauvignon,
Tempranillo and Merlot as well as
Monastrell. The firm set its sights on
making only red wines of the highest
quality. The brand name is Carchelo,
and there is a basic red *crianza* made
from a selection of grapes, as well
as varietals from *joven* to *reserva* level
made from Cabernet Sauvignon
and Monastrell. All are very good.
*Best wine:* the Monastrell *joven,*
which can be excellent in good years.

**Casa Castillo, Jumilla.**
*Founded 1991.* Casa Castillo has
250ha and makes about 4,200hl
of wine in all three colours. The wines
are better than average. *Best wines:*
the *rosado* (50% Monastrell/50%
Tempranillo) and the red *crianza*
(50% Monastrell/35% Tempranillo/
15% Cabernet Sauvignon;
12 months in oak).

**Induvasa, Jumilla.**
*Founded 1978.* Another bodega
which has made great strides in
recent years, especially in planting
French varieties. *Best wine:* Castillo
de Luzón *reserva* (40% Cabernet
Sauvignon/35% Tempranillo/15%
Monastrell/10% Merlot)'.

**San Isidro Cooperativa, Jumilla.**
*Founded 1935.* The biggest
producer in Jumilla, with 2,000
members farming 20,000ha and
turning out around 200,000hl per
year. Although a good deal of the
wine is sold in bulk, the co-op has
a very good track record for better-
quality wines, mainly under the
Sabatcha label. This range offers
white (Airén) and *rosado* (Monastrell)
*jovenes* and a red *crianza* (Monastrell;
12 months in cask), all of which
are good. There is also an unusual
*semiseco* made from Monastrell and

a delicious San Isidro red (Monastrell)
made by *maceración carbónica.*
*Best wine:* the red Sabatcha *joven.*

**Señorío del Condestable,
Jumilla.** *Founded 1968.*
Started by Bodegas y Bebidas
as the SAVIN company, this firm
has now become one of the front-
runners of new-style Monastrell
wines. In the mid-1990s, Señorío
del Condestable launched a
varietal Monastrell called Vilamar,
on the label of which the name
'Monastrell' was much more

prominent than 'Jumilla'. This
wine is part of a series of varietals
which the firm is marketing from
regions all over Spain. The main
brand is Señorío de Robles,
and the range offers *jovenes*
in all three colours: white (Airén),
red and *rosado* (Monastrell).
These are good, sound, well-
made wines, especially the
*rosado. Best wine:* the Vilamar
mentioned above. Excellent,
with a lighter, fruitier, modern
style, it retains all the region's
warmth and ripeness.

**Above: The village church of Mora de Santa
Quiteria, in the province of Albacete. Although
they originate in a different *autonomía*, wines
produced in Albacete still take the Jumilla DO.**

# Y Yecla

**Y**ecla occupies that part of the eastern secton of the Murcian province left vacant by Jumilla. The fact that Yecla is a separate DO may seem strange, considering it is the only one in Spain to cover a single town. This status, however, reflects its historic importance as a wine-producing area in the days when the Levant had an unquenchable thirst for everyday wines produced for blending and export. Those days are long gone, but they gave Yecla the opportunity to wrest its independence from the surrounding areas – a status it does not intend to lose. Since the mid-1970s, this little DO has resolutely ploughed ahead to establish its wines as unique in their own right.

The town of Yecla itself is unexceptional. It exists mainly because of its location at a major crossroads. The settlement that grew up around these two thoroughfares offered the modest accommodation and pleasant cuisine of any small rural Spanish town, catering for heavy traffic trundling by. If no one had made the effort, Yecla might well have remained in what amounts to vinous obscurity, turning out everyday wines of average quality and selling them locally.

## Geography and climate

There is no reason why Yecla should not make excellent wine. After all, its vineyards are high – 400 to 700 metres (1,312 to 2,297 feet) – the climate is continental and the soil is composed of good, thick loam spread over a limestone bedrock. The main grape, here as in neighbouring Jumilla, is Monastrell. We have seen what can be accomplished with it, so all the ingredients for success have been in place for many years.

Yecla's major co-op is workmanlike in its output, but not to the extent of exciting potential export markets. What was needed to push the region into the modern wine arena was something to encourage the bodegas to think beyond the local bulk market and experiment, invest and develop instead. In Jumilla, the catalyst was phylloxera. In Yecla, it was Bodegas Castaño.

Bodegas Castaño set out to open up world markets for the wines of Yecla. It was willing to invest, make good wine, help win the DO for the area – and then get out into the international marketplace and sell. The risks were palpable: there was no guarantee that new winemaking equipment or careful vineyard husbandry would persuade anybody outside southeastern Spain to take an interest in Yecla wines. Still, Bodegas Castaño took the plunge, and the world noticed. Because of this, the (admittedly still modest) export situation of wines from the DO owes a considerable debt to the Castaño family.

## Grape varieties and wine styles

What makes the wines of Yecla different? Certainly not its grapes, which are roughly the same as those of neighbouring DOs. The main grape for red wines is Monastrell, though Garnacha is also permitted. For white wines, Merseguera, Macabeo and Airén are prominent. There are also the usual experimental plantations of Cabernet Sauvignon, Tempranillo and Merlot. It is fairly obvious, however, that Monastrell is still Yecla's workhorse – certainly in the short-term.

If grapes are not vastly different and vineyards are not quite high enough to produce the early-ripening, thinner-skinned, higher-acidity grapes that turned the tide for Jumilla, then the answer for Yecla must lie in the way its wines are aged. From experiments conducted at Bodegas Castaño, winemakers learned how to make judicious use of oak to tame the ripeness and strength of the chief grapes. They also adopted an intelligent approach to bottling in order to capture the wines at the right moment – even if that does not square with the official regulations in certain years.

The result is wines which, if not taking the world by storm, are at least appearing on the shelves of northern Europe's major supermarket and specialist wine-merchant chains. In terms of style, they are mainly *jovenes* in all three colours. Some of the reds are made by *maceración carbónica* and there is even a little oak-aged red produced (usually from Monastrell) up to *reserva* level. There is still a long way to go, of course, but Yecla is definitely on the move.

# Notable bodegas

**Bodegas Castaño, Yecla.**
*Founded 1972.* The family firm that started the ball rolling. The firm owns 300ha and also buys in grapes to produce around 40,000hl, much of which is still sold in bulk. Bottled wines, however, have broken into world markets under three brand names. Viña las Gruesas is the label for traditionally made wines, including two whites: a *joven* (70% Airén/20% Macabeo/ten per cent Verdejo) and a *crianza* (70% Airén/30% Macabeo; eight months in oak). There is also a *rosado joven* (80% Monastrell/20% Garnacha); and a red *crianza* (80% Monastrell/15% Garnacha/5% Merlot). All are very good. Next, the Castaño label offers a good Monastrell red made by *maceración carbónica.*
*Best wines:* those made under the Pozuelo label, which offers reds at *crianza* (70% Monastrell/10% Garnacha/10% Merlot; ten months in oak) and *reserva* (70% Monastrell/15% Garnacha/15% Merlot; 20 months in oak) levels. Arguably the best wines of Yecla.

**Dominio de la Torres, Yecla.**
*Founded 1989.* Well-equipped with modern technology and its own 170ha. Annual production is around 3,000hl. As well as traditional Monastrell-based wines under the label Torrepalomares, there is also a varietal Cabernet Sauvignon called Coto del Moro. Wines with potential.

**La Purísima Cooperativa, Yecla.**
*Founded 1954.* Giant, with 1,400 members farming 4,500ha, making over 100,000hl. The co-op takes an 'ecological' approach to its wines (sort of halfway between standard and organic practices). *Best wines:* the reds made under the Alféizar label, from Monastrell with some *maceración carbónica.*

Below: The high vineyards of the Yecla DO are well positioned to grow Monastrell, which is the DO's main variety.

Below: A cart-load of Bobal grapes, much of which is destined to be turned into light red and *rosado* country wines.

# Country Wines of the Levant

## Valencia

### VC Benniarés (Alicante)

This is a small area located between the city of Valencia and the city of Alicante, covering five municipalities and approximately 450ha of vines. Recommended grapes are Garnacha, Monastrell and the obscure local variety Tortosina, with Moscatel as a secondary variety. However, much of the vineyard is given over to the Valenciano 'regulars' such as Bobal and Merseguera.

Production is small-to-domestic in scale, and although wines of all three colours are registered, most of the production consists of light reds and rosados as well as sweet wines made with Moscatel and Pedro Ximénez.

### VC Sant Mateu (Castellón de la Plana)

Northernmost of the Valenciano winelands, the Sant Mateu zone is the rump of what was once a major wine-growing area dating back to Roman times. It covers approximately 1,000ha of vineyards which stretch over nine towns and villages. Many of these vineyards are used in mixed cultivation with other crops, and a good deal of the area's production is old-fashioned and/or domestic.

Sant Mateu is registered for the making of red and white wines from the Garnacha, Monastrell and Macabeo grape varieties, although the obscure Esquitxagos and Bonaire are also very widely planted. Most of the zone's production is devoted to strong, dry white wines – 13% abv – and these can be reasonable country fare. Reds and rosados, however, tend to be of rather poor quality.

### VC Lliber-Jávea (Alicante)

This area is situated just outside the northern part of the Alicante DO and covers nine towns and villages north of Benidorm and between Lliber and Jávea. It is registered to produce red and white wines made from Garnacha, Monastrell and Merseguera, with Moscatel as a secondary variety.

One of the towns and villages is the town of Denia, widely regarded as the birthplace of paella. Make of this what you will.

### Notable bodega

**Carmelitano, Benicasím.** A small bodega of monkish (Carmelite) origins turning out a very passable sweet white made from Moscatel, called Carmelitano.

## Murcia

### VdlT Campo de Cartagena

Campo de Cartagena wines are produced around the town of Cartagena itself, which is situated on the southeastern coast of the province of Murcia. There are 143ha currently classified as vino de la tierra, growing 80% Merseguera and 20% Monastrell, and producing about 12 hl/ha. The new regulations recommend Merseguera and Cencibel as the principal grape varieties, with Pedro Ximénez and Airén recommended as back-up selections.

The soils in this wine zone are admittedly not very good, consisting mainly of loose clay, but with some carbonates, at altitudes of around 200 metres (656 feet). The climate, however, is dry Mediterranean, and manages an average annual rainfall of 280 millimetres (11 inches). This district actually takes up about half of the original 300ha area of Campo de Cartagena, the rest of which has lost the right to the name. In the new VdlT zone, winemaking is improving, although the main product is a rather old-fashioned blanco dorado aged according to the crianza artesanal – ie, in tinajas. As a result, a good deal of the wine is suitable only for local consumption. There are 23 bodegas, all privately owned.

### VdlT Abanilla

This area is contiguous with the Alicante DO; indeed, parts of the town of Abanilla are included in the Alicante DO zone. It includes vineyards in Abanilla and Fortuna. Some 2,000ha of vineyards are planted with Monastrell and subsidiary varieties such as Garnacha Tinta, Merseguera and Airén.

The wines have something of the character of Jumilla and Alicante about them, although they are not really in the same league in terms of quality.

# The Meseta

The Meseta is the high, central plateau that forms the centre of Spain. This vast tableland is highest in the northwestern section of Old Castile (Castile-León), where it reaches up to 1,000 metres (3,281 feet), and lowest in the southeastern part of New Castile (Castilla-La Mancha), where it falls to just 500 metres (1,640 feet). Tilting downwards from northwest to southeast, it is split in two by the mountain ranges of the Sierra de Guadarrama and the Serrania de Cuenca. Its temperatures are extreme: high and hot in the summer, freezing in the winter. It is hard to believe that wine-grapes grow here, but grow they do – and with great success. This part of Spain is home to the country's largest wine region, La Mancha, and one of its best known, Valdepeñas. Both turn out a wide range of quality wine that is happily snapped up by the world's export market. Meanwhile, producers in the Vinos de Madrid DO supply the Spanish capital with its own particular styles – a real taste of 'local' Spain.

**Below:** Hallmark of the Meseta. In a region that includes the legendary land of La Mancha, windmills such as this are an intrinsic feature.

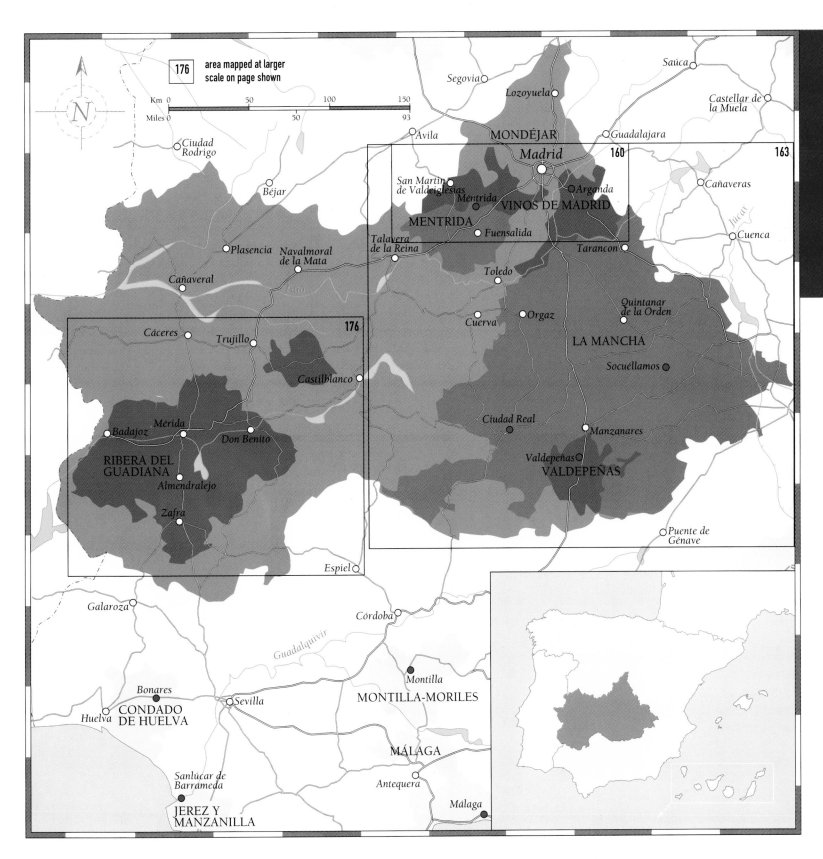

area mapped at larger
scale on page shown

Km 0          50          100          150
Miles 0          50          93

Saúca

Segovia
Lozoyuela
Castellar de
la Muela

Avila
MONDÉJAR
Guadalajara
Madrid
160
163

Ciudad
Rodrigo
San Martin
de Valdeiglesias
Arganda
Cañaveras

Béjar
Méntrida
VINOS DE MADRID

MENTRIDA
Cuenca

Plasencia
Navalmoral
de la Mata
Talavera
de la Reina
Fuensalida

Cañaveral
Tarancon

Tajo
Toledo

Cáceres
Trujillo
Cuerva
Orgaz
Quintanar
de la Orden

176
LA MANCHA

Castilblanco
Socuéllamos

Mérida
Badajoz
Don Benito
Ciudad Real
Manzanares

RIBERA DEL
GUADIANA
Almendralejo
Valdepeñas
VALDEPEÑAS

Zafra

Espiel
Puente de
Génave

Galaroza

Córdoba

Guadalquivir
Montilla

Bonares
MONTILLA-MORILES

Huelva
Sevilla
CONDADO
DE HUELVA

MÁLAGA

Sanlúcar de
Barrameda
Antequera

Málaga
JEREZ Y
MANZANILLA

# Vinos de Madrid

## Madrid: the heart of Spain

*Madrid did not become capital of Spain until the mid-16th century, when Philip II moved his court there lock, stock and barrel. Today's Madrid is home to around three million people, and sits in the centre of the autonomía of the same name. Most development occurs around the major roads out of the city, but nestled among the industrial estates and suburbs are places where the pace of life has hardly changed in a hundred years. Wine is made, cows are milked and farming life continues just out of earshot of the impatient traffic-horns of the Plaza de las Cibeles. Just a few kilometres away, a a farmer's wife is serving up bowls of the steaming cocido, Madrid's classic regional dish: a nourishing winter stew based on chick-peas and made with meat, game, or other vegetables according to individual taste. The only other menu item native to Madrid is callos a la Madrileña: a hot, spicy dish of boiled tripe that is now enjoyed all over Spain.*

Not content with being both capital and *autonomía*, Madrid also gives its name to the wines produced in three areas situated southwest and southeast of the city. Wine has been made in this area since the *Reconquista*; it seemed to be an act of faith by the advancing Christian armies to re-establish the vine in all the lands they recaptured.

The creation of the city of Madrid presented a ready market for these wines but, by the time the *bodegueros* got their act together, La Mancha had become its major supplier. Thus, growth of the local wine industry was gentle and sustainable. The wines of Madrid gained a slow but steady foothold throughout the region and within the city as its vineyards matured and its bodegas became more commercially minded.

Throughout the 20th century, Madrid's vineyards have made a comeback. Once La Mancha turned its attention to export markets, Madrid's producers worked hard to fill any gaps which arose in terms of supply. When the DO was awarded, they had a golden marketing opportunity to offer Madrid restaurants their own 'local' wine. Those bodegas that had invested and improved their wines did good business.

Vineyards are found in three subzones: San Martín de Valdeiglesias, east of the city, where the soil is brown earth over granite; Navalcarnero, east and south of the city where poor-quality soil lies over sand and alluvial clay; and Arganda, southwest of the city, with clay and marl soils over granite and some good active limestone content. Vineyard sites range between 500 and 800 metres (1,640 to 2,625 feet). The nearest (around Getafe in Navalcarnero) are barely 12 kilometres (seven miles) from Madrid's city centre.

The main grapes used to make red wines are Tinto Fino and Garnacha Tinta, along with the usual plantations of Cabernet Sauvignon and Merlot. For whites, the main varieties have always been Malvar, Albillo and Airén, but an amendment to the wine laws in 1996 added Viura, Torrontés, and Parellada in an attempt to raise standards.

At present, wines are made as *jovenes* in all three colours, generally from the basic varieties. However, some bodegas have taken the trouble to re-equip, invest and pay more for their grapes, with the result that there are better wines (particularly reds with a little oak-ageing) emerging, made from Tinto Fino, sometimes with a little Cabernet and/or Merlot. These are very much wines to watch.

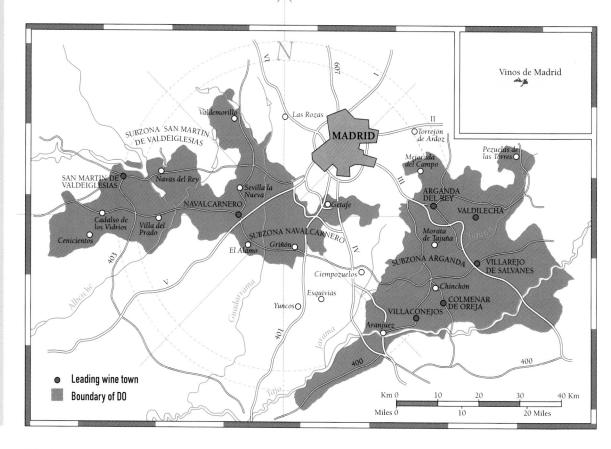

## Notable bodegas

N = Navalcarnero; A = Arganda.

**Aigaco/Compañía de Comercio y Bebidas, Villarejo de Salvanés (A).** *Founded 1988.* An incarnation of an older company founded in 1956. The firm owns 50ha and also buys in grapes. Its methods and equipment are among the most modern in the region, with new stainless-steel tanks for fermentation. The best-known brand name is Jeromín, which offers a basic range of white (Malvar), *rosado* (Tinto Fino/Malvar) and red (Tinto Fino) *jovenes*; all are good, but the white is best. There are also Jeromín *crianza* wines, both white (Malvar; six months in oak) and red (Tinto Fino; eight months in oak), as well as a range of two wines called Puerta del Sol, *rosado* and red, made principally from Cabernet Sauvignon, and both technically *jovenes*. The *rosado* (90% Cabernet/10% Malvar) is for immediate release and the red (100% Cabernet) has four months in oak. These are very good wines with tremendous potential.
*Best wine:* the Jeromín red *reserva* (Tempranillo; 12 to 14 months in oak).

**Jesús Díaz e Hijos, Colmenar de Oreja (A).** *Founded 1900.*
This bodega has won the most prizes in the region for its wines and is one of the most respected. Originally family owned and now a limited company, the firm has 60ha and buys in additional grapes to produce around 3,500hl of wine. All wines carry the bodega name. The basic range offers two varietal *jovenes* in white (one Malvar, the other Macabeo), *rosado* (Tinto Fino) and red (Tinto Fino). There are also two older reds, a varietal Cabernet Sauvignon *joven* (sometimes with up to 15% Tinto Fino) and a *reserva* made from Tinto Fino with just a little Malvar, and a year or more in oak. All these wines are uniformly

good. The firm also makes a fascinating *espumoso* called Oriella, from Verdejo and Parellada. *Best wines:* the young whites and older reds show particularly well.

**Orusco, Valdilecha (A).**
*Founded 1896.* Family firm currently run by the third generation, and farming 11ha of vines as well as buying in grapes from around the region. Orusco has ancient and modern technology – stainless-steel tanks rub shoulders with concrete *tinajas* – although all fermentation is now carried out under controlled conditions. The brand name is Viña Main for the three *jovenes*: white

(Malvar), *rosado* (Tinto Fino) and red (Tinto Fino). These are good, workmanlike wines, well made at modest prices. Orusco has also pioneered the making of oak-aged wines and these are some of its best works. *Best wines:* the Main Crianza label (100% Tinto Fino; minimum six months in oak). These can be very good and may be wines to watch as Madrid's 'new wave' continues.

**Ricardo Benito, Navalcarnero (N).**
*Founded 1940.* Large family firm with 80ha, although most of the grapes are bought in to produce 8,000hl. The primary range of wines is called Tapón de Oro and consists of a

white *joven* (Malvar/Airén), *rosado joven* (Garnacha) and red *crianza* (Tempranillo with a little Garnacha; eight months in oak). A barrel-fermented white under the same label has been very well received. All of these wines are very good.

# Castilla–La Mancha: hot and high

**Above: The great plain of La Mancha, studded with vines. Conditions are extreme, both in summer and winter, yet half of all the vineyards in Spain are located in this region.**

'In a place in La Mancha... of which I do not remember the name...' So begins the story of *The Adventures of the Ingenious Gentleman Don Quixote of La Mancha*, the masterpiece of Miguel Cervantes. The first-time visitor to the great plain of La Mancha might forgive him for forgetting the name. The landscape is endlessly flat, ringed by distant mountain ranges; the relentlessly straight roads seem to go on for ever. Towns flash past and are gone, and everywhere lie vineyards full of red soil and short, stubby vines.

The windmills, too, are short and stubby, turned by the prevailing winds that howl across the plain in winter, contributing to some of Spain's lowest temperatures

(the record is -22°C/-8°F). They also blast across the plain in summer, braising the vines and causing some of the highest temperatures (the record is 44°C/106°F).

Cervantes, the man who made this inhospitable region famous, was a young Spanish sailor, born in the province of Madrid. Wounded and decorated in the Battle of Lepanto against the Turks (1571), he was subsequently captured and sold into slavery in what is now Algeria, before being rescued five years later and returned to Spain. Here he became a tax collector – a job that made him popular in Madrid, but not in La Mancha, his tax-collecting patch. When he arrived in the small Manchego town of

Argamasilla de Alba in the early 17th century, the local *alcalde* (mayor) was away. Cervantes was imprisoned in the local jail until his identity could be proved.

From the jailer and the local priest, Cervantes learned about the local *hidalgo* (squire), an elderly gentleman of noble birth who was addicted to novels of Arthurian legend. Slaying dragons, rescuing maidens and finding the Holy Grail was precisely what the *hidalgo* wished to do – despite the fact that the local doctor forebade him to set foot outside his door. The locals called him *Don Quijada* ('old lantern-jaws') or *Don Quejido* ('old moaner'). Cervantes rechristened him *Don Quijote* (later Quixote). While still in prison, he wrote the first two chapters of a book which was to become a classic throughout the world.

But what does this tell us about today's La Mancha? For one thing, you can still visit the towns and villages mentioned in the book and recognise aspects of life, light and landscape just as Cervantes described them. Even the vineyards remain the same; only the odd sparkling, new state-of-the-art winery reminds visitors that a revolution in winemaking has taken place here in the past 20 years.

Sheep farming is Castilla-La Mancha's biggest industry, and the local sheep's-milk cheese, *queso Manchego*, is so popular that it is almost a generic term for similar cheeses made all over the country. In its home patch, it comes *fresca*, *madura* and *reserva*. The first is a delicious, soft-textured cheese usually offered with *tapas*; the second has been stored for a time and has a harder, crumbly texture. The *reserva* may have been marinated in olive oil for years and takes on a dark, powerful style much favoured by *aficionados*. One of the region's most popular starters is *queso frito* – strips of *Manchega fresca* dipped in beaten egg, rolled in breadcrumbs and fried: it is excellent with a glass of the local red.

The most flambuoyant of all Manchego dishes is the *gazpacho de Castilla-La Mancha*. Cast aside all memories of cold cucumber soup: this is a feast for two people, starting with a tortilla the size of an occasional table. Into this is poured a rich, meaty stew containing pheasant, partridge, lamb, *chorizo*, rabbit and just about anything else in season. With a bottle of something good, old and red, it can take up most of the evening.

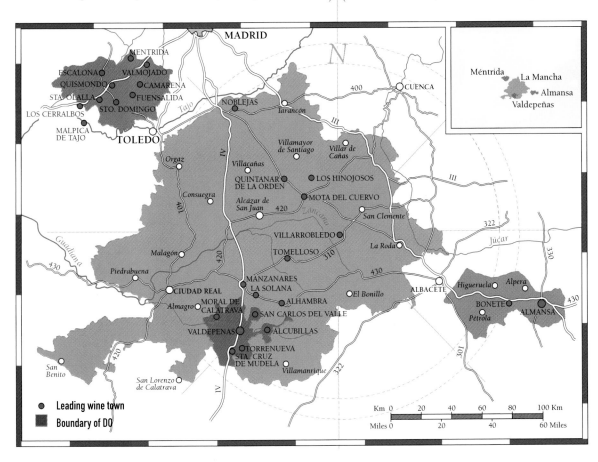

# Almansa

If a Moorish invader from the relatively wet Mediterranean coast arrived in this area 1,000 years ago, he would have wondered at the highland plains stretching out under clear blue skies for as far as the eye could see. He would also discover that the dry soils were laced with limestone, that there were almost no rivers and that the climate bordered on the semi-arid. He might well have remarked that this was indeed 'the dry place': *Al-Amankha*. If this is truly how Almansa got its name, then it sheds an interesting sidelight on the area, since the region of La Mancha received its name in the same way.

In geographic terms, Almansa could be considered 'the forefinger' of Castilla-La Mancha, attached politically and administratively to New Castile while at the same time pointing towards the Jumilla, Yecla, Alicante and Valencia DOs. Its Levantine roots seem obvious – and indeed roots there are, in business terms. The wine history of Almansa has been one of producing high-strength reds to blend with others from the region, mainly with the aim of eventually shipping them abroad. The new standard for quality bottled wines from the region is the result of tireless work by one company over many years: in this case, Bodegas Piqueras (*see* 'Notable bodega').

Culturally and socially, however, Almansa is quite different from the Levant. The town itself is dominated by a castle, the last of many to be built and razed during the *Reconquista*, and its architecture is more north-Castilian than Mediterranean. Almansa is the chief town of the DO, but wine is made in a further eight towns and villages throughout the region. Vineyards spread over a sausage-shaped area from the eastern outposts of the city of Albacete to the western border of the Alicante DO.

## Geography and climate

Unlike those of its Levantine neighbours, the vineyards of Almansa all tend to be positioned in rolling foothills on the same level: about 700 metres (2,297 feet) in altitude. The land here is watered by streams from the Embalse de Almansa, a manmade lake-cum-reservoir up in the Sierra Mugrón which lies northwest of the town. Natural rainfall is reasonably good for these latitudes – about 400 millimetres (16 inches) – and the soil is fertile and well-supplied with carbonates. Like that of the vast La Mancha DO to the east, the general climate of Almansa is high continental, with very hot summers and very cold winters.

The main grape is Monastrell, which takes up nearly half the vineyard, followed by Garnacha Tintorera: a great blending grape if nothing special on its own. A long way behind these comes Cencibel (Tempranillo), and there are also a few experimental plantations of Cabernet Sauvignon. Red wine makes up 85 per cent of production while *rosado* accounts for just five per cent. Whites make up the final ten per cent, made mainly from Merseguera and Airén.

In wine terms, a good deal of Almansa's production is still sold in bulk. Although basic quality has improved, such wine would make little impact on the export market. There is potential here for producing good- to excellent-quality red wines from *joven* all the way to *gran reserva* level. Soils, altitude and the Monastrell grape have delivered similar results in much less-favoured parts of Spain. All that is needed now is the will to succeed.

**Below: The town of Almansa is dominated by its impressive 15th-century castle, the last to have been built during the *Reconquista*.**

**Today, vineyards flourish on the old battlefields, with half of the harvest (far right) likely to be made up of Monastrell grapes.**

## Notable bodega

**Note:** Bodegas Piqueras has shown what Almansa is capable of. Of the five other companies that belong to the *consejo regulador*, at least one – Bodegas Carrión – has been established long enough (since 1886) and seems big enough to have the necessary investment capability to follow its example. Even a couple of local co-ops, Santa Cruz and Santa Quiteria, have some impressive new equipment on show, but as yet, they are not making wines worthy of export.

For the moment, then, just one bodega manages to make it into the list below.

**Piqueras, Almansa.** *Founded 1915.* This family-owned company owns no vineyards but buys in all its grapes from contract growers, whose vineyards, methods and picking dates it helps to supervise. It maintains an average annual production of approximately 7,000 to 8,000hl. The wines are so much better than anything else from Almansa that Piqueras' is the only wine known outside the region, let

alone nationally or internationally. The bodega itself is small and has a slightly art deco air about it; it also features a giant two-storey barrel in which celebrations are occasionally held. The brand name is Castillo de Almansa, and the range includes good white and *rosado jovenes*.

*Best wines:* the bodega's oak-aged ranges. Castillo de Almansa reds range from *crianza* to *gran reserva* and are typically made from 75% Cencibel and 25% Monastrell, with 18 to 28 months in oak. There is a parallel (and slightly cheaper) range called Marius, which is made in both

*crianza* and *reserva* versions, and is typically composed of 60% Cencibel, 30% Monastrell and 10% Garnacha Tintorera. These are excellent wines by any standards, and the 1989 Castillo de Almansa *crianza* was generally considered outstanding, listed by the *Madrid Club de Gourmets* guide as one of the top 100 wines of Spain.

# La Mancha

La Mancha is, and has always been, the largest DO in Spain, and all attempts to cut it down to size have so far been to no avail. Originally, in 1966, one *consejo regulador* was set up to police what are now the DOs of La Mancha, Almansa and Méntrida, on the basis that all were producers of bulk wines and that any competition among them would be counter-productive.

The designated area proved so large and unwieldy that it was dismantled in the mid-1970s, and Méntrida and Almansa went their separate ways. La Mancha remained the largest DO in the country, however, and plans were made even then to divide it into smaller, more manageable units. Since the *consejo regulador* failed to come up with any proposals at the time, the idea faded out of sight.

It resurfaced in 1993, and a special commission was appointed to report on the prospects for rationalisation. The members of the *consejo* duly responded in 1996, recommending some reduction in the planting area while at the same time allowing for the planting of new grape varieties and permitting new types of wine – but there was still no change in terms of any proposed divisions. At present, contingency plans are in place in case a decision is taken to fragment the DO, but there is nothing to show whether, when or if that will ever happen.

## Successful evolution

The reason for this is simple: La Mancha is a brilliant success. After a shaky start caused by working with inappropriate grapes (mainly Airén) in the late 1960s and early 1970s, the DO's quality has evolved in leaps and bounds. Arguably, the progenitor of all this was the Rumasa Group (later disgraced but, at the time, respected), which built what was then a state-of-the-art winery in Manzanares in 1977, calling it Vinícola de Castilla.

The directors of the company may well have been more attracted by the price of land and the development opportunities than by wine. Still, the fact remained that the north-European market was opening up in a big way; Rumasa had determined that La Mancha could be relied upon to provide a reliable, low-cost, endless supply of light, herby, slightly fruity, squeaky-clean white wine – which was what northern Europe just happened to be demanding.

Rumasa was right, of course. Mass-market buyers from the UK, the Benelux countries and Scandinavia took to the wines with delight. Many a medium-sized bodega in the doldrums of commercial development was revitalised by orders from abroad. These profits allowed them to re-equip,

invest and discover that Airén was capable of producing much better wine than late-picked, hot-fermented, high-strength, headache-in-a-bottle bulk wines.

So far, so good. By the mid-1980s, most of La Mancha's major bodegas had learned the new ideas of early picking, cool fermentation, rapid turnaround and effective quality-control. Since then, La Mancha has come just as far again, confident in its own abilities and buoyed up by the world's willingness to trust its name and try its wines.

## The region and its vines

First, the region. Yes, it is vast, baking hot in the summer and freezing cold in the winter. It is also dotted with short, chubby windmills and whitewashed towns set about with olive groves, almond orchards and (of course) an endless, undulating sea of vineyards. Their red-brown sand and clay soils are occasionally dusted with white where outcrops of chalk and limestone come to the surface.

The vineyards themselves are unmistakeable, easily identified by their curious, chessboard-style pattern called *marco real*. This is a method of planting in which the vines are spaced 2.5 metres (around eight feet) apart in all directions to allow sufficient access to any available water in the ripening season. It also allows the vines themselves to be trained *en cabeza* – with the head of the vine positioned very low to the ground in order to use its own leaves to protect the grapes from the worst solar excesses.

The altitude of the plain of La Mancha rises from 489 metres (1,604 feet) at Aranjuez in the north to 645 metres (2,116 feet) at Manzanares in the south – meaning that the entire plain tilts gently northwards. The average sunshine enjoyed by La Mancha amounts to eight hours and 23 minutes per day, 365 days a year. Allow for the fact that it must rain or be cloudy at least some of the time, and that the days in winter are much shorter than those in summer, and you will find that, during the ripening season, grapes in La Mancha receive the equivalent of around 120 days of solid sunshine, with an average of about 12 to 14 hours each day.

The problem of drought notwithstanding, there are several advantages to this sunny state of affairs. For a start, the extreme climate (hot/cold but always dry) means that very few insect pests and vine diseases survive to affect the crop. It has been calculated that every hectare of vines needs only about 20 days of work per year, including harvesting. As a result, La Mancha is home to large numbers of part-time or absentee farmers with very small holdings who sell to the major producers.

The grapes themselves are mainly Airén and Cencibel (Tempranillo); the latter is heavily recommended for replanting. Airén continues to flourish because it survives almost any weather conditions. It got started in the vineyards after the Civil War, when Franco offered to buy every drop of unsold wine for distilling in order to keep the peasants quiescent. The upshot was that a good deal of high-production vine-stock was planted during those years. However, once producers discovered that, with the right winemaking, Airén could produce light, fresh white wines of a pleasant character at minimal cost, its future was assured.

Other white grapes include Pardilla and Macabeo (Viura), and there have even been rumours of some Chardonnay being planted. For red wines, Cencibel (Tempranillo) is highly recommended, but there are also Moravia, Garnacha Tinta, Cabernet Sauvignon and Merlot.

La Mancha's wines tend to fall into three groups. First are the basic *jovenes* made for local consumption by giant co-ops and village wineries. These may still be fermented in concrete *tinajas* and sold in bulk at the bodega gate. The second group consists of low-cost, high-value wines

intended for the export market. Grapes for these are picked much earlier than the local variant, and the wines are cool-fermented in stainless steel and carefully blended to meet the buyers' specifications and price.

The third group of wines are those produced by the inevitable mavericks who exist in every corner of Spain. Someone is always working with an obscure vine or a new strain of yeast, and La Mancha is no exception. Indeed, greater La Mancha (beyond the DO zone) is home to one of the greatest mavericks of all time, the Marqués de Griñón (*see* 'Country Wines of the Meseta', page 180).

Likely finds on the home market include *jovenes* in white (Airén), *rosado* (Moravia and/or Garnacha) and red (Cencibel) as well as oak-aged wines (though not yet up to *gran reserva* level) made from Cencibel and perhaps a little Cabernet Sauvignon and/or Merlot. The most recent development has been the addition of a *vino espumoso* to the list of permitted wines, made by the *método tradicional*. The rules provide for it to be made from any of the permitted grape varieties, but the sudden upsurge in interest in Macabeo may be significant.

**Above:** Windmills stand sentry duty above the village of Consuegra. It may not be the exact location of the 'Encounter with the Windmills', but it would probably seem familiar to Cervantes.

# Notable bodegas

Provinces: AB = Albacete;
CR = Ciudad Real; CU = Cuenca;
Toledo = TO.

### Altosa, Tomelloso (CR).
*Founded 1985.* Established on the back of a distillery that was founded in 1972, this firm belongs to the Sherry company Bobadilla. Its main business consists of producing brandy for Jerez. However, it also makes non-vintage *joven* red and white wines under the La Posada label.
*Best wine:* the white can be very good.

### Ayuso, Villarobledo (AB).
*Founded 1947.* Ayuso is a large family firm turning out around 175,000hl of wine, which is reckoned to be among the best in the modern-wines category of La Mancha. All the wines are good, with workmanlike *jovenes* in all three colours under the Ayuso label. There are also some particular high-spots: Armiño is a unique *semidulce* white made from Airén and Viña Q includes good *jovenes* in white and *rosado* as well as an excellent red *joven* (70% Cencibel/30% Garnacha).

*Best wines:* any wines in the Viña Estola range, all of which are made from 100% Cencibel. The *reserva* spends 24 to 36 months in cask, according to the quality of the vintage; the typical *gran reserva* has 48. These are excellent, powerful, ripe, full-bodied wines.

### Centro-Españolas, Tomelloso (CR). *Founded 1991.* Centro-Españolas is one of the most modern bodegas in the region, complete with the very latest winemaking kit and an annual production of approximately 16,000hl. Eschewing (almost) the temptations of new-wave vine-crazes, the company makes exemplary whites and reds from 100% Airén, and 100% Cencibel (here called Tempranillo) in both *joven* and *crianza* styles. Allozo and Verdial are the labels for *jovenes* in white (Airén), *rosado* (Tempranillo) and red (Tempranillo). However, there is also an Allozo *crianza* with 12 months in oak. All the wines are very good. *Best wines:* opinion is divided over the relative merits of the Allozo Tinto *joven* (75% Tempranillo/25% Cabernet Sauvignon) and the Verdial red *joven* (100% Tempranillo). Both are splendid wines crafted in the classic, powerful, ripe-fruit style of modern La Mancha reds.

### Cosecheros Embotelladores, Noblejas (TO). *Founded 1979.*
This is an independent cooperative with 14 members farming some 300ha of vines. Production consists mainly of white wines under the labels Cuevas Reales and Donante. The whites and *rosados* are generally good. *Best wines:* the reds, particularly the excellent Cuevas Reales *joven* and the Viña Donate *crianza*.

### Cueva del Granero, Los Hinosos (CU). *Founded 1987.* Cueva del Granero makes wine only from its own 400ha of vineyards, where Cabernet Sauvignon, Garnacha,

Below: Airén grapes are havested in La Mancha. The variety's ability to survive the harsh climate has made it the region's most widely planted grapes.

Chardonnay and Viura grow side by side with Cencibel and the Airén. The wines carry the bodega name and the range includes good *jovenes* in white (Airén), *rosado* (50% Cencibel/50% Garnacha) and red (Cencibel) as well as a very good varietal Cabernet Sauvignon. *Best wine:* the *crianza* version of the Cabernet Sauvignon varietal.

### Evaristo Mateos, Noblejas (TO).

*Founded 1963.* This bodega makes mainly white wines from its own vineyards and bought-in grapes, with an annual production of roughly 60,000hl. Most of the wines are *jovenes* in all three colours: Evaristo white (Airén), Sembrador *rosado* (Garnacha) and Evaristo red (Cencibel). There is also a Sembrador *crianza* (Cencibel; nine months in oak). All the wines are well made. *Best wines:* the white and *rosado jovenes*.

### Julián Santos, Quintanar de la Orden (TO). *Founded 1900.*

This family firm is now shared between two branches of the original family and has recently overhauled its equipment and winemaking processes. The company owns 800ha of vines and produces about 175,000hl of wine. The label is Don Fadrique and the basic range offers *jovenes* in white (Airén), *rosado* (Garnacha) and red (Cencibel), all of which are excellent. The red range continues right up to *gran reserva* level, and the wines can be very good. *Best wines:* the joven wines carry the reputation of this bodega – and deservedly so.

### Nuestra Señora de Manjavacas Cooperativa, Mota del Cuervo (CU).

*Founded 1948.* Although this is a co-op and still uses concrete *tinajas* for storage, its approach to new equipment and modern winemaking has been very enthusiastic. It was one of the

first – back in the early 1980s – to produce light, fruity, low-strength, cool-fermented *joven* wines. These were going into the export market when most other companies were still devoting themselves to the boil-in-the-bottle styles which had been made in country districts for centuries. Today, there are some 2,000 members farming 8,000ha, turning out 20,000hl of wine. Much of this is still local production sold in bulk. The bodega's flagship wine is called Zagarrón and the range includes *jovenes* in all three colours made from Airén and Cencibel. There is also a little *crianza* red made from Cencibel. These are good wines, and this is probably the second co-op of the region in terms of quality wines.

### Nuestro Padre Jesús del Perdón Cooperativa, Manzanares (CR).

*Founded 1954.* In answer to your question, this is the premier co-op of La Mancha. The winemakers here spotted the benefits of new-style winemaking at the same time as their colleagues at Manjavacas, but they turned over more of their production to quality wines and invested quickly in newer technology as well as continuing to produce local wines for bulk sale. The main brand is Yuntero and encompasses a white *joven* with four months in oak and a white *crianza* with eight months in oak (both Airén). There is a *rosado joven* (50% Cencibel/50% Garnacha) and a red (Cencibel) called Mundo de Yuntero. There are also *crianza* and *reserva* versions of Yuntero red which are made from Cencibel but which may have up to 25% Cabernet Sauvignon. These wines are all excellent.

### Rodríguez y Berger, Cinco Casas (CR).

*Founded 1919.* This company re-equipped itself in the mid-1980s with the offer of a major contract to supply a UK chain with everyday white wines. It follows this discipline quite competently, with a total production of some 100,000hl.

Its main own brand is Viña Santa Elena, with good, well-made *jovenes* in all three colours.

### Torres Filoso, Villarobledo (AB).

*Founded 1921.* This is a family firm with two bodegas, one very traditional, complete with old-style *tinajas,* and one (dating from 1988) that is very modern indeed, with all the latest stainless-steel technology. The annual production is about 1,500hl for DO wines, plus the same amount again of local wines. The basic range is called Torres Filoso and offers *jovenes* in all three colours made from Airén and Cencibel. These are decent enough. *Best wines:* the bodega's major work is under the Arboles de Castillejo label, with a white *crianza* Chardonnay (six months in oak), a red *crianza* (50% Cencibel/50%Cabernet Sauvignon with six months in oak) and a varietal Cabernet Sauvignon called Juan-José. Excellent wines.

### Vinícola de Castilla, Manzanares (CR).

*Founded 1977.* Vinícola de Castilla was the first bodega to be built entirely using new, squeaky-clean, stainless-steel, computer-controlled technology. At the time, it was among the most modern wineries in Europe, and belonged to the doomed Rumasa empire. Since then, however, as an independent company it has consistently turned out some of La Mancha's finest wines and continues to do so. Brand names include (among others) Castillo de Alhambra (*jovenes* in all three colours plus a splendid varietal Cencibel); Castillo de Manzanares *blanco* (Viura; three months in cask) and *tinto* (Cabernet Sauvignon; three months in cask); and Señorío de Guadianeja with a *reserva* Cencibel and *gran reserva* varietals from Cencibel and Cabernet Sauvignon. These wines are excellent as a matter of course,

and often outstanding. Nothing ordinary comes out of Vinícola de Castilla.

### Vinícola de Tomelloso, Tomelloso (CR).

*Founded 1988.* This bodega set out to make the best possible varietal wines in La Mancha and has achieved its objective in fine style. In white wines, the Abrego label offers a simple Airén *joven* as well as a fascinating *semidulce* from the same grape. Añil is a very good Viura. Rosado Abrego is an excellent varietal *joven* Cencibel and the red version has an added 10% Cabernet Sauvignon. These are excellent wines. *Best wine:* the top-of-the-range *crianza* called Torre de Gazate, which is made from 100% Cabernet Sauvignon with 12 months in oak.

### Virgen de la Viñas Cooperativa, Tomelloso (CR). *Founded 1961.*

This co-op is located on the road to Agamasilla de Alba, where Cervantes was imprisoned (the original 'place in La Mancha, of which I do not remember the name...'). This is a sound, modern co-op using Airén and Cencibel to turn out good *jovenes* in all three colours as well as some decent *crianza* red. Brand names are Don Eugenio, Lorenzete and Tomillar.

# Méntrida

## Notable bodegas

**El Barro, Camarena.** *Founded 1973.*
El Barro grows Cabernet Sauvignon and
Merlot as well as Cencibel. The main
brand is Mazajul: the *rosado* is a pleasant
*joven* (a blend of Cencibel, Syrah and
Garnacha). The red is also *joven*, but a
bold Cabernet Sauvignon/Merlot mix.

**Condes de Fuensalida Cooperativa,
Fuensalida.** *Founded 1974.*
This co-op's 130 members farm
1,000ha, making about 24,000hl.
Condes de Fuensalida is the brand
name for *joven rosado* and red,
both made from 'a mix of grapes'
(up to 15% abv).

**Poveda, Valmojado.** *Founded 1947.*
Big bodega (50ha plus bought-in grapes
to produce 30,000hl) aiming to make
wines up to *reserva* level. The brand
name is Poveda, the grape is Garnacha.
Makes a red *crianza* (24 months in oak)
as well as *jovenes* in both colours.

**San Isidro Cooperativa, Camarena.**
*Founded 1974.* Co-op whose 157
members farm nearly 900ha, producing
about 20,000hl. Bastión de Camarena
is the label for *jovenes* in both colours
made from Garnacha. Quality is
generally good.

**San Roque Cooperativa, Escalona.**
*Founded 1964.* With 224 members,
one of the more old-fashioned
bodegas of the region. Castillo de
Escalona is a red *joven* made from
Garnacha (16% abv) which has
massive weight and an altogether
weird-but-wonderful style.

**Santo Cristo de la Salud
Cooperativa, La Torre de Estebán
Hambrán.** *Founded 1975. Jovenes*
(both colours) are sold under the
Señorío de Estebán Hambrán label.

Méntrida has had a bad press for as long as most people can remember. It was promoted to DO status in 1960, when the world could not get enough Spanish bulk wine for blending. The region's advantages in this department were considerable: Garnacha cropped copiously in the well-drained, fertile, carbonate-rich soils, and the local yeasts obligingly provided naturally fermented wines at up to 18 per cent alcohol by volume (abv).

While not particularly favoured for drinking, these wines, like the *doble-pasta* wines of the Levant, were exported to other regions of Spain, Europe and beyond to beef up lightweight wines made from grapes grown in less sunny vineyards. And Méntrida's vineyards are certainly sunny. Temperatures can be blazing in summer and freezing in winter, but in both seasons they are ameliorated by the DO's location on the northern borders of Toledo province.

As the market for bulk, heavyweight wines fell off, Méntrida's exports faded away and finally petered out altogether in 1987. The *consejo regulador* duly lowered the minimum abv for its wines from 14 to 12 per cent for reds and from 13 to 11 per cent for *rosados* (the DO allows no white wine) in the hope of picking up more business from the voracious Madrid market. By this time, however, the winemakers of what was to become the Vinos de Madrid DO had already gained a foothold in the city's red-wine market. La Mancha, which had been shipping whites into the capital for generations, had also got its act together, with new-wave wines setting a new-wave standard.

Despite this disheartening scenario, Méntrida is fighting back. Garnacha still reigns supreme, with 70 per cent of the vineyard, and Cencibel is being recommended for replanting where the local Tinto de Madrid is currently grown. New methods are slowly being introduced, although these are more likely to take the form of cooling *placas* inserted into concrete tanks than stainless steel.

Thankfully, the wines currently on offer have shaken off the image of the over-strength, boiled-to-death stuff that used to be Méntrida's stock-in-trade. Today, there are robust red and *rosado jovenes*, the pinks made with Garnacha, the better reds with Cencibel. There is also scope for red *crianza* with six months in oak; one or two bodegas are approaching that standard. There is a long way to go, but Méntrida is working hard to win a new reputation for its wines, with the full backing of the co-ops that dominate its production.

# Mondéjar

**M**ondéjar is the most recent DO in La Mancha. It is also the only winemaking zone of any importance in the province of Guadalajara, covering 20 towns and villages around Sacedon and Mondéjar itself. It was originally a VdlT zone called Sacedón-Mondéjar, or Mondéjar-Sacedón, presumably depending upon which part the speaker came from.

Geographically, Mondéjar splits into two sub-regions about ten kilometres (six miles) apart. The northern zone is centred around the town of Sacedón, 51 kilometres (32 miles) east of the city of Guadalajara, and the southern one centred on the town of Mondéjar, about 80 kilometres (50 miles) east of Madrid. The Mondéjar DO is contiguous with the Vinos de Madrid DO in the southwest, and just touches the La Mancha DO in the south.

Vines and winemaking have been a significant part of the local economy ever since the town became a staging post on the royal road between Valencia and Madrid. So why didn't Mondéjar achieve more prominence in its earlier history? Perhaps because it was a little too close to Madrid – just a day's journey by coach – and the call for accommodation and livery was that much smaller.

Today, Mondéjar winemakers grow three principal grapes – Malvar, Macabeo and Torrontés – for use in the production of white wine; there is also some Airén. For red wines, the two main varieties are Cencibel and Cabernet Sauvignon, followed by some Tinto de Madrid, Garnacha and Jaén. In good-quality, red-brown soils with mainly limestone bedrock, there is no reason why good wines should not be made here.

## Winemaking and wine styles

Traditionally, the majority of Mondéjar's wines have gone into the bulk market. However, one or two bodegas are trying to produce something a little more adventurous: cold-fermented whites from the Malvar (*jovenes* as well as some white *crianza*), reds from Cencibel (up to *reserva* level), and even a sweet white made from Malvar and Airén with 13 per cent alcohol by volume (abv). There is also a strong incentive to work with varietals from the five main grape varieties, as well as plenty of encouragement to experiment with red wines in oak. These are early days yet for a region which has been making wine for more than 400 years.

## Notable bodega

**Mariscal, Mondéjar.**
*Founded 1913.* Mariscal has pioneered oak-aged wines but focuses on its *jovenes* sold under the Vega Tajuña label. There is also a 70% Tempranillo/30% Cabernet Sauvignon mix called Señorio de Mariscal. This is a bodega to watch. *Best wines:* are called Mariscal and include a very good *rosado joven* (100% Cencibel; here called Tempranillo) and a promising *reserva* with 12 months in oak.

**Left:** Just outside the Méntrida DO is the Casadevacas, the headquarters and country home of Carlos Falcó, the Marqués de Griñon. Wines made here are called Dominio de Valdepusa.

# Valdepeñas

**V**aldepeñas is one of those *denominaciones de origen* that go against the received wisdom of Spanish winemaking. Surrounded by an area that, for generations, was known only for producing everyday wines, Valdepeñas has managed to turn out wines of remarkable quality up to *gran reserva* standard since time immemorial – or, at the very least, since the 13th century.

That was when Queen Berengula brought together a number of small villages in the newly reconquered *Valle de la Peñas* ('Valley of the Rocks') and in doing so, created the town of Valdepeñas. At that time (1243), the town was used as a strategic position for Castilian forces against the retreating Moors, and its importance as a military base far exceeded its prominence as a trading entity.

## The influence of market forces

Where there are people (especially those on government salaries), however, there is always a market, and trade and industry grew up to service the comings and goings of both the civil servants and the soldiers. The Moors left Spain in 1492, but with the establishment of Madrid in 1561, Valdepeñas was set for another boom. Naturally the town was already well known to the government, and this government was now only two days' travel away.

The royal road to Córdoba, Granada and points south passed conveniently through Valdepeñas, and a thriving coaching industry was born, once again servicing the royals, officials, clerics and other travellers who regularly headed from the capital to the cities of the south and the coast. There is nothing like a ready market for quality wine to inspire quality in the supply-chain, and Valdepeñas had long ago discovered that when its customers had money to spend, they were particular about what they ate and drank. The market came closer still when the railway arrived in 1861. Suddenly, Valdepeñas was just a few hours' journey from Madrid, and the town boomed once again.

Modern travellers heading south from Madrid into Valdepeñas on the NIV will cross the great plain of La Mancha. This vast tableland rises gently before dropping down into the town itself, which is set within a ring of mountain ranges. The vines of the Valdepeñas DO are planted on a small plain surrounded by mountain peaks. To the west, the vineyards are known as *Los Llanos* ('The Plains') and to the north *Las Aberturas* ('The [mountain] Passes'). Both are considered the best areas for vines.

Like that of La Mancha, the soil throughout Valdepeñas is fertile and thick, lying over a good chalk bedrock which provides excellent water retention during the ripening period. This has been one of the contributing factors in the ability of Valdepeñas to grow good-quality Cencibel grapes even in years when, just over the border in La Mancha, the heat has been so intense that they simply withered on the vine.

## Grape varieties and wine styles

Traditionally, the wines of Valdepeñas have been light reds (known as *claretes*), though of course, *rosado* and white wines are made here, too. The last two tend to be *jovenes* made with Airén (white) and a mixture of Airén and Cencibel (*rosado*). There are also low-cost *joven* and

locally consumed reds made from a mixture of grapes, but all wines for ageing in oak must, by law, be made entirely from Cencibel.

The reason for the dominance of Airén in the vineyards dates back to the phylloxera disaster, which reached Valdepeñas in 1911. Cencibel in these vineyards produces about half as many grapes as Airén does, and many growers opted for quantity rather than quality. Just as in the La Mancha DO, the situation was compounded during the Franco era, when cheap, low-quality wines were bought in by the government for distilling purposes. As usual, some producers opted for an easy, if low-paid life rather than for one which involved the hard work of replanting, re-equipping and investing. As a result, even in the 1990s, Airén occupies

more than 80 per cent of the Valdepeñas vineyard. Cencibel is recommended for replanting everywhere, and there are also the inevitable experimental plantations of Cabernet Sauvignon and Chardonnay.

## The modern DO

The best wines of Valdepeñas in regular years seem to be the *crianza* and *reserva* reds, which show all the warmth of the southern heat and are burnished with American oak. Although the *gran reservas* win the medals, they make up a relatively much smaller part of the export market. However (and on the subject of export markets), one area in which Valdepeñas has achieved an enormous amount of progress is that of international sales. Its classic red wines are to be found all over the world.

**Above:** The vast landscape of Valdepeñas. The region is a vinous enigma, producing average, everyday gluggers alongside some of Spain's classic vintage wines.

## Notable bodegas

**Casa de la Viña, La Solana.**
*Founded 1987.* Casa de la Viña now belongs to the giant Bodegas y Bebidas Group, which invests in promising companies throughout Spain. This one is no exception: it owns an agricultural estate of 2,850ha, 900 of which are planted with Cencibel. The winery itself is situated very close to the vineyards. Its winemaking kit was heavily modernised at the time of the takeover and the results are easy to see in the excellent wines made here.

The basic range offers *jovenes* in all three colours (Airén for white, Cencibel for *rosado* and red), but the bodega's greatest work is in its reds made from 100% Cencibel. There are also *crianza* and *reserva* wines with up to 24 months in oak. Labelling is a little confusing, with Señorío del Val for *jovenes*, Vega de Moriz for *jovenes* and a red *reserva*, and Casa de la Viña for *reservas* in export markets but also for *jovenes* within Spain itself. However, the Casa de la Viña name is generally a guarantee of excellent quality-control and reliable, good-quality wines – even in average years.

In great years, they can be exemplary. *Best wine:* the 100% Cencibel *joven* is truly excellent, year in and year out.

**Espinosa, Valdepeñas.**
*Founded 1967.* Its trademark is a chubby La Mancha windmill. Its industrial look shouldn't hide the fact that good wines are made here, even though much is still sold in bulk. The brand name is Concejal and the wines are white and *rosado jovenes* and a good red *crianza* made from 100% Cencibel called Cencipeñas. One example of new thinking is the Señorío de Valdepeñas Cabernet Sauvignon.

**Below: The vineyards of Casa de la Viña contain the largest plantation of Cencibel in the entire region.**

### Félix Solís, Valdepeñas.

*Founded 1945.* A family company of impressive reputation, and one of the three top bodegas of Valdepeñas (*see* Los Llanos and Luís Megía, below). Its extensive bodega comprises both ancient and modern technology. Grapes, must and ready-made wines are bought in, but the bodega also uses grapes form its own 1,000+ ha of vines, and production and exports are on a large scale. The best-sellers in Spain are basic *jovenes* called Soldepeñas and Los Molinos, but the bodega's international fame rests on a subsidiary company called Viña Albali Reservas. *Best wines:* the Viña Albali label represents some of the best value-for-money quality wines produced in Valdepeñas. In reality, Viña Albali comes in a number of guises other than *reserva*: there is a white *joven* made from early-picked Airén, a *rosado joven* made from Cencibel, and two reds. The eponymous *reserva* has 12 months in oak and is excellent, as is the *gran reserva*, with 24 months in oak.

Both of these also experience a further two years' ageing in traditional clay *tinajas*, which gives them traditional Valdepeñas warmth and style. The quality is, quite frankly, out of all proportion to the price: these are some of the best-value wines made in Valdepeñas and, indeed, in all of Spain. There is also a varietal Cabernet Sauvignon *crianza* with 15% Cencibel and ten months in oak.

### Los Llanos, Valdepeñas.

*Founded 1875.* Despite its founding date, Los Llanos has been owned since 1975 by the Grupo Cosechero Abastecedores. If Félix Solís is the king of the *reservas*, then Los Llanos is the king of the *gran reservas*. This is the other bodega which has proved that Valdepeñas produces better than the pleasant everyday *claretes* which made it famous. There are 270ha, mainly Cencibel. In the bodega, new-

wave technology sits side-by-side with the traditional methods to provide the best of both. The results are spectacular. A pleasant white and *rosado* called Armonioso are made, and there is a range of decent *jovenes* in all three colours called Don Opas. *Best wines:* those under the Señorío de los Llanos label. These are all 100% Cencibel, and, typically, the *crianza* spends 12 months in oak. The *gran reserva* usually has two years in oak but, according to vintage quality, may spend anything up to eight years in the vat, taking on its classic Valdepeñas style. In outstanding years the company produces a *gran reserva* called *Pata Negra*, or 'Black Leg' (for the origin of this phrase, *see* page 177). The 1983 vintage had six years in the vat and two in oak. As with Félix Solís, the prices asked for these wines are derisory when compared with the quality.

### Luís Megía, Valdepeñas.

*Founded 1947.* Valdepeñas has a 'triumvirate' of top bodegas and this is the third, along with Félix Solís and Los Llanos (above). This company produces almost a quarter of a million hectolitres of wine each year. Since 1989, it has belonged to the Grupo Collins, a Hispano-Japanese food and drinks group. The bodegas are spread throughout the town in small units, and the firm buys in grapes, must and wine to suit its needs. The company's name is associated with a number of labels. Marqués de Gastañaga and Duque de Estrada are new-wave *jovenes*, the whites made with Airén and the reds from Cencibel. There is another range called Luís Megía offering white and *rosado joven* wines, but which also includes oak-aged reds made from Cencibel, a *crianza* typically with 24 months in oak, and *reserva* and *gran reserva* with 30 months.

### Miguel Calatayud, Valdepeñas.

*Founded 1960.* Family firm with 100ha which also buys in grapes

to make up its needs. The bodega has been extensively modernised – although *tinajas* still stand side-by-side with stainless steel and oak *barricas*. The brand name is Vegaval and the basic range offers *jovenes* in all three colours made from Airén (white), and an Airén/Cencibel mix (*rosado* and red). Vegaval Plata is a premium range offering *joven* Airén (white) and Cencibel (*rosado* and red) but also oak-aged reds made from 100% Cencibel, typically with 12 months in oak for the *reserva* and 24 for the *gran reserva*.

### Miguel Martín, Valdepeñas. *Founded 1934.* A traditional bodega turning out workmanlike wines under the Valdemesa, Miguel Martín and Destellos labels. There is a pleasant red *reserva* under the Valdemesa label. *Best wines:* the white and rosado *jovenes*.

### Rafael López Tello, Valdepeñas.

*Founded 1973.* This is a family firm turning out well-made wines mainly for the Madrid market. *Best wines:* those under the Gran Mohino label, most notably a white *joven* and a red *reserva*.

### Real, Valdepeñas. *Founded 1989.* A forward-looking bodega with 350ha of vines, mainly Cencibel but also with

some Cabernet Sauvignon and Merlot. The white wine is a good Airén *joven* called Viña Luz. *Best wines:* the reds. Vega Ibor is the brand name and the *reserva* (100% Cencibel) has 24 months in oak.

### Vicente Navarro y Hermanos, Valdepeñas. *Founded 1959.* This is a small family bodega with 70ha of vines selling mainly in southern Spain. *Best wine:* a red *reserva* (Cencibel) called Racimo de Oro.

### Videva, Valdepeñas. *Founded 1968.* A merger of six vineyard owners with 1,000ha (70% Cencibel/ 30% Airén), Videva has evolved into a major force, producing around 35,000hl. The main brand name is Viejo Videva and the wines come as white, *rosado* and red *jovenes* as well as red *crianza* and *reserva*. *Best wines:* the older reds.

# Extremadura: a fertile landscape

**A**nyone driving through the rolling plains of Extremadura could be forgiven for thinking the entire region existed purely to support endless flocks of sheep. In fact, this region is where fertility of all types was invented: if it grows in Spain, it will grow in Extremadura. Good soil, plentiful rainfall and excellent drainage provide generous agriculture, with everything from cereals, cotton and olives to cork and tobacco flourishing here. Indeed, one of the greatest delicacies of Spain (and Europe) is produced in the region – but more of that in a moment.

Extremadura comprises two provinces, Cáceres and Badajoz, the latter of which is the largest province in Spain. A saying has it that there are more sheep and vines in Badajoz than there are people. To the north lies Old Castile (provinces of Salamanca and Avila); to the east, La Mancha (provinces of Toledo and Ciudad Real). To the south is Andalucía (provinces of Huelva and Sevilla); to the west, Portugal – specifically, the region known as the Alentejo. Just to confuse matters, there is a Portuguese region called Estremadura, but it is located on the west coast, north of Lisbon. The meaning of the word (in both languages) is 'the [extreme limit of the] land beyond the River Duero/Douro'. In Portugal, the 'limit' is the Atlantic ocean. In Spain, it is formed by another of the original frontiers between Christian and Moslem Spain – or, indeed, the no-man's-land created by scorched-earth retreats and pitched battles between the two forces in the 13th century.

Extremadura's history goes back much further than that. The Romans settled in the region around 25BC at a river-crossing on the Guadiana, founding a town called *Emerita Augusta* (now Mérida). It became the capital of Lusitania (Greater Portugal), and still has well-preserved Roman remains. Cáceres, by contrast, is a splendid, walled medieval city with fine Renaissance architecture. Badajoz, meanwhile, still bears traces of its stint as capital of a Moorish kingdom that stretched from Seville to the Atlantic.

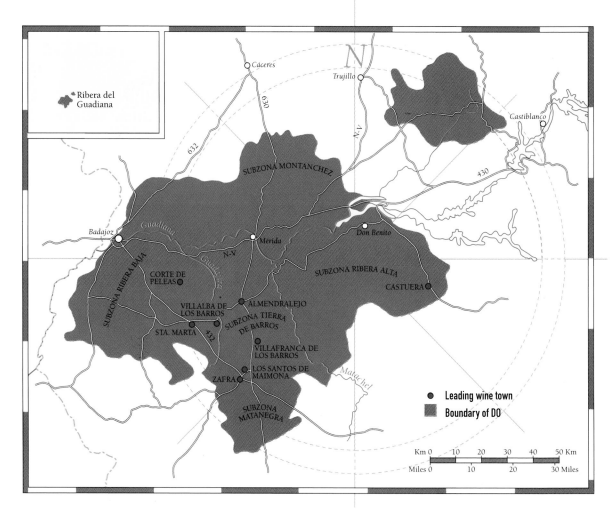

Apart from the roast, grilled and baked lamb that is the staple diet in these parts, Extremadura is home to one of the world's great delicacies: the *jamón serrano* (sliced ham) of the *Pata Negra* (black leg) pig. This black-legged pig is legendary in Spain, and it is believed that all the *jamón serrano* made in the country is an attempt to copy its success.

Pata Negra has its own *denominación de origen*, and to qualify, the following regulations must be observed. Each pig must have exclusive free-range access to one-and-a-half hectares of land. The pig lives for five years in this wilderness, foraging for itself until its final three months, when it is fed exclusively on acorns. After slaughter, its four legs are buried in salt for three years, while its other body parts are used for *embutidos*, *chorizos*, *morcillas* and the other piggy products for which Extremadura is also famous.

Once the salt-curing is complete, the legs are hung in special warehouses to dry completely before they are sold. Typically, the leg is placed in a special holder and sliced thinly with a very sharp knife by an expert in the craft. The meat is very dark, and quite heavily marbled with fat, but the taste is unbelievably subtle and delicious. The price is roughly equivalent to that of fresh Scottish smoked salmon.

Cheese is the third classic product of Extremadura. In addition to a generic cow's-milk cheese under its provincial name, Cáceres produces a range of interesting goat's-milk cheeses. Badajoz also makes goat's-milk cheese, but its best-known is probably *La Serena*, made from cow's milk. Some *aficionados*, however, insist that there is nothing to compare with the cheese they call *Torta del Casar*. This comes in a small, round, yellow 'cushion' shape, the outside of which is hard and waxy. When ripe, a circular 'lid' is cut in the top, which allows the interior soft cheese to be spooned out. It is quite sensational – and very expensive.

Small wonder, then, that with such strong flavours to contend with, the wines of Extremadura have grown up bold and red.

**Above:** The fertile countryside that is Extremadura. With its good soils and climatic advantages, it is a region that supports a wide number of crops, livestock and vines.

# Ribera del Guadiana

At present, Macabeo or Viura grapes (above) are in the minority in Ribera del Guadiana, yet it is just such varieties that hold the key to the DO's future.

Ribera del Guadiana is one of Spain's most fascinating new (1997) DOs. It partly points the way forward for the shape of things to come if the classification system is overhauled or reformed in central and southern Spain.

As mentioned earlier, a special dispensation in Valencia allows the Valencia DO to take a measure of grapes from the Utiel-Requena DO and sell the result under the former DO's name. The reasons boil down to a flexibility that allows styles of wine made in various parts of the region to be blended together in order to supply whatever the market requires (*see* page 142). The situation is similar in Ribera del Guadiana. Originally, what is now the Ribera del Guadiana DO comprised six *vino de la tierra* areas, each making its own style of wine. These are now subzones of the DO, and each has the right to make wine in its own style, or in any combination of other styles.

The wine region takes its name from the River Guadiana, a major river of southern Spain. It rises in the highlands of Ciudad Real (La Mancha), south of Tomelloso, and runs westwards through the La Mancha DO (part of the way underground). From there, it heads northwards to the foothills of the Montes de Toledo and southwest through Mérida and Badajoz to the Portuguese border.

The river forms the border with Portugal for about 50 kilometres (31 miles) southwards, then continues south through the Portuguese region of Alentejo. Back on the border in the province of Huelva, it joins the River Chanza some 120 kilometres (74 miles) south, and then forms the border between the two countries once again for its final 50 kilometres before emptying into the Gulf of Cádiz.

The river skirts four of the six subzones of the Ribera del Guadiana DO as it runs west and south, with Cañamero and Montánchez (in the province of Cáceres) on its north bank, and the remaining four subzones – Ribera Alta de Guadiana, Ribera Baja de Guadiana, Tierra de Barros and Matanegra – on its south and east banks, (province of Badajoz).

The driving force behind the region's promotion to DO status has been a small number of bodegas in the Tierra de Barros subzone, most particularly Bodegas InViOSA in the town of Almendralejo. The largest of the Ribera del Guariana subzones, Tierra de Barros accounts for 80 per cent of the vineyard. It was awarded a provisional DO in 1979, and since that time, its major players have worked tirelessly to encourage neighbouring bodegas and regions to invest and re-equip for promotion. At present, Tierra de Barros is also the DO's most advanced subzone in terms of production, winemaking and export experience;

in contrast, Ribera Alta de Guadiana could be considered the straggler. No doubt the *consejo regulador* hopes the example of the former will inspire the latter.

## Geography and climate

Although the entire DO zone is a large one, its soils and climate are relatively similar, well-irrigated by the Guadiana and its tributaries. Soils are fertile, and lie over alluvial clay in the river valleys, with outcrops of limestone in the better, more elevated sites. Altitudes range from 300 to 350 metres (984 to 1,148 feet), and the combination of more than adequate rainfall and excellent sun exposure means that there is no reason why excellent wines should not be made here. Indeed, Tierra de Barros in general and Bodegas InViOSA in particular have amply demonstrated that any company prepared to shake off bad past practices can turn out wines of exemplary quality.

A wide variety of grapes is grown in the region, most notably the Andalusian varieties Pardina, Malvar, Cayetana and Pedro Ximénez, plus the Portuguese grapes Borba and Morisca (*aka* Mourisco; believed by some to be a Pardilla and Cayetana cross). There are also other high-croppers, including Bobal, and local specialities such as Eva, Mantúa (or Montúa) and Alarije. Even so, the future of Tierra de Barros probably lies with what in this region are 'minority' grapes: Tempranillo/Cencibel, Garnacha and Macabeo/Viura. Good work is also being done with Merlot, Cabernet Sauvignon, Chardonnay and Sauvignon Blanc. The fertility of the area aids experimentation with new grape varieties.

Traditionally, this area has produced white wines, since white grape varieties make up about 80 per cent of the vineyard. In addition, it has always been a major source for base wines which provide the grape brandy used by distilleries to produce Brandy de Jerez. The natural future of Ribera del Guadiana, however, should lie in red wines, for which its climate is ideally suited.

Early work by leading bodegas is providing excellent fresh *jovenes* in both white (Alarije, Viura, Chardonnay) and red (Garnacha, Tempranillo), as well as some very promising oak-aged examples up to *reserva* level, and specialty varietals with Cabernet Sauvignon, Merlot *et al.* Even the cooperatives are joining in the general quest for quality – usually a very good sign. If the trend that began in Almendralejo ten years ago continues to gather momentum, this may turn out to be as bountiful an area for wines as it seems to be for every other agricultural product.

# Notable bodegas

Mat = Matanegra; RAG = Ribera Alta de Guadiana; RBG = Ribera Baja de Guadiana; TdB = Tierra de Barros.

### Castelar, Almendralejo (TdB).
*Founded 1963.* Makes *jovenes* in red and white and reds to *crianza* level, sold under the bodega name. The basic white is a good, everyday wine (60% Cayetana/40% Pardina); the red is 85% Tempranillo/15% Garnacha. *Best wine:* the red *crianza* (85% Tempranillo/15% Garnacha; ten months in cask).

### Coloma, Alvarado (RBG).
*Founded 1966.* Coloma is seen as the leading bodega in Ribera Baja de Guadiana, with 198ha providing 80% of its needs. Only red wines are made, under three labels. Viña Amelia is a pleasant *joven* (50% Garnacha/ 25% Merlot/25% Cabernet Sauvignon). Torre-Bermeja is the *reserva* (50% Cabernet Sauvignon/25% Merlot/25% Garnacha; 24 months in cask). The *gran reserva* is an older version of the latter, but may also have some Cencibel and may be under the Torre-Bermeja or Castillo Al-Ruwiya labels.

### Dolores Morena, Los Santos de Maimona (Mat). *Founded 1944.*
Big family concern with 80ha; annual production is around 9,000hl. There are three wines of importance: a white *joven* made from the local Eva grape under the Zagalón label; a red *joven* called Tío Meliton (Cencibel/ Garnacha); and a *dulce* (16% abv) called Vino Para Consagrar (Eva/ Vidueño). Good work is done here. *Best wine:* Tío Meliton.

### InViOSA, Almendralejo (TdB).
*Founded 1931.* Bodegas Industrias Vinícolas del Oeste, to give it its full name, has been the catalyst that brought Ribera del Guadiana up to DO status. In 1981, present boss Marcelino Díaz planted more

Tempranillo, picked with more care and aged his wines judiciously in oak. In 1983, he expanded into sparkling wines under the Cava DO. In the early 1990s, he planted Cabernet Sauvignon, Chardonnay and Sauvignon Blanc. Exported worldwide, the range includes white (Macabeo) and *rosado* (75% Tempranillo/25% Garnacha) *jovenes* and a red *reserva* (75% Tempranillo/20% Garnacha/5% Graciano; 12 months in cask) under the Lar de Barros label. There's also a white barrel-fermented Lar de Barros made from 100% Pardina. Lar de Lares is a *gran reserva* with the same grape-mix as the *joven*, but 24 months in cask, and Lar de Oro is a varietal Cabernet Sauvignon *crianza* with 12 months in oak.

### Medina, Zafra (Mat). *Founded 1931.*
Family firm with 66ha, widely regarded as the leading bodega in the Matanegra subzone. Two ranges: Jaloco Zafra *joven* white (Cayetana/ Mantúa/Pardina/Macabeo) and *rosado* (Cencibel/ Garnacha); two reds: a *joven* (Cabernet Sauvignon/ Cencibel/Garnacha) and a *reserva* (same grapes but with the regulation period in oak) called Jaloco. Marqués de Badajoz is the label for a similar range with similar grapes but different *cuvées*. Quality is usually high.

### Montevirgen Cooperativa, Villalba de los Barros (TdB). *Founded 1962.*
This co-op's 465 members farm 2,700ha and make around 15,000hl. Marqués de Villalba offers a white *joven* (80% Pardilla/20% Macabeo) and a red *crianza* (Tempranillo). Señorío de Villalba is a very good *joven rosado* made from Cencibel and Garnacha.

### Romero, El Raposo (Mat).
*Founded 1954.* Romero has 60ha and is modestly sized by local standards. The brand name is Almonazar, offering *jovenes* in white

(70% Pardina/30% Mantúa) and red (95% Cencibel/5% Garnacha). *Best wine:* an excellent red *crianza* (100% Cencibel).

### San Isidro Cooperativa, Villafranca de los Barros (TdB). *Founded 1960.*
Co-op whose 460 members farm 2,136.5ha of vines. *Best wines:* the *jovenes* Macabel white (Macabeo), and Valdequemao red (Cencibel).

### San José Cooperativa, Villafranca de los Barros (TdB). *Founded 1963.*
With 547 members farming 4,000ha, San José has the most land under vine in the region. Production is 150,000hl, but room has been found for quality wines. The brand name is Canchal de Viera and includes a pleasant, off-dry white *joven* (Pardina/ Cayetana). *Best wine:* the red *joven* (Cencibel/Garnacha).

### San Juan Cooperativa, Castuera (RAG). *Founded 1968.*
With 240 members farming 900ha, San Juan is small by co-op standards but takes its turn at quality *joven* wine. Most unusual is a fascinating white *joven* invoking obscure local varieties (and flavours) like no other. Called Palique, it is made from Pedro Ximénez, Cigüente, Perruno, Cayetana and Alarije.

### San Marcos Cooperativa, Almendralejo (TdB). *Founded 1980.*
Some 510 members farm 3,250ha and turn out 120,000hl. The brand name is Campobarro, with *jovenes* white (95% Pardina/ 5% Cayetana), *rosado* (85% Cencibel/ 15% Garnacha), and red (same grape mix). *Best wines:* the whites are very good.

### Santa María Egipciaca Cooperativa, Corte de Peleas (TdB). *Founded 1978.*
Co-op whose 145 members work 1,397ha. The brand name is Conde de la Corte, with good *jovenes* in white (Pardina) and red (Cencibel/Garnacha).

### Santa Marta Virgen Cooperativa, Santa Marta de los Barros (TdB).
*Founded 1963.* Has the most members in the region: 567 farming 3,200ha, turning out around 170,000hl. The label is called Blasón del Turra and it offers *jovenes* in white (Cayetana/Pardina) and red (Cencibel). *Best wine:* a Blasón del Turra *afrutado* (100% Macabeo).

### Santiago Apóstol, Almendralejo (TdB). *Founded 1979.*
Owns 250ha and makes wine under two labels. Doña Francisquita offers white (Cayetana) and red (Cencibel/Garnacha) *jovenes*, both of which are very good and well made. De Payva offers a (white) barrel-fermented Cayetana and a (red) Cencibel/Graciano *crianza* with astonishing fruit. All are excellent.

### Viña Extremeña, Almendralejo (TdB). *Founded 1970.*
This bodega is fully equipped with new winemaking technology. The basic range is called Montaraz, of which the red (Cencibel) can be very good. Monasterio de Tentudia is a premium range, with *joven* white (80% Moscatel/20% Macabeo) and *rosado* and a *crianza* red (90% Tempranillo/10% Macabeo; 18 months in cask). *Best wines:* the red Palacio de Monsalud *crianza* and Vega Adriana *gran reserva* (90% Tempranillo/10% Macabeo; nine and 24 months in oak, respectively), and an interesting Viña Almendra *semidulce* (100% Macabeo).

# Country Wines of the Meseta

## Castilla-La Mancha

### Vino de Mesa de Toledo

This is the legal nicety that allows the Marqués de Griñón to put a vintage date on his wines. There is no wine-producing area – just this one estate.

### Notable bodega

**Viñedos y Bodegas de Malpica, Malpica de Tajo.** *Founded 1973.* Established at the Finca Dominio de Valdepusa in Malpica de Tajo, on the N-V between Madrid and Talavera de la Reina, this is the former hunting-lodge and now main bodega of a firm that also produces wines in the Rueda DO and the Rioja DOCa. The owner is Carlos Falcó y Fernández de Córdova, the Marqués de Griñón. He studied agricultural engineering at Louvain in Belgium and œnology at the University of California at Davis, and planted his first Cabernet Sauvignon at Valdepusa in 1973 as an experiment. He also installed the latest winemaking equipment and a California drip-feed irrigation system fed by a reservoir on the estate. The vines did well. Around 1980, when the vineyard was mature, the Marqués consulted French expert Alexis Lichine, as well as Bordeaux oenologist Professor Emile Peynaud about the possibility of setting up a commercial venture.

Peynaud recommended specialising in Cabernet Sauvignon and Merlot, and refined some of the winemaking techniques, while Lichine consulted on marketing and presentation. This resulted in the first commercial vintage in 1982, released in 1985. Subsequently, Griñón took further advice from American winemaker Randall Grahm (of Bonny Doon vineyards in California). The later wines in the Malpica stable owe a good deal to his input.

At this point, the question of a name cropped up. The nearest classified regions are the Méntrida DO to the north and the La Mancha DO to the east, but Valdepusa is outside both and has nothing in common with either. The fact that the estate grows French grapes and irrigates them negated any kind of formal recognition, so the Marqués went ahead and simply marketed the wines under his own name from his own estate. The only formality was to register the wines as the non-existent *Vino de Mesa de Toledo* so that he could put a vintage date on the label. The wines won prizes all over the world and generally gained great acclaim.

The example provided by Griñón has inspired more than a few winemakers in parts of Spain originally considered too hot or too arid to produce great wines. It also helped change the minds of officialdom on the subject of drip-feed irrigation – once banned outright but now permitted by individual *consejos reguladores* as an experimental measure, and likely to considerably raise the standard of southern-Spanish wines in the future.

The Valdepusa wines today are among the best in Spain – and, indeed, of Europe. Without the burden of a *reglamento*, the Marqués can bottle his wines when they are ready for bottling, regardless of whether they have spent a minimum term in cask. This expensive option involves tasting every cask every month, but it results in magnificent wines.

The wines are sold under the Dominio de Valdepusa label, typically 90% Cabernet Sauvignon and 10% Merlot, although there is also a varietal Syrah. The terms *crianza*, *reserva*, etc, are not used; one wine may have eight months in cask, another 18. It all depends on how they have developed.

**NB** The bodega is also responsible (although not at this site) for the non-DO Durius wines, red and white. They are both made with grapes from more than one DO region, the white with Verdejo and Viura from Rueda and Ribera del Duero; the red with Tinto Fino from Ribera del Duero and Toro. These, too, are everything we would expect from the Griñón name.

### VdIT Manchuela (DOp – Albacete and Cuenca)

Manchuela is a vast area in east-central Spain, contiguous with the following DOs: La Mancha in the west, Utiel-Requena (in the *autonomía* of Valencia) in the northeast, Almansa in the southeast, and Jumilla (*autonomía* of Murcia) in the south. The chief town is Albacete, and the 75,000ha of vineyards that come under the DO are located partly in that province and partly in Cuenca.

Manchuela was originally part of a much larger provisional DO (DOp) which included La Mancha, Almansa and Méntrida before those three areas achieved their own DO status. It, however, became a provisional DO in its own right in 1982, and since then, has done little to warrant its promotion. There have been suggestions that it should simply be reclassified as a permanent VdIT area.

The main grape is Bobal (as in neighbouring Utiel-Requena), which accounts for 70% of the vineyard. The permitted varieties include Cencibel, Monastrell, Macabeo and Albillo as principal varieties and Bobal, Moravia, Coloraillo, Airén and Pardilla as secondary.

The wines tend to be *jovenes* in all three colours, although there is some new-wave thinking, and the occasional red *crianza* and barrel-fermented white have been spotted. However, most of what is produced here is sold in bulk.

### Notable bodega

**Iniestense Cooperativa, Iniesta (Cuenca).** *Founded 1944.* The most forward-looking co-op in the region. The label is Señorío de Iniesta and provides pleasant *joven* wines. There are also *reserva* and *gran reserva* reds (both Bobal, with 12 months in oak).

### VdIT Pozohondo (Albacete)

This tiny area covers a triangle of three small towns about 30km (19 miles) south of Albacete. Principal grapes are Monastrell and Airén, and wines tend to be *jovenes* in all three colours.

### VdIT Gálvez (Toledo)

This is a large area to the southwest of the city of Toledo covering nine towns and villages. It is classified for red wines only, made from Cencibel and Garnacha Tinta, mainly *jovenes*.

### VdIT Sierra de Alcaraz (Albacete)

With the exception of Manchuela, this is probably the only serious contender for promotion in Castilla-La Mancha. It became a VdIT zone in 1995, due largely to the number of hard-working new bodegas trying to raise the profile of the area. The classification covers the west of the province of Albacete up to the border with the La Mancha DO.

This area has never been considered appropriate for vines, but good soils with a high carbonate content in highland vineyards (up to 1,000 metres/3,281 feet) provide excellent sites with good microclimates. French varieties and French oak predominate, and small-scale, low-production and high-quality is the goal. As the vineyards mature and the wines develop, don't be surprised if this area leapfrogs all the others and becomes Castilla-La Mancha's next DO. Remember: you read it here first.

### Notable bodegas

**Baronia, El Bonillo.** *Founded 1993.* A small estate with 50ha under vine and a brand-new winery. The main label is Viña Consolación, which includes a varietal Chardonnay *joven* and a red *crianza* (60% Cabernet Sauvignon/40% Tempranillo). There is also a Cabernet Sauvignon varietal called Baronia. All are excellent wines.

**Manuel Manzaneque, Ossa de Montiel.** *Founded 1993.* At 1,000 metres (3,281 feet) these must be the highest vineyards in mainland Spain. The grapes ripen in the summer and do not freeze in the spring. There are 35ha planted in small plots in selected microclimatic sites. The brand name is Manuel Manzaneque, and includes a barrel-fermented Chardonnay with four months on its lees, a red *crianza* (80% Cabernet Sauvignon/10% Merlot/10% Tempranillo; 12 months in cask) and an estate wine called Finca Elez, with the same grape mix. All are excellent.

## Extremadura

### VC Azuaga (Badajoz)

This area covers ten towns and villages centred around Azuaga and makes mainly *joven* wines in all three colours. Principal grapes: Cayetana, Eva, Pedro Ximénez, Garnacha Tinta and Cencibel. Secondary varieties: Alarije, Borba, Mantúa and Pardina.

### VC Cilleros (Cáceres)

Tiny area covering the two towns of Cilleros and Villamiel, close to the Portuguese border. The wines tend to be *jovenes* in all three colours, made from principal grape varieties Verdejo, Garnacha Tinta and Cencibel, and subsidiary variety Malvar.

**Right:** Airen grapes are unloaded at Señorío de los Llanos. The variety is a mainstay of country wines as well as of the chief DOs.

# Andalucía and the Canaries

**A**ndalucía is a region of changing fortunes. When the Moors ruled the land they knew as *Al-Andalus*, it was almost a terrestrial paradise, carefully shaped into a huge garden that reflected the same intricate geometry of its great mosques. Then came the *Reconquista*, and in a few hundred years, what had once been one of the most prosperous areas in the world was transformed into one of its most impoverished. Thankfully, today's Andalucía has bounced back, due in large part to its tourist industry – the largest in Spain. This it has in common with the Canary Islands, whose economy is also largely dependent upon an annual influx of visitors.

But what of the wines of these two areas? Both have a long and respected wine history. Indeed, Andalucía is the oldest wine region in Spain, home of what some would call the most quintessentially Spanish of wines: Sherry. The Canaries, too, have exported fortified wines for centuries. Nowadays, both areas make other wines, but their proud heritage lives on – to the delight of wine-lovers everywhere.

**Right:** El Hierro, one of the Canary Islands. While no match for Andalucía in terms of quantity, wine has been produced here since the 16th century.

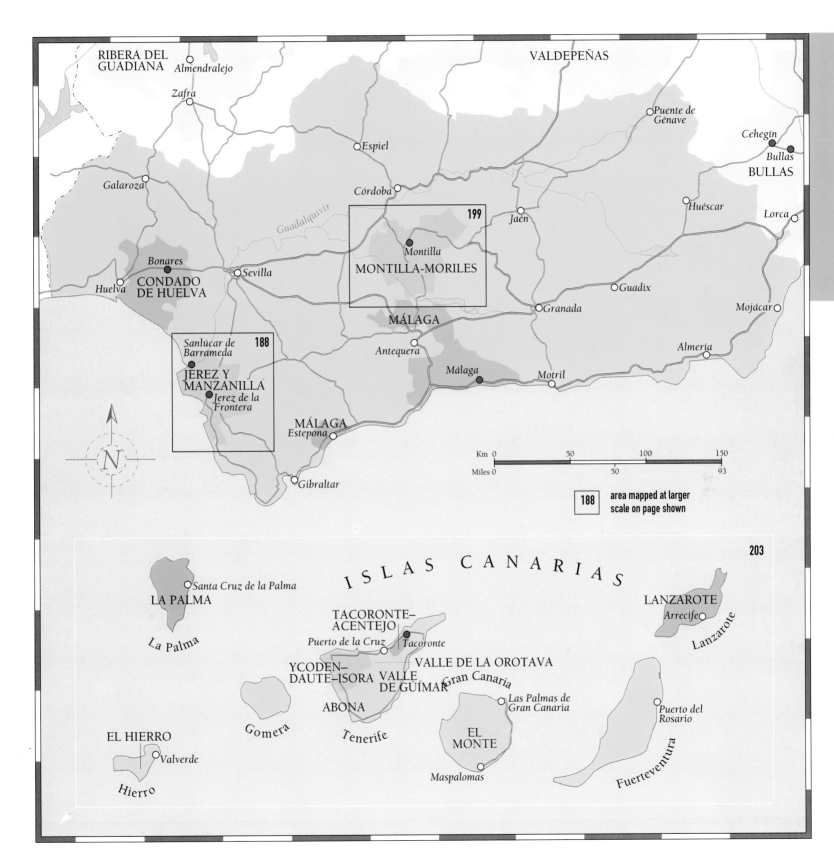

RIBERA DEL GUADIANA

Almendralejo

Zafra

VALDEPEÑAS

Puente de Génave

Cehegín

Bullas

BULLAS

Espiel

Galaroza

*Guadalquivir*

Córdoba

Jaén

Huéscar

Lorca

199

Montilla

MONTILLA–MORILES

Bonares

CONDADO DE HUELVA

Huelva

Sevilla

Guadix

Mojácar

Granada

MÁLAGA

188

Sanlúcar de Barrameda

JEREZ Y MANZANILLA

Jerez de la Frontera

Antequera

Málaga

Motril

Almería

MÁLAGA

Estepona

Km 0    50    100    150

Miles 0    50    93

Gibraltar

188   area mapped at larger scale on page shown

203

I S L A S   C A N A R I A S

Santa Cruz de la Palma

LA PALMA

La Palma

TACORONTE– ACENTEJO

Puerto de la Cruz

Tacoronte

LANZAROTE

Arrecife

Lanzarote

YCODEN– DAUTE–ISORA

VALLE DE GÜÍMAR

VALLE DE LA OROTAVA

Gran Canaria

ABONA

Gomera

Tenerife

Las Palmas de Gran Canaria

EL MONTE

Puerto del Rosario

EL HIERRO

Valverde

Maspalomas

Fuerteventura

Hierro

# Andalucía: birthplace of Spanish wine

Above: The Alhambra, the fortified palace of the Moorish Nasrid kings, still stands guard over the modern city of Granada. Inside is a labyrinth of elaborately decorated rooms...

... such as the *Sala de las Dos Hermanas* (the Hall of the Two Sisters, far right, bottom), which boasts an extravagant domed ceiling, a speciality of Granadan artists.

It is difficult to extract the wine history of Andalucia from the wine history of Spain as a whole – or, indeed, from that of western Europe. A good deal of it was covered in the introductory section of this book, and much may be repeated in the chapter on Sherry (see pages 10 and 188, respectively). However, a brief recap is necessary in order to understand how the wines of this region developed.

When the Mediterranean Sea formed the centre of the western world, and the Pillars of Hercules stood on either side of the straits of Gibraltar, traders from the Middle East set up staging posts, entrepôts and settlements in what is now Morocco as well as in the region that makes up present-day Andalucía. The first city to be established in Spain was Gadir (modern Cádiz), which was founded in or around 1100BC by the Phoenicians, and the first vines on the peninsula were probably planted in the hinterland beyond Gadir in what is now the Sherry Country.

In those days, all the wine made in the region was sweet and strong, the better to withstand long journeys in hot climates, not to mention the poorly sealed vessels in which it was carried. The hot, lowland slopes of Andalucía proved to be ideal for the kind of high-yielding vines that had been brought from Syria, Lebanon, Israel and Egypt. Pruning was unknown, and it seems likely that the traders simply planted the vines in sunny places and waited for them to perform.

## A horticultural paradise

Meanwhile, early settlers were discovering that the climate of western Andalucía was also ideal for a variety of crops. The prevailing westerly winds from the Atlantic kept temperatures at a manageable level, and the high chalk content of the soils helped to retain moisture during the dry season, thus feeding the roots of whatever was grown: oranges, figs, olives, rice, almonds and cotton as well as vines. This was a trader's paradise, and it was situated right at the crossroads of world trade.

A thousand years on, the Romans also recognised the natural advantages of Andalucía, which they called *Baetica*. They were able to feed a good deal of the western Empire on the wheat, olive oil and wine that was grown and produced here, shipping it along the Atlantic coastline to Gaul and Britain. In 711, the Moors landed at what is now Gibraltar and ruled the region from Seville and Córdoba, exporting the produce of their new territories back home to north Africa. Once Spain was reunited in 1492, Andalucía was to go through yet another boom with the export of its (by now fortified) wines to the newly discovered Americas, northern Europe, the Indies and countries all over the world.

As Spain became industrialised during the 18th and 19th centuries, Andalucía, as a largely agricultural region, became considerably less important to the country's national economy. Yet tourism countered this decline in prosperity from the mid-20th century onwards, and a whole new generation of invaders – this time bearing cash and cameras rather than the weapons of war – did an enormous amount to restore the area's fortunes.

Andalucía is Spain's second-largest *autonomia*, with eight provinces (Castile-León has nine) which divide roughly into three parts. In the west, Cádiz, Sevilla and Huelva are very much the 'classical Spain' of vines, horses, bullfighting and Flamenco. In the east, Granada, Almería and Málaga have become some of the most successful holiday resort areas, particularly along the coast. In the middle, Córdoba and Jaén continue the tradition of agriculture that brought the region its original prosperity.

The Moors ruled in Andalucía longer than anywhere else in Spain, and their influences in terms of language, architecture and town-planning are strongest in these parts. The city of Granada was the last Moorish capital, and the Alhambra Palace serves as a lasting monument to a people who lived in opulent luxury at a time when most of Europe was still building houses out of mud and straw.

Such is the strength of this Arabic influence that it appears everywhere, even in modern artistic styles, décor and architecture. The traditional Andalucían house, for example, consists of four rooms around a central courtyard – a Moorish design that was developed to maintain cool quarters in the heat of the afternoon, In fact, architectural design throughout the region reflects the Islamic archways, courtyards and tracery of an empire which collapsed 500 years ago.

Above: The other face of Andalucía. Christian effigies such as this one appear inside mosques, evidence of the effects of the *Reconquista*.

## Andalucían gastronomy

As would be expected from a region with a coastline, Andalucían cuisine features fish in a big way. The warm, shallow, coastal waters breed big, bold shellfish and every imaginable white fish, from sole and monkfish to sardines. These are usually eaten poached or baked, accompanied by a cold fino or manzanilla Sherry in the west, or a light *joven afrutado* (*see* page 186) in the east.

In contrast, Jaén and Córdoba are herding country, so beef and lamb steaks, chops and roasts are the mainstays of the menu. *Churrasco*, the grill on which meat is cooked (and by extension, the meat itself) is a speciality of many restaurants. In addition, local cheeses are made in profusion from goat's, cow's and sheep's milk, and there is ubiquitous *gazpacho* to be tasted. For pudding, try the speciality known as *tocino de cielo* (a meringue-based dessert) or opt for a dish of fresh, locally made ice-cream with a glass of thick, black Pedro Ximénez from Montilla poured over it.

# Condado de Huelva

## Notable bodegas

**SoViCoSA, Bollullos del Condado.** *Founded 1983.* This company was established by the founding bodegas as an acknowledgement that *joven afrutado* wines were the way forward for the Condado de Huelva. The bodega is kitted out with the most modern winemaking equipment, and most of its production appears under just one label: Viña Odiel (Zalema). This is possibly the best of the new-style wines of the region.

**Vinícola del Condado Cooperativa, Bollullos del Condado.** *Founded 1955.* The largest co-op in the region, with 1,800 members farming 4,500ha of vines and turning out 250,000hl of wine. In spite of its size, the co-op recognised some while ago that things were changing in the market, and shifted a large part of its production to new-style wines. White *jovenes* include Privilegio del Condado and Don Condado *semiseco* (both 100% Zalema and 10.5% abv). *Generosos* include a palatable *pálido* called Mioro (90% Listán/5% Garrido Fino/5% Palomino; 15.5% abv), a decent *viejo* called Botarroble (100% Zalema; 18% abv) and two *vinos de licor*: Misterio and Puesta del Sol (both 100% Zalema; 15% and 18% abv, respectively).

During the 16th and 17th centuries, worldwide demand for sack (the forerunner of modern Sherry) exceeded supply. The main producers were Jerez, Madeira and the Canary Islands, and the last two simply sold what they had and put up 'out of stock' signs. Jerez, however, did not. This region and its neighbours continued to keep exports flowing with powerful, sweet, fortified wines for several centuries. The region of Condado de Huelva grew up in this enterprising climate, cheerfully making and selling its own wines as well as supplying them to Jerez, where they were transformed via the *solera* system.

Today, of course, much has changed. The Sherry zone has not been permitted to buy wine outside its home area for many years. The Condado de Huelva has since expanded its winemaking styles, but its whole existence was built upon making *generoso* wines – many of which are very good.

As they ought to be, for the main ingredients are readily available. The Condado's vineyards are situated just above sea level at heights of around 25 metres (82 feet), and it has a relatively generous amount of rainfall. The soil is alluvial and sandy, with a trace of chalk in some places. The main grape variety is Zalema, which occupies 80 per cent of the vineyard, but other varieties are grown as well: Palomino/Listán (the Sherry grape), Garrido Fino, Moscatel and Pedro Ximénez. The DO applies only to white wines, but an enormous amount of experimentation goes on here: everything from Monastrell to Syrah, Chardonnay to Vermentino is on trial in the region's vineyards.

## Winemaking and wine styles

Wines fall into two groups. Condado *pálido*, which is 15.5 per cent alcohol by volume (abv), and Condado *viejo* (17 to 23 per cent abv) are old-style, semi-fortified wines. They can be very good, especially at the sweeter end where they resemble a decent old oloroso. *Joven afrutado* is a new-style, cool-fermented, light white wine made from the local grapes. Zalema, however, is a bit neutral when vinified in this style – hence the great interest in other white varieties.

At present, the wines of the Condado de Huelva are in the doldrums. However, with a change of regulations, some new grape varieties and a bit of marketing effort, this is an area that could achieve a great deal.

**Right:** Using horses to plough vineyards is still common practice in the Condado de Huelva DO. Here, much of the production consists of traditional, semi-fortified wines.

MÁLAGA

A sad story, this. The Málaga DO, that once-great stalwart of Victorian morning-rooms, is down to just eight bodegas and even some of those are struggling. To make matters worse, the DO has to import grapes from Montilla just to make up its numbers.

Such was not always the case. Málaga wine was one of the great success stories of the wine-export boom that took place during the Renaissance. It flourished alongside sack from Jerez and the Canary Islands, and its rich sweetness, staying power and high alcohol brought a blush to many a maidenly Victorian cheek. Known in the 19th century as 'Mountain Wine', no civilised sideboard could be seen without it.

Yet tastes change. As bottling became more widespread and trade routes opened up around the world, a wider range of wines became available to the consumer. Matters were made worse with the tourist boom that followed the Second World War. Parts of Málaga's coastal areas were hived off for redevelopment, and local winemakers found a ready cash market for their wines closer to home.

Málaga survives, nevertheless. There are two vineyard areas: one in the east which stretches from the city of Málaga to the border with Granada; the other in the west, around Estepona and up to the border with Cádiz. Moscatel is the main grape grown in the latter, but the eastern vineyard still provides the classic Pedro Ximénez (PX) grapes used to make traditional Málaga wine.

The eastern vineyard is split into three subzones. Axarquía runs along the coast from Málaga city to Nerja and inland along the border with Granada; it, too, grows mainly Moscatel. The two remaining areas are quite small: Molina, around the town of the same name, and the original 'Mountain' vineyards around the town of Cuevas de San Marcos. These are the only two areas that grow PX, and although there are about 12,000 hectares of vines in the DO zone, fewer than 1,000 are actually classified for the Málaga DO – which is why grapes are brought in from Montilla.

## Geography and climate

Altitudes range from near sea level on the coast to 700 metres (2,297 feet) and more in the Mountain subzone. Soils become increasingly clay-based with altitude, but there is a fair sprinkling of chalk throughout the region, which provides the PX with its quality. Climates range from Mediterranean on the coast to continental inland, with some suprisingly cold nights up in the mountains; this, too, is good for the vines.

Málaga's best wines are made purely from PX, although there are blends and varietals with Moscatel. To make classic Málaga, grapes are picked fully ripe and then laid out in the sun on esparto grass mats to dry in a process known as *soleo*. Most of the water content evaporates, leaving behind something resembling a soggy raisin that produces highly concentrated juice, rich in natural grape-sugar.

Yeast ferments only briefly at these sugar levels, so once fermentation has begun, the wine is fortified with grape spirit to up to 23 per cent alcohol by volume (abv). Then it is sent for ageing. This may be static (in casks or butts) or dynamic (in a variant of the *solera* system; *see* page 192), but the end result will be a blend that suits the bodega, probably with a dash of ancient wine thrown in to add a final burnish.

Producers have experimented with a dry, fully fermented Málaga; there is also a semi-sweet Málaga *abocado*, with up to 50 grammes per litre (g/l) of unfermented grape sugar. Moscatel is pleasant, too, but real Málaga (up to 600g/l) is unmistakeable: dark or golden in colour, it is chocolatey on the nose, and offers blockbusting, raisiny fruit, rich toffee notes, and consummate grace on the length. It is also expensive and hopelessly unfashionable – hence one of the world's great wines is dying peacefully before our very eyes.

## Notable bodegas

**Larios, Málaga.** A giant drinks and distilling company that makes about 5,000hl of good-quality Málaga wine each year – keeping the dream alive, some would say, and using the Larios distribution network to keep the name alive throughout Spain. Benefique is an 'oloroso' made from 100% PX, and the traditional Málaga *dulce* is PX with 5% Vidueña.

**López Hermanos, Málaga.** *Founded 1885.* The biggest (25,000hl) surviving Málaga house working hard to keep the wine alive by diversifying into different styles. These include a 15% abv Málaga *pálido* called Cartojal, and some excellent Moscatels. Flag-carrier for the traditional style is the 17% abv Málaga Virgen (75% PX/25% Moscatel). All wines are excellent value for money and are made in the best traditions of Málaga. *Best wine:* a 'dry oloroso' style called Trajinero (18% abv).

**Scholtz, Málaga.** *Founded 1807.* Scholtz closed in 1996, but it held such vast stocks that they are likely to be in the supply-chain for some considerable time. Everything made here was exemplary, so if you see the label, buy the wine – especially Lágrima 10 Años, or, best of all, PX Añejo. We shall not see the like of these wines ever again.

**Above left:** The old town of Ronda stands precariously above the gorge of the River Tajo in the province of Málaga.

# Jerez

The Jerez DO has the longest name in the business – *Jerez/Xérès/Sherry y Manzanilla de Sanlúcar*, to give it its full title – mainly because it has had to fight the longest of any wine in the world in order to protect it. The struggle has been complicated by both history and linguistics: the town of Jerez itself was called *Ceret* by its earliest settlers, *Scheris* by the Moors and *Xerez* by the re-conquering Castilians of the 13th century. It is astonishing to record that it took until January 1, 1996, for Sherry to become a protected quality-wine name within the European Union. Imitative flattery certainly had something to do with it.

One reason for the long haul to 'copyright' status was that so many wines from so many countries around the world called their own wines 'Sherry' in an effort to bask

in its reflected glory. Although the wine had been known in England since 1340, it was not until 1587 that it became particularly fashionable – largely because Sir Francis Drake attacked Cádiz harbour, set fire to most of the Spanish fleet and made off with nearly 3,000 barrels of the stuff. London was suddenly awash with 'sherris sack', creating a market that was to boom almost unhindered for nearly 400 years – give or take the odd war.

Twelve years after Drake had thus 'singed the King of Spain's beard', in part two of *Henry IV*, Shakespeare's Sir John Falstaff discoursed at length on the peculiar benefits and quality of sherris sack. It was so much better than all the others, he declared, because it

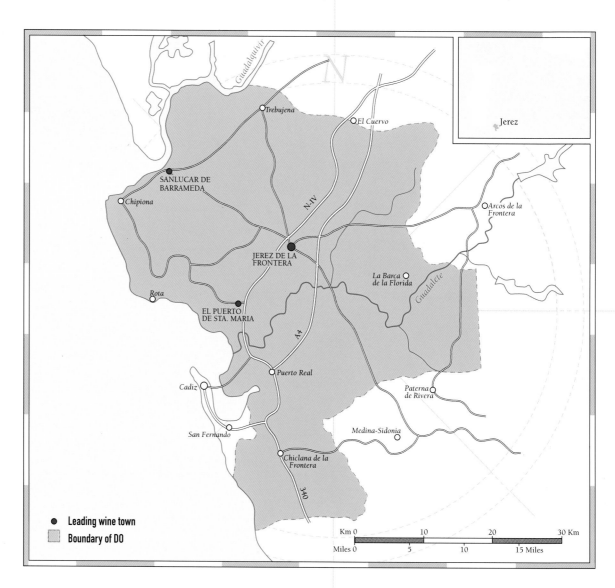

- ● Leading wine town
- Boundary of DO

'...ascends me into the brain and dries me there all the foolish and dull and crudy vapours which environ it...' Well, he enjoyed it, at any rate.

The early history of Sherry has been related elsewhere in this book, since it is inextricably linked with the early history of Spanish wine. By the 19th century, Sherry had become an established favourite all over the world. Its stability and ability to travel well (thanks to fortification and oxidation in cask) made it a valuable trading commodity. In fact, the name 'Sherry' had become a generic term for fine wines in certain quarters. One surviving Victorian wine merchant's list, for example, describes a wine as 'Château d'Yquem – finest Sherry'. A producer could scarcely ask for a better association of qualities.

Sherry sales boomed yet again in the final quarter of the 19th century, as England and Holland (then, and now, the two largest markets) as well as Belgium, Germany and Scandinavia discovered the benefits of a glass or two of this noble, warming liquid in the depths of a dark, north-European winter. Note that, at this time, the wines known today as fino and manzanilla were not the light, fresh, *flor*-flavoured examples available to modern consumers. There was little in the way of refrigeration, and transport was slow, hot and cumbersome. As a result, all Sherry wines would have been fully cask-conditioned and more like what today's *aficionado* would regard as amontillado in style.

## The first regulations

The Spanish government made the first attempts to regulate wine production by national law during the early 1930s. Prior to that time, any regulation had been performed by local and regional committees and guilds. Sherry's first *consejo regulador* was established in 1933, its creation partly a response to the increasing trade in 'Sherry' from almost every wine-producing country in the world, little of which reflected well on its role model.

As well as setting the rules and regulations for every aspect of vine planting, winemaking, ageing and marketing, for the first time the *consejo* also provided accurate statistics about how much wine was being made and shipped, and who was buying it. In 1940, Jerez exported 240,000 hectolitres of wine before the market temporarily collapsed due to the Second World War. Sherry, however, was back in business right after the war: 206,000 hectolitres were exported in 1949 and 300,000 in 1959. It seemed as if the boom would go on for ever, but in the end this proved to be far from the case.

To continue the statistics: in 1969, Sherry exports stood at 700,000 hectolitres; in 1979, they were 1,500,000 hectolitres – the equivalent of two hundred million bottles. Such a figure would never be achieved again, as trends in the drinks market changed. A new generation of drinkers, born after the war, associated Sherry with their ancient relatives and dusty old bottles gathering cobwebs in the sitting-room sideboard. Meanwhile, the wine market was booming. With examples of every style from every country in the world becoming available, poor old Sherry somehow got pushed into the background.

## Problems within the industry

In many ways, the Sherry industry was the architect of its own downfall. It had become complacent after centuries of unending prosperity, and unwilling to change and react to the market. There was also far too much poor-quality wine overloading the market and being shipped around the world in bulk containers, collecting export subsidies and compensatory amounts – despite the fact that it had never been intended for drinking at all.

Jerez found itself in the midst of a crisis. There were too many hectares of vines, too many people in the industry, too much wine and too many overheads. Companies got into serious difficulties; there were strikes in the vineyards as promised and generous pension agreements suddenly ran out of money. A spate of mergers and takeovers took place as the export market halved in ten years to just 783,000 hectolitres in 1989. It was a very painful time for a very large number of people.

Stability eventually returned in the early 1990s. Obviously, the days had ended when anything with the word 'Sherry' on the label would sell itself off the shelf. But the reason Sherry had achieved so much in the first place was due to its basic, inherent, solid-gold quality. That quality had not gone away; it had simply been masked by the appalling, bland, branded, advertising-led monstrosities that had done so much to destroy the wine's image.

**Above:** Fino Sherry is poured straight from the cask in the bodegas of Emilio Lustau. Cellarmen often demonstrate their skill by filling glasses from distances of a metre or more.

## The Sherry renaissance

The new generation of wine drinkers who had turned their backs on the old brown sticky stuff suddenly rediscovered Sherry, but in a different guise. Here were young, cool, crisp, lower-strength finos and manzanillas, fresh with the yeasty flavour of *flor*, delicious with light, fishy and vegetarian foods – or wonderful by themselves, returning to their original roles as perfect *aperitivos*. The more adventurous went on to explore glorious old olorosos and ancient *solera* sweet wines and, like every generation, imagined that it had discovered them for the first time. No matter: Sherry was, once again, back in business.

True, Aunt Maud had died and the new vicar was a vegetarian who drank only organic Sauvignon. There would never be a return to the rivers of bland, sticky stuff that had (to be fair) funded the industry throughout most of the latter half of the 20th century. Less wine was coming out of Jerez, but it was of a much better quality. Sold at higher prices, it provided the profit margins needed for the bodegas to re-equip, reinvest and fight back. As the century draws to a close, the wines of Jerez are as good as or better than they have ever been. The choice is excellent, and in terms of value for money – year for year in maturity terms – they have no rivals on Earth.

## The Sherry Country

Geographically, the Sherry Country covers the 'golden triangle' of land that lies in the eastern part of the province of Cádiz, with an incursion northwards into the province of Sevilla. It is centred around the three towns of Sanlúcar de Barrameda, Jerez de la Frontera and Puerto de Santa María. One of the earliest controls placed on Sherry was that it could only be shipped from one of these three towns, and that is still the case today.

The soil of Sherry Country comes in three distinct types: sand, clay and chalk, called *arenas*, *barros* and *albarizas*, respectively. Grapes used to be grown in all three soil types, but the sand and clay vineyards have mostly been grubbed up, and the vines are grown only on the *albarizas* – which, after all, produce the highest-quality grapes.

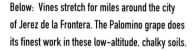

**Below:** Vines stretch for miles around the city of Jerez de la Frontera. The Palomino grape does its finest work in these low-altitude, chalky soils.

This chalk, which is as white as flour on the surface of newly ploughed land, is one of what could be called the three secrets of Sherry.

The best vineyards face the Atlantic Ocean and benefit from the westerly winds and generous rainfall that are particularly important for a wine-producing area this far south. Even so, the daily heat in the ripening season causes massive evaporation, and much of the water would be lost were it not for the chalk. Its spongy nature soaks up every last drop and holds it underground, where the temperature varies much less. In addition, after the rains, the surface of the soil dries in the sun like icing on a cake, forming a hard crust which also helps to prevent evaporation. The result is healthy grapes in good quantity.

*Albariza* land is divided into *pagos* (individual vineyards), and there are about 150 of these, some as small as a hectare, the largest covering several thousand hectares. Each has its own particular characteristics. Hotter and higher *pagos* tend to grow grapes that will make good oloroso wines; cooler and more coastal *pagos* favour the fino tendency. Vineyard names likely to be found on bottles are usually only those of the biggest and most important *pagos*, and there are eight of these. Añina, Balbaina, Carrascal, Macharnudo and Martín Miguel are located in the interior of the region, around Jerez; Miraflores and Torrebreva are in the coastal area, near Sanlúcar; and Los Tercios is situated in the coastal area, near Puerto de Santa María.

## Grape varieties

The second secret of Sherry is the grapes that are used to make it: the Listán, or Palomino, or Listán Palomino. Moscatel and Pedro Ximénez (PX) grapes are also grown here; the former is often made into a varietal wine while the PX is used for sweetening as well as in the production of some rare and expensive varietals of its own. For most purposes, though, the Listán is king. A heavy cropper, it makes wines of insipid quality elsewhere in Spain but here, with the chalky soil and the unusual, very hot but relatively wet climate, it is the perfect ingredient for the third secret of Sherry: the Sherry process itself.

**Above:** The traditional tools of the Sherry *bodeguero's* trade. *Jarras* (jugs; centre) pour wine into the *canoas* (funnels; top), which in turn are used to channel wines into new butts.

# The Sherry Process

There are wine regions of the world favoured with a perfect climate, rich soils, alpine altitude and noble and complex vine varieties, but Jerez is not one of these. The greatness of its wines is the result of a determination to make something good from the fairly humble ingredients provided by Mother Nature, backed up by a couple of thousand years of trial and error, evolution, fine-tuning and just plain hard work.

The process starts in the vineyard. We have seen how the land, sea breezes and high levels of active chalk are used to maximise the quality of the Listán Palomino on the vine. Over a considerable period of years, the *bodegas* have come to know those areas that are likely to produce the best grapes for fino wines and those that will provide better oloroso wines, and the grapes tend to be harvested according to this knowledge. However, the Sherry process is nothing if not a model of equal opportunities, and all types of wine are generally encouraged to grow *flor* in their early days, just to see if they have it in them to become fino at the end of the *solera*. This is how it works:

## The first year

All Sherry starts its life dry. After full fermentation, the wines will have achieved 12 to 13 per cent alcohol by volume (abv) and may be stored in tanks until the January after the vintage, when they will be assessed for quality. The best wines are fortified to 14.5 per cent abv and any substandard ones to 16.5 per cent. The former then go into cask and the latter tend to be sold off or stored for eventual blending use.

In the cask is where *flor* grows. This strain of yeast feeds off residual elements in the wine and forms anything from a very thin film to a foaming crust on its surface. In the spring, those wines that have grown the most vigorous *flor* are re-fortified to 15.5 per cent abv (an ideal strength for *flor* to thrive). These will become fino wines. The rest will be fortified to 17.5 per cent – too strong for *flor*. These will become olorosos.

At this stage, these are wines of a single vintage, known as *añadas* ('yearlings', perhaps). Very little single-vintage Sherry comes to the market, although Emilio Lustau lists a 1918 amontillado, and Williams and Humbert keeps a library of vintages dating back to the 1920s for visitors to the *bodega*. The vast majority of wine, however, goes into that triumph of Jerezano technology known as the *solera*.

## The *solera*

Imagine a three-row pyramid of barrels with, say, seven along the bottom, six on the row above and five along the top, and you have a mental image of how the *solera* system works. The barrels are typically *botas* (butts) of 500 litres, and the bottom seven are known as the *solera*. In any one year, only a third of the wine in these butts may be sold, and they are topped up by adding wine from the row above, which is known as the first *criadera* (nursery).

These, in turn, are topped up with wine from the row above them, known as the second *criadera*, and these are topped up by new wine from the latest year's *añadas*. The wines are carefully selected to bring something unique to the *solera*. By the time a new wine has gone right through the system, anything from five to 100 years may have passed. More importantly, the new wine will have had the chance to

Below: One of the key factors in the Sherry process. The yeast known as *flor* grows on the surface of wine in the *solera*, imparting a characteristic flavour to the finished product.

take on the characteristics of its forebears in the system. This natural quality-control gave Sherry its early ascendancy in export markets. Finally, the wines are assembled into a final *cabeceo* (what the French call a *cuvée*). This may result in anything from a modestly priced supermarket own-brand to an impressive single-*solera* wine of immense breeding.

## The wines

**Fino** is the lightest and driest of Sherries, carrying the delicate, fresh, yeasty flavour of the *flor*. In cooler coastal areas such as Sanlúcar de Barrameda (where fino is known as manzanilla), *flor* grows vigorously all year round, giving a great deal of flavour to the wine and preserving its delicate pale-straw tint. In hotter, inland areas such as Jerez itself, the *flor* dies back in mid-summer, and the wines are darker and more aromatic as a result. They are normally released at five to ten years old.

    **Amontillado** wines start out as fino but spend much longer in the *solera*. At around 15 years old, amontillado takes on a darker colour and a more robust aroma, but maintains the savoury character of its youth.

    **Oloroso** wines develop through the *solera* without growing *flor*, and are darker, richer and more powerful in aroma, although not sweeter. Olorosos are among the longest-lived wines in the world, lasting up to 100 years or more. The best have a golden, nutty fragrance and rich, powerful palate with a long, bone-dry finish.

    **Palo Cortado** is a rare deviant, a wine that started life as a fino developing *flor*, and then lost it to undergo kind of vinous sex-change in an effort to become an oloroso. The result has some of the savoury character of a young amontillado, but with the enduring yet bone-dry finish of an oloroso.

    **Cream Sherry** and other types have been concocted to appeal to individual markets. All Sherry is naturally dry, but *soleras* of sweetening wines are made from Pedro Ximénez or Moscatel grapes (the former is used increasingly in dry Sherries). *Dulces* (sweetening syrups) made with reduced grape juice (*arrope*) or pure sugar (*almíbar*) add sweetness to the finished *cabeceo*. Many commercial amontillado styles are made from a blend of young wines and sweetening agents to create what is perceived as a popular medium-dry style. Like many attempts to please everybody, these wines usually end up pleasing nobody.

    The greatest sweet wines of Jerez go back into a *solera* after sweetening, and may spend another 20 years or so developing before they are released for sale.

# Notable bodegas

**Agustín Blázquez, Jerez.**
*Founded 1795.* This bodega was an early enthusiast for the new, lighter, fresh styles of fino, and its excellent Carta Blanca is one of the best. It's also one of very few with the confidence to date-stamp the back-labels so the customer knows how long the wine has been in bottle. The range also includes Carta Oro and Carta Plata (amontillados), Carta Roja (oloroso) and Medal (cream).

**Argüeso (Herederos), Sanlúcar de Barrameda.** *Founded 1822.* Beware! There are two Argüesos. This one owns 40ha and specialises in manzanilla, and La Medallas de Argüeso is an outstanding example of the craft. Some prefer San León, which is the manzanilla *pasada* version, but they are both classics of their kind. There is also an amontillado and an excellent Moscatel, but these together only represent 5% of production.

**Barbadillo, Sanlúcar de Barrameda.** *Founded 1821.*
Formerly a major supplier to John Harvey, this is another outstanding producer of manzanilla. With a total production of around 100,000hl, it is one of the biggest winemakers in Sanlúcar. *Best wines:* the best manzanilla is Soleo and is outstanding, but the range is wider than that. Eva manzanilla and cream are excellent; Príncipe (two versions of amontillado) is superb, as is Cuca oloroso *viejo*.

**Bobadilla, Jerez.** *Founded 1882.*
Bought by Osborne in 1990 but still making wines in its own style from its own 38ha of vineyard. Alcázar (amontillado), Capitán (oloroso), La Merced (cream) and Romántico (PX) are all very good. The firm also makes a best-selling brandy under the DE Brandy de Jerez. *Best wine:* the excellent classic fino Victoria.

**Croft, Jerez.** *Founded 1970.* The Croft company had been exporting Sherry for more than 200 years via its offices in Oporto, Portugal, but it wasn't until 1970 that it set up a proper bodega in Jerez. As a result, the equipment, cellars and handling are all thoroughly modern, and the firm makes wine from its own 350ha, producing about 80,000hl per year. The wines are all sold under the Croft label. Delicado is a pleasant fino, Classic a good amontillado and Original the enormously popular mass-market, sweetened-fino blend. *Best wine:* (also the rarest) the excellent Croft Palo Cortado.

**Delgado Zuleita, Sanlúcar de Barrameda.** *Founded 1744.*
An excellent house turning out some 10,000hl of Sherry and *jovenes afrutados* under the VdlT Cádiz. There are good wines under the labels Barbiana (manzanilla *pasada*) and ¿Quo Vadis? (amontillado), and a very good amontillado called Zuleta. *Best wine:* the most famous name in its stable – the excellent La Goya manzanilla *pasada*.

**Emilio Hidalgo, Jerez.** Beware! There are two Hidalgos. This one is situated in the heart of the old town of Jerez, and makes wine in the classic styles: Charito manzanilla and Panesa fino are good, Magistrál cream and Privilegio PX are very good, and Gobernador oloroso and Tresillo amontillado are excellent.

**Emilio Lustau, Jerez.** *Founded 1896.* Splendid old firm in a beautiful bodega in the old town, this is one of the leading quality names in the business. Founded by a lawyer with a liking for good Sherry, the enterprise was purely a family bodega for the first few years, until the founder's son-in-law, Emilio Lustau, put it on a business footing. The company registered the name *Almacenista* (storekeeper) to

describe special wines which it buys in from individual, often amateur and enthusiast stockholders, of whom there are a number in Jerez; José Berdejo, Lustau's founder, was just such a one. Almacenista wines are bottled under the Lustau name with details of the individual bodega owner on the label, and have become some of the highest-quality and most sought-after wines in Jerez. Certainly, they won for Lustau a reputation for unrivalled quality that was well earned and continues right up to the present day. Emilio Lustau's successor, Rafael Balao, was in failing health as the 1980s drew to a close, and the company was taken over in 1990 by Luís Caballero of Puerto de Santa María. This firm has a successful reputation, providing good-quality wines for the supermarket trade, and there were initial worries that Lustau might simply be assimilated. The reverse was true. Not only did the new ownership give Lustau access to the 170ha Montenegrillo *pago* (previously all grapes had been bought in), but Caballero provided encouragement and investment for Lustau to develop its quality business. The result is that it's now one of the top bodegas in Jerez. The Almacenista range changes on a rolling basis according to what wines are mature and available from individual suppliers, but they are never less than exceptional in quality and may include such rarities as palo cortado and even manzanilla amontillada. The Solera label offers a traditional range of wines made to Lustau standards, including Puerto fino, Reserva Los Arcos amontillado, the magnificent Emperatriz Eugenia oloroso and an impressive Reserva Moscatel called Emilín.

**Garvey, Jerez.** *Founded 1780.*
Major export bodega with 500ha and two bodegas: one in the old town and one outside Jerez. Garvey was the first bodega to experiment with 'light' Sherry wines (finos), in the early 1820s, when the vast majority of production was of olorosos. Its reputation has been built largely on the fino San Patricio, which is still

excellent despite a few changes in ownership in recent years. Other wines include Tío Guillermo, a very good amontillado and Flor de Jerez oloroso. *Best wine:* San Patricio.

### González-Byass, Jerez.

*Founded 1835.* An old warhorse of the Sherry trade with magnificent bodegas in the centre of Jerez and 800ha, producing over 200,000hl of wine. Recent ownership changes threatened to rock the boat in the late 1980s, but were finally sorted out in 1991, with the family still firmly in charge and the IDV Group (International Distillers and Vintners) with a minority stake in the company. The international fame of González-Byass (GB) rests on the shoulders of one wine: the fino Tío Pepe. This was allegedly named after an 'Uncle Joe' who had a special cask of particularly light, dry fino kept to one side for his personal use. Unlike most leading Sherries in the international marketplace that survive on their name, tradition, anecdotal history or sheer advertising spend, Tío Pepe as sold in Spain really is an outstanding example of a mature fino – very unusual, considering the quantity that gets exported. The firm had to build a vast new three-storey bodega (the only one of its kind in Jerez) just to accommodate Tío Pepe. GB has also entered the new 'lighter, fresher' market with an excellent, delicious manzanilla called El Rocío, and also maintains a range of workmanlike, middle-ranking everyday wines. Most romantic, however, are the Apóstoles: 13 huge oak barrels in the centre of the main bodega complex, each one named after one of the 12 apostles, roughly in the order of Michaelangelo's *Last Supper*. The central one is unnamed and contains brandy. 'Judas' contains *vinagre de Jerez* – Sherry vinegar. The others harbour wines from various ancient *soleras*, some going back to the middle of the last century. A small quantity of oloroso *seco* is released from these casks each year under the brand-name Apóstoles, and this is the classic style that our great-great grandparents would have recognised as very fine Sherry indeed. In the same range as Apóstoles come Matúsalem – a glorious, golden, honeyed oloroso *dulce* which tastes as old as its name implies; Amontillado del Duque – an exceptionally fine, concentrated, dry amontillado; and Noë, a PX of enormous smoothness, richness and maturity. These are wines to dream about.

### John Harvey, Jerez. *Founded 1970.*

This firm was actually active in Jerez in 1769. Since then and until 1970, its base was Bristol, England, and its wines were sourced from among the myriad producers on the ground in Jerez and Sanlúcar (notably Antonio Barbadillo). In 1970, the company bought Mackenzie & Co and re-established itself in a smart, new but traditionally styled bodega in Jerez with all the latest equipment. John Harvey went on to buy once-familiar names such as Marqués de Misa, Diez Merito, De Terry and Palomino y Vergara. This last bodega was famous for only one wine, the fino Tío Mateo, but all the *soleras* and the name were sold onward to the new bodegas of the Marqués del Real Tesoro in its new incarnation from 1990. Most of the vineyards acquired in this buying spree (some 1,000ha in total) have been given over to the world's unquenchable thirst for Bristol Cream, which remains Harvey's premium product and, as sold in Spain, is still surprisingly good, given its 'branded' status. Bristol fino is a good, clean wine, and there's also a Bristol medium dry, but these are a bit half-hearted compared with the Cream. Harveys is a member of the Allied-Domecq group, and the reasoning at boardroom level seems to be that the group's major fino should be La Ina (*see* Pedro Domecq) since there's not a lot of point in competing with itself at that quality level.

### Los Infantes de Orleans-Borbón, Sanlúcar de Barrameda.

'The Royal Children' might be a suitable translation of the name of this bodega, which is jointly owned by Barbadillo and the Spanish Royal Family. The wines are generally very good, and the range includes La Ballena manzanilla, Alvaro fino, El Botánico amontillado, Fenicio oloroso and Carla PX. *Best wines:* the excellent Torre Breva manzanilla (from the *pago* of the same name) and a splendid cream called Orleans 1884.

### Internacionales (Bodegas), Jerez.

The Medina group owns a number of very large bodegas, including part of what was once the Rumasa empire. Total production is about 170,000hl. The main quality interest here is Rumasa's flagship wine: Don Zoilo. The fino has always been one of the best in the region (albeit at a premium price) and this remains true today. The rest of the range – manzanilla, amontillado, oloroso and cream – are very good but seldom achieve the quality of the fino.

### Jesús Ferris, Jerez. *Founded 1975.*

A relatively small bodega by Jerez standards with 35ha and a particular passion for sweeter wines. Las 3 Candidas is a range of three wines: amontillado, oloroso *seco* and *dulce*, all very good. *Best wines:* two *dulces* under the J Ferris M label: an excellent pure Moscatel and an exceptional PX.

### Luís Caballero, Puerto de Santa María. *Founded 1830.*

A family-owned company with a long and respectable reputation on the home and export markets. Since 1933, it has owned the house of Burdon, and Sherries under this name (which the company describes as its 'fighting wines') are sold in the export market. The present Luís Caballero is an enthusiast for finos, and has developed an interesting method of maximising the freshness and *flor* flavour of the bodega's Pavon fino. Once the main *cabeceo* has been selected, a little *sobretabla* (new wine from the latest vintage's *añada* selection) is added and the wines are allowed to mix in bottle. Certainly, Pavon is a good wine of great freshness and delicacy. There's also a very good Moscatel *dulce* called Lerchundi, but Caballero's main business has been turning out good-quality, reliable wines for the supermarket trade, in Spain and abroad. Indeed, since the company bought Emilio Lustau in 1990, a good deal of its quality focus has shifted. However, Caballero remains a company that manages to maintain the quality and traditions of the classic Sherry house while doing excellent business in the mass market.

### Manuel de Argüeso, Jerez.

This is a relatively small bodega (9,000hl) which belongs to Valdespino. Its greatest work is an exceptional PX, so black that it's almost opaque and so rich you could almost stand a spoon up in it. One of the world's greatest dessert wines.

### Marqués del Real Tesoro, Jerez.

*Founded 1860.* The residuals of this dormant company were bought and re-established at the beginning of the 1990s in a spanking-new and very elegant bodega on the edge of town. The existing *soleras* were very small and a bit ad hoc, so the bodega began by buying up the *soleras* and name of the excellent fino Tío Mateo from Harveys, which had purchased it from the original owners, Palomino y Vergara. It remains an excellent example of classic Jerez fino. There is enormous room for expansion here, and the new owners have

shown themselves to be unafraid when it comes to investment and quality. We shall hear more of this bodega.

### Osborne, Puerto de Santa María.
*Founded 1772.* The Osborne name didn't appear until 1890. Still family-owned, Osborne is, of course, the originator of the famous black bull silhouettes which still dot the hillsides and motorways of Spain even now that roadside advertising has been banned. The firm has beautiful headquarters in Puerto de Santa María. In recent years, it has taken over Bobadilla in Jerez, so expansion is all part of the plan. However, the classic wines go on, it seems, for ever. In some export markets they're still called Duff-Gordon, but the Osborne name reigns supreme in Spain. Bailén oloroso and Coquinero amontillado are very good wines. *Best wines:* the excellent Fino Quinta is the flagship wine. There's also an exceptional Pedro Ximénez 1827.

### Pedro Domecq, Jerez.
*Founded 1730.* The family is still in control, but ownership is vested in the Allied-Domecq stable, along with John Harvey, *inter alia.* The bodega owns 750ha and turns out around 80,000hl of wine, and it has an enviable reputation for quality-control and innovation. Beltrán Domecq has been in control for some years, although his father Ignacio (known as 'the nose' because of his uncanny tasting ability) was a regular sight, riding to the office every day on his battered old moped, complete with pet dog in a carrier on the pillion, well into his 80s. Sadly, Ignacio died at the end of 1997, but the Domecq name continues as it has done for more than 250 years. Since the agglomeration with John Harvey, the main wine from the Domecq stable has been La Ina: a classic, elegant and exceptional fino which rather puts its oloroso *dulce* counterpart, Bristol Cream, in the shade. Domecq also produces

a full range of wines, from the decent mass-market Celebration Cream to a very good Viña 25 PX. However, the premium range is outstanding by any criteria: as well as La Ina fino, there are Capuchino palo cortado, Rio Viejo oloroso *seco*, Sibarita oloroso *viejissimo* and the mind-blowing Venerable PX. The least of these wines is excellent, most are exceptional, and if any fans were worried that membership of the Allied-Domecq leviathan would take away Domecq's individuality, style and quality they may breathe a sigh of relief. It's perhaps also worth mentioning that Domecq produced the first Brandy de Jerez – Fundador – in 1874.

### Rainera Pérez Marín, Sanlúcar de Barrameda. *Founded 1825.*
This specialist manzanilla house produces the classic La Guita ('the string'), named after the piece of string sewn through the cork to ensure that the drinker doesn't lose it and can recork the bottle. The straight manzanilla (with a white label) is sold widely in the region and is an excellent example of fresh, *flor*-flavoured wine. More widely available is the manzanilla *pasada* version (with a yellow label) which is also a classic of its kind (and travels better). All are excellent wines.

### Sanchez Romate, Jerez.
*Founded 1781.* Sanchez is probably best known these days for its outstanding Brandy de Jerez, Cardenal Mendoza, but it still farms 80ha of vines and turns out some 30,000hl of Sherry. Marizmeño is a good, classic fino and Iberia Cream and Dulce Gloria are very good. *Best wines:* the oldest. NPU (Non Plus Ultra) is an excellent Amontillado and Don José a dry oloroso of equal standing. Best of all is the Cardenal Cisneros PX, which is an exceptional example of the genre.

**Sandeman, Jerez.** *Founded 1790.* This company (Sandeman-Coprimar, to give it its full name) started out rather like Croft, shipping Sherry to England via its office in Oporto, Portugal. However, it was forced into Jerez in a takeover with the collapse of one its major suppliers (Pemartín, now part of Bodegas Internacionales). Today, it farms 358ha of vines and produces some 90,000hl of wine. The main range of wines includes Armada Cream and Don Fino (both good wines), and a new departure: a 'very special dry' which is aimed at the young fino/manzanilla market and is called Soléo. *Best wines:* most commentators rate the company's older wines highest, notably the Character Medium-Dry (a rather anodyne name for such an excellent wine with 5% PX) and – most of all – the Royal Corregidor oloroso (with 10% PX).

**De Terry, Puerto de Santa María.** *Founded 1865.* A bodega with Irish origins that now belongs to John Harvey (as part of Allied-Domecq), who wanted it purely for its famous and excellent-value Brandy de Jerez. However, the bodega continues to turn out a small quantity of good Sherry, most notably Maruja: a very good manzanilla labelled under the mellifluous-sounding brand 'Sherry de Terry'.

**Valdespino, Jerez.** *Founded 1837.* This firm's origins go back very much further. In the 13th century, Castilian forces were beating the Moorish forces back towards Granada. For some considerable time, the region around Jerez formed the frontier between the two Spains (hence its full name: Jerez de la Frontera). The legend is that, in 1264, 12 knights of King Alfonso the Sage led their forces into battle against the Moors and retook Jerez. Twenty years of siege and battle ensued, but Jerez never fell again. In gratitude, Alfonso made gifts of land and vineyards to the 12 knights, and one of them was a Valdespino. If true, that puts the family's tenure in Jerez at 735 years in 1999, which is impressive by any standards. Today, there are five bodegas in Jerez (including Manuel Argüeso) and two in Sanlúcar, and the winemaking philosophy has a traditional style. The range is wide, and includes own-brands for major export clients as well as the bodega's individual labels. There are 155ha of vineyard and annual production is around 45,000hl. *Best wines:* the superb fino Inocente (spelled *Ynocente* in Spain), which comes from the Macharnudo *pago* and is still fermented in oak; and the *viejo dulce* oloroso. Valdespino Coliseo amontillado is over 90 years old. The current head of the family, Don Miguel Valdespino, keeps a few special casks in a small bodega behind his office for selected visitors. He is a mild-mannered, polite and self-effacing man, but a giant among Jerezanos, with a passionate love for his wines.

**Vinícola Hidalgo, Sanlúcar de Barrameda.** *Founded 1792.* This family firm has 70ha of vines and makes about 15,000hl of wine, 90% of it pure Manzanilla La Gitana, adjudged by some to be the best of them all. There's also Napoleon amontillado and oloroso, and a palo cortado called Hidalgo. These are all excellent wines.

**Williams & Humbert, Jerez.** A very old, established company which has gone through several changes of ownership – including the collapsed Rumasa group – and is now part-owned by a Dutch consortium that includes the distilling company Bols. However, it continues to thrive, with 288ha of vineyards and a production of 60,000hl. The main export market has always been England, and the brand-names reflect the connection. Dry Sack is an oloroso with five per cent PX which has been a best-seller in England for many years (and which was the subject of a lengthy brand-ownership court case with the receivers of Rumasa, which W&H finally won). Other good wines include Alegría manzanilla, Canasta Cream, Dos Cortados oloroso and Pando fino. The English connection is well-represented with the sweetened amontillado As You Like It and the oloroso *dulce* A Winter's Tale. *Best wines:* Canasta Cream and Alegría, but W&H has another fascination for those fortunate enough to visit the bodegas. The company has set aside a 'library' of *añadas* (single-vintage Sherries) for nearly every harvest dating back to 1921, and the opportunity to taste a selection of these is not to be missed.

Above: The bodega at Pedro Domecq is known as 'La Mezquita' – for obvious reasons. It is safe to say there are no casks inside the original, however.

Far left: Casa blanca, Jerez-style. The blue sky, the palm and the sunflowers are in place; all that is missing is the manzanilla.

# Montilla-Moriles

**Above:** *Tinajas* stand at attention inside Alvear, the oldest and largest company in the entire Montilla-Moriles wine zone.

In many ways, Montilla could be classed as the 'comeback kid' of Andalucía. Until the beginning of this century, a good deal of what was once produced here would have found its way into Sherry bodegas. In 1933, however, when both Sherry and Montilla were each appointed with its own *consejo regulador*, this practice was put to an end. (There are still periodic arguments over the rights to use the terms 'fino' and 'oloroso' in some export markets.)

Yet even with the loss of the Sherry market, Montilla bounced back and began to focus on its own wines. These are largely unfortified, made from the Pedro Ximénez (PX) grape, and are allowed to ferment naturally into high-strength wines that are then aged in *tinajas*.

The DO zone surrounds the two towns of Montilla and Moriles, both located in the province of Córdoba. The city of Córdoba was a Moorish capital, and its architecture reflects Moorish tastes. The jewel in the crown is La Mezquita: the magnificent 1,000-year-old mosque in the city centre that maintains all the majesty of the Islamic original – despite the fact that it incorporates a 13th-century Christian cathedral.

## Geography and climate

Soils here fall into two groups: *albarizas*, the chalk-white topsoils seen elsewhere in Andalucía, and *ruedas*, sandy regions on the borders of the region. The central area of about 2,670 hectares of vineyards is classified as *superior* and produces the best grapes, most of which go into export wines. The altitude is between 300 and 700 metres (984 and 2,297 feet), and the climate is hot and continental, bordering on the semi-arid in places, in spite of relatively generous rainfall. The trouble is that the rain tends to fall all at once, leaving the rest of the year mainly dry.

The main grape in the Montilla-Moriles DO is Pedro Ximénez, or PX, and this is the only one likely to be found in the classic Montillas that get into the export market (apart from the occasional Moscatel). There are other grapes, used especially in the new-style *joven afrutado* wines. These include Lairén (Airén), Baladi and Torrontés.

When the Sherry export locomotive hit the buffers in 1979, it took most of the other fortified wines of Andalucía with it, and Montilla suffered similar setbacks on the export market. However, the wine's second comeback, which began in the late-1980s, has been more sustainable. Sherry eventually returned to the market shorn of the undercurrent of cheap wines that had sustained it for so long. Now, quality Sherry had to stand on its own financial feet and charge the going rate. In addition, once the Sherry name finally won its

case for European-wide protection in 1996 (effectively sweeping away *ersatz* 'sherries' that had clouded the market), Montilla had a much clearer run.

## Improving styles and fortunes

The region took a twofold approach to improving itself, beginning with *joven afrutado* wines. These are made typically from the Baladi or Torrontés varieties, but often PX and even Moscatel is used to create light, fresh, cool-fermented wines that are offered for sale immediately after the vintage. *Joven afrutados* proved popular in the everyday-wine market, bringing much-needed cashflow back into the Montilla wine business as a whole. As a second step, Montilla producers began to look at the region's classic wines. Fortunately, most decided that their unique selling points were worth preserving, enhancing and promoting.

Whatever their styles, all Montilla wines start out the same way. Grapes are picked and pressed, and the juice is run off into tanks for fermentation, divided into free-run, first pressing and second pressing *mosto*, or must (third-pressing juice goes straight to the distillery). The vats undergo normal fermentation, usually in stainless-steel tanks under strict temperature control.

Once fermentation is complete, the winemaker decides which wines will become *joven afrutado* and which will go forward to become traditional Montilla. The former will be chilled, filtered and bottled; the latter will go into malolactic fermentation to prepare them for the next stage of production. The fully fermented wine goes into tanks, which may be giant concrete *tinajas* or large oak vats, to wait for the development of *flor*, just as in the Sherry process (*see* page 192).

Wines showing the most vigorous growth will be racked off into barrels on *ullage* (a gap of air between the surface of the wine and the top of the barrel which encourages further yeast growth). These will ultimately become the pale, dry style of Montilla that is known in Spain and most export markets (though not the UK) as fino. Wines that show little or no growth go into barrels that are filled to capacity, providing no opportunity for *flor* growth.

The natural strength of a Montilla wine may achieve 15.5 per cent alcohol by volume (abv), but there is no fortification at this stage. Both types of wine go into an appropriate *solera*, where they take on characteristics of the older wines. However, PX has more natural sugar than the Palomino of Jerez, and it is this characteristic that forms the main difference between the Montilla and Sherry.

Modern Montilla wines fall into three groups. First are light, fresh *jovenes afrutados* made from PX or other grapes, picked early to retain acidity and not exceeding 12 per cent abv. These tend to be pleasant, rather neutral wines that offend no one. The second group is made up of *vinos crianzas*: wines aged statically in *tinaja* or cask and usually sold under retailer brand names as dry, medium or sweet. The third group comprises *vinos generosos*, known as fino and oloroso in most markets.

The finos are generally unfortified, but amontillados and olorosos achieve up to 18 per cent abv, with a little help from fortification where necessary.

The only wines routinely fortified in Montilla are PX dessert wines. For these, the grapes are 'sunned' before pressing and then fortified with *aguardiente* (local clear brandy) during fermentation to produce a wine of immense body, richness and sweetness. This is the stuff that locals pour onto rich ice-cream for dessert.

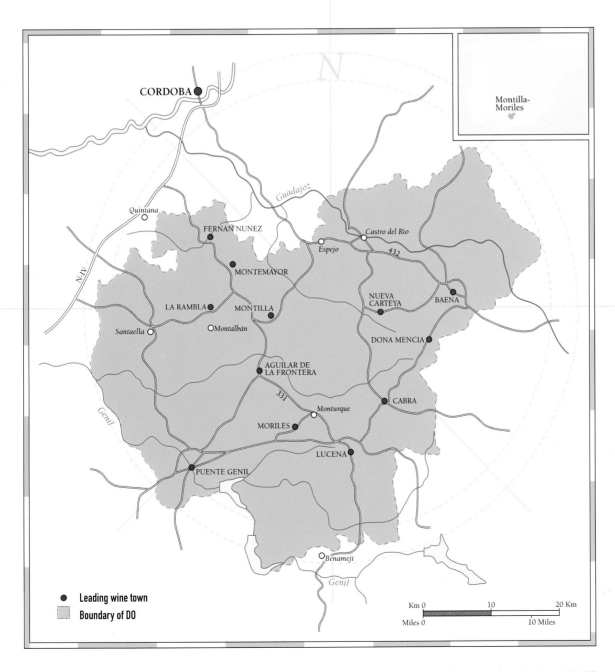

# Notable bodegas

**Note:** assume that all the wines listed below are 100% Pedro Ximénez (PX) unless otherwise stated.

**Alvear, Montilla.** *Founded 1729.* Alvear is the oldest and biggest company in the entire Montilla-Moriles region. It is still family-owned after nearly 300 years in existence. There are 128ha of vines, and the annual production is about 100,000hl, made in a combination of concrete tanks and stainless steel. The quality is exemplary, with all wines reaching the highest standards. There are two finos: Capataz and CB (the latter is named after the initials of a long-serving cellar-master); two amontillados, Carlos VII and Solera Fundación (the second isn't really as old as the firm's foundation but is nonetheless very old); an Asunción *abocado* oloroso; and finally two PX wines, Alvear PX 1927 and Alvear PX 1830. The last two do carry the date of the foundation of the *solera*, and the 1830 is one of the finest wines of this type in Spain. Alvear was also one of the first bodegas to market a *joven afrutado* white called Marqués de la Sierra.

**Aragón, Lucena.** *Founded 1946.* This is a relatively old-fashioned bodega still fermenting its wines in cement vats and selling more than half of its production in bulk. However, the wines it bottles can be excellent. *Best wines:* Moriles 47 fino, Pacorrito amontillado and Araceli PX.

**Cobos, Montilla.** *Founded 1882.* This company – along with three others in Montilla – is a member of the NaViSA food and drinks group. Wines are very much mixed and matched among Bodegas Cobos, Montebello, Montulia and Velasco Chacón. *Best wines:* Cobos is generally reckoned to be the label on the best. The company makes a very good PX called Tres Pasas, and two good finos called Cobos and Pompeyo (the latter is better).

**Conde de la Cortina, Montilla.** *Founded 1973.* Conde de la Cortina now belongs to Bodegas Alvear (*see above*) and turns out 100,000hl of wine in its own right. There are two good sweet wines: Cortina Pale Cream and Gran Vino Dulce (75% PX/25% Moscatel). *Best wines:* Monumental fino and a varietal Moscatel Dulce, both of which are excellent.

**Crismona, Doña Mencía.** *Founded 1904.* This bodega has modernised heavily and makes wine from its 90ha of vineyards in modern tanks as well as in traditional *tinajas*. *Best wine:* a very good *dulce* called Samarra.

**Gracia Hermanos, Montilla.** *Founded 1945.* Gracia Hermanos is a small but fully modernised bodega which belongs to the Compañía Vinícola del Sur (as do Pérez Barquero and Tomás García). It turns out some splendid wines, including Corredera and María del Valle finos (the latter is outstanding) and Montearruit amontillado *viejo*. While the sweeter wines are good, they don't quite hit the heights of the others. *Best wine:* the Oloroso Cream.

**Pérez Barquero, Montilla.** *Founded 1905.* Another of the larger bodegas of Montilla which also belongs to Compañía Vinícola del Sur (along with Tomás García and Gracia Hermanos) and works 125ha of vineyards. The winery has been extended in the past few years and fitted out with the latest modern equipment. There is a range of good basic wines, including Los Amigos fino and Los Palcos pale cream.

There is also a *joven afrutado semiseco* called Viña Amalia, made with 75% PX and 25% Vidueño, which is very good. *Best wines:* those sold under the Gran Barquero label: fino, amontillado, oloroso and PX.

### Rodríguez Chiachio, Cabra.

One of the smaller bodegas by Montilla standards, with 50ha of vineyards and an annual production of approximately 4,000hl of wine sold under various brand names. *Best wines:* those bearing the Los Mellizos label, with two good finos; the better of the two is known as Solera Fundación.

### Toro Albala, Aguilar de la Frontera.

*Founded 1922.* Toro Albala stands on the site of an old heating plant – which is how it chose the brand names for its wines. The firm owns seven hectares of vines and buys in grapes to make up a total production of some 1,500hl. It may be small, but its wines are exemplary. There are two finos, Eléctrico and Fino de Lagar, both of exceptional quality; two amontillados, Toro Albala Viejisimo Solera 1911 and Viejisimo Eléctrico Solera 1922 (both outstanding); and three sweet wines: Mistela PX (unfermented grape juice and spirit;

excellent), Don Pedro Ximénez (outstanding), and the greatest of them all Eléctrico PX, one of the very finest wines of the region. There is also a *joven afrutado* called (you guessed it) Joven Eléctrico, which is an outstanding wine. It actually manages to be more than a squeaky-clean, bland, dry white wine. All these wines are handmade in the old tradition, and are among the best that Montilla has to offer.

Above: Vineyards and olive groves cover the hills near Montilla. The former are planted with the Pedro Ximénez variety, which gives fortified Montilla its characteristic flavour.

Far left: *Criaderas* rest inside Alvear's La Monumental bodega. The portrait is of D Juan Rodríguez, foreman of the bodegas until 1932.

# The Canary Islands: wines in obsidian?

In some ways, wines from the Canary Islands have remained frozen in the volcanic rock of time since the days of the *conquistadores*. The islands have never known phylloxera, so no grafting has been necessary. Varieties of vines that died out on the mainland still soldier on here and there. The tradition of sweet *vinos de licor* is still alive and well, yet there is also a new wave of winemaking using the latest technology in modern bodegas. To understand winemaking in the Canary Islands, however, it is essential to consider their complex geography.

The Spanish *autonomía* of Canarias is divided into two provinces covering seven main islands and some scattered islets. Santa Cruz de Tenerife includes the four western islands of Tenerife, La Gomera, El Hierro and La Palma;

Las Palmas de Gran Canaria covers the three eastern islands of Gran Canaria, Fuerteventura and Lanzarote. The regional government is based in Santa Cruz de Tenerife, and most of the islands' wines and wine zones – five of the nine DOs – are also to be found on Tenerife. The nearest part of mainland Spain lies some 1,100 kilometres (682 miles) to the northeast; the southwest coast of Morocco is 100 kilometres (62 miles) to the east.

The islands have a rather arcane history. The Romans landed on Fuerteventura and found it inhabited by packs of wild dogs; hence, they called it *Insula Canaria*, or Dog Island, and the name spread to the neighbouring islands. Over the next few centuries, the Canaries received occasional visitors, including the mysterious fair-skinned, long-eared, red-haired people commemorated in a bewildering number of places throughout the Atlantic and the Pacific from Easter Island to Asturias. In 1402, Jean de Béthencourt, a French captain of a Spanish ship, landed on Gran Canaria to find a tribe called the Guanche still living in stone-age conditions. He claimed the islands for Spain, naming them *Las Islas Canarias:* The Dog Islands.

Then as now, these volcanic peaks rising from the bed of the Atlantic provided fertility in profusion. Northern Europe was once the biggest market for Canary sack, and it remains the biggest market for Canary produce. The islands offer an extensive range of microclimates, ranging from subtropical, palm-fringed beaches to the heavily wooded craters of extinct volcanoes, whose vegetation and humidity levels are almost like those of an equatorial rainforest.

The Canaries have plentiful freshwater springs, and the volcanic craters often fill with water during the rainy season. Much of this percolates through the rocks to refresh natural springs, but some also flows down the *barrancos*, ravines cut by ancient lava-flows which stretch from the craters to the sea. This is the nearest the islands have to what would count as rivers and streams on the peninsula.

## Changing wine styles

Wine is still made in these subtropical areas. In the mountainous north of La Palma, for example, it is made just as it was 500 years ago in caves hewn out of the rock. Here, old *rancio*-style wines are aged in the open air; as brown as mahogany, they are sold to anyone who arrives with a suitable empty vessel. But as times have changed, so, too, have the wines and the manner of making them. The main change for the Canary Islands has been the tourist business, which now underpins the economy.

Below: Black sand, a legacy of the volcanic eruptions that formed the archipelago, distinguishes the Canary Islands from other Spanish beaches.

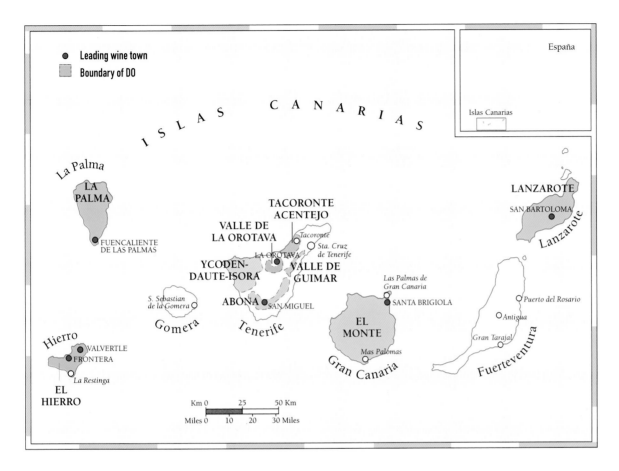

Vast numbers of holiday-makers swell the local population throughout most of the year, and a good deal of what the island produces goes to the satisfy this seasonal appetite. It is possible to miss the indigenous cooking altogether amid the coastal fast-food chains, themed restaurants and specialities from the UK, Germany, Scandinavia and the US.

Once inland and out of season, though, there are identifiable local specialities. Fresh fish and other seafood abound, and the fertile landscape also provides a wealth of fresh produce. Tomatoes, potatoes and bananas are the three most important crops, but the islands also offer brassicas, onions, pumpkins, sweet potatoes, carrots, garlic, pulses and beans of all kinds.

One of the classic dishes of Tenerife is a stew called *puchero Canario*, made from some, all or most of these, along with beef, chicken and/or *chorizo*. It may be eaten with *gofio*, a coarse local grain that appears in anything from stew to a loaf of bread. Potatoes – particularly small new potatoes – feature in nearly every meal, usually boiled in salt water and eaten as a side-dish. These are known as *patatas arrugadas* or, more simply, as *papas*.

In terms of fruit (as well as grapes, of course), figs grow wild by the roadside as well as in cultivated orchards, and mangoes, oranges, pineapples and even paw-paws have been planted here and there. Avocados are a major crop, and wild mushrooms feature in many dishes.

Another particular speciality is the *mojo*, which means 'sauce' but is more like a vegetable stock. Classic *mojos* are based on peppers, coriander, garlic, saffron and cheese; the latter can be very thick and is used as a sandwich spread. Each island makes its own classic cheese: *Conejero* (Lanzarote), *Palmero* (La Palma), *Majorero* (Fuerteventura), *Herreño* (El Hierro), *Flor de Guía* (Gran Canaria), *Gomera* and *Tenerife*.

Puddings generally take the form of fresh fruit or are pastry-based. Typical examples are the *rosquetes* of Tenerife: small cakes either fried in syrup or covered in egg-white and sugar and served with lemon juice. Strangely enough, one of the islands' biggest fruit crops – the banana – has produced almost no speciality dishes at all. It is occasionally fried in a variant of rice pudding, but mainly eaten simply as a fresh fruit at the end of a meal.

The Canary Islands: wines in obsidian? **203**

# La Palma

**Above:** *La Isla Bonita*. A good deal of La Palma's coastline is rocky and dramatic, but the island's beaches are golden — not black like its neighbours.

**Far right:** Eye on the sky. The observatory on La Palma's Roque de los Muchachos makes good use of the clear, clean atmosphere that surrounds the island.

La Palma is *La Isla Bonita*, The Beautiful Island. Around the coast, the cliff-top corniches provide occasional *miradores* (viewpoints), where visitors can admire the impossibly blue sea, the cloud-wrapped peaks of its volcanoes, the immaculate, white-painted villages and the green-velvet carpet of the banana plantations. Sometimes it seems as if every spare square metre of ground has a banana-palm planted in it, but there are vines here, too.

At vintage time in La Palma, bodegas put up signs on their gates stating *no aceptamos uvas de plataneros*: 'We do not accept grapes from banana-growers'. Apparently the banana-palm has such a voracious appetite for moisture and nutrients that it tends to leave neighbouring vines a bit bereft. On an island where some deliveries of a contract grower's entire vintage arrive in a dozen plastic boxes out of the back of a Toyota hatchback, it pays to be careful. Small may be beautiful, but very small and planted around the palms can be underripe and low in sugar.

La Palma's towns are delightful, a strange mixture of rural Spanish and South American colonial architecture that is reminiscent of Cuba or the Dominican Republic. Early prosperity came as a result of its position at the northwestern-most extent of the archipelago. This location turned it into a last (or first) staging post for ships sailing to and from the Americas. La Palma was licensed to revictual ships and trade with them (a privilege granted only to Seville and Vigo on the mainland), and it grew rich as a result.

The island's calm is occasionally shattered by its volcanoes. Just as the Montañas del Fuego on Lanzarote grumble and smoke from time to time, La Palma's volcanoes remind locals that they are still there: the last major eruption here was in October, 1971. It didn't do too much damage, but it did remind everyone that the centre of the earth is still on fire and La Palma is one of its chimneys.

## The structure of the DO

The La Palma DO has three subzones: Fuencaliente-Las Manchas, surrounding the town of Fuencaliente in the south; Hoyo de Mazo around Mazo in the west-central region; and Norte de Palma in the north. The lats is a fascinating area, further subdividing into the northeast (where vinegrowing and winemaking are relatively modern) and the northwest (where everything is handmade, nothing is bottled, and little has changed in several hundred years).

High up towards the Caldera de Taburiente — the crater of an extinct volcano — lies a misty, steep, inaccessible, humid pine forest strewn with small, *artesanal* bodegas hewn out of volcanic rock. Here, the *viñeros* make wines called Tea from (mainly) Albillo grapes trained perilously in rows on the slopes above. *Tea* is the Canary-Spanish word for the species of pine that dominates the forest, and from which the 500-litre barrels are made in which the wines are aged.

*Vinos de Tea* are not eligible for the La Palma DO, but they do have a following among lovers of traditional *rancio* styles; they are also said to be effective as homeopathic medicines. The style varies from medicinal to what an Andalucían might describe as 'dry oloroso', and the pine casks add their own resinous notes to the flavour.

The *consejo regulador* supervises production in the hope that these wines will one day achieve something unique and spectacular for the La Palma DO. In the meantime, hire a jeep to visit the cellars and taste the wines. The views over the island, the subtropical landscape and the opportunity to meet the individuals (and they really are individuals) who make the wines are well worth the visit.

## Grape varieties

In other zones, most of the white wines are made in Fuencaliente-Las Manchas, while most of the reds are produced in Hoyo de Mazo. The permitted grape varieties are Listán Negro, Prieto and Negramoll for red wines (20 per cent of production); Albillo, Bujariego, Gual, Listán Blanco (70 per cent of the vineyard), Malvasía and Sabro for whites. There are also 11 subsidiary varieties, but all are common to the Canary Islands.

Soils are similar throughout La Palma, with fertile topsoil lying over volcanic bedrock. Vineyards are planted in terraces on the sides of the valleys and *barrancos* at altitudes of between 200 to 1,200 metres (656 to 3,937 feet).

In general, wines come as *jovenes* in all three colours, with the best reds from Hoyo de Mazo and the best whites from Fuencaliente. In the latter subzone (which provides about three-quarters of all production) the main grape variety is Malvasía, and the style of wine ranges from dry *jovenes* to sweet *vinos de licor* which may be fortified up to 22 per cent alcohol by volume.

Traditional sweet wines are generally rated highest of all, especially those affected by botrytis (noble rot). Yet some very good work is being done with dry-fermented Malvasía, and there are delicious fruity reds being made by *maceración carbónico*. Most fascinating to the enthusiast are the wines made from 'original' grape varieties such as Gual, Bujariego and Sabro, which died out long ago on the peninsula.

## Notable bodegas

### Carballo, Fuencaliente.
*Founded 1990.* Carballo is a small, family-run bodega using only grapes from its own 7.5ha to make about 150hl of organic varietal wines (mainly *jovenes*) from the island's classic grape varieties. The basic white is made from Listán Blanco and is very pleasant, but it is eclipsed by the varietal Bujariego, which manages to be rich without sweetness. More traditional are the Vidueño Seco (Verdello/Gual/Sabro/Bastardo Blanco; 14.5% abv; two years in bottle) which hints at a dry oloroso style. Better is Vidueño Dulce, made from the same grapes: a classic Canary sweet wine. Red wines take second place, but the Negramoll *joven* is very pleasant. *Best wine:* the Malvasía Dulce, which is very good and very traditional.

### El Hoyo, Villa de Mazo.
*Founded 1986.* A smart, new-wave bodega with all the latest winemaking equipment, El Hoyo makes wine from grapes provided by its shareholders, who farm 100ha locally. Legally, it is a SAT – *Sociedad Agricultural de Transformación* – which is a kind of halfway house between an old-style co-op and a limited company (SL or SA: *Sociedad Limitada/Anonima*). El Hoyo makes wine for other, smaller bodegas as well as for its own shareholders, but the brand name is Hoyo de Mazo. Some real work is being done here with the Negramoll grape; the winemaker believes it has a common ancestor with Pinot Noir and has been experimenting with different approaches, including making *rosado* wine by the *sangrado* (short-term skin-contact) method and making a real red *crianza* with eight months in American oak. This is all in addition to the standard red *joven*, and these are all very pleasant. Once again, however, whites come out on top. There's a straight Hoyo de Mazo white

*joven* (80% Listán Blanco; 13.5% abv) which is good; a Moscatel Seco (a non-DO wine) which takes dry-fermented Muscat to new levels of strength at a natural 15% abv. By contrast, the traditional Malvasía Dulce seems a little austere, but these are, in general, very good all round. Viña Etna Verdello Dulce is an astonishing sweet wine (90% Verdello; barrel-fermented in chestnut wood), with a natural 15% abv. *Best wine:* the excellent Sabro Dulce made from 85% of this 'original' grape variety, picked from vines that are 100 years old. Is this what Canary sack really tasted like, half a millennium ago? If so, it explains a lot. Outstanding stuff.

### Llanovid Cooperative, Fuencaliente.
*Founded 1948.* The main producer in the Fuencaliente-Las Manchas subzone, turning out about 5,000hl

of wine on a mainly varietal basis. The bodega is partly modernised, ferments its wines in stainless-steel and epoxy-concrete vats, and added a *crianza* cellar in 1993 to experiment with cask-ageing in Tronçais oak, mainly for white wines. Winemaker Carlos Lozano is also experimenting with different ways of working with Malvasía. The bodega maintains the quaint custom of bottling 90% of its wine and giving the rest back to the members. The main brand name is Teneguía and most of the wines are varietals. Reds and *rosados* are *joven* in style, made from Negramoll, the best of which is a delicious *maceración carbónica* wine called Escamez Teneguía. These are all very good. The bodega is also experimenting with sparkling wines made by the *método tradicional* from Listán Blanco, Bujariego, Malvasía and Xarel-lo.

Early results show some promise, but more work is needed. *Best wines:* the whites, including a barrel-fermented Malvasía Seco with three months on its lees; a botrytised Sabro Dulce (with 20% Gual) and two classic botrytised Malvasía Dulces, one *joven*, one with two years' bottle-age. All are excellent.

# El Hierro

## Notable bodegas

**Vinícola Insular del Hierro Cooperativa, Frontera.**
*Founded 1986.* This smart, modern bodega is fully equipped with the latest stainless-steel winemaking kit and turns out some 1,500hl of wine. The brand names are Herrero (*jovenes* in all three colours) and Viña Frontera (red and white *crianzas*). The main white grape is Vijariego; the reds are made from Listán Negro and Negramoll.

**Bodegas El Tesoro, Valverde.**
This bodega is a specialist in the classic white *vino licoroso dulce*, an inheritor of the original Canary sack tradition.

The first vineyards on the island of El Hierro were planted by an Englishman, John Hill, in 1526 to service the burgeoning taste for sack – the sweet, strong wine that dominated European and transatlantic trade during the 16th and 17th centuries. While Canary sack from the other islands went to England, Holland, Scandinavia and Germany, El Hierro's main export markets were in Central and South America – particularly Cuba and Venezuela.

Needless to say, as well as wine there has been a constant flow of young people from the island, off to seek their fortunes in the outside world. It should therefore come as no surprise to learn that there is a large expatriate community in Venezuela that buys wines from El Hierro to this day.

### Geography and climate

Geographically, the vineyards of the El Hierro DO are terraced into the slopes that make up the island's 'spine'; just as in many places throughout the Canaries, they are planted where there is access and exposure. While some of the other islands show peaks and craters of extinct (and sometimes not-so-extinct) volcanoes, El Hierro does not. It is actually part of the rim of a volcanic crater that is much larger than any of the others. All of the rest of it is under water.

The island's landscape varies considerably. There are bluffs and cliff-faces jutting out into the sea, semi-tropical forests, sandy beaches and steep valleys with terraced vineyards situated at heights of up to 700 metres (2,297 feet) above sea level. The soil is sandy or stony over volcanic bedrock, and in many places, vines are trained over the ground to make harvesting easier.

### Grape varieties

Listán Negro and Negramoll are the chief grapes grown for red wines, while Verijadiego (or Vijariego, known as Bujariego on other islands), Listán Blanco and Bremajuelo (Bermejuelo) are cultivated for whites. In addition, there are plantations of Uval, Verdello, Torrontés, Pedro Ximénez (PX) and Moscatel. The sweet-wine heritage of the Canary Islands as a whole still shows through.

Indeed, sweet and old classic wines make up a good slice of El Hierro's total production: 50 per cent is made up of white wine, plus a further five per cent *dulce* made from PX and Moscatel. The latter includes old-fashioned

*rancio* styles which are stored for many years in chestnut casks. Some of the best sweet whites are made from botrytised grapes (grapes that develop the desirable mould known as 'noble rot' or botrytis), but the classic Moscatel and PX styles made today would probably be recognised by the crew of a passing 17th-century ghost ship.

However, as bodegas modernise, there is an increasing emphasis on making lighter wines. *Jovenes* may be found in all three colours: *rosado* makes up 20 per cent of production while red wine takes 25 per cent. Interestingly enough, some good work is being done on the island with *crianza* wines, both white and red. Although there are only two or three bodegas active on El Hierro, the future looks quite promising from a quality point of view.

Though small in comparison to that of the other islands in the group, El Hierro's tourist industry manages to absorb most of its production. It seems likely that, given the sheer cost of shipping wine from the island (it has to go first to one of the major ports on Tenerife for trans-shipment), the homesick expatriates of Venezuela will remain El Hierro's biggest customers for the foreseeable future.

**Right, above:** Just like many of the vineyards that grow on the island, the Frontera Candelaria church of El Hierro takes a clifftop position.

**206** The El Hierro DO

# Abona

Vineyards grow at altitudes up to nearly 900 metres (2,953 feet) in mainland DOs such as Ribera del Duero in Castile-León. In the VdlT Sierra de Alcaraz (Castilla-La Mancha), vines flourish at 1,000 metres (3,281 feet). Neither would cut any ice with the *viñeros* of Vilaflor, one of the seven parishes of the Abona DO on the island of Tenerife. Here, the highest vineyards are planted at 1,700 metres (5,577 feet), halfway up Mount Teide, and they are almost impossibly difficult to work. However, work they do, and this DO zone, spread over the south and southeast of Tenerife, supplies much of the wine destined for the tourist industry along the south coast resorts.

Up to about 600 metres (1,969 feet; the average height of the vineyards), soils are volcanic, with sandy topsoil and sometimes clay and alluvial deposits. Above that altitude, topsoil is made up mainly of volcanic ash, often with a surface dressing of coarse volcanic gravel to retain water. The climate is subtropical: hot and dry on the coast but falling rapidly with increasing height, so that frost is a real danger in the high-altitude vineyards.

Estates grow typical Canary grapes. The main varieties are Listán Blanco for white wine and Bastardo Negro (one of the classics of old Canary sack), Listán Negro, Malvasía Rosada and Tintilla for red. There are also experimental plantations of Negramoll and Malvasia, Verdello (same as the Verdelho of Madeira) and the so-called 'original' grapes Bermejuela, Gual, and Sabro. The last three are particularly interesting as they were brought here by settlers from the peninsula some four or five hundred years ago, but have long died out in their original habitats. In the islands, they survive as (generally) low-yielding but very well-adapted varieties.

Wines tend to be simple: *jovenes* in all three colours aimed at the beachfront market. Production is 70 per cent white wine, 20 per cent *rosado* and ten per cent red. There are some exports of ecological (semi-organic) wines, since the island's climate (no insect pests; very little vine disease) is well suited to them. The experimental whites made from the three 'original' varieties are well worth seeking out. They are not cheap, but can provide an idea of what wines made here might have been like several centuries ago.

Left: The other side of Tenerife. Vineyards in the inhospitable Abona DO yield much of the wine that quenches the thirsty tourists who flock to the island's coastal resorts.

# Tacoronte-Acentejo

The name rolls off the tongue, doesn't it? But if the marketing-men had little input in naming what was Spain's second offshore DO (after Binissalem in the Balearic Islands), then its winemakers have more than made up for it. Tacoronte-Acentejo is the largest DO in the Canary Islands, as well as the most geared-up for development and exports. A modern, fully equipped, industrial-scale wine region with 42 bodegas (some are admittedly very small) and more stainless steel than a *viñero* could shake a pipette at, it is something of a culture-shock after the cottage-industry style of some of the islands' other DO zones.

This is the northwest coast of Tenerife. The 'spine' of the island runs northeastwards from the crater of Mount Tiede, and the capital, Santa Cruz de Tenerife, is situated on the northeast coast. Directly opposite, on the western side of the ridge, are the towns of Tacoronte and La Victoria de Acentejo, which give the region its name.

This bustling, businesslike part of the island lies between its second port, Puerto de la Cruz, and the northern airport, which gives access to all the other islands in the archipelago. It is one of the few places where tourists do not dominate day-to-day life. Once again, the architectural style hints at South American colonial. There are lovely old houses with open balconies and galleried upper storeys – although here, just as practically everywhere else on the Canary Islands, anything within half a kilometre of the coast is likely to be a modern holiday development.

## Geography and climate

Fortunately, that development has not taken land from the wine industry. Vineyards are planted up the mountainside at altitudes between 200 to 800 metres (656 to 2,625 feet), and the soils on the lower levels are mainly fertile loam spread over volcanic bedrock. As the altitude rises, so the topsoil thins out, but this does not necessarily affect the quality of the grapes. In fact, it gives winemakers a wider selection of different types to work with: riper, thicker-skinned berries from lower levels or grapes with more acidity and freshness from the highlands. The climate is subtropical, with rainfall fairly typical at about 300 millimetres (12 inches). Conditions are right for good-quality wine, and there is probably more opportunity for economy of scale in Tenerife than anywhere else.

Grapes grown in the Tacoronte-Acentejo DO are the Canary Island stalwarts. Listán Negro and Negramoll are preferred for red wines, with Tintilla, Moscatel Negro and Malvasía Rosada also permitted. For white wines, the preferred varieties are Gual, Malvasía, Listán Blanco and Marmajuelo, with Pedro Jiménez (the local spelling) Moscatel, Verdello, Vijariego, Forastera Blanca and Torrontés used as subsidiary varieties.

A fair amount of old-fashioned winemaking in large wooden vats still goes on, but most major bodegas have re-equipped themselves with stainless steel (to impressive levels in some cases), with built-in room for expansion. This is a region with attitude: export is not just a dream nor even a prospect, but something for which the *bodegueros* have planned, invested, and worked.

One of the prime movers behind the drive, first for DO status, then for modernisation and now for export marketing, is the president of the *consejo regulador*, Lourdes Fernández López. A chemist by profession, she has been instrumental in most of the advances made by the wine industry on the island of Tenerife. Under her leadership, Tacoronte-Acentejo has provided an example and role model for other regions bringing themselves up to DO status.

## Winemaking and wine styles

This district is placed firmly out of white-wine country. Around 90 per cent of production is devoted to red wines, with just eight per cent to whites and two per cent to *rosado* wines. *Crianza* styles are really starting to happen here. *Jovenes* in all three colours are still the mainstay of production, but more and more bodegas are installing oak (Spanish and French rather than American). Some of the new red wines being made – particularly from the Listán Negro – are showing very well.

Interestingly enough, it is still quite common in this DO to put a small amount of white grape juice into red wines to add 'fire and brilliance' to the finished blend. This used to be commonplace in Châteauneuf-du-Pape in the Rhône Valley in France, in Chianti in Italy and, of course, in Rioja. The custom has all but disappeared from these other regions, but it survives in Tacoronte-Acentejo.

Here and there, new-style winemaking makes its presence felt. There is fermentation in French oak for some white wines, *maceración carbónica* for delicious, fruity reds. Some serious work is also being carried out with *crianza* wines made from particularly good selections of grapes harvested in good years – again, ageing in French oak. If Tacoronte-Acentejo fails in its bid for international status, it will not be for lack of trying. The signs are that it is already succeeding.

# Notable bodegas

**AFECAN, Tegueste.** *Founded 1990.* A small, modern, well-equipped bodega making *jovenes* in white and red under the El Lomo label from its own four hectares. There are two very good whites (both 90% Listán Blanco); one is made in stainless steel, the other is barrel-fermented. *Best wines:* two reds, one made in the normal way (80% Listán Negro/15% Negramoll/5% Listán Blanco), and one made from 100% Listán Negro by *maceración carbónica*. Both are excellent.

**Flores, La Matanza.** *Founded 1972.* A very small, family-run bodega making only red wine from its own four hectares under the Viña Flores label. The wine is a *joven* (75% Listán Negro/22% Negramoll/3% Listán Blanco) and is very pleasant.

**Insulares Tenerife, Tacoronte.** *Founded 1992.* This is a SAT (shareholders' cooperative) and the biggest producer in the DO. There are 375 members, of whom one is another co-op with 170 members; thus, total ownership exceeds 550 growers farming 250ha. Annual production is around 5,000hl. The bodega is impressive, spotlessly clean and laid out to the most efficient specifications. It has a built-in extra capacity that makes it capable, when the time comes, of almost doubling its production. Meanwhile, the main brand name is Viña Norte, and the wines are among the best in the Canaries. There are two whites: one made in steel, and an Alliers-barrel-fermented white made from Listán Blanco (three months in oak) can be very good. The *rosado* (95% Listán Negro/5% Negramoll) is equally good. *Best wines:* the reds. There are three of them, all made from 90-95% Listán Negro, the rest Negramoll. Viña Norte Tinto is a *joven del año* made with a good balance of fruit, tannins and acidity; an excellent wine. There is also a delicious *maceración carbónica* version that is enormously popular. Others, however, prefer the Viña Norte Tinto Madera, with four to five months in Alliers oak. Since the 1996 vintage, there has also been a full-crianza red with six months or more in oak which is extremely promising. This bodega is an example to the rest of the DO.

**La Isleta, Tejina-La Laguna.** *Founded 1869.* La Isleta is another small, family-owned bodega making some 500hl of wine from its own 12ha. There are red and white *jovenes* made from Listán Blanco and Negro, and the quality is good, with the red having the edge.

**Monje, El Sauzal.** *Founded 1956.* The Monje family owns 14ha and produces about 600hl, mainly red but also white, *rosado* and a small amount of *dulce*. Some wines are still made in old stone *lagares* above the ancient barrel-cellar. Although small, Monje's influence is considerable because of its attention to detail and quality winemaking; the bodega has won a large number of prizes in international tasting competitions since 1977. There are four wines in the range. Dragoblanco is a pleasant white *joven* made from Listán Blanco. Bibiana is the *rosado joven*, made from Listán Negro. *Best wines:* the reds. Monje Tinto is a *joven* (80% Listán Negro/15% Listán Blanco/5% Negramoll) that spends a bit of time in oak. The excellent Hollera Monje is made by *maceración carbónica* from Listán Negro and regularly wins prizes in international tastings. There is also an older wine called Monje d'Autor which is the bodega's first full *crianza* (same grape-mix as the *joven*; ten months in oak).

**La Palmera, El Sauzal.** *Founded 1969.* Another small bodega with 43ha doing good work with white and red *jovenes* (some with a short time in oak) under the La Palmera label. The white is 90% Listán Blanco, 10% Malvasía. The red is 60% Listán Negro, 15% Negramoll, 10% Listán Blanco, 10% Gual and 5% Tintilla. These can be good.

**Below: The church of Santa Catalina, Tacoronte. The Tacoronte-Acentejo DO is the largest in the Canary Islands.**

# Ycoden-Daute-Isora

Above: Mount Teide, on Tenerife. This extinct volcano could well have been active when the ancient Ycoden, Daute and Isora tribes existed on the island.

Ycoden, Daute and Isora are the names of three areas that were occupied by the Guanche, the primitive tribespeople who inhabited these islands before the *conquistadores* came. These indigenous people have been commemorated by something with which they could hardly have been acquainted, since vines were not known on the Canary Islands before they were imported from the peninsula.

Today, however, the *denominación de origen* that is named after the Guanche covers the western tip of the island of Tenerife, comprising nine towns and villages, from Guía de Isora on the west coast across in a northeastern diagonal to La Guancha on the north coast. In the days when *vino de la tierra* was the area's stock-in-trade, there was a good deal of competition among winemakers and a fierce debate over whose was actually the best. The use of the ancient tribal names and a broadly based DO zone seems to have kept everyone relatively happy.

Interestingly enough – and fortunately for the locals – about the only internationally known tourist attraction in these parts (aside from the odd beach resort) is the famous Dragon Tree situated in the town of Icod de los Vinos. Looking rather like a giant floret of broccoli, the tree dominates the town centre. Botanically, it is not a tree at all, but a plant that grows sporadically only in the Canary Islands and on the African coast. It produces a new branch every eight years, and the tree is believed to be several thousand years old. An older example growing a little further up the coast at Orotava was provisionally given an age of 10,000 years.

## Geography and climate

Towards the coast, vineyards are planted in sandy soil, while those inland are situated in soils that contain more clay over the ubiquitous volcanic rock. Vines grow at heights of between 200 to 1,000 metres (656 to 3,281 feet) up the slopes of the volcano.

This is the hottest and wettest area of the island. More sheltered from the drying winds of the south, it is still open to the dampening influence of the *alicios* (humid winds) from the west, which means that the vines are well-watered. The temperate-to-hot climate favours the production of white-wine grapes, so it stands to reason that Ycoden-Daute-Isora should be best known for its white wines.

## Grape varieties

The main grape cultivated in the Ycoden-Daute-Isora DO is Listán Blanco, which accounts for around 70 per cent of the vineyard. Listán Negro occupies a further 20 per cent, with Negramoll at five per cent, leaving only five per cent for all the rest of the Canary favourites: Gual, Malvasía, Vijariego, Moscatel, Bermejuela, Forastera, Sabro, Pedro Ximénez, Torrontés and Verdello for white wines; Malvasía Rosada, Moscatel Negro, Tintilla and Vijariego Negro for reds.

Winemaking is modern in Ycoden-Daute-Isora. The region is the second-largest producer of wines in the islands (after Tacoronte-Acentejo), and most installations feature stainless-steel tanks, temperature-control and all the various bells and whistles of modern winemaking technology. However, there are still a few *artesanal* bodegas, and barrel-fermentation has made something of a comeback in recent times. *Crianza* is in its infancy; only two bodegas regularly put their wines into oak, and the results are still being evaluated.

## Winemaking and wine styles

Whatever the methods used, the wines here can be excellent – especially the whites that are made from Listán, sometimes with a small amount of one of the more expensive grapes thrown in to add another dimension. Sometimes these are barrel-fermented, but most are made as straight *jovenes*. There is a kind of unspoken 'deal' in Tenerife that Tacoronte-Acentejo makes the best reds and Ycoden-Daute-Isora makes the best whites. There is actually a grain of truth in this – although no one would want to make such a claim at the annual dinner of the *consejo regulador* in either place, of course.

*Rosados* make up approximately 15 per cent of the DO's total production while reds take up 20 per cent; the majority are still *joven* in style. However, given the economy of scale in Tenerife (small in comparison to the mainland DOs, but generous for those of the Canaries), the basic good, sound quality of the wines coupled with the unquenchable thirst of the tourist industry should see the Ycoden-Daute-Isora DO progressing as a growing and prosperous wine-producing area in the future. Whether this success will ever lead to export business, however, is entirely another matter.

# Notable bodegas

### Cueva del Rey, Icod de los Vinos.

This bodega is so small that it's hardly there at all, but the owner is such an enthusiast that he deserves a mention. An English teacher during the day and a self-taught œnologist in his free time, Fernando González' bodega contains 11 small fibreglass tanks with a capacity of 250hl. Temperature control consists of a compressor taken out of an old chest freezer. González has connected this to an oil drum filled with cold water in the room next door, where the red wines are fermented at rather higher temperatures. Some of the grapes grow in what used to be the kitchen garden (he buys the rest, and prefers them a little under-ripe), and the old stables have been converted into a private museum of the González family, which Fernando will cheerfully open for anyone who comes along to buy his wine. Although self-taught in the winemaking department, his small tanks and careful sampling have allowed him to experiment much more quickly than larger installations, and his wines – all *jovenes* – are usually good and occasionally excellent. There is a good white (Listán Blanco) that manages to keep the fresh, clean herbiness of the grape without descending into blandness. The *rosado* is made mainly from Listán Negro with one day's maceration to keep in the freshness, and the red is an excellent, ripe, warm Listán Negro. If this man ever gets his hands on any investment money, he will be a force to be reckoned with in this DO.

### La Palmita, Icod de los Vinos.

*Founded 1992.* La Palmita is another small house that produces 500hl from its own 2.5ha and bought-in grapes. The wines are non-vintage *jovenes* made in all three colours, with Listán (Blanco and Negro) and Negramoll being the dominant varieties.

### Viña Donia, Icod de los Vinos.

This is a cooperative with 125 members farming 600 to 650ha, with a premium paid for the best grapes, a sign banning *plataneros* on the door, (*see* page 204) and a particular interest in white wines. The winemaking kit is smart and modern, and the bodega expanded into new premises just before the vintage of 1996. Normal production is about 1,500hl, and expanding. The wines are all *jovenes* and the basic white is a good, fresh, crisp Listán Blanco. The bodega has an ambition to make a classic varietal Vijariego – the pure Canary style – and produces an experimental *cuvée* every year which is very promising. There's also a fascinating *aguja* (slightly sparkling) white made from Listán Blanco. The *rosado* is made from a mix of 80% Listán Negro/20% Listan Blanco pressed together in a pneumatic press, with 12 hours' maceration, and is very pleasant. The red is a soft, fruity mix of 95% Listán Negro and 5% Negramoll.

### Viña La Guancha, La Guancha.

One of the few bodegas making real progress with *crianza* in red wines. It has also invested in modern equipment and thinks seriously about its wines, which are sold under the Viña Zanata label. One of these is a good white *joven* made from Listán Blanco which manages to avoid the blandness it so often has in other regions. *Best wine:* the red *crianza* (eight to ten months in Alliers oak), showing excellent style and length. This could be a pointer for other producers. A bodega to watch.

### Viñátigo, La Guancha.

*Founded 1990.* A family firm that is actually much older than its official founding date. Viñátigo makes wine largely from its own vineyards, which surround the winery at an altitude of around 500 metres (1,640 feet). There are three whites, all *joven* and all made from Listán Blanco: dry, *semiseco* and Viñátigo Tradicional (barrel-fermented). The last is a very good, well-made, 'post-modern' style of wine which has an enthusiastic following. *Best wines:* the straight dry white is one of the best of the region – yet again demonstrating that it is possible to make wine from Listán Blanco that has freshness, character and a proper acid balance if you try hard enough. The best red is made from 75% Listán Negro and 25% Negramoll by *maceración carbónica*. These are, in general, excellent wines.

**Below: The famous Dragon Tree of Icod de los Vinos, which is believed to be several thousand years old.**

# Valle de Güímar

## Notable bodegas

**Valle de Güímar Cooperativa, Güímar.** *Founded 1991.* The largest bodega in the area, it turns out some very respectable wines under the brand name Brumas de Ayosa. There are two white *jovenes* made from Listán Blanco, one fermented dry and one *semiseco*, both of which can be good.

**Viña El Machado, Güímar.** *Founded 1987.* A tiny but hard-working bodega with half a hectare, making about 50hl with the help of bought-in grapes. In many ways, it is typical of the small-scale bodegas that make up this DO. The brand name is Viña Melozar and the wines are pleasant enough.

In the old days of *vino de la tierra*, if you had flown into the southern airport (Aeropuerto Reina Sofía) on Tenerife, then travelled north up the TF-1 *autopista* towards Santa Cruz, you would have travelled through an area known as Abona-Valle de Güímar, which stretched almost to the Santa Cruz city limits. Since elevation to DO status, the two regions have split into the Abona DO (situated around the southeastern corner of the island) and this, the Valle de Güímar DO, which is based around the two towns of Arafo and Güímar between Los Cristianos and Santa Cruz.

The valley from which this DO takes its name extends on either side of the road, almost down to the coast and right up into the mountainside. It is very fertile and heavily planted with the island's most important crops – bananas, tomatoes and potatoes – as well as vines. The DO extends to 11 towns and villages along this strip of coastline, many of which have been harvesting grapes and making wine for a century or more, usually on a very small scale.

The vineyards are planted from 200 to 1,400 metres (656 to 4,593 feet), typically with rich, fertile soil on the lower slopes and exposed volcanic subsoils further up. The classic Canary Islands grapes are grown: Listán Negro, Negramoll and Tintillo for reds; Listán Blanco, Malvasía. Moscatel, Gual and Vijariego for whites.

### Winemaking and wine styles

Although most of the producers in the Valle de Güímar are relatively small-scale (the average vineyard holding is a little over one hectare), winemaking equipment is generally modern, and the wine style follows that of the other Tenerife DOs, all of which, of course, share much the same market.

Wines consists mainly of white *jovenes* (made from Listán Blanco) along with sweet wines made with varying amounts of Malvasía and Moscatel. Some *rosado* and red wines are also made, and there is some experimentation being conducted with barrel-fermentation and even a little *crianza*.

# Valle de la Orotava

## Notable bodegas

**El Mocán, Los Realejos.** Family firm whose six hectares and partly modernised winemaking equipment turn out about 400hl a year. *Best wines:* the sweeter whites made from Listán Blanco, including a good *joven semiseco* and an excellent botrytis-affected *dulce* at 15% abv.

**Valle de la Orotava Cooperativa, La Perdoma-La Orotava.** *Founded 1988.* Co-op with 120ha, turning out around 6,000hl under the Gran Tehyda label. Wines are *jovenes* in three colours: dry and *semiseco* white (Listán Blanco), and *rosado* and red (Listán Negro).

Orotava is a lovely old colonial-style town situated near the coast, on the northwestern side of the island of Tenerife. Today, it lies close to holiday development along the beautiful coastline, but originally the area was one of the earliest to be planted with vines, not long after the island was taken by Spain in the 15th century. While the encroaching needs of modern tourism and the business of banana plantations have rolled back the carpet of vines to a certain extent, the recognition of the Valle de la Orotava DO shows that there is life in the old industry yet.

The vineyards are planted in a doughnut-shaped area centred around Orotava, and the DO includes the neighbouring towns of Los Realejos and Puerto de la Cruz. Vines are planted from about 200 to 800 metres (656 to 2,625 feet) up the mountainside, and they grow in volcanic-sandy soil over clay on the volcanic bedrock. Rainfall is lower here than on the other side of the island, but the prevailing *alicios* (humid winds) help keep the vines watered by condensation – a phenomenon known locally as *precipitaciones horizontales*, or horizontal rain.

All the favourite Canary grape varieties are grown in the Valle de la Orotava DO, but for red wines, Listán Negro is the main choice, while Listán Blanco and Gual are chosen for whites. The two Listáns account for 90 per cent of the vineyard; 60 per cent of production is devoted to white wine. The other permitted varieties are Malvasía Rosada, Tintilla, Vijariego Negro and Negramoll for red and *rosado* wines, and Malvasía, Verdello, Vijariego and Torrontés for whites. The grapes are trained in a unique way: along low pergolas about 60 centimetres (23 inches) above the soil. Locally, this is known as *cordón*, although the term means something quite different on the mainland.

Wines are mainly dry white and light, fruity, red *jovenes*, although there are sweeter whites from higher sites when botrytis is in town. A small amount of experimentation is being done with *crianza* in American oak, but this is in its infancy. All the wine the DO makes is swallowed up by the local market; thus, while there is pressure to maintain quality-control and development, it seems unlikely that this will lead to export potential.

# El Monte

The El Monte DO is an island-wide classification covering Gran Canaria. In effect, however, all the vineyards are situated in the northeast of the island, in the areas formerly known as Santa Brígida and San Mateo, and in a semi-circle spreading inland from the capital, Las Palmas.

Some 450 hectares of vines are spread over 15 towns and villages, planted in the *barrancos* and on the slopes in typically volcanic soil from 300 to 800 metres (984 to 2,625 feet). The best vineyards are those between La Caldera de Bandama and Monte Lentiscal, where the island's most famous wine, known as 'Mountain Red', is made.

Grape varieties are legion, but the most important is unquestionably Listán Negro (known here as Negro Común). Other main grapes include Breval, Malvasía, Moscatel, Pedro Ximénez, Negramoll (also known here as Mulata), Malvasía Rosada and Vijariego. Subsidiary varieties include Albillo, Marmajuelo, Forastera, Gual, Listán Blanco, Torrontés, Verdello, Moscatel Negro, Tintilla and Vijariego Negro.

The best-known red in the islands is the *Tinto del Monte*, or 'Mountain Red': a surprisingly powerful *joven* of 12 to 13.5 per cent alcohol by volume (abv). It is made from Negro Común and is consumed enthusiastically all over the island. This is the wine that encouraged the relevant authorities to promote El Monte to DO status.

In higher vineyards, the Negro Común produces lighter-coloured, thinner-skinned grapes which are often made into pleasant, refreshing *rosados*; there are also some white *jovenes* produced from Breval and Listán Blanco. All of these wines are ideally suited to the local climate and gastronomy – not to mention the tourist industry, of course.

Being the Canary Islands, someone has to make *dulces* to complete the canon. These may be produced from Moscatel, with a natural strength up to about 15 per cent abv, or they might be fortified *vinos de licor* made from Malvasía *et al*. Production is small and, at this stage, seems unlikely to be seen outside the archipelago.

## Notable bodega

**San Juan del Mocanál, Santa Brígida.** The only local bodega of any size. Most of the wines sold commercially on the island (as opposed to 'over the bodega gate') are likely to have been made here. All are *jovenes* and include a white (80% Breval/20% Listán Blanco), a red (Tinto del Monte; 100% Negro Común) and a *dulce* (100% Moscatel). *Best wine:* the red is quite acceptable.

**Below:** The majestic peak of Mount Teide, as viewed from the Mes del Mar, north coast of Tenerife. Here, vines grow as high as 1,400 metres.

# Lanzarote

Lanzarote is a spectacular island. The landscape is like another planet: jet-black soil over jet-black bedrock; vines planted in hollows scooped out of the ground, or in chequerboard layouts surrounded by low walls to protect the ripening grapes from the prevailing winds. No weeds grow in this *ceniza* (ash); indeed, nothing grows in it until the farmer has dug deep enough to find retained moisture and fertile soil, which is sometimes as much as 60 centimetres (23 inches) below the surface.

In the centre of Lanzarote is the Timanfaya national park, a piece of history frozen in the 18th century which tells its own story of the past. There are more than 30 volcanoes on the island, and several of them still grumble, smoulder and threaten to erupt when the mood takes them. In 1730, an eruption began in the centre of the island which lasted for six years; when it had finished, everything was covered with black ash and the centre had become an area of solid black lava, with lava hills and lava valleys, lava humps and hollows, and lava ash – all pitch black.

To their credit, the tourist authorities did no more than lay a tarmac road through the area and declare it a national park – perhaps one of the most minimal in Europe, but also one of the most breathtaking. Aside from the fact that the lava is, of course, cold, that six-year-long eruption could have taken place last weekend rather than nearly 300 years ago, for there is not a blade of grass in sight.

## Climate and viticulture

It was the ash that brought the vines, subsequently. Volcanic soil is very fertile, but the coating of *ceniza* inhibited the growth of unwanted wind-borne seeds, and vines thrived in the aftermath of the big burn. The wind, however, remained a problem: The *alicios* (humid winds) that blow from the west are not particularly strong, but they are hot, humid and relentless, and they do tend to shrivel and dry the grapes on the vines.

For this reason the growers scooped out hollows known as *hoyos* in the ash, or built cairns (*abrigos*) around the vines to protect them from the winds. This means, of course, that the vines are planted a good distance from each other – the result being that already low-yielding varieties produce even less. Yet growing vines is a struggle almost everywhere in the Canary Islands. Lanzarote is the easternmost island of the archipelago; Africa is only 100 kilometres/62 miles away. It is also the warmest and driest: rainfall is a pathetic 150 millimetres (six inches), and every drop of that moisture has to be conserved by the ash.

Although the DO covers the entire island, it is divided into three subzones: La Geria, in the south around the town of Yaiza; Tinajo/San Bartolomé in the centre, and Haría-Ye in the north. Divisions aside, the wines each subzone makes – and, indeed, the problems faced by the growers – are very similar. One way and another, yields are small, costs are high and the sheer distance of the islands away from the mainland makes the prospect of exports unlikely. So, what happens to the wine in this unique, almost extra-terrestrial vineyard?

## Grape varieties

First, a look at the grapes. Lanzarote has been growing vines only since the mid-1730s; most of the other islands started in the 15th century. Once again, Listán Negro (known here as Negro Común) and Negramoll are the main varieties grown to make red wine, while Listán Blanca and Malvasía are cultivated for whites. As well as the Canary varieties Diego and Burra Blanca, Moscatel is also grown for the production of sweet wines.

For some of the best-quality wines, the vines may be anything up to 100 years old, with production even lower than the already-minimal average. A hectare of vines on Lanzarote in an average year might yield ten to 15 hectolitres of wine. By comparison, the arid plains of La Mancha might yield 25 hectolitres per hectare.

Sweet white wines are still a major part of production, although the needs of the tourist market have engendered a good deal of interest in *jovenes*. Sweet wines are made with Moscatel and Malvasía and account for more than half the white wine produced on the island. They may be naturally sweet or fortified *vinos de licor*, up to 22 per cent alcohol by volume (abv). For the tourist trade, *jovenes* are made in all three colours (including popular semi-sweet whites), and there is even a small production of sparkling wine, although this does not qualify for the Lanzarote DO.

Four times as much wine is consumed on the island as it makes, so exporting is not a major imperative, although a small amount does go abroad. It seems likely that the bars and restaurants on the black beaches along the coast will continue to be the most important market.

For a taste of the real thing, travel to a small town called Teguise, about 12 kilometres (around seven miles) north of Arrecife, and seek out a shop called La Bodeguita del Medio. The proprietor, Jesús López, is a missionary for all things *Canario* in wine and food. He has one of the best stocks of Canary wines in the islands.

## Notable bodegas

### Barreto, San Bartolomé.
*Founded 1950.* This bodega has about 35ha of vines and operates a partly modernised bodega with stainless-steel tanks for fermentation and traditional epoxy/concrete vats for storage. Wines produced at this bodega are all white and sweet and made from either the Moscatel or Malvasia variety under the Campesino label.
*Best wine:* the Malvasía is very pleasant.

### El Grifo, San Bartolomé.
*Founded 1775.* El Grifo has been operating in this company format since 1980. This is the premier bodega of Lanzarote, complete with its own wine museum as well as a sparkling new bodega full of stainless-steel equipment and the very latest winemaking kit. It has 40ha of vines planted mainly with Malvasía and Moscatel, and produces some 4,500hl of wine annually, including *jovenes* in all three colours. The white (90% Malvasía/10% Listán Blanco) is good. There are also Malvasía wines dry-fermented, *semiseco* and barrel-fermented, and there is a red that is lined up for *crianza* when the time is right. It also makes a sparkling Malvasía by the *método tradicional* which promises much but needs work. *Best wine:* what El Grifo does best is classic, old-style Canary sack – sweet white wines from the Malvasía. There is probably a good deal more to come. This is a bodega to watch.

### Mozaga, Mozaga. *Founded 1974.*
Mozaga makes some 2,500hl of wine, all under the brand name Mozaga.

There are white *joven-semidulce* and *crianza* wines made from Malvasia as well as a varietal Diego *reserva*; a *rosado semiseco* and reds in both *joven* and *crianza* style from Listán Negro; a *dulce-crianza* from Malvasía; and a *dulce-gran reserva* from Moscatel. The level of experimentation here shows the will to succeed. Another bodega to watch.
*Best wine:* the *semiseco* white *joven*.

**Far right:** Insurance, Lanzarote–style. Growers scoop out hollows (*hoyos*) or build cairns (*abrigos*) around the vines to protect them from the winds.

# Country Wines of Andalucía and the Canaries

## Andalucía

### VdlT Cádiz

This is the VdlT zone that was created to take advantage of surplus Sherry grapes by using them to make a *joven afrutado* dry white wine. The grapes are picked early to retain acidity and the wine is served chilled in the seafood restaurants of Puerto de Santa María and Sanlúcar de Barrameda. The principal grape is Palomino, but secondary varieties include Moscatel de Chipiona, Mantúa and Perruno.

The VdlT zone more or less duplicates the Sherry Country, and specifically covers ten towns and villages including Jerez, Puerto, Sanlúcar, Trebujena, Chipiona, Chiclana and Arcos. There is still some debate about whether wines made entirely from the Moscatel grape – and especially *mistelas* (mixtures of unfermented grape-juice and spirit) should be allowed the Jerez DO or should be consigned to this VdlT classification. In either case, only white wines are allowed.

### Notable bodega

**Barbadillo, Sanlúcar de Barrameda** (*see* DO Jerez). Castillo de San Diego is one of the best examples of this wine, made from 100% Palomino.

### VdlT Contraviesa-Alapujara (Granada)

This region covers 13 towns and villages along most of the Granada coast and is centred inland from Almuñécar. Contiguous with the VC area of Lopera to the northwest, it used to be called Costa-Albondón, covering some 7,000ha. Principal grapes are Garnacha Tinta, Jaén Blanco, (90% of the vineyard) Mantúa, Pedro Ximénez, Tempranillo and Vigiriega (or Vijiriego), with the Perruno as a secondary variety.

The area is classified for wines in all three colours, but the traditional wine from this area is an old-fashioned, east-coast *rancio*, kept for many years in the barrel and sold straight from the tap to those who bring their own containers.

The style is reasonably appreciated locally, although it has little or no export potential. Some small amount of conventional wine is also made by bodegas which might have ambitions beyond the region, but there is a long way to go here if these ambitions are likely to be realised.

### VC Laujar (Almería)

This region covers three towns around Laujar itself. It posseses something like 400ha of vines, growing (officially) Jaén Blanco for white wines with a natural minimum strength of 13.5% abv. In practice, some Airén is also grown, and light red wines are made from Jaén Negro. Production is bucolic, and there are no bottlers.

### VC Villavicosa (Córdoba)

Only two municipalities make up this zone: Espiel and Villaviciosa de Córdoba itself. One cooperative dominates production with less than 5,000ha of vines. Officially, the grapes are Airén and Pedro Ximénez, backed up by Palomino, for the making of white wines.

### Notable bodega

**Gomez Nevado, Villaviciosa.** This bodega makes sub-Montilla wines of interesting quality, mainly from 70% Airén, 20% Palomino and 10% PX. The best wine is a decent 'amontillado' called Roble Viejo.

### VC Lopera (Jaén)

Lopera and four other towns make up this area, where the official grape is Pedro Ximénez and the official wine is white, with a minimum strength of 13% abv. The style is sub-Montilla and there are approximately 350ha of vines.

### VC Aljarafe (Sevilla)

Two of Spain's most obscure grapes, Garrido Fino and Zalema (but *see* the Condada de Huelva DO, page 186) are grown here for the making of white wines. The vineyards amount to around 1,000ha and are situated between the city of Seville and the border with the Condado de Huelva, where they take in 22 towns and villages.

The main town is Bollullos de la Mitación. The style of wine reflects those of Condado de Huelva in style, fortification and maturation, but only two bodegas bottle their wine.

### Notable bodega

**Góngora, Villaneuva del Ariscal.** A small outfit making very acceptable and modestly priced sub-Sherry *generosos* and *jovenes afrutados*. The former are labelled Aljarafe, Pata de Hierro ('finos') and PX Góngora (*dulce*). The *jovenes* are called Marqués de Eliche.

### VC Lebrija (Sevilla)

This area covers only the town of Lebrija in the west of the province of Sevilla, almost in the Coto Doñana national park. The area is registered for white wines made from Palomino, backed up by Perruno.

### VC Los Palacios (Sevilla)

Three towns east of Seville and radiating around Los Palacios officially make white wines from the Palomino grape. There are some 1,400ha, the most prevalent grape being the local Mollar. There are also plantations of Airén and Zalema. All sales are in bulk, and most of the Mollar production is made into *mistelas*.

## The Canary Islands

### VdlT La Gomera (Santa Cruz de Tenerife)

With El Hierro galloping off into the distance and even El Monte on Gran Canaria winning its DO 'spurs' in 1997, only the island of La Gomera is left champing, as it were, at the bit. This area covers six towns and villages over about 350ha on the northwest part of La Gomera – effectively, all the vineyards on the island. The island is rich in volcanic soil; vines in the best sites are trained on trellises while those on the poorer sites are trained lower to the ground. The climate is typically Canary: hot, dry and moderated by sea breezes and with plentiful rainfall.

Wines consist of *jovenes* in all three colours, made from a bewildering array of grapes. The principal varieties are: Bermejuela, Gual, Malvasía, Moscatel, Torrontés, Verdello, Vijariego, Listán Negra and Negramoll. Subsidiary varieties include Forastera, Listán Blanco, Pedro Ximénez, Malvasía Rosada, Moscatel Negro, Tintilla and Vijariego Negro. In practice, Forastera is the most widely planted, and most wines are powerful whites (up to 15% abv) with the usual Canary warmth and sub-tropical style. Some light red can be found, often made with an admixture of white grapes to lighten the colour.

Three bodegas turn out workmanlike wines with some potential for improvement. Perhaps La Gomera will appear in the ranks of the DO some time in the near future.

Below: Harvest time in Andalucía.
Country wines of the region include
*jovenes afrutados* and *generosos*.

Country Wines of Andalucía and the Canaries **217**

# Glossary

The following terms have either been used in this book, or might be found on Spanish wine labels.

**Adega** Galician word for bodega *(qv)*.

**Afrutado** Wine that has been vinified particularly to emphasise the fruit element.

**Aguja** Slightly sparkling wine, often helped along by a 'charge' of sugar before being bottled.

**Albariza** White soil that is made up primarily of chalk.

**Añada** A wine of a single vintage.

**Aperitivo** Apéritif.

**Arenas** Sandy soil.

**Arrope** Reduced grape juice that is used to make sweetening syrups *(dulces)*.

**Artesanal** Wine that is hand-crafted by a small bodega or made in the old-fashioned style.

**Autoevacuaciones** Small tanks, shaped liked flying saucers, used to ferment grapes without pressing.

**Barrica** A hogshead or barrel with a capacity of 220-230 litres.

**Barros** Clay soil.

**Blanco** White wine.

**Bocoy/Bota** A butt or barrel with a capacity of 550 to 600 litres.

**Bodega** (and adega, celler, cava) (1) an above-ground cellar; (2) a winery, and/or the company that runs it; (3) a wine-merchant's shop; (4) a restaurant's cellar of wines.

**Bodeguero** A representative of a bodega, who may be the owner, winemaker, or a member of staff.

**Cabeceo** The *cuvée*, or final blend, that results after a wine has passed through the *solera* system.

**Cava** (1) A sparkling wine (*see espumoso*); (2) Catalan word for bodega; (3) an underground cellar.

**Celler** Catalan word for bodega.

**Consejo regulador** Official organisation set up to govern the defence, control and promotion of a *Denominación de Origen*.

**Criadera** The top rows of barrels used to age wine in the *solera* system.

**Cosecha** Harvest.

**Crianza** Term referring to the ageing of wine. Wines bearing this distinction must have spent at least six months in oak (more in some cases), plus a year in bottle. Reds are released after two years, white and *rosado* wines after one year.

**Cubo/Deposito** A vat, usually of concrete lined with epoxy-resin, sometimes tiled, sometimes made from wood in older or more traditional bodegas.

**Conjunto de Varias Cosechas (CVC)** A blend of different vintages.

**Denominación de Origen (DO)** Quality Wine region.

**Denominación de Origen Calificada (DOCa)** Classification for wines of the highest quality. Has applied to Rioja since 1991.

**Doble pasta** Hefty, red blending-wine which is made using a double quantity of black or red grape skins over a single quantity of must (fermented over two batches of lees).

**Dorado** An older, lightly fortified version of *pálido (qv)*.

**Dulce** Sweet. Applies to sweetening syrups or sweet wine – fortified or not.

**En cabeza** Method of training vines by positioning the head of the vine downwards.

**En vaso** Method of training vines in which several upright vine shoots are trained in a goblet shape (called *gobelet* in French).

**Enverado** Wine made from grapes picked early or when under-ripe in order to maintain acid levels.

**Espumoso** Sparkling wine, subdivided into: *Cava* – fermented in bottle from grapes grown only in the Cava *Denominación* zone. *Espumoso método tradicional* – fermented in bottle. *Espumoso* – made by the transfer method, in which the wine is fermented one bottle and filtered into another. *Granvás* – sparkling wine made by the *cuve close* method, in which the wine is fermented in tank, then filtered into the bottle. *Gasificado* – sparkling wine made by injection or dissolution of carbon dioxide.

**Fino** Term for the lightest, finest Sherries: completely dry, very pale, delicate but pungent.

**Flor** A floating yeast peculiar to fino Sherry and certain other wines which imparts a characteristic flavour.

**Generoso** Fortified wine; mainly in the form of apéritifs or dessert wines.

**Gran Reserva** Good-quality wine that has been matured for a long period, at least two years in oak and three in bottle. Reds may be released after five years; whites and *rosados* after four years.

**Joven** A young wine that undergoes no ageing at all, (or less than the minimum for *crianza* wines) and is intended for immediate release.

**Lagar** Stone trough where grapes are crushed or pressed.

**Maceración carbónica** (carbonic maceration). Traditional method of fermentation in which whole bunches of uncrushed grapes are fermented inside a sealed container.

**Manzanilla** Sherry, normally fino, which has acquired a peculiar, bracing salty character from being aged in bodegas located in Sanlúcar de Barrameda, on the Guadalquivir estuary near Jerez.

**Método industrial** Commercial winemaking (as opposed to Metodo rural, *qv*); originally involving basket presses and oak barrels. First used in the DOCa Rioja.

**Método rural** Method of making wine made by traditional crushing in troughs and fermenting in open vessels under its own blanket of carbon dioxide – typical of the origins of the DOCa Rioja and still practised here and there.

**Método tradicional** Method of making sparkling wine in which natural secondary-fermentation takes place in bottle.

**Oloroso** Style of Sherry, heavier and less brilliant that fino when young, but maturing to greater richness and puungency. Rich and powerful, with a bone-dry finish.

**Orujo** Term for grape skins. Also refers to the fresh or fermented spirit that is the residue of the grapes, similar to French *marc* or Italian *grappa*.

**Pago** An individual vineyard.

**Pálido** Naturally strong or lightly fortified pale white wine with some ageing, often in *tinaja* rather than oak.

**Palo Cortado** Style of Sherry that is close to oloroso, but shows some of the character of an amontillado as well. Dry, rich and soft, and rarely seen.

**Placa** A device lowered into a fermentation vat in order to cool the fermenting wine.

**Rancio** Wine aged 'on ullage' (in the presence of air) until it darkens and takes on a fully oxidised flavour.

**Reglamento** Set of rules designed to govern a *Denominación de Origen* enforced by a *Consejo regulador*.

**Reserva** Good-quality wine that has been matured for a long period, at least a year in oak and a year in bottle. Reds may be released after three years; whites and *rosados* after two.

**Roble** Oak.

**Rosado** Rosé wine, made from red grapes or from a mixture of red and white where fermentation takes place in the absence of grape skins, limiting the amount of colour the wine can achieve.

**Seco** Dry.

**Sin cosecha (S/C)** A non-vintage wine.

**Semidulce** Medium-sweet.

**Semiseco** Medium-dry.

**Solera** Term used for the process of ageing wine 'dynamically' through a series of barrels. It also refers to the row of barrels closest to the floor.

**Tinaja** A vat, often shaped like an 'Ali-Baba' jar, traditionally made of earthenware but more usually of concrete and lined with epoxy resin.

**Tinto** Red wine.

**Varietal** Wine made from at least 85% of the stated variety (the remainder can be up of any other grape/s).

**Viejo** Literally 'old'. In wine terms, it refers to quality wine which undergoes a minimum three years of ageing.

**Vendimia** Harvest or vintage.

**Viñero** A vineyard owner, grower or vineyard worker.

**Vino Comarcal** Table wine that exhibits some regional character. Roughly equivalent to the French classifications *vin de pays de région* and *vin de pays de département*.

**Vino ecológico** Wine made as naturally as possible, with minimal use of chemical sprays and insecticides.

**Vino de licor** Sweet, often lightly fortified wine, usually white but occasionally red.

**Vino de Mesa** Literally, 'table wine'. A type of wine made by blending wines from various regions of Spain.

**Vino de la Tierra** 'Wine of the land'. Type of table wine that is likely to apply for promotion to Quality Wine status; roughly equivalent to the French classification *vin de pays de zone*.

# Statistics: vineyards and yields

Area of vineyards, average production, maximum permitted and actual average yields for each DO are given below. Please note that many areas – especially those which were awarded the DO since about 1990 – are unlikely to be anywhere near full production or even full plantation: Monterrei, for example, has 3,000ha of vines, but only 500ha were available for the production of DO wines for the 1998 harvest. Average yields may look low simply because much of the vineyard is, as yet, immature. Those marked with a — have yet to file a full set of figures.

| Denominación de Origen | Autonomía | Year certified | Area in ha | Good average prod in hl | Max yield in hl/ha | Average yield in hl/ha |
|---|---|---|---|---|---|---|
| Abona | Canary Islands | 1996 | 1,053 | 5,000 | 70 | 5 |
| Alella | Catalonia | 1932 | 355 | 4,750 | 45 | 13 |
| Alicante | Valencia | 1957 | 13,159 | 350,000 | 49 | 27 |
| Almansa | Castilla-La Mancha | 1966 | 7,600 | 120,000 | 35 | 16 |
| Ampurdán-Costa Brava | Catalonia | 1975 | 2,977 | 70,000 | 49 | 24 |
| Bierzo | Castile-León | 1989 | 3,475 | 200,000 | 84 | 58 |
| Binissalem | Balearic Islands | 1991 | 300 | 9,500 | 63 | 32 |
| Bizkaiko Txakolina | Basque Country | 1994 | 56 | — | 94 | — |
| Bullas | Murcia | 1994 | 2,500 | 45,000 | 56 | 18 |
| Calatayud | Aragón | 1990 | 9,529 | 170,000 | 56 | 18 |
| Campo de Borja | Aragón | 1980 | 6,847 | 148,000 | 56 | 22 |
| Cariñena | Aragón | 1932 | 21,597 | 400,000 | 52 | 19 |
| Cava | Catalonia (+) | 1959 | 32,904 | 1,500,000 | 80 | 46 |
| Cigales | Castile-León | 1991 | 1,926 | 25,000 | 49 | 13 |
| Conca de Barberà | Catalonia | 1989 | 10,150 | 200,000 | 49 | 20 |
| Condado de Huelva | Andalucía | 1964 | 6,432 | 400,000 | 70 | 62 |
| Costers del Segre | Catalonia | 1988 | 4,081 | 115,000 | 65 | 28 |
| El Hierro | Canary Islands | 1996 | 250 | 2,200 | 18 | 9 |
| El Monte | Canary Islands | 1997 | 450 | — | — | — |
| Getariako Txakolina | Basque Country | 1990 | 85 | 5,000 | 94 | 59 |
| Jerez y Manzanilla | Andalucía | 1933 | 11,624 | 850,000 | 103 | 73 |
| Jumilla | Murcia | 1966 | 42,300 | 250,000 | 28 | 6 |
| La Palma | Canary Islands | 1994 | 883 | 9,620 | 56 | 11 |
| La Mancha | Castilla-La Mancha | 1966 | 178,543 | 750,000 | 85 | 4 |
| Lanzarote | Canary Islands | 1994 | 3,270 | 28,000 | 35 | 9 |
| Málaga | Andalucía | 1937 | 830 | 40,000 | 70 | 48 |
| Méntrida | Castilla-La Mancha | 1960 | 12,931 | 100,000 | 42 | 8 |
| Mondéjar | Castilla-La Mancha | 1997 | 3,000 | 14,000 | 42 | 5 |
| Monterrei | Galicia | 1996 | 3,000 | 8,000 | 91 | 3 |
| Montilla-Moriles | Andalucía | 1933 | 12,900 | 650,000 | 56 | 50 |
| Navarra | Navarra | 1958 | 13,171 | 550,000 | 56 | 42 |
| Penedès | Catalonia | 1960 | 26,389 | 1,800,000 | 54 | 68 |
| Pla de Bages | Catalonia | 1997 | 350 | — | — | — |
| Priorato | Catalonia | 1954 | 1,820 | 11,000 | 42 | 6 |
| Rías Baixas | Galicia | 1988 | 1,923 | 70,000 | 87 | 36 |
| Ribeira Sacra | Galicia | 1997 | 1,550 | 15,000 | 77 | 10 |
| Ribeiro | Galicia | 1957 | 3,100 | 225,000 | 91 | 73 |
| Ribera del Duero | Castile-León | 1982 | 11,874 | 450,000 | 49 | 38 |
| Ribera del Guadiana | Extremadura | 1997 | 3,388 | 82,000 | 45 | 24 |
| Rioja | La Rioja (+) | 1926 | 50,733 | 2,444,684 | 63 | 48 |
| Rueda | Castile-León | 1980 | 6,253 | 140,000 | 56 | 22 |
| Somontano | Aragón | 1985 | 3,000 | 73,500 | 63 | 25 |
| Tacoronte-Acentejo | Canary Islands | 1992 | 938 | 28,000 | 70 | 30 |
| Tarragona | Catalonia | 1933 | 18,422 | 450,000 | 59 | 24 |
| Terra Alta | Catalonia | 1985 | 8,171 | 330,000 | 56 | 40 |
| Toro | Castile-León | 1987 | 3,364 | 30,000 | 63 | 9 |
| Utiel-Requena | Valencia | 1957 | 39,843 | 1,600,000 | 49 | 40 |
| Valdeorras | Galicia | 1957 | 2,700 | 42,500 | 70 | 16 |
| Valdepeñas | Castilla-La Mancha | 1964 | 29,212 | 900,000 | 42 | 31 |
| Valencia | Valencia | 1957 | 17,355 | 600,000 | 56 | 35 |
| Valle de Güímar | Canary Islands | 1996 | 529 | 9,000 | 70 | 17 |
| Valle de la Orotava | Canary Islands | 1996 | 430 | 9,000 | 74 | 21 |
| Vinos de Madrid | Madrid | 1990 | 11,758 | 300,000 | 56 | 26 |
| Ycoden-Daute-Isora | Canary Islands | 1994 | 875 | 10,500 | 70 | 12 |
| Yecla | Murcia | 1975 | 12,000 | 120,000 | 28 | 10 |

*Conversion factors:*

1 hectare (ha) = 2.471 acres
1 hectolitre (hl) = 100 litres
= 21.997 Imperial gallons
= 26.42 US gallons
= 11.111 cases of a dozen standard (75 cl) bottles
= 133.33 standard (75 cl) bottles

1 hectolitre per hectare (hl/ha) = 8.9 Imperial gallons per acre
= 10.69 US gallons per acre
= 53.96 standard (75 cl) bottles per acre

*Measurements used elsewhere in the book:*

1 metre (m) = 3.28 feet
1 kilometre (km) = 1.601 miles
1 kilogram (kg) = 2.2 lbs

1 Celsius degree (°C) = 1.8 Fahrenheit degrees (°F)

So a temperature expressed in Celsius (C) may be converted to Fahrenheit (F) as follows: (C x 1.8) + 32 = F

# Index